CHARLES MACKERRAS:

A Musicians' Musician

CHARLES MACKERRAS:

A Musicians' Musician

by

NANCY PHELAN

with appendices by
Sir Charles Mackerras

' . . . in our profession, you have "musicians'
musicians" and you have the "stars" for the public
at large . . . the ultimate, for a musician, is to be
appreciated by one's own kind. Charlie is. In my
opinion, he is one of the very best.'
Dame Janet Baker

LONDON
VICTOR GOLLANCZ LTD
1987

First published in Great Britain 1987
by Victor Gollancz Ltd,
14 Henrietta Street, London WC2E 8QJ

British Library Cataloguing in Publication Data
Phelan, Nancy
  Charles Mackerras: a musicians' musician.
  1. Mackerras, *Sir* Charles 2. Musicians
  —Great Britain—Biography
  I. Title
  785'.092'4   ML422.M1/

ISBN-0-575-03620-6

Typeset at The Spartan Press Ltd, Lymington, Hants
and printed in Great Britain by
St Edmundsbury Press Ltd, Bury St Edmunds, Suffolk
Illustrations originated and printed by Thomas Campone, Southampton

For
Judy
and in memory
of
Catherine

'A man can rise to the
greatest heights solely
through the help of
women.'

Since I do not think it possible to write a complete biography of a living person, this book does not profess to do more than show aspects of a complex man and his career.

Where important features of Charles Mackerras's work, described for the general reader in the main text, have been dealt with in more detail by Mackerras himself in the Appendices, a certain amount of overlapping has been unavoidable.

N.P.

CONTENTS

LIST OF ILLUSTRATIONS

Following page 96

1928: Charlie aged three with his mother and brother Alastair.

1935: with his flute.

*c.*1935: Charlie as Ko-Ko, in *The Mikado* with Alastair as a Maid from School.

1946: Charlie conducting the Sydney orchestra, watched by Walter Susskind.

August 1947: the wedding at Cleeve Hill, *l.*: Judy; *r.*: Charlie (*photos by Judy's mother*).

Prague, July 1948: Charles and Vaclav Talich.

March 1951: Charles arranging music for *Pineapple Poll*, in the flat at Pembridge Crescent.

1952: Judy and Charles at the Forth Bridge.

1927: Janáček in the garden of his house at Brno (*courtesy department of Music History of the Moravian Museum at Brno*).

1960: Charles with the composer Chlubna, at Hukvaldy, outside the schoolhouse, Janáček's birthplace (*photo by Judy*).

Janáček's house in Hukvaldy (*photo by Judy*).

1960, Essex House: Fiona, Charles, Judy and Catherine (*photo John Fairfax*).

1962: Charles and Judy outside Essex House.

1960: Charles conducting in Sydney (*photo Elizabeth Barrett Studios*).

1963: on tour with the Queensland Symphony Orchestra.

1959: rehearsing *Noyes Fludde* with Benjamin Britten (*photo Auerbach*).

Martinů.

Janáček in 1924 (*courtesy department of Music History of the Moravian Museum at Brno*).

Following page 224

1970: Charles and Fiona in San Gimignano (*photo by Judy*).

Nepal, 1973: the maestro's wife recharges herself (*photo Inge Henderson*).

1962: Edinburgh Festival. Shostakovich advises Charles on conducting his Ninth Symphony (*photo Scotsman*).

Rome, 1968: Charles and Tatiana Troyanos. Visit of Hamburg State Opera.

Charles rehearsing with Mischa Elman (*photo Black Star*).

Behind the scenes with *Tristan*. The dying Tristan (a super); television technician; Birgit Nilsson (Isolde); Patricia Foy, producer; Charles Mackerras, conductor (*photo Dominic*).

Number 10 Hamilton Terrace (*photo by Judy*).

1975: Charles and Judy at the Coliseum.

Charles on Sydney Harbour, Opera House in background (*photo Sue Ingham*).

Elba: Charles sailing *Emilia Marty* into Zuccale Bay (*photo by Judy*).

1982: Charles with daughters Fiona and Catherine and grandchildren Nicholas and Alice (*photo Sarah Quill*).

1982: Judy and Charles with their two eldest grandchildren (*photo Sarah Quill*).

1985, Australia House: double birthday party for Charles (60) and Catherine (35). Alice helps cut the cake (*photo Geneviève Thomas*).

1986: Judy and Charles at 14,000 feet on the continental divide, Colorado, USA.

1984: Charles with Janet Baker (*photo Clive Barda*).

ACKNOWLEDGEMENTS

I SHOULD LIKE to thank all those who co-operated with me in producing this portrait of Charles Mackerras, and Lord Harewood in particular for writing the Foreword.

I am most grateful to Dame Janet Baker for letting me use quotations from her own book, *Full Circle*, (London, Julia Macrae, 1982), one of which appears on the title page and suggested the sub-title; Lady Barbirolli for permission to quote the words of Sir John Barbirolli with which the book finishes; the late Professor Sir Edward Ford for an extract from his obituary of Josephine Mackerras; Fritz Spiegl for part of the programme notes he wrote in 1958 for the Elisabeth Schwarzkopf concert in the Royal Festival Hall; James Mallinson, former Artists' Manager for Decca, for his letter describing the Janáček recordings in Vienna; Alan Blyth for excerpts from his article, 'The Right Man', which appeared in the *Daily Telegraph*.

Among the artists, friends and colleagues of Charles who helped with reminiscences, advice and suggestions I thank Lady Harewood, the late Richard Merewether, the Mackerras family, Charles's daughters Fiona and Catherine, Pamela Munks, Denby Richards, Geoffrey Chard; Noel Davies, Edmund Tracey and Rupert Rhymes of the English National Opera; Margaret Carter of the Australian Broadcasting Corporation (previously Commission).

For permission to use quotations and extracts in the main part of the book I thank the Britten Estate (letters from Benjamin Britten to Charles Mackerras), and for articles and reviews, the proprietors of the *Daily Mail*, the *Daily Telegraph*, the *Sunday Telegraph*; *The Times*, the *Sunday Times*, *The Times Educational Supplement*; the *Guardian* and *Manchester Guardian*; the *Gramophone*; Brevet Publications (*Music and Musicians*); *Opera* magazine; the *Scotsman*.

For the Appendices, Harold Rosenthal, Editor of *Opera*, generously allowed us to use material originally published in his magazine; Universal Edition A. G., Vienna (Alfred A. Kalmus Ltd), gave kind permission to use musical examples from *The Makropulos Case* and Brevet Publications to quote from an article by the late Hans Keller in *Music and Musicians*. My thanks are due to all these, and above all, to the three people without whom the book would not have been finished: Elizabeth Kingsley, who willingly typed and retyped; Judy Mackerras, not only an endless source of information but who checked it all, and my husband, R. S. Phelan, who made it possible for me to do the writing.

N.P.

FOREWORD

by Lord Harewood

I WENT TO hear Charles Mackerras conduct *The Marriage of Figaro* more than 35 years ago, to some extent by accident. An RCM contemporary of my first wife's had told her she had married a very talented musician who was getting his first conducting opportunity at Sadler's Wells, and we should go to hear him. I thought he conducted the opera well, which is what one would with hindsight have expected of Charles, and years later he told a journalist who was interviewing us at the Coliseum that I had given him his first good notice, which is almost more than one could expect, even with hindsight, of even *his* phenomenal memory.

Since then, Charles has moved a long way. From slim beginner with a tendency to flail, to mature conductor with immaculate stick economy; from the facile musician who could swot up Wieniawski or Minkus (for instance) for an impromptu recording session next morning, to the authority whose mature series of Janáček operatic recordings commands universal approbation and world sales. Scholar he always was, as my wife, who was at the Conservatorium of Music in Sydney with him, confirms, and he apparently always had the flair to find 'different' works and ur-texts, to edit eighteenth-century music, to turn historical small change into hard artistic currency. The crucial factor is that in the last 20 years he has developed a formidable ability as performer to match the scholarship.

It was through Charles that I was invited to become Managing Director of Sadler's Wells, and he was the most congenial of colleagues during our time together there. To be on top of the work was natural to him so that his touch was habitually light. Planning repertory with Charles was not only to work constructively and responsibly, which is as it should be in the public context we found ourselves in, but fun as well, which is rarer. As a musician, he seemed to me as encyclopaedically knowledgeable as anyone I have ever met, and as resourceful in crisis as even an administrator could hope for.

During those years with Sadler's Wells and English National Opera, our friendship ripened and it was based on a shared passion for music and opera and cemented by the facility to laugh at the same things. Staying with Charles and Judy in their villa on Elba — unpretentious, apart from the generosity of the hospitality and the magnificence of the view — made me discover not only, as I had begun to suspect at the Coliseum, that he was in the matter of operatic tags never willingly outquoted, but that he possessed the secret of doing just enough work early in the day to keep ahead of next season's challenges and then putting up the shutters in order to spend the rest of it in genuinely holiday mood. That I believe is one of the secrets of his success: he is so thoroughly prepared that when it comes to rehearsal and performance, he is not only in complete control but the results appear spontaneous and the music second nature to him.

I suspect what our infinitely experienced orchestral manager whispered to me as Charles went into the pit in the Coliseum for the opening rehearsal of my first season with the company was no more than the truth: 'Well, there goes the best all-round operatic conductor in Europe!' It was not in Charles's nature, as it was in for instance Karajan's, to orchestrate his career. Rather, like Topsy, it just growed. With his specialization in Handel, Mozart and Janáček, his natural affinity with Puccini and Verdi, his growing aptitude for Wagner, and the versatility which brought the same 'lift' to Donizetti, Massenet or Offenbach as to Dvořák or Britten, it might still be no more than on the threshold.

September 1986

CHARLES MACKERRAS:

A Musicians' Musician

AFTER CONDUCTING JANÁČEK'S *Jenůfa* at the Vienna State Opera, Charles Mackerras rushed to his hotel and flung last-minute oddments into his carry-on flight bag. He threw in the latest addition to his collection of gadgets, a little plastic cassette rewinder, and set out for the airport. He was on his way to London to conduct a concert at the Barbican, a late wedding present from Rostropovich to the Prince and Princess of Wales.

At the airport the British Airways Executive Club was full of well-dressed Englishmen and Americans enjoying a quiet drink. Charles sat down and gave his order. He was very tired. He had just returned from a season in Australia, where he had been appointed Chief Conductor of the Sydney Symphony Orchestra, and had spent the long exhausting flight with a score on his knees, earphones on head and Walkman switched on, immersed in Handel's *Semele* which he was shortly to conduct in his own edition at the Royal Opera House, Covent Garden.

As he took his drink his carry-on bag slid to the floor and the little rewinder inside began to whirr. There was a sudden hush all round, then the dignified Englishman next to Charles put down his glass, stood up and quickly made for the door. As the whirring sound continued more 'executives' hastily left their drinks and headed for safety. By the time he had opened the bag and turned off the rewinder the room was empty.

Charles, who enjoys telling this story, probably does not realize how many facets of his life and personality it reveals. There is his connection with the music of Janáček; with the Vienna State Opera; indirectly with Australia; his habit of non-stop work, his constant movement from one part of the world to another, the pressure under which he lives, even his incurable childlike fascination with new and ingenious toys — all typical of this man whose life is given to music.

I

Origins

WHEN CATHERINE MACKERRAS named her first son Charles, her husband's schoolgirl cousins assumed as a matter of course that it was in honour of Charles Edward Stuart, the Young Pretender. Not only had Catherine's ancestors been loyal Jacobites, they had passed down to her a lock of hair from the head of Bonnie Prince Charlie, a romantic relic that set her apart.

In fact, the baby, Alan Charles MacLaurin Mackerras, was named for his father, Alan, and maternal grandfather, Charles MacLaurin. He was the first MacLaurin-Mackerras grandchild and though both parents were Australian he was born, on 17 November 1925, in Schenectady, New York State. On 8 May 1924, two weeks after their wedding, Alan Mackerras and his bride had left Sydney for the USA. By the time they returned to Australia Charles was nearly three years old.

His parents' nationality and the fact that he was born on American soil gave him dual citizenship but he grew up as an Australian; yet his family had only been in that country for two generations. Catherine's grandfather, Henry Normand MacLaurin, was a Scot whose wife was brought out in childhood from England; Alan's maternal grand-parents came from Ireland and his paternal grandfather, James Mackerras, had emigrated from Scotland to New Zealand, where he married a Scottish girl.

The name Mackerras is said to be either a corruption of Mac-Fhearghusa or an Anglicized version of Kilkerran, the part of Argyllshire where the Ferguson clan held lands. (The Mackerras family are entitled to wear the Ferguson tartan.) By the time Alan's father, James Murray Mackerras, married, old James was a prosperous merchant in Dunedin, an elder of Knox church, a member of the Harbour Board, Director of Railways and of various companies.

Alan's mother, Elizabeth Creagh, known as Lizzie, was descended from a very old Catholic family of Limerick and County Clare. Some time in the 1820s or '30s Jasper Creagh, who was in the army, sailed for the British West Indies where, in 1833, in Antigua, he married Mary Auchinleck who bore him four children. When she died he brought his family to Australia, sold his commission, remarried and eventually settled in Sydney. His eldest son by his first wife, Patrick William, married an Irish girl and also produced four children. Patrick founded a firm of solicitors, became a distinguished yachtsman and gave up the Catholic Church.

Biographica Britannica describes the MacLaurins as 'an ancient family in Argyllshire long possessed of the island of Tyrrie'. Most of them were crofters with a leaning towards education and in the eighteenth century Colin MacLaurin was an eminent mathematician and friend of Isaac Newton. Young Henry Normand MacLaurin, the son of a dominie, was a graduate of Edinburgh University who came to Australia in 1867 as surgeon in HMS *Challenger*, flagship of the Australia Station. He married, resigned from the Navy and settled in Sydney where he became a successful surgeon and held many important positions in the city. He was a Member of the Legislative Council, became Chancellor of Sydney University in 1896 and was knighted at the coronation of Edward VII for services to the University.

All these people were worthy and eminent in their way but the woman who married Normand MacLaurin brought to the family an exotic strain even more romantic than Bonnie Prince Charlie. Eliza Anne Nathan was the daughter of Dr Charles Nathan, FRCS, the surgeon who first introduced anaesthetics into Australia, and grand-daughter of Isaac Nathan, sometimes known as the Father of Australian Music.

Isaac was the son of a Jewish scholar, Menehem Mona, Cantor of the Jewish Community of Canterbury. According to family legend, Menehem was the illegitimate son of Stanislaus Poniatowski, the last king of Poland, by a Jewish mistress. It was said that during the troubles following the first partition of Poland in 1772 the little boy and his younger brother were sent away from Warsaw for safety in the care of a servant. They crossed the Polish border into Germany and lay down to sleep in a forest but when they woke in the morning the younger brother was gone. He was never seen again. Menehem was adopted and brought up in Germany by a Jewish family, from whom he probably took the name Nathan, but he never forgot his little brother and when he was twenty he moved on to England still searching for him. In England he married, became Cantor of the Synagogue at Canterbury and his son, known as Isaac Nathan, was born there in 1790.

Isaac was given an excellent education for it was intended that he should be a rabbi, but he showed such obvious musical talent — the Poniatowski family were 'outstandingly musical' — and so neglected his studies for practice that, although musicians were then regarded as little better than servants, his father finally allowed him to make music his career. In London he was apprenticed to Domenico Corri, the renowned teacher of singing, who also composed, and had himself been trained by Haydn's music-master, Nicolo Porpora.

Isaac became Corri's chief assistant and a very popular singing-master to the aristocratic young females of Regency London. His pupils included the Princess Charlotte, daughter of the Prince Regent, and the prince appointed him Royal Music Librarian. 'Tall, handsome, slightly exotic, his pale face framed with glossy black curls, he was charming in manner and highly educated. His voice was small but beautifully trained and he could compose sentimental songs by the dozen for his pupils to sing.'* He was twenty-two years old when he fell in love and eloped with one of them, Rosetta Worthington, a pretty, well-bred Irish girl of seventeen who was henceforth disowned by her family.

To supplement his earnings from teaching Isaac set to work on a number of 'ancient Hebrew melodies' which he claimed to have discovered and proposed to adapt for the voice, gracing the music in the eighteenth-century manner of his teacher, Domenico Corri. Since only the greatest poet of the age was worthy of providing words for these sublime airs he began to make 'servile and flattering'† approaches to Byron, inviting him to collaborate. Byron disliked and had no ear for music but he responded and though Isaac had asked humbly for but one or two lyrics the poet produced 26, now known as the *Hebrew Melodies*. They were extremely successful, one long outliving Isaac's fame.‡ He met many celebrities, was visited by Walter Scott and taken up by Lady Caroline Lamb; but prosperity did not last. Byron fell into disgrace and left England for ever, Princess Charlotte died and Lady Caroline went mad; then Rosetta died in childbirth, leaving a new baby and six young children. Though Isaac remarried and started another family his fortunes were in decline, his life became unsettled and rather mysterious. It is said that he was engaged by George IV as a secret agent to spy on Queen Caroline, that he dealt with the king's

The Hebrew Melodist, by Catherine Mackerras. Sydney, Currawong Press. 1963.
†Ibid.
‡*She Walks in Beauty like the Night*. In 1961, as part of an Australia Day BBC programme, Charles Mackerras conducted the first performance for many years of this song. It was sung by Marie Collier, the Australian soprano.

debts, a job he may have performed also for William IV, but all this came to an end with Victoria's accession. The throne became respectable, the government refused to reimburse him for his expenses, debtors pressed, it was time to flee. In December 1840 Isaac embarked with his family for Australia.

In Sydney he set up once more as a teacher of singing and was soon a well-known figure and respected authority on musical matters. He composed the first opera written in Australia, *Don John of Austria*, genteel, anaemic and derivative, as well as many sentimental and inferior songs. He was one of the first to show interest in, and certainly the first to try and set down, the music of the Aborigines. As a composer he was of little account but he was a dedicated servant of music and Australia's first professional musician and when in 1864, at the age of 74, he was accidentally killed by Sydney's first horse-drawn tram he had perhaps earned the title of Father of Australian Music.

Catherine MacLaurin and Alan Mackerras first met as infants when they were wheeled out in their prams by nursemaids, though it was not until they were both at Sydney University that they really came to know each other. Their families were friends; Alan's grandfather, Patrick Creagh, was Sir Normand MacLaurin's solicitor and Normand's son Charles was a friend of Patrick's son William. This was the period of dutiful sons and Charles, who longed to be a musician, obediently became a doctor, while Willie, who wanted to join the Navy, took over his father's law practice. As well as frustrated ambitions, Willie, who was witty and lively and Charles, who was quiet and spoke with a stammer, shared a passion for literature, music and sailing.

While Charles was doing post-graduate work at Edinburgh University he met his future wife, Anne Croal, a member of a puritanical Calvinist family. She joined him in Sydney, where they married and where Catherine was born. Books, music and boats were a vital part of her girlhood but though there was always sailing in Alan's early life there was not much music. His mother, who had played the piano with brilliance but little feeling, had turned her back on music and there was no father with whom he could, as Catherine did, listen to Wagner or sing parts of Beethoven's *Missa Solemnis*.

It was through their fathers that Alan's parents had met. James Mackerras of Dunedin was a client of Patrick Creagh and when young Murray Mackerras visited Sydney he was entertained by the Creagh family. He was handsome and charming and though five years younger than Lizzie he proposed and was accepted. Patrick did not approve: Lizzie was his favourite and he was doubtful about the suitor's prospects. Murray had not gone into his father's business but set himself up on an apple orchard at Balclutha, 65 miles south of Dunedin. Lizzie, accustomed to having her own way, was determined. The marriage took place and she left for New Zealand where, for a time, she stayed happily at the comfortable Mackerras house in Dunedin.

Life at Balclutha was very different. Brought up in luxury and thoroughly spoilt, she was horrified to find herself expected to live as a farmer's wife in an isolated part of the country. Her son, Ian Murray, was born in 1898 and two months later she was pregnant again. Her elder sister Lily came over and took her back to Sydney where Alan Patrick was born in the Creagh house, The Peel, at Elizabeth Bay. Lizzie returned with the boys to New Zealand but when in 1902 an avalanche, following a bad drought, ruined Murray's orchard she departed for Sydney where she stayed for the rest of her life, supported at first by her father, then by her brothers, finally by her sons. Despite the break, the Mackerras and Creagh families remained friends.

Lizzie was a handsome woman but without warmth or magnetism. She gave the impression that she could not be bothered. Her speech was languid, slightly condescending and hinting at martyrdom; one was always faintly on sufferance. Fussed over by her charming but rather silly mother, her plain admiring sister, she sat in the drawing room making exquisite lace and embroideries. Disappointment had warped her, she became a malicious gossip, a snob. To her brother Willie's children she seemed an insufferable bore and her grandson Charles remembers her as a tedious old woman, which is sad because she adored him.

The two little boys, Ian and Alan, lived surrounded by women in the big house at Elizabeth Bay. Their dignified grandfather had soon died, their uncles, Albert and Willie, had left home; there were only their withdrawn mother, their affectionate but fussy grandmother and aunt. There may have been some fun from the Irish servants but mainly the children depended upon each other. Separated by only eleven months they were almost like twins yet though both were exceptionally clever they were different in every way. Ian was handsome, dashing, outgoing, full of charm, everyone's favourite; Alan was shy and reserved, rather plain, with red hair, described by the Creagh's housekeeper as 'lovely horanjair', but he never showed resentment or envy for his popular brother. His love and admiration for Ian were as constant and touching as Ian's affection for Alan. To the end of their lives the brothers were devoted friends.

The rather formal chilly atmosphere of the Creagh ménage had little outward effect on Ian, but Alan became careful, secretive, inhibited. As he grew up he developed an almost split personality. Warm and animated with outsiders, at home he was guarded, cautious about showing affection, as though fearing to be rejected. His aunt and grandmother doted on him and Lizzie would never have been deliberately cruel or unkind, indeed she was boringly proud of both boys, but Alan may have sensed an unconscious resentment towards the child she possibly had not wanted. His endless scholastic triumphs could have been an attempt to win her love.

Yet she was not entirely to blame for her coldness. Apart from the disappointment, shame and humiliation of her failed marriage there was in the Creaghs a deep kind of shyness which at its worst became almost paralysis when faced with emotion. Though such natures respond to a warm spontaneous approach they hesitate to reveal themselves, to show vulnerability and are judged to be cold. Once bitten they take no more risks. No doubt Lizzie's pride, her Victorian training in keeping a stiff upper lip and not losing face, helped increase her reserve and blight her emotions, but, however innocent, however much of a victim herself, it was her younger son who suffered most.

II

Parents

CATHERINE MACLAURIN WAS a precocious girl, impulsive, high-spirited, never backward in airing her opinions or correcting the ignorance of others. Though this habit, which lasted all her life, was mainly due to enthusiasm it did not endear her to all recipients, and was the origin of the myth later known as The Mackerras Manner. Her remarkable command of the English language, which she loved and respected, increased her reputation for arrogance. Her vocabulary, written and spoken, was Churchillian, her use of words fluent, elegant and correct.

Yet she was not really formidable; her nature was warm and feminine, passionate and romantic. Impatience and a quick brain led her to make sweeping statements but she was easily disarmed and discomforted if she saw she had gone too far.

As a girl she was full of vitality, eager to try everything that could be done in life. When she expressed this ambition one day, her mother mildly suggested that she would do better to marry and have sons who could do all the things forbidden to women. This remark, which sums up the position of female Australians at the time, has been made much of, even, to her sons' amusement, used for a Ph.D. thesis on the Mackerras family, but no one who knew Catherine would believe she set out to produce sons for use as substitute achievers. As an only child herself she simply wanted a big family.

While she was being educated at Shirley, a progressive school founded by two pioneers of higher education for women, Ian and Alan were distinguishing themselves at Sydney Grammar School. (In Australia *Grammar* means Public School and *High School* means run by the State.) Apart from their endless prizes and scholarships the boys were good at tennis and often played at Balvaig, the MacLaurins' house at Rose Bay. By the time they were both at the university Catherine and Alan had become friends. She was studying Arts, specializing in History and French, and he was an engineering student, but they spent their spare time together. For all her exuberance she

was a serious young woman and Alan was not afraid of her brains as
other young men seemed to be. Her extrovert nature complemented
his own repressed one; they both loved music and sailing, and
Catherine was intrigued by his clear sight and logic, his rational
attitude, his interest in mathematics and astronomy. They had so
much to say to each other that friends claimed they never stopped
talking. Each was attracted by the very qualities that later helped to
divide them.

Alan, who had specialized in Electrical Engineering, graduated in
1923 and joined the Electricity Undertaking of the Sydney Municipal
Council. Catherine took her degree in 1922 and was runner-up for the
University Medal in History; in fact it is said that she was the winner
but was not awarded it because of her sex. She went abroad for a year
with her parents and when she returned late in 1923 she found Alan
had arranged to go to America. He was to do post-graduate work at
the Central Station Electricity Department of General Electric at
Schenectady, New York. Two days after Catherine's arrival from
Europe she and Alan announced their engagement.

Meanwhile Ian, on graduating brilliantly from Medical School, had
proposed to a quiet, gifted fellow-student named Josephine Bancroft,
the third generation of a Brisbane family distinguished in medicine
and research. Their courtship deserves description:

> They had, even in their student days, started the collaboration that
> was to be lifelong and highly productive. For in those days Ian
> owned a small sailing skiff in which he would take them fishing off
> North Head, making smears of the heart blood of the fish they
> caught. . . . On reaching home Jo would cook the fish, Ian would
> stain the films and after dinner they would spend the rest of the
> evening over their microscopes looking for parasites. The result
> was a joint paper in 1925, the first of the long list they later
> published together.*

To his mother's indignation, Ian and Jo were married in Queensland, under a tree. Alan and Catherine's wedding was at St Andrew's
Scotch Church, Rose Bay, where the bride's parents had married,
with a great reception afterwards at Balvaig, on the shores of the
harbour. Two weeks later, down at the docks to send off the young
couple on their way to America, Willie Creagh was concerned to see

*Professor Sir Edward Ford: Obituary, Mabel Josephine Mackerras. *The Medical
Journal of Australia*, 18 March 1972.

that Charles MacLaurin looked ill and depressed. He seemed to feel he would never see his daughter again.

By March 1925 Catherine was pregnant. Her parents began to talk of coming to America but shortly before the baby was born Dr MacLaurin collapsed and died of heart failure. His marriage had been ideally happy and his widow was devastated. She set out alone for Schenectady and Alan went across to Seattle to meet her, visiting astronomers and observatories on the way.

In Sydney, the birth of Catherine's son threw Lizzie Mackerras into transports. Instead of embroidering tray-cloths she, her mother and sister Lily now made exquisite baby clothes, shawls, pillows, pram-covers, even stuffed toys. Photographs and reports came of the infant's progress. He was said to be exceptionally bright; at the age of thirteen months he was given some blocks and had deeply impressed a child psychologist who had watched him building a tower. When it was finished the psychologist had given him another block to see what he would do and instead of demolishing the tower as expected Charles had carefully put the new block on the top. This was said to signify remarkable intelligence.

In 1927, when he was eighteen months old, the family set out for Sydney by a leisurely roundabout route. In Edinburgh Charlie met his mother's grim Scottish aunts, in London he was taken each day to Kensington Gardens, where, to Catherine's amusement, the infant Princess Elizabeth could be seen in her pram, waving obediently to her subjects. The Mackerrases sailed for home in a ship that took them down into the Roaring Forties where the weather was frightful and everyone was sick. Back in Sydney they moved into a house with a harbour view, in Fisher Avenue, Vaucluse. It was not far from Catherine's old home, where her mother still lived.

At three, Charlie was a bright little boy with curly red hair and alert reddish-brown eyes, the colour of Kalamata olives. He was energetic, excitable, nervous and highly strung. While he was still very young he was given a puppy which bit him and so frightened him that for the rest of his life he avoided dogs, yet he early developed a love of sailing and showed no fear of the sea. Music and boats were soon part of his life. With his parents he went sailing and camping in Alan's boat, *Maricita* and at home he was surrounded by music. When Catherine and a violinist friend played sonatas together he would neglect his toys to listen. He liked to sit on the floor by the piano when his mother played and she was struck by the remarkable awareness and concentration he showed whenever he heard music, classical or otherwise. His ear was very sensitive; he was always slightly worried by the metallic hammering he could hear when the wind blew from the west, where the Harbour Bridge was being built.

His parents loved Gilbert and Sullivan. Catherine often played the scores on her piano, Alan had early recordings and whistled airs from the operas round the house. One Sunday when Charlie was three his mother took him to church at St Michael's, Vaucluse. He sat quietly till the congregation began to sing 'Onward Christian Soldiers' at which he exclaimed with excitement that the music was like *The Gondoliers*. This was taken as a sign of precocious awareness of style in composition since he certainly did not know that Sullivan had also composed the hymn, but Charles himself has never taken the incident seriously. He feels it would have been forgotten if he had not become a musician.

Alastair, the second Mackerras son, arrived in 1928, when Charlie was already a kindergarten pupil at Kambala, a nearby girls' school. He was sent to stay with his grandmother at Balvaig during Catherine's confinement. Mrs MacLaurin was not musical but she had kept her husband's gramophone and collection of records and soon found them the easiest way to entertain the little boy. Though he could barely reach the turntable he handled the discs very carefully and would sit for hours completely absorbed. Dr MacLaurin had been a passionate lover of Wagner and his records included selections, the best then available, from the operas — from *Parsifal, Die Walküre, Götterdämmerung* and *Siegfried*, conducted by Leo Blech, Bruno Walter, Siegfried Wagner, with such singers as Lotte Lehmann, Elisabeth Schumann and Lauritz Melchior. There was also a Weingartner recording of Beethoven's Seventh Symphony.

The old wind-up gramophone and the pre-electric records, some of them single-sided, were a revelation to Charlie. Each time a new Mackerras baby was born he was sent to Balvaig and though he remembers his grandmother as a dour Scot he went happily because of the music. As he grew up and recordings improved, though living so far from the great musical centres, he probably heard more good symphonic playing and more good operatic singing than many people in London. The finest conductors and singers gave him such high standards that when he first saw opera in England and Europe he was sometimes bitterly disappointed at the poor quality of performance.

Catherine had been very fond of her father, whom she greatly admired. He was a cultivated intellectual, a gifted amateur musician and the author of two distinguished books of medico-historical essays,* probably the first of their kind, in which he examined historical figures from contemporary medical evidence and made new diagnoses. He was a kind and affectionate father but he was an atheist and had deliberately ensured that his daughter should be kept from any contact with religion. His devoted wife did not share his views but respected his wishes.

As the only child of parents absorbed in each other, Catherine often felt strangely alone and adrift. In a vague way she was afraid and longed for reassurance. Even in childhood she had realized that material wealth and privilege gave no security in this world; she would envy the devout Irish maids going off to Mass on Sundays, poor, ignorant, hardworking yet seeming so much safer and more secure than she. Travelling in France with a favourite aunt she had been taken into Catholic cathedrals, even to High Mass, which had made a tremendous impression. In a different way she had also been impressed by her Scottish aunts in Edinburgh who, when the little girl said she loved sausages, told her it was a sin to love food. She began to associate Protestants with coldness, austerity, puritanical correctness and joylessness while Catholicism meant life, colour, warmth and safety.

As she grew older and began to question and think for herself she was increasingly repelled by her father's atheism and distressed by his nihilism. They often argued bitterly. She had realized that she needed a religion but it was not until 1928, as a married woman, that she made a decision. After years of deep thought, reading and searching she began to take instruction at the Sacré Coeur Convent, Rose Bay and in 1930, having said not a word about her intention to Alan, was received into the Catholic Church.

Her family and friends were startled, even shocked. It says a great deal for Lizzie's devotion that she did not lose her admiration for Catherine, and even defended her action. The Creaghs had been Catholics in Ireland, in fact being great ones for honour, loyalty and indifference to worldly affairs had been persecuted for their faith in the reign of Elizabeth I; but in late nineteenth, early twentieth-century Sydney, *Catholic* meant poor Irish immigrants, illiterate servants and labourers. Catholics were believed to be deceitful (because of confession), vaguely disloyal (because of hating Queen Victoria), even regarded with suspicion (because of being anti-British), and though by 1930 these fantastic ideas were fast dying out prejudice still existed,

Post Mortem (1923) and *Mere Mortals* (1925). Jonathan Cape.

particularly in families who like the Creaghs had once been Catholic themselves. Catherine always suspected that Patrick Creagh left the Church out of snobbery, though his family said it was because of his pagan wife. He was buried in a Catholic cemetery.

Brought up in this atmosphere of intolerance Alan was the most shocked of all by his wife's conversion. Not only did he distrust outward show and public display of any kind, both he and Ian were atheists, like Dr MacLaurin. He must also have been hurt and humiliated by being presented with a *fait accompli*; yet it is hard to see what else Catherine could have done, given Alan's cool scientific dismissal of religion in any form, and hostility to the Catholic Church in particular. His clear rational thinking which she had once admired was now anathema to her. She often said he was like a nominal Anglican who had given away religion but kept all the narrow puritanical restrictions of the Protestant church.

There was also the question of children. Alan had felt that two were enough, but Catherine wanted more and was backed by her church. (She used to startle and amuse people by telling them that she had had to fight for every one of her children.) Alan could not consent to the family having a wholly Catholic upbringing but agreed that they should go first to Catholic, then to non-denominational schools. Religion was not to be forced upon them and they were to be left to make their own decisions when they were old enough. Though neither he nor Catherine was happy with this arrangement both were to observe it faithfully.

III

'Harpenden'

BY THE TIME Neil, the third Mackerras son, was born in 1930 the Sydney Harbour Bridge had opened and trains were running from the city to the suburbs across the water. In 1933 Catherine and Alan decided to buy land and build at Turramurra, then a semi-rural district on the North Shore Line, about twelve miles from town. A house, big enough for all the children Catherine intended to have, was designed by Alan and an architect friend and named Harpenden — Alan's choice — after a village in Hertfordshire.

Alan, who was a specialist in the economics of electricity supply in industry, had rejoined the Sydney City Council, where he later became Assistant Distribution Engineer. His offices were not far from Wynyard station, the terminal of the North Shore railway, and the journey from Turramurra was easier and more comfortable than from Vaucluse, but he was never really happy away from the water and his boat, which he visited faithfully at weekends. Though Catherine had also grown up by the harbour she quickly adapted to rural life. She started a kitchen garden, bought hens, ducks, cows, a pony, and hired people to look after them. She also engaged domestics for she hated housework, apart from cooking which she taught herself from books. She loved her poultry and animals and enjoyed pottering about in deplorable clothes.

Harpenden was large to start with and grew as the family increased. If the actual building was influenced by Alan's ideas, the interior expressed Catherine's personality and tastes: fine Persian rugs and handsome inherited furniture, a huge hospitable mahogany dining table, a long sitting room with lamps, sofas and open fireplace, a grand piano. Books were everywhere and shelves of Rockingham, Newhall, Coalport, Worcester. There were family portraits on the walls and eighteenth-century silk embroideries. The kitchen was large, cheerful, efficient, with larders and an old-fashioned pantry for vases and crockery. Upstairs were the bedrooms and balconies for sleeping-out. Alan had his study downstairs and later one was added for Catherine and an Italianate terrace with pergola and grapes and steps down to the garden. It was a house for comfort and expansive living, where children brought their friends and cats slept on chairs. As the family grew it was full of noise, voices, barking dogs, people practising musical instruments, Catherine playing her piano, Alan playing the electric gramophone he had designed and made.

Two girls were born, Joan in 1934, Elizabeth in 1937 and, in 1939, a few weeks before the outbreak of World War II, twin boys, Malcolm and Colin. Catherine put on weight and became very fat but continued to ride her pony; Alan retained his slim figure but lost most of his lovely horanjair. He wore a perpetual air of bemusement confronted with so many children, surrounded by so much noise. At weekends he would disappear, in summer to sail, in winter to work on the boat. *Maricita* had been replaced by *Bettina*, named after Patrick Creagh's yacht. He pursued his astronomy and mathematics, wrote papers and gave lectures to learned societies. He was never without occupation and though the word was then unknown had become a workaholic.

When the children were old enough they travelled by train to Milsons Point, the boys to St Aloysius College, the girls to Loreto Convent. They were all alarmingly clever and precocious. At the age of three Neil knew by heart all the railway timetables of New South Wales and by the time he was four had been taught to read and write by his two elder brothers. Alastair had an outstanding gift for mathematics and Charlie, as well as his talent for music, had remarkable powers of concentration. Soon after moving to Turra-murra, when he was six or seven, he began taking violin lessons. His teacher was Sister Mary Lawrence at Mount St Bernard Convent, about fifteen minutes' walk from Harpenden, across the cow paddock and over the open fields. Before long he was working out chords and harmonies. At eight he was setting to music poems he had learnt at school from the Jesuits and at twelve he wrote a piano concerto, assuring Catherine that he knew perfectly well how it would sound when played. He had taught himself instrumentation from a nineteenth-century textbook (Ebenezer Prout) that he had found and bought second-hand at Paling's music shop when he was ten.

He had also bought a pocket score of Beethoven's Seventh Symphony, which he studied and analysed, for he had already decided to be a conductor. His mother once found him checking the score of *Messiah*, to verify that 'good composers don't use consecutive fifths or octaves'. He had been very young indeed when his parents began taking him to orchestral concerts and had discovered opera when he

was seven. In 1933 an Italian company had toured Australia and he had
seen *Carmen*. He was immediately opera-struck, enthralled by the
music, the story, the colour and drama. It was a *coup de foudre* that was
to influence his life.

He thought of nothing but music and had no interest in sport, apart
from swimming and sailing which he loved, but even in the boat his
mind was on music. At the time he was working on his piano
concerto, Alan asked one of his Creagh cousins to sail *Bettina* in the
Ladies Race at an End of Season regatta. It was a very long race and a
difficult day, flat calms alternating with violent gusts from different
directions. She was anxious to win, her father Willie and brother John,
racing in different boats, had both won their events, but it was
impossible to concentrate. Charlie, brought along to be useful, talked
incessantly about his concerto; at the most critical moments his mind
was on strings and woodwinds instead of sheets and sails. Alan,
looking tolerant, slightly sheepish and humorously resigned, made
mild but ineffectual efforts to stop the flow. It is a mystery how *Bettina*
won the race and how the skipper refrained from pushing the
composer overboard. He has since confessed that in those days it
would not have occurred to him that his concerto should not take
priority over the race, for everyone.

Yet despite brains and musical tastes neither Charlie nor the other
children were swots nor did they sit indoors all day playing chamber
music. When they were small there were scooters and billycarts, made
by Alan, and a tree-house in the big oak at the back of Harpenden.
There was plenty of swimming and endless pets and though Charlie
disliked dogs, and quite hated his sister Joan's puppy, he was very kind
to her when it died. The little boys, who were all very independent
and confident, liked to spend the day making train trips round
Sydney. They would decide where to go and plan a route, Neil, the
expert on timetables, would work out the connections and they would
set off early, with sandwiches and their mother's blessing. They chose
long journeys for preference (6d return) and having reached their
destination would get out, cross the platform and wait for the train
back to Turramurra. Sometimes they went to a cinema but it was
really the train trip they had come for. Catherine did not worry about
them and they were soon known to guards and station-masters all
over the district.

The Savoy operas loomed large in family life. Quotations from
Gilbert were known by heart and Sullivan's music played on the
gramophone or sung to Catherine's accompaniment. (Gilbertian
jokes are still a private family language — Germans are always

'mystical Germans', the name 'Basingstoke' shouted aloud with varying inflections.) There was even Gilbert and Sullivan at school, for every year St Aloysius produced one of the operas. Performances were at the Sydney Conservatorium of Music and all the parts were played by the boys. The Mackerrases were usually in the cast. One year Charlie was in the chorus of *Pinafore*, at other times he played Kate in *The Pirates of Penzance* and a fairy in *Iolanthe*; but his main triumph was when, at the age of twelve, he was given the part of Ko-Ko in *The Mikado*. Of this, the *Sydney Morning Herald* reviewer said, 'The interpretation of Ko-Ko, the Lord High Executioner, by Charles Mackerras kept the audience chuckling', and a family letter describes the production as 'excellent, beautifully staged . . . Ko-Ko couldn't have been better acted or sung . . . it was wonderful how the little fellow entered into the part and understood the lines and the wit so well . . . and NO SHOWING OFF! They are certainly well-trained by those priests.' One of the Jesuits wrote in the school magazine that Charlie had 'stolen the show . . . his brilliant presentation of Ko-Ko vitalized the whole piece. He seemed really to grasp the Gilbertian situation and his cool and confident acting while it over-shadowed none, brought out the best in all who played with him. . . . Never once did his antics distract the scene to himself and the applause he received was a spontaneous tribute to his really fine work.'

Though Ko-Ko was a star role Charlie had not told the family that he was to play it. Perhaps to ward off the Evil Eye, when he made the announcement he pretended he did not realize the part was important. His mother would have been shocked to find him already susceptible to superstition.

Though outwardly nothing had changed, Catherine and Alan were drifting apart. In the past when their views differed it had meant healthy argument but since Catherine's conversion disagreements had taken on a personal note. She was far too eager a convert to be calm or detached and Alan's air of unexpressed disapproval put her on the defensive. They no longer shared sailing, which they had once enjoyed together; Catherine, often pregnant or with a young baby, went out in the boat less and less. She knew that to Alan sailing was serious, the boat sacred, no place for children who would crawl round the deck and drop crumbs.

There was still their love of music but whereas Catherine's tastes included works that Alan considered bombastic — Wagner and the heroic Beethoven — he preferred chamber music, Mozart and Haydn quartets, the late Beethoven. They could not even discuss history without clashing over religion. The solution was not to talk; there were no acrimonious disputes, when Catherine made sweeping statements Alan quietly left the room — far more provoking to her temperament than a flat contradiction. He never fought back, he simply withdrew and let silence fall; he retreated into his work and his hobbies and she concentrated on her religion, her reading and her family.

The children, absorbed in their own affairs, were unaware of any strain. They were all good friends and never quarrelled, in fact rows between them were strictly forbidden. Catherine might campaign for a child or a cause but she considered fighting primitive and demeaning. Alan also despised conflict; he was a natural Quaker, a pacifist parent ahead of his time — he took away the toy soldiers that someone had given to Alastair. Prohibition on fighting makes good sense in a large family yet may cause inner conflicts in later life.

Competition was also discouraged; there was something contemptible about the suggestion of pushing and shoving and trampling on others. The children's artistic talents were encouraged and fostered but general training was based on the old-fashioned cult of modesty and distaste for display. Boasting was odious, too-obvious worldly success despised, flaunting of material wealth unspeakable, self-advertisement and self-promotion the last word in vulgarity. Catherine was rarely seen wearing jewellery, was indifferent to what clothes she wore, what kind of car she drove.

This attitude, which presumably originated in consideration for those less well-off than oneself, is seen by some as a kind of snobbery, an implication that there is no need to proclaim one's superiority. Harold Nicolson has described it as 'arrogant reticence'; yet in certain natures it breeds not arrogance but chronic apology and bashfulness, a compulsion to reject or ridicule praise or at the other extreme over-self-assertion and bumptiousness covering uncertainty. Since few bothered to look deeper, most of the Mackerras family, and Charlie in particular, were regarded as arrogant.

Catherine encouraged her children but was never a complacent mother; to the end of her life when congratulated on her family she replied 'I have been very fortunate'. Alan was privately pleased with them but publicly modest, even faintly deprecating. In their different ways both parents had extremely high standards which may have seemed to the children impossible to attain. Everything was measured against the best, nothing less would do. It was an attitude that discouraged easy self-satisfaction and encouraged self-questioning, but aiming for the highest at the same time as playing oneself down is an indigestible mixture. In Charles, enthusiastic and ambitious by nature but non-competitive by training it developed a chronic uneasiness that drove him on but deprived him of satisfaction. Now, when as adults the Mackerras family hear themselves described as 'achievers' they are faintly amused and wonder by what standard of achievement they are judged. No matter how well they have done they know there is always the impossible goal ahead.

Charlie was not very happy with his violin lessons at Mount St Bernard. He practised religiously but progress was not good, mainly because he disliked his teacher. He looks back now with admiration on the elderly nuns who did so much for music-teaching in Australia, often in remote parts of the country, but at the time he found Sister Mary Lawrence 'too tough and rough' and not very good with little boys.

It was better when he changed to piano lessons with a young friend of the family. Olive Wilmore had just graduated from the State Conservatorium and was full of enthusiasm. She encouraged Charles to compose and organized a chamber orchestra of students. As the children grew older they made up their own family chamber orchestra and gave concerts at Harpenden with Charlie conducting his own compositions, like Schumann at thirteen with his brothers and sisters. In preparation for his career he would shut the glass doors into the sitting room, play concertos and symphonies on the gramophone and watch himself in the glass while he conducted.

He had become interested in the organ. The Harpenden cow was milked by a neighbour named Ernest Bormann who played the hymns in his church and owned a harmonium. His whole family were musical; his daughter Dulcie and her husband, a tenor, sang for many years in Sydney choirs. The Bormanns, who recognized Charlie's talent, were sympathetic and encouraging and he liked to spend time with them, improvising on the harmonium, learning about the stops and experimenting with effects.

He was also learning the flute. One of Alan's colleagues, an electrical engineer named Edwin Foster, was a good amateur flautist and gave him his first lessons. Mr Foster, who lived nearby, often held musical evenings for his flute-playing friends and sometimes invited Charlie to join the quartets and trios. He began with a borrowed flute but soon bought his own, second-hand, from a student at the Conservatorium. It had a beautiful tone but Continental pitch, about half a tone higher than standard pitch in Australia. It was too high for Catherine's Steinway and to play with her he had to learn to transpose.

Some years later he bought a metal flute with standard pitch in the hope of playing in an orchestra.

He had not forgotten the opera. Alan had built a little theatre for marionettes, made from wooden crates, with a curtain that could be raised and lowered. He had carved the marionettes with his fretsaw and Catherine had dressed them and sometimes wrote plays for them. Charlie was stage manager and manipulated the strings, music came from the gramophone and dialogue was spoken by older members of the family. His first productions were *Snow White* and *Rumpelstiltskin* but as he became more ambitious he moved on to Wagner, with sets inspired by the Arthur Rackham illustrations in Catherine's copy of *The Ring of the Nibelung*. The sombre Teutonic colours, great trees and grotesque writhing roots of these illustrations impressed him so profoundly that he has never felt really happy with any other kind of settings for Wagner operas. The little wooden figures played with great success to young neighbours and even when Charlie himself had outgrown them he was always ready to put on plays for his younger brothers and sisters or for birthday parties.

Inspired by the Gilbert and Sullivan productions at St Aloysius he organized public performances of *Iolanthe* and *The Gondoliers*. He stage-managed, trained the cast of local schoolchildren and rehearsed the chorus, rather over-estimating their abilities and his own to direct them, but the operas were given several times in Turramurra Masonic Hall to appreciative friends and relations.

According to the agreement that the children's education should be part Catholic and part non-denominational, when Charlie was twelve he left St Aloysius for Alan's old school, Sydney Grammar. He had spent his first years with the Jesuits but had not become a Catholic. Apart from Elizabeth, the rest of the family followed their mother, for though both parents had honourably refrained from persuasion Catherine had an advantage. Her interests, rooted in European, often Catholic culture, were more congenial to the family than Alan's scientific pursuits, her devout warmth more attractive than his cool rationalism; yet, though Charlie rejected his mother's religion with its wonderful musical heritage, for after all some of the most sublime music ever written was composed for the Catholic church, her conversion was an important influence on his development. He had no adolescent spiritual crises; for him music replaced the need for an orthodox faith but he has always regarded his Catholic background as a tremendous enrichment. It gave him an understanding of the great religious music, the Masses and Requiems of Mozart, Schubert, Beethoven, Verdi — even the Catholic attitude that informs so many operas; it also prepared the way and cultivated the feeling for the baroque that has been so much a part of his life and career. He was ready to fall in love with the period when he encountered baroque cities in Europe, it was all familiar, he felt at home. The architecture seemed to him the music made visible so that on seeing the Wies Kirche in Bavaria he instinctively cried, 'Why, it's the Jupiter Symphony!'

At St Aloysius music had been encouraged and the Jesuits were far more sympathetic to the arts than the average Public School master but Charles does not seem to have suffered from the change of schools. It would not have made much difference where he was sent, for, like Beethoven, who rejected formal education as soon as he was able to read and write and who never learnt to do mathematics, Charlie did not intend to let any school interfere with his music. Sydney Grammar is in the city with playing fields at Rushcutters Bay, some distance away; the school is also barely ten minutes' walk from the Conservatorium of Music and when the boys went off for cricket or football Charlie would make his way there, down Macquarie Street or across the Domain and Botanical Gardens. The 'Con' is a charming confection of scallops and crenellations and turrets; with its mild gothic doors and window embrasures, its shallow slate roof and two elongated palms in front, it has more than a touch of a folly or garden pavilion. Modern additions at the back have not spoilt its vaguely Regency character. Originally the stables for Government House it stands by the vice-regal gates, on the edge of the Gardens which stretch away down to the harbour. Music floats from windows and students lie on the grass in the sun, talking and eating their lunches.

For Charlie it was a magnet. His parents, who had agreed that he should have music lessons twice a week after school, had no idea how much time he was really spending at the Con. They had not yet realized the strength of his determination. It was obvious that he would be a musician but, they assumed, with a solid profession behind him like medicine or law. Gifted amateurs were admired and respected but there must first be a good general education.

When not hanging about the building envying the full-time students, Charlie went to his piano lessons and studied harmony and counterpoint in a small mixed class. Some of the girls, including an extremely pretty violin student, found harmony difficult and before long he was doing their homework. Their teacher, Dr Barnard, was not deceived and when there were no mistakes would write on the girls' books, *Well done Charles!* The pretty violinist, Patricia Tuckwell, who is now the Countess of Harewood, claims that she owes her incomplete knowledge of harmony and counterpoint to Charles.

He was thirteen when he conducted a student performance at the Con of Mozart's *Bastien and Bastienne*. He had orchestrated the opera from a vocal score for Sidney de Vries, a Dutch baritone then teaching in Sydney, and some of his pupils. It was not till Charles was an adult in Europe that he could compare his orchestration with Mozart's and realize that his had been far more ambitious and advanced than the original. He had modelled it on the late operas, the only ones he had heard, and tried to produce something more like the composer's mature work than the score written in childhood.

He had also continued composing, helped by Arnold Mote, one of the masters at Grammar, and had written an opera in collaboration with a school friend, Roderick Bowie. There is no trace now of *The Sultan* or *The Magic Carpet* but a more interesting effort survives: *Marsyas*, a cantata in the style of a Purcell masque. Based on the story of the Phrygian flute-player who challenged Apollo to a contest, the music was very much influenced by the eighteenth century. Catherine wrote the libretto and one of Charlie's friends, Freddie Foxley, trained the chorus and also conducted when the cantata was performed in 1939. Marsyas was sung by the tenor Raymond Nilsson and Apollo by Charlie's cousin, John Creagh. Friends and relations were there in force.

'We all went on Friday night to the Conservatorium to hear Charlie's cantata, *Marsyas*. It was a wonderful piece of work for a boy of his age — the music is full of depth and melody and through it all you can hear the influence of Bach and Handel. . . . Catherine wrote the libretto and the words are very good. She took the small hall and invited all the representative people who were terribly impressed. . . . Charlie played the oboe in the orchestra and received a great ovation at the end. . . . It is going to be repeated for the Red Cross and Catherine wants John to do Apollo . . . the music is very high and strained for a baritone but Charlie is going to transpose it for him. They are really wonderfully clever little fellows.'

The Australian Broadcasting Commission Bulletin of 7 July 1940, said: 'Something of a prodigy is Charles Mackerras of Turramurra. Recently his composition, *Marsyas*, a pastorale, was performed in the small hall of the Sydney Conservatorium. Charlie is now fourteen but this work was composed, orchestrated and everything by him when he was thirteen. His mother, who wrote the libretto, is justly proud of the achievement.'

There was a reason why Charles was playing the oboe in the orchestra instead of the flute. He had read in the paper that in order to build up Australian orchestras the Conservatorium was offering scholarships in oboe, french horn and bassoon. Good flautists were plentiful but oboes were always scarce and becoming even harder to find since the start of World War II. To Charlie, a place in an orchestra was a step on the way to the podium. He applied for an oboe scholarship and was given one immediately, in fact he was lent an instrument so he could start lessons straight away. His teacher, Jan Brinkman, was a Dutchman who had settled in Sydney. He was not an inspired musician but gave his pupils a good solid grounding.

Charlie's friend, Richard Merewether, who was exactly the same age and lived at Turramurra, had also won a scholarship, for horn and timpani. He was a pupil at Shore (Sydney Church of England Grammar), and the two boys travelled to and from their schools together. In the train they talked loudly and continually about music, shrieking with laughter and startling suburban commuters with weird orchestral imitations. At the end of the journey they were so reluctant to part that they would stand talking for hours on the overhead bridge at Turramurra station till the local policeman asked if they had no homes to go to.

In later days, Richard, Charlie and several others formed a kind of gang at the Con. They were always together: Patricia Tuckwell was studying the violin, Maureen Jones and Richard Farrell the piano, Lois Simpson the cello. They spent hours in a favourite coffee shop in Castlereagh Street, talking and arguing about music. Music was their obsession: when Patricia and Charles went to a musical film together they were both annoyed if the dialogue prevented them hearing the score, which Charlie wanted to memorize and transcribe. He had an extraordinary ear and a flair for writing music in the style of any composer. He and Richard Farrell, the brilliant New Zealand piano student, concocted a fake Delius sonata for piano and oboe which they claimed to have discovered and which they played to all who would listen, including the Director of the Conservatorium.

Though one secluded room at the Con was known to them as the Seduction Room, by present standards their amusements were almost childlike. Lady Harewood remembers standing outside the entrance to Wynyard station with Charles, Maureen and Richard Merewether singing the horn parts of the trio from the *Eroica*. She lived at Neutral Bay and travelled by ferry across the harbour, but Charlie and Richard often took the long way back to Turramurra to escort her home. At Neutral Bay, where Claire and Lois Simpson also lived, they would all paddle about in a dinghy, shouting musical phrases across the water. It was Richard who gave young Barry Tuckwell his first horn lesson.

Charlie's high spirits, good nature and sense of humour made him popular with his cronies but less so with his elders. His own teachers understood his singleminded eagerness but others, including the parents of his friends, thought him cocksure and conceited. It is bad enough when a young person claims to know everything but when he or she is usually right it is quite unforgivable. He was too full of enthusiasm to be tactful; like his mother, when others were wrong he had to correct them. It did not endear him to adults.

Most of his friends found Catherine alarming, even terrifying and felt safer with Alan, though he rarely appeared; they liked his quiet manner and old-fashioned courtesy. Catherine seemed not to mind how much noise they all made; she enjoyed the young people and despite twin babies and wartime lack of domestics was always ready to leave the chores in order to play accompaniments. When Charlie and Richard played Strauss and Wagner records full blast, shouting at each other over the music . . . *Horn! Oboe! Horn!* . . . identifying their instruments, she remained imperturbable though Alan would come from his study with fingers in ears to beg them to turn down the volume.

It was not always noisy. One day when Beryl Kimber, in her teens but already a fine violinist, came to lunch Charlie accompanied her in the Beethoven Violin Concerto. She had come without music and he had no piano score but played the orchestral parts from memory, singing and humming the notes he had forgotten.

He was happy with life at the Con and not unhappy at Grammar but his school reports were abysmal. He was always slipping away or not turning up and, like his ancestor Isaac Nathan, neglected his studies for music. Catherine was also concerned about what she called Unsuitable Influences among the older students and professional musicians with whom he consorted. When he scraped through the Intermediate Exam with 4 Bs and one A (for music), a shameful pass for a Mackerras, his parents decided that Grammar was too near the Con to be safe, and the only way to prevent him spending so much time there was to send him to boarding school.

IV

'Is he a piper?'

GRAMMAR HAD BEEN an orthodox Public School but not oppressively philistine,* in fact on Charlie's last disgraceful report the headmaster, F. G. (Sandy) Phillips wrote: 'This is of course a very bad report; however, *Ars longa, vita brevis est . . .*' a gesture that Charles appreciated and has never forgotten.

He was enrolled at The King's School, Parramatta, about sixteen miles from Sydney. It had been chosen because of its distance from town but it would be hard to find a more unsuitable place for a musician. The fees are high, most pupils are the sons of wealthy graziers or of socially-aspiring *nouveau riche* parents. It is the oldest public school in Australia and the boys still wear a semi-military uniform, introduced in 1868 by a headmaster who had been an army chaplain. King's has produced some fine men but few distinguished in the arts. Sport and Anglo-Saxon philistinism prevail.

For Charlie it was out of the frying-pan. He loathed the uniform, the discipline, the emphasis on games. As a day boy at Grammar he had been free after school; now there was only a weekly trip to the Con for his lesson on Friday, a concession made by the sympathetic headmaster, despite the opposition of Charlie's disapproving house-master.

The one gleam of light was the modern-languages master, A. W. B. Webb, a Cambridge man who was musical and aware how totally uncongenial the boy found his surroundings. Webb went out of his way to befriend him and gave him organ lessons, which Charles remembers with gratitude, but it was not enough, and one day Catherine and Alan arrived back from a weekend in their Blue Mountains cottage to find Charlie at Harpenden. After his Friday music lesson he had taken the train to Turramurra and spent a peaceful

*These days it is sometimes reproached for not being more so and the headmaster, Alastair Mackerras, is accused of elitism. The school has a very good orchestra and a lively musical life. Old Boys complain that pupils are often to be seen carrying violin cases instead of football boots.

time at home. Catherine at once drove him back to King's, ready with excuses and explanations, but finding he had not been missed for two whole days quickly launched into indignant accusations.

During the next six months Charles concentrated on getting himself expelled; he ran away several times and eventually the headmaster, Mr Hake, regretfully obliged. He understood the boy's predicament but felt that discipline must be maintained. Charlie was removed from King's.

Though expulsion did not worry him his parents were disturbed. The younger boys were not told why their brother was home again and Catherine is reputed to have said she would have to resign from the Queen's Club — an unlikely story. It was not disgrace that worried her and Alan, it was the question of their son's future for they were now forced to realize that he would let nothing stand in the way of becoming a musician.

They had done everything to foster his musical talent. At the Con he had had the best tuition with a series of excellent teachers and Catherine had spent hours driving him across country for extra piano lessons with the brilliant Polish virtuoso, Ignaz Friedmann, a great Chopin exponent who had come to live in Australia, but none of it had been intended to make him more than an accomplished amateur. He was only sixteen, which they believed far too young to finish his education; as well, there was at that time, even among cultivated people, a kind of snobbery about earning a living by music. Great artists and safely-dead geniuses were one thing but ordinary musicians, particularly if unsuccessful, were somehow seedy, a relic perhaps of the strolling player. Catherine and Alan may have laughed at Dr Johnson's gaffe about Johann Christian Bach ('Is he a piper?'), but in fact their own attitude was not really so different. They felt that Charlie must finish his education, must go to the university. Once he had a profession he could do what he liked. Plenty of doctors and lawyers were excellent musicians, Catherine's own father had been one.

The arguments and persuasions continued; family friends were called in to advise, use their influence. The eminent father of one of Charles's friends warned that professional musicians *had to belong to a union!* The example of David Maddison, a fellow-pupil at Grammar, was held up. He was a gifted musician who had let his parents talk him into doing medicine instead of becoming a concert pianist. (He became a leading psychiatrist and died at the height of his career.) The Law School was suggested; after all, Handel had studied law to please his father, Schumann had enrolled at the Law School because his mother thought music 'an unprofitable pursuit'. Charles would not compromise. In the end he was allowed to return to the Con as a full-time student.

As well as oboe lessons with Jan Brinkman and piano with Ramsay Pennicuick, Frank Hutchens and Alexander Sverjensky, Charles began to study with Father Joseph Muset Ferrer, professor of music at St Patrick's, the Catholic seminary at Manly. Father Muset set him a stiff course in free counterpoint in which he had to harmonize eleven Bach chorales every week, taking as his standard the rules drawn up by César Franck for the *Scuola Cantorum* in Paris. Father Muset was impressed by his ability and urged Catherine to find him the best possible teacher, one that he could not easily surpass. The priest also predicted that the boy would soon earn enough by playing the oboe to send himself abroad and before he reached thirty would have thrown away the oboe for the conductor's baton.

Despite this encouragement Charles disliked his teacher. He described him as 'oily' and made scandalous remarks about Father Muset's *Hymn to the Virgin*. It sounded, he said, as though the priest had composed it while having unlawful thoughts about parts of the Virgin's anatomy.

Charles himself had given up serious composition: he had begun to realize that he was better at imitating the styles of others than at true creation. He knew his work would always be derivative, that, apart from great geniuses like Mahler, conductors who spend their lives searching into the minds of composers and playing the music of others are rarely original thinkers.

Waiting one day at the Con for his lesson with Ramsay Pennicuick, he strayed into the library and noticed a pile of music set aside to be thrown away. He began to turn over the scores and came upon an opera, *La buona figliuola* by Niccolo Piccinni, a Neapolitan contemporary of Mozart. He had read about Piccinni but never heard his music. He knew that *La buona figliuola*, which was rather like Mozart without being Mozart, had been immensely popular in eighteenth-century Europe, and he was shocked to think of the score being destroyed. When the librarian said he could have it he took it home and studied it till he knew it well. Years later, in London, he conducted the opera on the BBC Third Programme.[*]

---

[*]Piccinni, described by Dr Burney as a 'pleasant honest little man' was born in 1728 and lived in Naples where he wrote very successful comic operas in the local dialect. Invited to Paris by Marie Antoinette, he found himself, through no wish of his own, pushed into rivalry with Gluck. The libretto of *La buona figliuola*, (The Good Girl) was by Carlo Goldoni, adapted from Richardson's novel, *Pamela, or Virtue Rewarded*.

La buona figliuola was the first eighteenth-century score Charles had seen, but soon after the incident family friends, the musical Hollanders, invited him to help himself to some of their old chamber music scores. Every member of this large, rich Jewish family played an instrument and they had formed their own private orchestra. In the great ballroom of the Hollander mansion, where the concerts had been held, Charles and Neil found hundreds of scores, orchestral parts, symphonies, quartets, trios, concertos, some very old, of Haydn, Mozart and Mendelssohn. Several of the Haydn works were first editions. The boys took away as many scores as they could carry and some of the music is still in Charles's library.

As far back as he could remember he had been attracted to the eighteenth century. It was Catherine's favourite period and she had encouraged his interest. He had read all he could of the early days of Sydney, which was founded in 1788, the year of Mozart's G Minor Symphony and Haydn's Oxford Symphony, and the thought that the colony had begun its existence while the two composers were alive and working had seemed to bring them closer. The music of Mozart and Handel had been part of his life since birth: some of his earliest musical experiences had been singing alto in *Messiah* in the local church choir with Dulcie Bormann or listening to Hamilton Harty conduct his own arrangement of the *Water Music* with the Sydney Orchestra. Later, when Alan had made a gramophone with an electric pick-up, there were electrical recordings of Beecham's *Messiah*, in the Prout arrangement, the London Philharmonic playing the Harty version of the *Water* and *Fireworks Music*, and Sargent conducting Elgar's arrangement of a Handel *concerto grosso*.

It would never have occurred to Charles that his views on Handel and Mozart interpretation might change or that he would become a pioneer in a new way of performing their music, but even then, despite his youth and inexperience, he felt that for all Beecham's fondness for overblown orchestrations it was he who had the proper lightness of touch for Handel's morning-freshness, the right feeling for his bouncy rhythms, the humour to understand the composer in all his facets. (In Brisbane, rehearsing 'For unto us a child is born' with the elderly ladies of the Choral Society Beecham once lost patience and implored them, 'Ladies, ladies, please think of the enjoyments of conception, not the agonies of childbirth.')

The Mackerras children were still unaware of the rift between their parents. On the surface there was nothing unusual, they were used to Alan's silences, Catherine's solo performances. Though often frustrated she was less alone than her husband: she had the company of the children, while his isolation had increased. At home he seemed to live defensively. Away from the house he was friendly and talkative, his staff knew him as approachable and kind, he was popular with his boating and astronomer friends, respected as a scholar and lecturer. If his family did not care for his interests there were others who liked to sail with him and study the stars. His own children were far too impatient and talkative to want to stand out in the dark waiting to look through the telescope. Only Alastair was interested in mathematics and though Charlie loved sailing he had red hair and freckles and suffered miseries from sunburn, which Alan should have understood. He himself had had such bad sunstroke in his teens that he had missed months of school and had to postpone matriculation. The younger children did not want to go out in the boat because he was so deadly serious about it. They complained that sailing with Daddy was like going to church. So mild ashore, afloat he was a martinet.

While Catherine and the family went to orchestral concerts together Alan went to chamber-music recitals. He made no attempt to compete for his children's affection, perhaps through pride, perhaps because he had learnt very young to avoid taking emotional risks. It was many years before Charles realized that there was a human side to his father.

Alan's mother Lizzie and his aunt Lily Creagh had died and Ian was living in Canberra. His only relations were Uncle Willie, always ready to talk about boats, and his younger Creagh cousins. He enjoyed meeting their friends, who liked his dry sense of humour. He never discussed his home life or gave a hint of complaint, in fact seemed always pleased at the family's achievements. If Catherine were criticized in his presence he immediately changed the subject.

All the same, a number of people, including some of Charlie's friends, could see the situation and understand why he had become a kind of loner, why he withdrew to his study after dinner. 'Why should he risk being shot down in flames by a child of four?' said Richard Merewether. 'They were all so bright, so vociferous and full of energy and *they all talked at once.*'

Alan had now been seconded to the new Electricity Commission of New South Wales. This had been established to plan an integrated high voltage transmission system in the State and he was responsible for the Sydney area. So modest was he about himself that some of his family were never quite sure what his work was. One day, when he surprised his cousins installing illegal powerpoints, there was panic till he assured them, with great amusement, that domestic wiring was not really his province.   ★

Charlie was back at the Con full-time on his own terms but not as a conventional student. His disregard for routine and preference for his own methods of study brought him into conflict with the Director, Edgar Bainton, whom he considered stuffy, academic and dull. In fact Dr Bainton knew a great deal about composition from which Charles could have benefited if he had spent less time running round looking for jobs. Some of his friends had already left the Con and started their careers and though he did not need money he felt that only by earning could he claim professional status and hope to be taken seriously. It was not enough to play in amateur chamber-music groups or the orchestras of musical societies, or even to take jobs as organist in Protestant churches. On Sundays he played for Baptists, Methodists, Anglicans, it was all the same to him, he went where he was asked. Sometimes out of boredom or devilment he would improvise or experiment with his voluntaries or play airs from Gilbert and Sullivan dished up like Mendelssohn or slowed down to a liturgical tempo. The younger children, taken to hear him one day, quickly recognized 'The World is but a Broken Toy', from *Princess Ida* and there were others who realized what he was up to. His old school friend, Roderick Bowie, who had collaborated in *The Sultan or The Magic Carpet*, had become a curate (he is now a Dean) and after Charlie had played in his church had told him sternly, 'I'm afraid that you and I now serve different masters!'

Jan Brinkman, his professor of oboe at the Con, was often engaged for theatre work at night but was growing tired of doing two jobs, and when he was asked to play at the Theatre Royal for a season of Gilbert and Sullivan he suggested Charlie might take his place. Charles, now sixteen, was delighted, particularly since Richard Merewether was also engaged as a horn player. Night after night the boys sat in the theatre pit, conducted first by the amiable Leo Packer, then the formidable Andrew McCunn, and as Charlie played the music he knew so well he would think what a wonderful ballet it would make. Through Richard Farrell, who was working as ballet pianist for the Hélène Kirsova Company, he had sometimes played for rehearsals and practice and had been very intrigued by the music of *Gaieté Parisienne*, a mish-mash of Offenbach tunes by Manuel Rosenthal. He could not see why the same should not be done with Sullivan and on their train journeys home after the theatre he discussed the idea with Richard. Richard agreed and was full of suggestions, but for all their enthusiasm there was nothing the boys could do, for the music was still under copyright.

After the Theatre Royal, to the family's slightly scandalized amusement, Charles took a job as pianist with the State Theatre orchestra.

The State was a grandiose cinema, full of carpets and chandeliers and brawn-like marble. There were huge plush seats and an organist who appeared from the darkness, lit by a spot-light, playing lush tunes. The orchestra, and Charlie with it, in uniforms with many buttons, rose from the pit with crashing chords and the rich swooning sound of strings. It rose and played and sank before the film and during the interval. The conductor was known as Tiny Douglas, but though the musical menu was rather third-rate the musicians were not and several became distinguished players when they moved on to higher things.

Two Sydney press cuttings give an idea of Charles's life at this time.

'The orchestration to be used in the broadcast performance (of *Bastien and Bastienne*) has been done by a sixteen-year-old Australian musician, Charles Mackerras, oboe player in the State Conservatorium and a pianist. He has been heard from national stations in oboe solo recitals. Mr de Vries met young Mackerras at the Con, where the lad holds a scholarship in composition and oboe. "He is the nearest approach to a genius I have met in this country," remarks Mr de Vries. "He can orchestrate in any style. *Bastien and Bastienne* he has orchestrated perfectly in Mozart style." Recently Mackerras orchestrated some Schubert songs for a broadcast over the national relay by Mr de Vries. The ABC bought the parts.'

And in another paper, 'Charlie Mackerras, former pianist with Tiny Douglas, has gone over to the new Colgate-Palmolive Radio Unit, *Calling the Stars*. This sixteen-year-old lad is proving his ability in many fields, for besides being an excellent pianist he plays the Hammond organ, oboe and cor anglais and is busy turning out some really good arrangements for Clive Amadio's Mode Moderne Quintet.'

It was through Clive Amadio, brother of Neville, the flautist, that Charlie had left Tiny Douglas and moved into commercial radio. In 1941, with many men away at the war, good musicians were so scarce that very high pay was being offered. When Charles heard that Station 2GB was looking for players he applied and was engaged. The George Patterson advertising agency had embarked on two musical broadcasts, *Calling the Stars* and *The Youth Show*, sponsored by Colgate-Palmolive. There were to be five broadcasts a week, and a good orchestra was needed for programmes of popular light music and songs from the shows. Charles was engaged to play the oboe but before long he had asked the conductor, Montague Brearley, to let him do orchestral arrangements. Brearley was a pleasant man, a good violinist with years of experience in England and, when he found the boy was really competent, gave him work orchestrating accompaniments of songs.

During the war many orchestral scores were unobtainable in Sydney but Charles could transcribe from records, setting down every note of every instrument. He became flooded with work. His brothers and sisters helped write out the bar lines for the parts at so much a page (pay deducted if there were blots), but they also had to endure often trivial music played over and over, with constant interruptions and endless fresh starts. The *Warsaw Concerto* was bad enough but Ravel's *Bolero*, though not trivial, was worse with its insistent beat and few notes repeated many times.

Charles had already started his lifelong pattern of doing too much at once. As well as playing in the orchestra, orchestrating, adapting and arranging he had agreed to write a ballet score for Hélène Kirsova. The commission had come through Richard Farrell and was based on *Waltzing Matilda*. There were to be dances for various Australian animals, and the ballet would end with a genuine fugue. He worked very hard on the score and took great trouble with the fugue but the ballet was never choreographed, apart from the *Jumbuk's Dance*, which was performed as a solo.

Reluctant to waste the work he had done on the score Charles turned it into a symphonic suite in the style of Weinberger's *Švanda, the Bagpiper*, and put it away. Several years later, Eugene Ormandy, conductor of the Philadelphia Orchestra, came to Australia for a season. Charles was deeply impressed by the maestro and what he had achieved with the local players. One day during rehearsal in the Sydney Town Hall, Patricia Tuckwell, now a violinist in the orchestra, was astonished to see him walk in looking very determined and approach the conductor. He handed some music to Ormandy and asked if he would play it. Ormandy looked at it, then said he would rehearse it if Charles would write out the parts.

Charles, Richard Merewether and other friends sat up all night copying them and Ormandy played the *Waltzing Matilda Fugue* through with the orchestra. COMPOSER CRASHES ORMANDY REHEARSAL, said a Sydney paper and quoted Charles as saying that if he had followed official channels it could have been weeks before the score reached the conductor. 'So I pushed into the rehearsal . . . through a side door, dodging uniformed officials and other watch-dogs.' The music director of the Broadcasting Commission said he would consider broadcasting the suite if it were submitted and Ormandy, who seemed impressed, was very encouraging. He advised Charles to go to the Juilliard School in New York and predicted for him a bright future.

Charles was now working extremely hard and under constant

pressure, for orchestrations and adaptations were usually needed for the next day's rehearsal. He was also making a great deal of money, so much in fact that one year the taxation department sent back his returns thinking them a mistake. They could not believe that a teenage boy could be earning so much. He was thin to the point of emaciation, chain-smoked, drank too much and in Catherine's opinion consorted with Most Unsuitable People, many of them much older than himself. He was perpetually falling in love and she lived in terror that he would become entangled and marry the wrong girl.

His brothers and sisters rarely saw him — they were often asleep when he came home at night and had gone off to school before he woke in the morning — yet though he now lived in a totally different world they remember him as being an extremely kind elder brother. He had a naturally amiable nature and since they made no demands on him and he had no responsibility towards them he found it easy to be pleasant. He was funny, good-tempered, never superior, always ready to play the piano for musical chairs at birthday parties (and stop when the birthday child reached the empty chair) or to accompany when people had to practise their instruments (though inclined to mess up simple pieces by playing conventional tunes with harmonies in the manner of Delius or Strauss). He paid his little brothers and sisters to clean his shoes (more if they were shiny, less if they weren't), and would help Joan with her theory homework, though he was often impatient when she did not understand. The younger children greatly admired him and thought him a brilliant wit, and the more they laughed the wittier he became. At meals he would convulse them with thrilling pantomimes, pretending to crash his glass on the table and at the last minute setting it down very gently, or making appropriate quotations from Gilbert and Sullivan — 'The acknowledged wit has but to say *Pass the mustard* and they roar their ribs out', which they all knew but still found excruciatingly funny.

He worked late and irregular hours, Turramurra was far from town and sometimes he reached home in the early hours rather the worse for wear. If he had forgotten his key Catherine would go down and surreptitiously let him in. For all her concern she rather enjoyed the touch of adventure. 'Why are you whispering?' he demanded one night when she warned him not to wake Alan. 'Anyone would think you were entertaining a lover, not your son.' Occasionally, when he missed the last train he would stay the night with Richard Farrell who lived at King's Cross, and eventually he decided to move to the Cross himself.

Catherine could see that the move was practical but she was uneasy; she worried about his health, he was a typical TB candidate, deathly pale with black shadows under his eyes. America was well into the war and King's Cross was enjoying a boom with US troops and girls who had come from everywhere to make the most of it. Though she envisaged late parties, drink, dissipation, all sorts of goings-on, either she had no idea how wild her son really was or she shut her eyes to what she did not want to see.

V

Professional

IT WAS A great relief to his parents when in 1943 Charles was offered a job as second oboe in the ABC Sydney Orchestra. There was no longer a good reason for him to live at King's Cross; trains ran direct from Turramurra to the Town Hall, where concerts were held, and to Burwood where the orchestra rehearsed. Charlie had accepted the offer at once. He had been playing in the orchestra from time to time and doing odd work for the ABC, always in the hope of moving closer to his ambition. He had learnt much at Colgate-Palmolive but it was time to leave.

His first concert was conducted by Dr Bainton, Director of the Con, with whom he had often had words. The wartime shortage of musicians was still acute and the principal oboe in the orchestra was a former house-painter named Snowy Waterfield who had taken to music a little late in life. By 1945 Charles had been asked to replace him, a move which Waterfield always believed he had engineered. It was very awkward when Snowy was engaged to paint the house next to Harpenden; Charles took to sneaking in and out by a side door like a thief but inevitably he was seen and recognized by Snowy and his workmen who let fly with loud abuse, jeers, accusations and catcalls whenever Charles appeared.

At nineteen Charles was principal oboe in the orchestra and had been appointed professor of oboe at the Con (the youngest ever to hold a professorship there), yet he still was not satisfied. He began to pester William James, the Director of Music at the ABC, for a chance to conduct. Though James later became one of his strongest supporters, at that time there was little love lost between them. A minor composer, James considered Charles bumptious and arrogant, too inexperienced to be given charge of an orchestra, while Charles did not conceal his poor opinion of the Director's compositions.

Eventually James relented and agreed that Charles should audition for him and two conductors, Percy Code and John Farnsworth Hall, on condition that he would abide by their decision. They set a very difficult test; after playing the Beethoven First Symphony he was asked to sightread music with which he was quite unfamiliar and which was full of traps, but he passed successfully and was told he might conduct studio broadcasts.

For the first of these concerts, which was also his first public performance with a symphony orchestra, he was allowed only one rehearsal, but he had made his own preparations. He had chosen to play Walton's *Portsmouth Point* which is notoriously difficult, and had studied it constantly from a pocket score and an Adrian Boult recording. By the time the rehearsal came the music was engraved on his mind and he conducted so well that at the end the orchestra broke into spontaneous applause. Flushed with triumph and very relieved Charles asked if they would mind playing it again and this time conducted without the score.

But conducting was only an occasional event; he was still an orchestral player and though Malcolm Sargent, who was touring for the ABC, thought so highly of his work that he requested him as principal oboe for all his concerts, Charles was not really consoled.

Because of his birth in the USA he still had dual nationality and as his eighteenth birthday approached he decided to enlist with the American forces. They were prepared to accept him but only if he obtained a clearance from the Australian army. This Australia refused to give and eventually he was called up for his medical examination by the local military. The army doctor looked with disgust at his hollow chest and emaciated form and said scathingly, 'You don't seem to have done much sport, do you?' He did not consider Charles to be much use in defending Australia and classed him as B grade. The Americans then summoned him for a preliminary examination, classed him as fit for service and sent him his papers; but as these required him to present himself in the United States, an order he could not obey, he became technically a deserter, which suited him very well since he had no wish to join the army. The Americans were not concerned but by now the ABC had become alarmed at the thought of losing their principal oboe. Claiming that in cases of dual nationality the country of domicile took precedence, that Charles was urgently needed for the Sargent concerts in Adelaide and Brisbane and that as a British subject he was reserved under the Manpower Act, they refused to release him from the orchestra, which was where he remained. He was still there when the war came to an end in 1945.

It was while he was in Brisbane with Sargent that Charles first began to realize that the Handel performances he knew and loved might not be quite as the composer had intended them. Dr Dalley Scarlett, the city's chief organist and musicologist, had shown him a facsimile of the *Messiah* autograph and for comparison, a copy of the Ebenezer Prout version. There was also an old full score in which Mozart's accompaniments were printed in a type distinct from Handel's original. Charles was particularly fascinated to see that both Handel's high trumpet parts and Mozart's low ones were included.

He next saw scores of the original version of the *Water Music* and the *Fireworks Music* and read the account of their first performances in the open air. He tried to imagine how they would have sounded from Handel's scores and to compare that sound with Hamilton Harty's sleek twentieth century orchestration. It seemed to him extraordinary that eminent conductors, who took such pains over details of orchestration in nineteenth-century symphonies could even consider playing Handel in a style so far removed from anything the composer would have imagined. He found the whole subject so absorbing that he wanted to know more. It was the beginning of an investigation that still continues. (See Appendix III, p. 291.)

Catherine believed that if you were going to do a thing you should do it as well as possible. She was also determined that though she might not like the careers her children chose she would give them all the help she could. She had not wanted Charles to be a professional musician but having accepted it she had supported him and now that the war was over, though she would miss him terribly, she encouraged him to go abroad. He did not need her financial help, he had made so much money that he had enough to live on in London for quite some time, but she was worried by thoughts of War-torn Europe and shortages, and reports that the English winter of 1946–47 had been the worst on record. As alarming stories appeared in the press she packed great quantities of soap and toothpaste, heavy woollen combinations, long-sleeved vests and underpants and urged Charles to buy as many good clothes as possible before he sailed. Food parcels were to be sent at regular intervals. She arranged for him to go to his cousins, the Grants, in London when he arrived and besought him not to marry the first girl he met.

Charles was busy up to the very last minute before his departure. As well as his work in the orchestra, he was recording music he had written for the films *Namatjira* and *The Rats of Tobruk*, he conducted a broadcast of *Bastien and Bastienne* and played an oboe concerto by the Israeli composer Boskovich, which had been sent to him by the Israeli pianist, Pnina Salzman. On 17 November he celebrated his twenty-first birthday at Richard Farrell's flat at King's Cross and there was also a large party at Harpenden, a mixture of family and musical friends. As usual at such affairs the noise was deafening and while Charlie and Catherine held court Alan soon retired to his study with a few congenial friends. Though he had said little it was clear that, if slightly baffled, he was proud of his eldest son. It would be thirteen years before most of the guests saw Charlie again and by then he would have changed from a thin, pale, hollow-eyed principal oboe to a rising young maestro, a substantial man of thirty-four with a wife and two children.

Shipping was far from normal in 1946 but he had managed to buy a one-way ticket in *Rangitiki*, one of the first passenger ships to leave Sydney after the war. On 6 February 1947 the whole family went with him to the docks to see him off. He was so anxious not to be late that they all arrived far too early. While he waited for hours to embark — he was almost the first on board — the others drove to Bradley's Head to wave as the ship sailed down the harbour, though in fact neither they nor Charles could see each other.

Rangitiki was packed; there were not enough cabins and people slept in dormitories. Nominally one-class, passengers ranged from un-kempt unshaven 'ockers' (tough Australians) to the Duchess of Gloucester, returning home with the Duke's entourage after his term as Governor-General. There were also 'millions of prelates and prelatesses'. Apart from several young journalists whom he knew, for Charles the most congenial passengers were a German-Jewish rabbi and his wife who loved music and gave him German lessons.

He started a long letter in diary form to be posted home, describing life on board. Having never roughed it he found meals and bathing conditions 'appalling'; the only way to get any sleep was on deck, which meant being hosed down at dawn. He was amused by the social distinctions in the 'one-class' ship and the fact that in many cases the only way to tell passengers from crew was that the latter were cleaner and tidier.

The journey, via Pitcairn, Panama and Curaçao, was long and rather boring. He was invited several times to the royal suite where he found the best way to keep the conversation going was to talk of Malcolm Sargent and fondle the Duchess's dogs. He practised his oboe and played in ship's concerts and by the time *Rangitiki* approached Tilbury was writing, 'Everybody has *had* this ship properly and we are all looking forward to getting in for the last time. . . . I have wired the Grants accepting their hospitality till I can find a flat. . . . In spite of my expectations I am missing you and the family very much and I wish you were going to be there when I arrive. With much nostalgic love, Charlie.'

On 20 March 1947 he landed at Tilbury.

While Charles was disembarking and moving in with the Grants, a pretty clarinet student named Helena Judith Wilkins was going to 'freezing rehearsals' at the Royal College of Music and skating in Regents Park where snowfalls had spoilt the ice surface.

At the beginning of the year she had come up from the Cotswolds for her final weeks at the RCM. The weather had been unspeakable, there was a transport strike, a fuel shortage, low gas pressure for cooking, unheated buildings; it was often too cold in her digs for practising and the RCM was also 'stinking cold'.

Judy had been born in Assam where her father, now retired, had been stationed. The family, which lived on Cleeve Hill, were musical though not professionals, and Judy had studied the piano. During her schooldays at Cheltenham College she had realized that though good she would never be a virtuoso and since she wanted to make her career in music and play in an orchestra she had also taken up the clarinet. She had gained her ARCM with top marks for her year when she interrupted her training for two years to serve in the WRNS. Six months after the end of the war with Japan she was demobilized and returned to the RCM with a government scholarship.

On 27 March 1947 she wrote in her diary, 'My last clarinet lesson in a.m. Played John Ireland . . . went to college dance which was pretty mouldy.' A week later she left for Paris, for two weeks' extra clarinet tuition. The previous year she had auditioned for Sadler's Wells Opera orchestra and was engaged as principal clarinet. By May she was in Southsea on tour with the company.

VI

Judy

———————————

WHEN CHARLES LEFT Australia he had had far more musical experience than most of his contemporaries in England. His training had not been interrupted by the war, which in fact had given him unusual opportunities; he had worked as pianist and oboe player in radio, theatre and symphony orchestras with all kinds of repertoires, had done a considerable amount of orchestration and arranging and played under distinguished guest conductors, all of whom had greatly encouraged him. Eugene Goossens, who had returned to take over the Sydney orchestra, by now known as the Sydney Symphony Orchestra, had given him letters to Adrian Boult and to his brother Leon Goossens from whom Charles hoped to have oboe lessons. There were also introductions to members of the BBC orchestra from Horace Green, the English oboist who was to replace him in Sydney.

In London he first stayed with the Grants at Highgate. It was still cold but he had the thick underwear Catherine had packed and the clothes she had advised him to buy. He often felt conscious that he and other Australians looked rather too prosperous beside the tired shabby Londoners. After the comfort, plenty and colour of life in Sydney it all seemed incredibly drab and for a time he found it hard to decide how much, apart from obvious bomb damage, was due to the war and how much to the normal British way of life. His reactions were still those of a sheltered and fortunate child.

Yet his letters from London were full of enthusiasm about places and things he had known of all his life but now saw for the first time: the countryside, which made him want to sing Vaughan Williams, the ancient houses and villages with wonderful names; porcelain and furniture in the Victoria and Albert; Greenwich College, where he dined on Visitors' Night, Windsor Castle where he visited the Gowries (a former Governor-General of Australia). At Oxford he was ravished by evensong in Magdalen and by the high standard of choral music, while the university itself so enraptured him that he wrote to Neil, urging him to continue his law studies there when he graduated from Sydney.

He planned to share a flat with his friend, the journalist Roland Pullen, who had travelled with him in *Rangitiki*; he had many introductions, and family friends invited him to visit, but he was homesick, he missed discussions with Catherine, he missed his brothers and sisters, to whom he sent descriptions of whatever he thought would interest them. Soon, however, the focus changed and music became the main, then the only subject of his letters. He had been to Covent Garden, to Sadler's Wells and seen *Figaro* with Arnold Matters (whom he had known in Sydney) as the Count; had been down to Sussex to Leon Goossens who lived in a 'marvellous Elizabethan house in a marvellous old village'. Leon, who 'looked and sounded like Eugene but shorter' and was 'mad about boats', was very nice, and willing to give oboe lessons. He had been in touch with Sargent; Adrian Boult had been exceptionally kind; the British musicians did not seem to resent him and were very helpful in suggesting jobs.

For Charles, London was not just a place of literary pilgrimage or historical associations; London meant music and what was happening in the musical world, particularly in opera. Before long, by haunting the pub frequented by members of Covent Garden orchestra he had met some of the players, one of whom, Richard Temple Savage, was also the librarian and became a lasting friend. Through these contacts Charles was able to slip into rehearsals and hear the musical director, Karl Rankl, conducting *Rosenkavalier* and, later, Wagner's *Ring*. He admired Rankl's work but thought him arrogant and patronizing towards the orchestra, behaving 'as though bringing the gift of European culture to the backward and barbarous British'.

He had no struggles or starving in garrets, no walking the streets looking for work; in those days labour permits were not needed and almost at once, despite competition, he was offered orchestral jobs. Walter Süsskind, under whom he had played in Sydney, wanted him for Scotland, Sargent rang several times and asked him to join the Liverpool Philharmonic but Charles refused the offer because Sargent was too busy to give him conducting lessons. Sargent was not pleased, annoyed perhaps at losing a good oboe player, perhaps at such brash confidence in rejecting an opportunity most young players would have jumped at.

In Sydney, Charles, with the rest of the orchestra, had liked Sargent, despite his social pretensions, but now he was surprised to find him unpopular among English musicians. (Beecham called him

Flash Harry.) Years later, as a rising young conductor, he shared a Prom with Sargent and found the maestro very lofty. Whether or not he recognized the impudent youth who had turned him down he refused to let Charles share his dressing room.

It was different with Adrian Boult. Though Charles would not have admitted it he was often nervous about approaching eminent people. He wanted to appear confident but knew that Australians had a reputation for being direct and that in his eagerness he sometimes went at things like a bull at a gate. Like Sargent, Boult, who was then conducting the BBC Symphony Orchestra, was also extremely busy but his secretary, Mrs Beckett, arranged an appointment almost immediately and Charles found himself welcomed by a modest, charming man who put him at his ease and invited him to attend BBC rehearsals. Boult also advised him against taking a permanent job as oboe with the Liverpool Philharmonic; once he joined such a good orchestra he could be there for ever.

By an odd chance Boult and Charles also shared a Prom, and a dressing room, many years later. (Boult was then over eighty and no longer strong enough to conduct a whole programme.) Charles, well into his fifties, was charmed to hear the old man say to Edgar Mays, the attendant of the BBC Symphony Orchestra, 'Nice to see young Mackerras again.'

The lessons with Leon Goossens were not very satisfactory, mainly because Goossens, who was notoriously unreliable, usually failed to turn up, but as Charles had not come abroad to play the oboe he was not greatly concerned. He took freelance jobs in several orchestras as an extra, notably the Royal Philharmonic under Beecham and with Beecham's protégé, Norman del Mar, the young horn player who was then starting his conducting career.

If he had gone to New York as Ormandy had recommended life would have been more comfortable but he had chosen England because it was closer to Europe. What he really wanted was to work in opera, to train in the European tradition which meant starting as repetiteur or coach in an opera house where he could learn every aspect of operatic conducting. There seemed little prospect of finding this in London and he had started to think of going to Austria or Germany, unaware that postwar conditions in both countries would have made serious study impossible. He was still undecided when he heard, through a British musician, of a vacancy at Sadler's Wells opera for a second oboe, for a thirteen-week tour. He applied and at the interview it was arranged that he should also work as a repetiteur.

Arrangements to share a flat with his friend Roly Pullen had fallen through and he had moved to Queen's Gate. He took most of his meals in eating places nearby and one day, as he waited for lunch in a crowded restaurant near South Kensington station, a middle-aged Central European asked politely if he would mind sharing his table. Charles agreed absently, barely looking up from his pocket score of Dvořák's D Minor Symphony, but presently the stranger leaned over and said, 'You are reading a score by one of my fellow-countrymen.' They began to talk; the Czech, Josef Weisslitzer, was an amateur cellist and a member of the Anglo-Czechoslovak Friendship League. When he heard Charles's plans for studying abroad he suggested that Czechoslovakia would be more suitable than Austria or Germany. Owing to the German occupation Prague had not been destroyed and conditions were better there than in many other parts of Europe. Weisslitzer, who had just come from a meeting of the Friendship League, where Anglo-Czech scholarships had been discussed, had with him a copy of conditions and arrangements. Six Czechs were to come to London and six British students go to Prague where they would receive a living allowance and where all education, including music, was free. The British Council was handling applications in England and he advised applying at once.

Though Charles was no longer a student, and had been a professional for several years, he decided to try for a post-graduate scholarship to study conducting. He quickly put in an application, giving Sargent and Boult as referees without waiting to ask their permission, then went off to Scotland for several weeks' work with the BBC Scottish Orchestra under Ian Whyte, before starting as second oboe-cum-repetiteur with Sadler's Wells Opera on tour.

On Monday, 12 May he arrived from Scotland at the King's Theatre, Southsea, just before the curtain rose for *La Bohème*. He barely looked at the girl, the principal clarinet, sitting behind him in the orchestra and she was far too nervous to notice him. It was the opening night of the tour and her first experience of playing an opera. By the third night first clarinet and second oboe had become aware of each other as Judy Wilkins and Charles Mackerras and two days later Judy wrote to her mother: ' . . . Well, here we are approaching the end of the first week and I haven't died yet, though I think *Tosca* tonight will just about finish me. . . . Everyone is being ridiculously nice and actually I'm enjoying myself enormously and feel that once the strain of the first three weeks or so is over, this will be an even better form of existence.

' . . . On Wednesday we went to a dance, if you please. I hadn't the slightest intention of going really but felt so relieved that *Bohème* second time through had gone a bit better that I was finally persuaded to. Sadler's Wells Co. were invited as guests and given drinks etc. on the house. . . . I had three partners . . . the female sex are definitely in demand here, there being few in number, anyway in the orchestra. Most amusing. I'm going to the Isle of Wight on Sunday with *Charlie*! Second oboe. Actually he's very nice. Australian, young, just arrived over here and wants to become a conductor. He was first oboe in the Sidney [*sic*] Symphony Orchestra and has taken this job simply as the best way of learning about opera.'

At the dance, given by the Southsea Council, Judy's partners had been the second clarinet, the principal flute and the second oboe. She found Charlie a terrible dancer but was very intrigued by him, particularly when he took her home to her digs and did not try to kiss her.

As newcomers he and she were much thrown together; they were both young, both sight-reading, both inexperienced in opera and finding it all rather strenuous. By 25 May, when the company moved to Bournemouth, they were already falling in love. At Bournemouth Judy stayed with her uncle and aunt and, since she knew the district very well, she took Charlie sightseeing. He was accustomed to discussing his plans and ideas with Catherine, and Judy was a willing listener. She was fascinated by his eagerness, his enthusiasm and talent, also concerned about his health, his thinness, his chain-smoking. He had always been looked after; before long she was sewing on his buttons and had taken over various small jobs for his comfort.

They were still in Bournemouth when at the end of May he heard he was being considered for an Anglo-Czech scholarship and was to go up to London for an interview. He was nervous and asked Judy to go with him. In letters home he had confided to Catherine several times that he was not very hopeful, and feared he lacked the necessary academic qualifications but that he intended to 'pitch them a good yarn'. The yarn was so well pitched that it nearly disqualified him. In his anxiety to impress at the interview he appeared bumptious and over-confident and his report recommended he *not* be awarded a scholarship. He was given no hint of this and after the ordeal took Judy for her first lunch in a Chinese restaurant.

On the last weekend at Bournemouth Mr Wilkins arrived to collect his daughter and on Sunday morning they drove to Cleeve Hill where she was to spend the night with her parents before joining the company at Leicester. Charlie went with them; it was 'a good chance to show him the countryside'.

After tea at 'Whistling Down', the Wilkins's house, Judy, her mother and Charles went for a walk. They called at the local pub, the Rising Sun, for a beer but supplies had run out and they had to make do with rum. They were all very cheerful when they started for home. On the way they stopped at the house of their friends, Mary and Mick Stern and were invited in for a drink. Judy and her mother felt they must hurry back and see about dinner but Charles was persuaded to stay. The two women were in the kitchen, giggling helplessly as they tried to concoct a pie from something out of a tin, when Mr Wilkins appeared at the door with a telephone message that Charles was on his way. 'I *say*,' he observed drily, 'that fellow sounds pretty ginned up!'

Charles was feeling far from well when he reached Whistling Down. After the rum at the pub he had drunk gin-and-vermouth with the Sterns and though he managed to come to the table he could not face dinner and hurriedly left to go upstairs.

When he woke in the morning he was not only hung-over but miserably aware of the impression he must have made on his hosts. He lay, feeling sick and dejected, till Judy arrived to comfort and reassure him. She was sitting on his bed when her mother came in and though nothing was said Mrs Wilkins could see that there was more than friendship between them.

Charles came downstairs feeling frightful, but not too ill to notice a pocket score of the Sibelius Second Symphony on the living-room piano. Unaware that it was one of his host's special favourites he sat down and began to play, bringing out all the parts in a masterly manner. Mr Wilkins, though still dubious, was impressed and began to thaw. He went out to the kitchen where the women were getting breakfast and said, 'Do you realize that fellow is playing like that from the *pocket score*!' Afraid that Charlie might stop Judy rushed in to him, saying, 'Don't stop! For God's sake don't stop! He's impressed! Keep it up!'

Charles played to the end, but though the performance showed his remarkable talent it did not completely restore his reputation. There was still a question-mark in the minds of Judy's parents when she and Charles left next morning to rejoin the company in Leicester.

When Charles joined Sadler's Wells in 1947 the job of repetiteur was still regarded as the first step on the path to becoming an operatic conductor and the best way of gaining all-round experience. A repetiteur had to know all the parts of all the operas and be able to play and sing them in order to teach the singers their roles. He also had to conduct at rehearsals and be responsible for off-stage effects. As well as playing the oboe Charles had a tremendous amount to learn; the repertoire of the tour included *Tosca, Bohème, The Barber of Seville, Cavalleria rusticana* and *Pagliacci, Figaro, Hansel and Gretel.* He wrote to his mother:

'In *The Barber*, which has one oboe only, except for the overture, I will play second oboe and then hop out of the pit and conduct the chorus off-stage and supervise various stage effects such as storms etc. . . . I have to coach bloody singers in their parts in the mornings so you can imagine that I might learn quite a lot. . . . I have always wanted to have some opera training and this is the chance.'

He was also learning by watching the two conductors, James Robertson and Michael Mudie. Mudie, who was young and brilliant and knew Charles's ambitions, was very helpful in coaching and correcting his mistakes.

In Leicester, to his astonishment, he heard that he had been awarded a scholarship to Prague. There were no other musicians, all the other winners were Slavists. (At this time Czechoslovakia was the only country where it was possible to study Slav culture and language.) He had not made a good impression at his interview but perhaps some perceptive official had seen through his over-confident manner. The news threw him into a state of confusion. He was excited and pleased but he also realized the time had come to find out where he stood with Judy. He knew that he did not want to lose her; they were very much in love but marriage had not been discussed and if he went to Prague for a year he might find her no longer free when he returned.

When he had told his mother about the visit to Whistling Down he had given the impression it was mainly to see something of the English countryside. Remembering her plea not to marry the first girl he met he had written from Leicester, 'By the way you don't need to be worried about my falling in love or getting engaged. The only girl I see a lot of is Judy Wilkins who is about my own age and is first clarinet in the orchestra and what's more she is one of the only friends (particularly girls) that I have ever had that you would whole-heartedly approve of. In appearance and manner and disposition she is like a mixture between yourself and Toni Roberts. And also we have a lot in common and she likes to show me round the place. So have no fear, my dear, I wasn't born yesterday.'

He may have meant these words when he wrote them or he may have intended them as a softening-up measure, for it was true that of all the girls with whom he had been in love Judy was the only one who would not have caused Catherine concern. He had not been anxious to invite the questions, persuasions and warnings he would receive if he confided his real feelings, nor could he expect his parents to understand that though he and Judy had met only a short time before, they had seen far more of each other, often under trying conditions, than they would have done in a normal year. The tour had thrown them together constantly, in their work as well as their free time, they were excellent friends and companions and though it was probably never spelt out, temperamentally each complemented the other. It was not only Judy's pretty face, her intelligence and sense of humour that made him anxious not to lose her but her strong maternal instinct which responded to his underlying, half-conscious need for reassurance. Since leaving home he had continued to seek Catherine's advice or approval for most of his plans, but though he might still write to her, 'I feel in need of your counsel more than ever,' the focus for his sense of dependence had already begun to change.

It was not easy to be alone in Leicester. The theatre was in the middle of the city and the only place for private conversation was a nearby churchyard garden. As they walked there together discussing the scholarship Charles came to the point.

'Well,' he said bluntly. 'If I'm going to Prague I want you to come with me.'

Judy remained calm. 'Is this a proposal?'

'Yes,' said the romantic suitor. 'I suppose it is.'

They decided to marry in August and leave in September for Prague. When Judy rang her parents from Manchester Mrs Wilkins was not very surprised but she and her husband were uneasy. They had liked Charles and recognized his talent but were doubtful about his stability. They may also have realized that their daughter, a brilliant student, would probably end by abandoning her career for his. Judy herself had no hesitation, she knew she was a good musician but she recognized Charles's 'enormous talent' and decided that helping it would be her career. Her parents could see she had made up her mind and did not try to dissuade her.

For Charlie, ringing to tell his family was only a courtesy which he felt could wait till the company reached Belfast; meanwhile he and Judy had already started on what was to be the pattern of their married life. Though England was having the hottest summer for years he was still carrying round in his luggage the six sets of heavy underwear brought from Australia. When Judy suggested he post them back to London he said, 'Good idea. Do you think you could do it for me?' 'All right,' she said unsuspectingly, so she packed them up and sent them. She has been packing for him ever since.

One of the leading singers with Sadler's Wells was the Northern Irish tenor, James Johnston. He had a splendid voice but was known for really living his parts. In *Pagliacci* he had once torn at Nedda's costume with such passion that the whole top came off and she had to rush from the stage. In Belfast Johnston gave a party for the company at the house of a friend. There was plenty of singing and most of the accompaniments were played, from memory, by a rather shy young man whom Charles did not know but who seemed to be part of the tour. Once or twice, when the pianist did not know the music, Charles took his place. He was astonished by the stranger's knowledge of opera and the way he accompanied so easily.

The young man, Norman Tucker, was about to become co-director of Sadler's Wells Opera with James Robertson and Michael Mudie (they were known as the Three Norns). Tucker was an Oxford graduate, exceptionally gifted, an intellectual with a passion for opera. He had wanted to be a concert pianist but an injured hand had made it impossible and he had had a varied career ranging from jobs with the Treasury to translating operas into English and even composing. Later, as sole artistic director at Sadler's Wells he was an important influence in Charles's career.

From Belfast Charlie rang Catherine but when it came to the point he lost courage and did not mention his marriage. In those days of international calls people spent most of their time shouting 'Can you hear me?' at each other. It was no way to break delicate news and finally he sent a letter.

' . . . Contrary to what I told you before we have quite decided to get married! Now please be calm read on. It's not such a bad scheme as you will immediately think. She is exactly the type of girl that I know you like and she is quite unlike (of course) any other girl I have ever been interested in. You would have no doubt about her if you could meet her and I know that your only worry will be that I am too young to make up my own mind on such a big subject. . . . I can't tell you anything much about her without sounding like a reference for a new domestic. However I will say that she has a lot of brains and common sense, a most sweet disposition, and tons of humour. . . . She has succeeded in making me spend half as much as usual and has even made me smoke less, also she was one of the most brilliant students at the Royal College of Music, has had a very fine education, a considerable knowledge of most things and speaks good French and

Italian. . . . Also she is very much what Dad likes, not much lipstick, out-door type etc. . . . I know you will have a fit at this news but I want to emphasize again that she is not like any other girl with whom I have been friendly and embodies everything I like to an incredible extent.'

By the middle of August he was writing from London.

' . . . I was really delighted as you can imagine that you are so favourably disposed to my proposed marriage. It was a great comfort to get your letter and also Dad's. . . . We have decided more or less that the best thing is for Judy to come to Prague, that is if the British Council will allow it. They don't seem too keen on the idea because apparently they have had some unpleasant experiences with students marrying. The allowance isn't meant to cover wives but they are going to look into it and tell me in a week. At any rate she could come in a couple of months and they couldn't say anything. I am off to Cheltenham tomorrow and I shall have a talk about it to Mrs Wilkins. Mr Wilkins . . . is so reserved that it is impossible to talk to him. He is so quiet and self-sufficient, he lives in his own little room and even eats meals by himself so as to avoid having to talk . . . like Dad, only carried to the most incredible lengths. . . . Mrs W. is full of fun and a good sense of humour and very good to talk to. Judy . . . will write to you soon, plus a photo . . . so there it is. We shall have to wait for the reply of the British Council before any more is decided. I introduced J. to Mrs Grant this morning and Mrs G. seems to like her very much.'

Aware that a report would be sent to Catherine, Judy had gone along good-humouredly to be vetted. Later, hearing more about some of Charles's previous girls she quite understood his mother's anxiety.

On Tuesday, 19 August they suddenly realized that if they were to marry before Charles went to Czechoslovakia they must do it almost at once. September was the latest date he could leave London if he was to be in time for the new term at Prague Academy. At the end of the tour he had three weeks' work to finish at Sadler's Wells and his only free day was Friday 22 August. That night Judy rang her parents and sent telegrams to her friends: GETTING MARRIED FRIDAY HOPE YOU CAN COME, and Charles wired to invite the Grants. Judy's diary says:

Tues 19　Made up our minds to get married next Friday.
Weds 20　Flap. Ringing up Susan, Winnie etc.
Thurs 21　Panic.
Friday 22　Noon Bishops Cleeve married great success. Dora drove us after reception to Farncombe Manor.

Mrs Wilkins and Judy's sister Jo worked frantically to prepare a wedding breakfast and even scraped up materials for a magnificent cake which they decorated and wrapped round with a strip of aircraft tin-foil. With no decorations available they scattered the top with rose petals. Judy's friends were there and the Grants came, partly to support Charlie, partly to report to Catherine:

. . . Charlie and Judy were married in a beautiful English church at Bishops Cleeve. The service was quite simple but the parson took it with quiet dignity and the music was specially chosen.* The day was perfect. Judy wore a blue dress with a little toque of blue flowers and she carried a small bouquet of red carnations. . . .

Everyone speaks very highly of Judy. She seems to be a general favourite and Mrs Wilkins told me that although musical she is very practical and a good cook. Mr and Mrs Wilkins both like Charlie. His easy, fresh manner, his general intelligence and attractive personality make a good impression wherever he goes. Judy and Charles are obviously happy in each other's company and you would agree that they are very suited to each other. The Wilkins house is situated in the Cotswold Hills and they have a marvellous view looking towards the Malvern Hills, with the Welsh mountains beyond. Several photographs were taken specially to send you.

The Wilkinses are a delightful family. . . . Judy and Charlie left the house about 2.30. . . . After they had said goodbye they walked hand-in-hand down the garden through the fruit trees. We all felt they had made a happy beginning to a long and happy married life.

In Sydney, the news of the marriage caused a small sensation. Some said they hoped Charles was not marrying in haste, others were thrilled and thought it romantic. Hearing that Judy was a clarinettist one of the female violins in the Sydney Symphony said dreamily, 'How lovely. Two woodwinds.'

Catherine made the announcement firmly; it was done and should be accepted. Alan, who had long given up being astonished by anything his family might do, seemed only mildly amused. Cheered by her cousin's favourable reports Catherine appeared reasonably

---

*Mr Schimmin, Judy's old harmony professor from Cheltenham College, was organist and played Bach chorale preludes. Charles did not want conventional wedding marches but Walton's *Crown Imperial*, which he had chosen, was too difficult for Mr Schimmin.

happy. The fact that she did say several times, 'I *do* hope he won't be unfaithful to her', suggests that she knew more of Charles's past than she admitted, despite her later bland assurance to Judy that she was marrying a virgin.

VII

Prague

NOW THAT THEY were married the British Council insisted that Charles go to Prague alone, repeating that the scholarship allowance was inadequate for two people. The Prague office objected strongly and sent a telegram saying ON NO ACCOUNT BRING WIFE, but since the Council could not prevent Judy going independently and living at her own expense she applied to the Prague Academy under her maiden name to study the clarinet. Charles hoped to study with Václav Talich, the leading Czech conductor.

They spent their last three weeks in London with the Grants. Though Charles was working at Sadler's Wells they both managed to take lessons in Czech, and even to arrange accommodation in Prague. Through Judy's aunt Rene they had met a Czech businessman, Dr Vojáček, and his Scottish wife, and, at their house in Buckinghamshire, had made friends with Eva Hustolesová, who had come abroad to improve her English. Eva's parents lived on a farm at Dušníky, outside Prague, but she had a flat in town which she offered to share with Charles and Judy. She would be back there before they arrived.

On Wednesday, 24 September, at 9.20 a.m. they left Victoria Station for Czechoslovakia. Judy wore a new green mohair coat specially bought for the European winter and they were seen off by her sister Jo and friend Liz. At the last moment there was a crisis, an enormous box of clothes, soap, toothpaste, etc., brought at Catherine's behest from Sydney, threatened to fall apart, but an official found a rope and tied it up, literally as the train was about to start.

Three days later Judy wrote to her mother from Prague:

> c/o J. Hoftichová,
> Praha XVI,
> Bozděchova 9.

My darling Mummy,

Here we are, well and safe and all our luggage! We fetched it this morning from the station with the help of Paul Krakeš, a very nice boy we met in England at the Vojáčeks. He dealt with the customs men in Czech, otherwise we'd have been very lost. The journey was interesting, comfortable and we didn't really get sick of the train until the last few hours on Friday morning. We rushed all round Paris the first night, had a good supper and met this friend of C's (Roland Pullen) who is a sub-editor on the *Continental Daily Mail*. The first night in the Arlberg Express I didn't sleep much, it was so noisy; the sleepers were very comfy though and by the second night I was well used to it. We arrived on the Swiss border early Thursday morning and spent all that day travelling through the most gorgeous mountainous country. The train went right along Lake Zurich and later followed the river Inn to Innsbruck. We certainly had the best part in daylight. On Thursday night we slept well barring interruptions from numerous police and customs on different frontiers. However they kindly left us sleeping and only looked at our passports which we left out. . . . We had a very nice little Frenchman on the train looking after the sleeping cars who helped us, lent us maps and brought Charlie hot water to shave with.

It was his first experience of European travel. For a young man from a country where people travel vast distances without passports, and border formalities are mainly concerned with control of agricultural diseases, everything was new and wonderful. It was exotic to sleep in a Wagon-Lit, eat in a restaurant car among different nationalities, the sound of foreign languages, the smells of European food and tobacco. The names on stations flashing past, places read of but not yet seen, the Swiss mountains under snow, were wildly exciting. Judy was amused and touched each time he jumped up and exclaimed at the sight of snow. He had never seen it before, never been interested in winter sports or gone with the school to ski in the Australian Alps.

At six o'clock in the morning they were woken and asked to make currency declarations, in Czech, but harassing formalities were forgotten when they heard voices calling outside on the platform and realized they could understand what was said. *Horký parky* (Hot sausages). . . . *Pivo* (Beer). . . . It was a marvellous moment. The feeling of having arrived, of really being there and part of it all was a far more wonderful welcome than the most impressive ceremony.

By half-past eleven they were in Prague. The train was forty minutes late but Eva Hustolesová and her father were waiting on the platform. They had brought their car to drive the travellers to their new address but also the news that Eva, through being abroad all summer, had lost the flat she had hoped to share with them. Accommodation in Prague was scarce but she had managed to find them a room in the apartment of a family friend, a widow with grown-up children.

Mrs Hoftichová lived alone, across the river in the suburb of Smíchov. She spoke almost no English and their Czech was not much better but she welcomed them warmly and they all liked each other at once. Their room was very comfortable. . . . 'Two beds with incredible bedclothes . . . quilts with sheets buttoned on and huge, very soft pillows . . . extremely good to sleep in. . . . Constant hot water and we can use the kitchen etc as we like. Mrs H. is very nice.'

Next day they went out and bought stamps and a map of Prague. Their efforts at shopping were hilarious. They also used a public telephone and sent telegrams to England and Australia. Feeling quite clever they went on to buy bread, some horrible margarine (there was no butter) and apples. It was all very amusing with much laughing and pointing and struggling to find the right words, but everyone was extremely friendly and helpful and they discovered a café opposite the house where for about threepence they could buy heavenly *černé pivo* — black beer.

Prague was spared major damage during the war, for the occupation had protected the economy in the German interest, but in 1947 there had been a very bad drought, crops had failed and the farmers had had to kill most of their animals. Apart from meat, food was extremely scarce, there was no milk, no other dairy products, very little fruit and few vegetables. To buy any one had to go to the markets very early which meant waking at five o'clock. There was no tea or coffee but Judy had brought supplies from London. Later, because of Charles's extreme thinness, he was allowed a tiny ration of milk (half a litre a week), and butter when possible. Eva's parents were generous with butter and fruit from their farm — Eva's mother was shocked at Charles's starved appearance — and after some time there were food parcels from Sydney and cigarettes from England. Meanwhile housekeeping was very limited, but there were good cheap restaurants and they soon learnt to order everything on the menu and take away what they could not eat in doggie bags. If there were stewed prunes Judy used them for making a kind of jam.

The shortages of fresh food did not improve but occasionally they could find frozen vegetables and at times there were onions and black-market eggs. They filled up a great deal on potatoes, black bread and beer. They did not starve but the diet was very limited and everyone suffered some degree of malnutrition.

They were both enchanted with Prague and the kindness, friendliness and hospitality of the Czechs, whom Charles described to Catherine as 'a charming, cultivated people'. He was deeply impressed by the general high cultural standards, the linguistic ability, the knowledge of music and interest in everything, also the fact that 'they work harder than the English and particularly the Australians'. It was the beginning of a genuine love-affair with Czechoslovakia and the Czechs which has continued to this day, and with baroque architecture, which he now saw for the first time.

They loved the ancient streets of the city, the churches and princely palaces, the river, 'the almost unbelievably beautiful view of the Charles Bridge and all the old towers with the castle on top of the hill.' The Bridge, which they crossed each day on the way to their classes became 'their' bridge when they found that its earlier name was Judita Bridge.

To immerse themselves more fully in the country's life and culture they began seriously studying Czech. Judy, who felt communication more important than perfect grammar, was soon speaking without inhibition but Charles was shy and preferred to wait till he had mastered the complexities of the language. These nearly drove him mad at times but he carried on until he could express himself correctly and fluently. Before they left the country they were both reading novels, if laboriously, in Czech.

For the Czechs life was not pleasant and Charles, who had never before encountered hardship, even at a distance, was appalled to realize the way many of the people lived, that 'there were men with distinguished minds whose bodies smell because they have no soap and can't get enough to eat'. For the first time in his fortunate life it came home to him that people were suffering acutely all around him. He had told his mother that artistically Prague was the best thing that had ever happened to him but it was also an enlightenment, a revelation of the aftermath of war.

Tomorrow is a holiday for all the universities . . . to commemorate the thousands of Prague students . . . massacred . . . at the beginning of the German occupation. The longer I live here the more I am horrified by the bestiality of the Nazis. . . . Every family that I have met had one person shot during the Occupation, or in a concentration camp or tortured, and I have heard the most sickening descriptions of torture from first hand. Wherever I go I hear the same thing. . . . The son-in-law of our landlady was for five years in Buchenwald and a lady I know was one of the three or four

survivors out of several thousands in Auschwitz. . . . She is
going . . . to Nuremburg next week to testify against the comman-
dants and officers of the camp at their trial. Also, it is painful to see a
young couple we know whose arms were burnt with red-hot
pokers. They showed me the scars. It seems that the stories in the
papers were not exaggerated. . . . I can understand why the Czechs
don't even like to hear the German language spoken . . .

Though Charles had gone to Prague on a British Council Scholarship
it appeared that through bureaucratic muddle the Academy had never
heard of him. They had a file on Judy and after paying about five
shillings' enrolment fee she was given an entrance test. At the RCM
she had been top of her year but was surprised to find here that she
failed in technique. She was accepted because of her 'outstanding
musicianship' and began lessons as an 'extra-ordinary' student, with
Vladimír Říha, principal clarinet in the Czech Philharmonic . . . 'an
awfully nice man and good teacher . . . so *patient*'.

Meanwhile Charles was left to fret and fume till his papers turned
up. It was several weeks before they did and then they were made out
for Charles Wilkins, born in Assam, which was Judy's birthplace. It
was not till the last week in October that he could tell his mother-in-
law that the confusion was sorted out.

. . . I thought you might like to know that I am now completely
fixed up in my studies and that everything is rosy in Praha. I know J.
was a bit dismal in her letter to you last week and I really was furious
that there was so much muddle over my simple request to be
allowed to study the subject for which I was awarded the
scholarship. . . . Apparently though although the Ministry of
Education had awarded me the scholarship it didn't seem to think it
necessary to tell the Academy I was coming. In fact, as far as they
are concerned I could have stayed here for the year, drawing my
salary and not gone near the Academy. As for their worrying about
wives, my dear, they couldn't care less if I had a harem and fifty
kids!

At any rate after much wrangling everything has fallen into shape
and I am now overflooded with work, I have so many subjects. I am
studying conducting with two people and a host of other subjects
thrown in for good measure. Actually Talich's class is the least good
of everything because he only has one every month or so. Other
times the class consists of attending his rehearsals, which are
certainly most absorbingly interesting. . . . Professor Doležil, the

other conducting teacher is a wonderful teacher, and most frightfully thorough, like everything in the Academy. In fact Judy and I
are agreed that it's almost TOO thorough, that they spoonfeed the
students and leave not much to their initiative. However I am glad I
have learnt the rough and tumble way for the last few years, because
it makes the very organized learning of this place seem so much
easier. At any rate at present it's all too marvellous and I feel I am
learning more than I have ever done before. Also we are beginning
to know quite a few people which helps a lot, not only with work
but other things too. . . . It is remarkable the number of people
who speak English and our studies in Czech are being much
retarded. . . . However, everybody seems frightfully willing to
help. . . . I am most happy here and I know Judy is too, although I
have suddenly so much work and study that we don't see so much
of each other as before, which is a blow, but it's all in the cause of
art!

Charles had been very disappointed to hear that he was not after all
to study with Václav Talich, the eminent Czech conductor, who had
formerly been in charge of the Czech Philharmonic. He was told that
Talich was fully occupied as Director of the National Theatre and had
no time free for teaching, for he also worked with a chamber orchestra
of young people which he had founded. Rafael Kubelík, who had
taken over the Philharmonic, was also too busy to teach, though he
suggested that Charles come to his orchestral rehearsals. Charles went
to see Talich, who was very friendly and after confirming that his
mornings were spent rehearsing the opera at the Theatre, invited him
to his afternoon sessions with the chamber orchestra.

Talich, who had been a violinist and was 'marvellous with strings'
was superb at work with his wonderful little chamber orchestra, but
though Charles felt he was learning by watching what he really
wanted was individual tuition. Eventually, impressed by his eagerness, Talich agreed to give him some private lessons and take him
through a score.

Student life was very sociable and Charles and Judy had both made
many friends. There were dances, musical evenings, gatherings in
cafés, meals in private houses. Parties ranged from receptions at the
British Embassy to sessions in cellars drinking delicious Slovakian
wine among hundreds of barrels. In view of the British Council's
attitude to wives Judy had been lying low but everyone knew she was
married to Charles and there were no repercussions. They both played
in the British Council's semi-amateur orchestra, went to the theatre

and operas as often as possible, gave English lessons and studied German as well as Czech. They rowed on the river and visited Bertramka, the Dušeks' house where Mozart stayed. Charles played on Mozart's harpsichord and found it out of tune. At weekends they went for long walks with other students into the lovely countryside and in the holidays to the mountains to ski. Judy enjoyed skiing immensely but though Charles made an effort he did not take to it much.

As well as their student friends there were older Czechs to whom they became very attached and who were to become a permanent part of their lives. Through the Hustoles they had met Jiřinka Kadainková, the wife of an army officer, and her friend Jana Skuhravá. Both worked in the United States Embassy and spoke good English; Jiřinka also had a piano on which she allowed Charles to practise. When times were hard she would come to breakfast, bringing rolls and any fruit she could find and they would share the coffee or tea from their English and Australian food parcels.

After classes there were recitals, concerts and operas and much of the music was Czech. Prague had suffered so bitterly under the Nazis that even German music was hateful. People preferred to hear the works of their own composers, Dvořák, Smetana, Janáček, and mainly Czech music was studied at the Academy. An exception was made for Mozart for there had always been a great Mozart tradition in Prague. The Czechs claimed, and rightly, that only in their capital did he receive the recognition he deserved. Talich was a great Mozart interpreter, said to be the equal of Bruno Walter, and they heard him conduct *Don Giovanni* in the theatre in which the opera was first performed.

On 15 October Judy wrote in her diary: 'Saw *Kát'a Kabanová* at Národní Theatre. Superb performance. Talich.' They had gone to the theatre that night on spec., perhaps because Talich was conducting, to hear two leading Czech singers, Beno Blachut and Marta Krasová in an opera by Leoš Janáček. They had never heard of *Katya* (as we spell it) and knew little about its composer, though Charles had played his wind sextet, *Mládí*.

The evening was a revelation. As Charles wrote later, here was a composer whose very name was barely familiar to them, who had been dead twenty years, writing an opera in an idiom entirely unlike anything they had ever known, who used the human voice, the inflexions of his strange-sounding language in an absolutely new way, and whose instrumentation and harmony produced colours and sounds such as they had never heard before.

The wind sextet had not prepared them for the dramatic impact, the yearning lyrical beauty of the opera, its inexorable momentum, the dramatic intensity of the vocal writing, the anguished passionate sounds of the music. For the first time they had encountered a work completely uninfluenced by that of any other composer, a masterpiece by an absolute original who used all the time-worn musical vocabulary to say something entirely fresh and individual. The music was neither like Bartók, though based to a certain extent on folk-music, nor like Debussy, though it used the whole tone scale constantly. It was simply itself, unprecedented and astonishing.

At the time Charles did not realize the tremendous influence that evening was to have on his whole musical life, but he and Judy knew they must hear more of this great composer's work, and for the rest of their time in Czechoslovakia they travelled about to other cities, particularly to Brno, seeking out Janáček compositions, operatic and symphonic. Their discoveries were a constant excitement and by the time they left the country they had seen nearly all the operas, some in two or three different productions, and had encountered the different styles of performance given in Czechoslovakia: the 'Prague style', led by Talich, who brought out Janáček's smooth lyricism, sometimes 'beautifying' his original orchestration to give the music more luscious, even Straussian colours, and the 'Brno style' which kept religiously to the composer's orchestration as he wrote it, warts and all. In Brno, the Moravian capital, where Janáček lived and worked, the rough, often primitive muscle of the music was more evident than in cosmopolitan Prague.

The more Charles heard, the more his admiration grew for the genius of Janáček. He determined to take scores of the operas back to London, where they were virtually unknown, and try to interest someone in producing them.

The beautiful Zdeňka Podhajská, whom they met later, was the daughter of a singer who had known Janáček, Brahms and other composers. Zdeňka had been part of the artistic world of Paris in the 1920s and as a young girl had been the model for the cover of the published piano score of *Katya Kabanova*. She owned many Janáček relics, some of which she gave to Charles who, always drawn to older women, developed for her a lasting affection.

Winter in Central Europe was far colder than they had expected and Judy's green mohair coat was not nearly warm enough. Charles of course had his famous long underwear. They both ordered high felt boots and he bought a cap with fur ear-flaps. It grew colder still in the

New Year, making life more difficult than ever for professional people who had already suffered under the Nazis and were now often hounded from their jobs by the new government that had taken over.

Charles had never been interested in politics. He had been aware of the Soviets' vast sway over Eastern Europe but had not believed, as many did, that the communists would win the next election in Prague. It was a shock to learn that people he knew were being victimized, that the Hustoles, Eva's parents, had had their land confiscated for redistribution to peasants in order, it was said, to win more votes for the communist party in the next election. Suddenly a crisis had arisen: anti-communist ministers resigned, there were demonstrations by students, the whole city was tense. Then a new government took over, nominally a coalition, entirely communist-dominated in fact. To the grief of the Czechs it was announced a few days later that the popular non-communist foreign minister, Jan Masaryk, had 'committed suicide'.

Judy drove with a friend towards Lány to see Masaryk's funeral but at Dobrá the roads were barred and they had to watch from the distance. In America Truman made a speech, and there were calls for conscription and mobilization. Charles was convinced that World War III was imminent and took to talking in his sleep. One night Judy heard him say, 'Milk. . . ? You mean red milk? You actually mean RED?'

She wrote to reassure her mother. 'You will have been hearing of the political upheaval here. It will naturally be made a lot of by England and America because Czechoslovakia is the vital link between preventing or creating a hard barrier between East and West; but don't take it too seriously and on no account worry about us.'

With the exception of Talich, who was very ill, there were many dismissals and replacements at the Academy. In Charles's opinion most were for the better, musically. He was very pleased with his first lesson with Karel Ančerl, conductor of the Prague Broadcasting orchestra, who had replaced his earlier professor.

His private lessons with Talich had fallen through because of the conductor's illness. Charles went to see him in hospital, partly no doubt in order to keep in touch, with future lessons in mind, partly because he found Talich's conversation about music so fascinating and instructive, but also because the great man whom he so admired had been sympathetic to the aspirations of an eager young student. Talich was very bored lying in bed, forbidden to read because his eyes were affected but mentally very alert. He seemed pleased to see Charles, who went again and continued his visits after Talich left hospital to recuperate at his country villa. It was the beginning of a relationship that continued even after Charles left the country and from which he learnt much.

With the communists in power and arrests and dismissals taking place all over the country, eventually Talich was sacked from the National Theatre and his chamber orchestra was dissolved. His friends had feared that he might be arrested. During the German occupation he had kept open the National Theatre so that his staff would not lose their jobs and possibly be sent to concentration camps. After the war the Minister for Culture, Nejedlý, had accused him of collaboration, but he was not arrested, perhaps because he was no longer young and was ill in hospital. He was allowed to 'retire' to his villa at Beroun, about fifteen miles from Prague, and later was given the job of forming another orchestra in Bratislava. When very old and ill he was allowed back to Prague and rehabilitated in time for a state funeral.

Talich was a cultivated cosmopolitan Central European who had travelled abroad and spoke several languages but he was also a devoted patriot. In a letter to Charles, in London, he wrote, 'I love my small country dearly and it is for me the greatest happiness if I can work for it in the field which I understand.' His field was music, particularly the music of Czechoslovakia, above all of Dvořák, to whose work he was devoted and for whom he campaigned all his life. He was regarded as the greatest interpreter of Dvořák's symphonies, rhapsodies, liturgical music and also the Slavonic dances, of which he wrote that he longed to prove the composer 'a poet of rhythm, not just a musician writing dance music'.

When Charles describes Talich as 'a conductor of the old school' he means an artist absorbed in his art, indifferent to personal promotion or the cult of charisma; a musician who had read widely and thought deeply and speculated about life, suffering and death. He was concerned with philosophical and spiritual values in life and in all art, not music alone. He was religious, humane and lived by a code based on dedication to music, Christian ethics and love of his native land.

Early in April 1948 Charles wrote to Catherine:

You have spoken about Talich losing his job. The other day we went to see him in his villa outside Prague where he is convalescing. He seems much better though he is still not allowed to read much. . . . He has taken his dismissal quite well and indeed predicted it . . . when I visited him in hospital. The new Minister of Education has apparently been his enemy for many years and all things cultural such as music, theatre are under the Ministry of Education. It is funny that there should have been so much enmity between Talich and Nejedlý because although they are on opposite political sides both have worked hard for Czech music. Talich's chief contribution has been in his wonderful rendering of Dvořák and Smetana and other modern Czech composers such as Janáček and Ostrčil, and Nejedlý has written a tremendous volume about Smetana and history of music, and his son is a composer. But unlike in England . . . it is impossible to be friends with a person with whom you disagree in politics. . . . It looks now as if he won't be teaching at all and will only continue to conduct his chamber orchestra. However he wants me to go out again to his villa and says he will do what he can to help me. I may go out next Sunday with the G minor symphony of Mozart.

Once a week Judy cut sandwiches and Charles went by bus to spend the day at Beroun. If Talich had visitors the lessons were interrupted, otherwise they continued for hours. Charles was avid for information and the conductor, forced into inactivity, was glad of occupation.

. . . I was out at Talich's place today and he was telling me of the wonderful chances young men had before the war and still more before the first war. He himself was assistant to Nikisch and he spoke of the wonderful opportunities one had to hear all the best artists and work with them and absorb what there was to learn . . . we were lamenting the fact that outside America there is so little to hear and so little opportunity for a young man to learn his job. . . . I am lucky to have these lessons from Talich. . . . Today was really fine. We are doing the *Eroica* at present and he has most interesting and remarkable ideas on nearly every bar of the music. Particularly interesting are his ideas on string orchestral playing and also on the sort of psychological reactions of the orchestra to a conductor and lots of other vital things. He has also given me permission to go to his house in Prague and take down the bowings etc and all his notes in his scores so that will be some valuable work done. The scores are full of interesting remarks and it is very nice of him to let me do this and to take the trouble with me when he is not too well and when he has this continual political nonsense hanging over his head. He is really most kind. I have also arranged to go more than once a week to him because it is really the only thing I am interested in now. I wish I could send the dear old boy out to Australia to end his days with food and sunshine . . . then of course I should rush out there.

Charles had asked Talich's advice about going back to Australia if the chance arose. It was so far from the world's music centres that he feared he would be out of touch there and slip back, having no standards higher than his own to work towards. Talich had assured him that to be out of touch for a time did not matter, he felt that Charles could not do better than return to Australia to gain experience, so long as he did not stay more than three years. He hoped, for Charles's sake, that any orchestra he conducted there would be very bad, for that was the most valuable experience of all. After that he should come back and listen and study with a famous conductor and take a job in Europe or in America. He stressed the fact that in conducting one could really only learn from studying and listening to good conductors *after* one had actually grappled with the problems oneself, that one gained more from study *after* practical experience than from the Prague Academy method of too much study and not enough practice.

Charles, as he told his mother, had become rather fed up with the Academy. Though he had thought Ančerl an improvement on the earlier professor the conductor had little time to teach and Charles spent most of his time with a student named Milan Munclinger, playing orchestral works on two pianos and conducting for each other. Apart from his friends, the two Richards in Sydney, he had never met anyone with whom he had so much in common. Munclinger was also obsessed with music and, like Charles, talked and thought of nothing else.*

In addition to their walks and expeditions with students, whenever possible Charles and Judy went exploring on their own. One day they set off very early to hitch-hike their way to Slovakia. They got a lift in an export lorry going to Yugoslavia and reached Bratislava at 8 p.m. The driver was extremely kind and generous, he insisted on giving them lunch and taking them out to dinner that night. They decided he must be a black-market dealer when two fishy-looking Slovaks joined him and they ran up a huge bill with bottles of wine. They all had a good deal to drink and Charles made friends with the cimbalom player of the Hungarian gypsy band in the restaurant. He was fascinated by the instrument, which neither he nor Judy had seen before.

After two nights in Bratislava, which they felt did not care for foreigners and where they saw the opera, which was poor and put them off trying for jobs there, they crossed the Danube and walked

*Milan Munclinger died in March 1986.

towards the borders of Hungary and Austria. They were only about 25 miles from Vienna but could go no further because they did not have the right permits; yet, even annoyed and frustrated, they both felt the strange excitement that comes in looking across a frontier. To all but the most blasé and obtuse, another country is always the unknown. For the first time they had 'a great feeling of being right in the heart of Europe with many nationalities all round'.

They had been pleased to find they could understand Slovak fairly well, though every word seemed to differ slightly from Czech. Going north, a charming Slovak picked them up and took them part of the way to Nové Město (New Town), found them a good hotel and insisted they come to his house for supper. His wife, a Slovak from the United States, spoke good English, or rather American. Charles and Judy had hoped to reach the High Tatras in Slovakia but the weather changed and a cold wind came up. Time was running out so they turned west through beautiful country to a pleasant town in Moravia called Olomouc. Next morning they hitched down to Brno, arriving at midday, visited the British Institute for information about a job there for Charlie and in the evening saw a very good performance of Smetana's opera, *Dalibor*. They had sworn they would not take a train but the wind was bitter, they both had hangovers and were tired and dirty. After trying for half an hour for a hitch on the main road outside Brno they returned to Prague by train. It had been a wonderful week, seeing the country and getting to know people; they had been taken for French, Poles, Germans, Hungarians, Austrians, Russians and of course Americans but as soon as they explained that they were English, everyone, Czech and Slovak, had overwhelmed them with kindness and hospitality.

Yet despite their love for the people and country, despite the offer of work, Charles knew he could not stay. He had written to Michael Mudie to enquire about the possibility of going back to Sadler's Wells and, after discussion with Tucker, Mudie had replied, offering him the job of repetiteur, with promise of future conducting. He was to start in September at £10 a week, training chorus and soloists, and later conduct opera or ballet. Charles was very pleased, though before accepting he asked for confirmation that he would conduct. Judy, who had hoped to work as deputy clarinet, in fact rejoined the orchestra full-time.

Charles wrote to his mother: 'I feel misgivings a little bit about going back to England. It will seem a bit tame and I'm sure the insular narrow minds of many English will drive me mad. However I am really looking forward to beginning in Sadler's Wells.'

During the last months there were walking tours in the lovely 'Bohemian Paradise', a visit to the Šumava Forest on the borders of Czechoslovakia and south-west Germany. The Prague Music Festival had started and though many stayed away for political reasons the Brno Opera Company was there and gave performances of wonderful Janáček operas. Among the Russian musicians, they heard a young pianist unknown to them but whom they recognized at once as a very great artist. His name was Emil Gilels.

They were suddenly desperately busy. The great Sokol Gymnastic Festival had begun and also a Festival of Broadcasting, during which Charles played a composition by a young Czech and was interviewed on the air, in Czech. All their friends were giving farewell parties, they had last-minute shopping to do and arrangements to make for their journey home through Poland and Sweden, with a holiday in Denmark.

In order to send their luggage in advance they had to pack up by a certain date. The authorities had discovered that foreigners were smuggling out clothes and valuables for Czechs who had escaped over the border and a heavy tax had been imposed on everything leaving the country, even on personal possessions brought in from abroad. Formalities included detailed inventories, inspections and valuations. For Judy and Charles the rush to be ready in time was complicated because he could not finish his packing until he had taken down and transferred to his own scores as many as possible of Talich's notes and markings. Eventually the luggage was despatched after 'one of the most frightful experiences of my life. We arrived at the Customs at 8 a.m. and did not get away till 4.0 p.m., not because there were any other people but because every handkerchief and score and tie etc was counted by the officials to see if it corresponded with the list of belongings which had been passed by the export board. For instance I had written 300 scores and there were 301 so I now have to get special permission again for that one and a few books we have bought here. Fantastic and most humiliating. They felt with their dirty hands through Judy's dresses to see if diamonds were hidden etc. Most of these things, by the way, were belongings from Australia and England. And we still have to pay duty to take them out again.'

At the last lesson with Talich his teacher repeated his advice that for Charles, at this stage, practical experience was more necessary than study. He suggested that after a year at Sadler's Wells Charles return for a few weeks' work with him. It seemed a good and feasible plan that delighted both Mackerrases. They longed to return to this country which they loved and to Prague which they thought as beautiful in its way as Paris or Rome. The new régime did not seem to trouble foreigners if they stayed only a short time and were not newspapermen.

They said goodbye sadly to their friends. Some had already left the country; those who remained loaded them with presents, Mrs Hoftichová, their landlady, was almost in tears, but there was a touch of comedy in their final scene with the dreaded Customs. Instead of the expected ordeal the officer did not even look at their bags, only raved about how well they spoke Czech.

'You aren't taking out anything for escapees, are you,' he said. 'No jewels or valuables. . . . No, of course *you* wouldn't do *that* . . . ha–ha–ha!' and so saying he walked away.

VIII

Pineapple Poll

BACK IN ENGLAND Charles suffered the anticlimax he had expected: he was depressed by the drabness of London and 'the extreme ordinariness and undistinctiveness of the English . . .'. He knew he should not be too sweeping but could not help comparing them, even educated people, with the cultivated Czechs who spoke four languages and could discuss politics, history, music, literature and art. The reaction was inevitable after a fascinating year.

London not only seemed drab, it was also crowded with visitors, in Europe for the Olympic Games. Sadler's Wells was away on tour and Charles, already worrying that he might not be given as much conducting as he hoped, could get no information. Flats were almost impossible to find. For some time Judy had been writing from Prague asking her sister and friends to search, even offering a commission but without success. When her former teacher at the RCM, the clarinettist Frederick (Jack) Thurston offered them a room in his house at Barnes they were very glad to accept.

They had also arrived back very hard-up after travelling across Europe from Prague to Sweden and on to Denmark to stay with a friend. Unlike Judy, who had been in London and Plymouth during the blitz, Charles had never seen bombed cities and was shocked by the devastation in Poland and Germany. Their money had run out in Holland, and on the train from Harwich to London they had had to borrow two pounds from 'a very nice Englishman' who turned out to be a private detective.

They spent a weekend with Judy's parents at Whistling Down before starting to look for a flat. Charles called on Adrian Boult (whom he also asked about a flat), and found him rather gloomy concerning the prospects for young conductors; but he promised to give introductions to the BBC and agreed when Charles asked him to take him through some British works. Boult was very kind but extremely busy and though Charles made the request from genuine eagerness to learn he also felt he was less likely to be forgotten if he kept more or less in sight.

At the end of the first week in August Judy wrote in her diary, 'FOUND A FLAT! and paid £150 premium [key money] to secure it.' It was an unfurnished maisonette at Notting Hill Gate, 12 Pembridge Crescent, much bigger than they needed but the key money was low (at that time £1000 was not unusual), and the agent agreed to paint it. The rent was £2.17 p.w. which they thought 'monstrous, though comparatively cheap by present day standards' and to help pay it they quickly let a room to a young Czech, Saša Kubin, for bed and breakfast.

Sadler's Wells came back to London and Charles was cheered when Michael Mudie assured him that though he would be given no conducting for a month or so there would be plenty of opportunities later. He could also make extra money by occasionally playing as deputy oboe in the orchestra.

They had been given some good furniture from Whistling Down, which had just been sold, but they still needed many things. For the first time Charles began to realize how much it cost to set up house. In his frail little Czechoslovakian diary, among names and addresses in spiky Continental handwriting, strange entries began to appear: *Ask about electric heater. . . . Cheap gas ring 6/4, nice one 12/2; must have chimney sweep also upstairs. . . . Toaster £3. . . . Immersion heater 28/– . . . . Kitchen tap doesn't work . . . armchairs coming . . . carpet coming . . .*

When the season began at Sadler's Wells he had fifteen operas to learn; as assistant conductor he might have to take over anything in the repertoire at a minute's notice. He was also to conduct ballet. It was a demanding job, combined with work as repetiteur, but he knew he was very lucky to have it. Mudie and James Robertson conducted the new productions, Charles and Leo Quayle, assistant conductor and chorus master, did the donkey work. Mudie, who was very helpful, had an 'absolutely wonderful operatic talent' but he was already ill with disseminated sclerosis.

In September 1948 Charles learnt that he was to conduct *Fledermaus* on 20 October. From then on he thought of nothing else. He was excited, nervous, anxious to succeed. Excusing himself to Catherine for not answering letters he said, 'You do not know how much work must go into a simple opera like *Fledermaus*. The conductor HAS to give every cue to the singers (because they can hardly hear the orchestra) and he MUST be dead sure always.'

On the night, Judy was playing in the orchestra, equally excited and nervous, but her diary says simply, '*October 20*. C. conducts *Fledermaus. Marvellous.* Everyone delighted.' Next day Charles wrote to his mother: 'I donned my tails for the first time in my life and went down in fear and trembling, having had one three-minute rehearsal with the orchestra and an hour with a few principals.' People were kind and encouraging but he knew there had been mistakes and could not wait for his next performance to correct them. 'Michael Mudie, who has had more operatic experience than nearly anyone else in England, was watching me the whole evening and today he took me through the opera showing me all the mistakes I had made and how to rectify them. . . . He was very nice, saying that he had expected it to be good but was quite astounded at my performance. He said he was only sorry that they couldn't give me more conducting but that there were unfortunately only six shows a week and that he and the other two conductors weren't bad enough to get the sack!'

Later in December of the same season Charles conducted *Cav. and Pag.* and in March 1949, *Rigoletto.* Of the first performance *The Times* critic wrote: 'The chief point of interest in this routine performance was the emergence of Mr Charles Mackerras as a conductor of promise. He kept the music flowing, secured a good ensemble and brought out such refinements as there are in this not so blatant score.'

During the 1949–50 season he substituted for Mudie and Robertson in London and on tour in *The Bartered Bride, Fledermaus, Pagliacci, The Barber, Madame Butterfly.* He usually conducted without rehearsal which was frightening at first but very good training. Taking over an orchestra rehearsed by another conductor meant he must prove himself to players and audience by his actual performance.

In the next few years he was given more conducting and as Michael Mudie's illness progressed frequently had to take his place. Charles has never forgotten how much he owed to Mudie who continued to teach and train him. In the morning he would watch and listen, then in the evening actually see carried out on the stage the ideas and theories they had discussed earlier. He was happy at Sadler's Wells; there were a number of Australians and South Africans among the singers and dancers and he felt it would be impossible to find 'two conductors more easy to get on with than James Robertson and Michael Mudie'.

At Pembridge Crescent there were now two lodgers to help finances. Judy also played in the orchestra and gave clarinet lessons. They both tried to keep up their Czech and study German — Charles's diaries are full of German phrases among his opera dates — and to hear as much music and see as many operas as possible. Charles was so overwhelmed by his first performance of *The Mastersingers* that he wept and they were both profoundly moved by one of Kathleen Ferrier's last appearances in *Orfeo* at Covent Garden, with John Barbirolli.

For all her intellectual interests and sense of adventure Judy was a home-lover and she wanted a family. Though Charles liked the idea in theory, he was afraid that children would interfere with his work. He told Judy that he was prepared to provide for them but that she would have to bring them up herself.

She was not discouraged and was already pregnant when in 1949 Catherine arrived from Australia. She had made a strenuous journey through Spain, inspecting the churches, dipped into Portugal to visit Fatima, which she described as 'just like Bondi Beach', and reached London in excellent spirits, eager to approve Charlie's wife. Judy, who was still playing full-time in the orchestra as well as running the house and looking after Charles, would come home from the theatre exhausted to find her mother-in-law full of energy, ready to start a dissertation on some learned subject — the Hapsburg Empire was a favourite — holding forth loudly in the kitchen while Judy struggled to prepare a meal. Eventually Catherine would notice her wan appearance and say with surprise, 'Judy, you look tired. I'll make you an egg-flip.' Like her son, she was kind and affectionate, but when caught up in an absorbing idea was oblivious to all else; however she was delighted with her daughter-in-law and announced to her family and friends that she herself could not have chosen a more suitable wife for Charles.

By the seventh month of her pregnancy Judy found breathing for clarinet playing was becoming too difficult. She left the orchestra and spent the next two months with her parents at Haslemere. On 8 August, while Charles and his mother were away in the Cotswolds, she produced a daughter, Fiona, three weeks earlier than expected. The baby weighed only 3½ pounds and was delicate, which, Judy felt, may have been partly due to her own poor diet in Prague. The following year, on Charles's birthday, a second daughter arrived and was christened Catherine.

Judy kept her side of the bargain about the children and devoted herself to them during their earliest years. Even after she had started teaching, and playing in public recitals, she managed to find time to listen and tie on bandages and sit on beds after nightmares. Charles was a kindly but abstracted parent; the girls, particularly Fiona, have a rather vague memory of him in their childhood. He was either away or he came and went with his mind full of music and at home usually had his head in a score. All his energies went into his work leaving nothing for such a new and difficult relationship as fatherhood. Babies were unnerving, unpredictable, liable to yell, be sick, keep one awake, interfere with one's plans. They were also foreign territory. During the war when the Mackerras twins were small and Catherine had no domestics, Alastair had helped to look after them but Charles had been working from dawn to dark at that time or living away from home. He had no experience of very young children and naively expected from them behaviour far beyond their years. He was also inept and squeamish when it came to coping with their physical functions. Having left him alone with the baby one day Judy came home and found him looking greenish and slightly phosphorescent. When she asked what was wrong he told her that he had just been sick.

'Fiona dirtied her nappy,' he said. 'So I took it off and emptied it into the loo and then I was sick. I didn't know how to put on a clean one so I put *The Times* under her.'

He was miserable and distressed but Fiona was happy, squealing delightedly as she kicked scraps of dirty paper all over her cot.

At the theatre Charles had been having discussions with Peggy van Praagh, the Sadler's Wells Ballet Mistress.* He had never abandoned his idea of making a ballet from the Savoy operas and when he realized that the copyright on Sullivan's music would expire at the end of 1950 he felt it was time to act. Peggy van Praagh was interested, she believed such a ballet would make a very good item in the company's 1951 Festival of Britain programme and suggested as choreographer the brilliant young South African, John Cranko, who was about the same age as Charles and equally enthusiastic. Cranko understood exactly what was needed and had the inspired idea of commissioning Osbert Lancaster for the sets and costumes. Lancaster had not worked for the stage before but he turned out to be the perfect choice, with a wonderful un-chi-chi flair for Gilbertian comedy.

Arranger and choreographer worked well together. After much thought and discussion Charles decided that rather than draw on an opera they should base their ballet on one of Gilbert's *Bab Ballads*, and

*After the war a number of the leading dancers, including Margot Fonteyn, Anton Dolin and Robert Helpmann, had moved from Sadler's Wells to Covent Garden where, under Ninette de Valois, they eventually became known as the Royal Ballet. A smaller company, the Sadler's Wells Theatre Ballet, remained at the old theatre with Peggy van Praagh in charge.

John suggested 'The Bumboat Woman's Story', the tale of Poll Pine-apple (a forerunner of Little Buttercup in *HMS Pinafore*). When Charles was free of the theatre he spent all his spare time in the D'Oyly Carte music library at the Savoy, working on the scores. He would choose the tunes he wanted, according to the kind of music he knew Cranko needed for his story, then at Pembridge Crescent would play them over on the piano so the choreography could be tried out. Cranko, who had an early wire recorder, would copy the music they chose and take it home to study, then he would tell Charles if it was what he wanted or if he must have something more. For Charles, making arrangements in this way was far easier than trying to compose for ballet, for if one tune did not suit the choreographer it could be swapped for another. As he worked he often thought of Tchaikovsky's ballets and marvelled that they were so good, considering that the composer wrote them to fit Petipa's exact instructions.

Pembridge Crescent became a kind of Sullivan factory. Hour after hour, week after week, month after month Charles played and John danced, working out steps on the sitting-room floor while the two little girls, Fiona and Catherine, slept peacefully in the next room and Judy got on with the chores.

The original piano scores had to be copied before orchestration could start and Joyce Bell, their young pianist lodger who lived in the attic, was called in to help. Charles had augmented the original orchestration, sometimes in Sullivan's own style, sometimes with modern 'brash' orchestration and Richard Merewether, who had just arrived in London and was looking for work, copied all the parts. Having been in the project from its conception he was amused and pleased to help with the final stages. He was in constant touch with Charles, for the copying had to begin long before the complete job was finished. Charles was under great pressure; he managed to keep just one jump ahead of the copyist but he was feeling the strain, orchestrating to a deadline at home, working as conductor and repetiteur at the theatre. Towards the end he became rather desperate and had to ask Norman Tucker's permission to be excused from one opera in order to finish the ballet. Tucker let him off but was rather annoyed and reminded him that he was being paid for a certain number of performance and rehearsal calls a year.

In John Cranko's story the heroine, Poll Pineapple, loved kind Lieutenant Belaye, (promoted to Captain for the ballet). He was by far the sweetest of all the kind commanders who anchored in Portsmouth Bay and commanded the gunboat *Hot Cross Bun*. ('She was seven-and-thirty feet in length and she carried a gun.') Not only Poll but all

the sweethearts and wives of Portsmouth were so infatuated with the
kind Lieutenant that they disguised themselves as crew and boarded his
ship. They swooned with delight when he danced the hornpipe,
collapsed (Poll fainted) when the gun was fired, were seasick, and 'spent
more time than a sailor should on their back back hair'. However, when
they found that Belaye was engaged to be married they revealed
themselves, Poll settled for a faithful suitor and all ended happily with a
typical G & S tableau grouped round Britannia and the Union Jack.

The first performance of *Pineapple Poll* was given at Sadler's Wells on
13 March 1951. Charles conducted the orchestra, Elaine Fifield, the
Australian ballerina was a perfect Poll and David Blair made a perfect
Belaye. The ballet was an immediate success. The cast made sixteen
curtain calls and choreographer, dancers, producer, designer,
arranger-conductor were all given rave reviews in almost every paper.
The Times critic, using the royal We, allowed that it disarmed criticism
'by its exuberant good humour' and found Charlie's arrangements
'splendidly exuberant'. The *Observer* rather cryptically called it a
breezy ballet which 'would be enjoyed by sea-faring persons of every
sex and by all who appreciated low life at the edge of the high seas . . .
even if they have never read Mr Auden's *Enchafed Flood*'. The
Manchester Guardian, describing the score as 'a jolly arrangement of
Sullivan tunes', admitted that it was a 'happy work . . . one of those
rare occasions when choreography, music and décor have blended, as it
were, irresistibly', while less pretentious reviewers went cheerfully
overboard with such words as delicious . . . enchanting . . . brilliant . . . witty . . . gaiety . . . ravishing . . . delightful . . . spirited
humour . . . uproarious success.

The ballet critic, Arnold Haskell, described it as being 'as truly
English as *Le Beau Danube* is Viennese and *Gaieté Parisienne* Parisian',
yet, though *Poll* is indeed 'truly English' in its origins, in a subtle way
the ballet music is not entirely so: it has even been said that Charles
made Sullivan sound like Offenbach. While remaining respectful and
faithful to the composer he had, through his orchestration, injected
lighthearted sex into the almost choirboy Englishness of the original
music, an extra warmth and dash that appealed to everyone, even
those who normally do not like Gilbert and Sullivan.

It is no reflection on the ballet's creators to say that the timing was
perfect. After years of war and postwar austerity people longed for
colour and fun, and from the very first moment that was what *Poll*
provided. Dashing choreography, witty sets, sparkling music (the
adjectives apply equally to each), create a marvellous sense of
freshness, youth and vitality which 35 years later still remains.

It is not hard to see why the ballet was such a triumph and why the music was said to fit the story like a glove. The humour and personalities of all involved had ensured harmonious collaboration, while Charles's whole past had contributed in a practical way: his intimate knowledge of Gilbert's librettos and Sullivan's scores, his years of arranging music for commercial radio, his knowledge of orchestration, his experience in ballet-conducting at Sadler's Wells.

After the first success, Chappell, who had been Sullivan's publishers, wanted to have the score, and gramophone companies were eager to record the orchestral arrangement with Charles conducting. When Columbia released their six 78s in 1951 the rave reviews were repeated: *The Times* wrote of the score's 'full-blooded brilliance, splendidly imaginative and effective orchestral texture and ingenious construction', and Desmond Shawe-Taylor considered that for skill and lightness of touch Charles's score deserved to rank as an English *Boutique Fantasque*.

People tried to spot the sources. One critic thought that much of the music came from *Pinafore*, while another, better informed, commended the deliberate avoidance of the more obvious selections from that opera. The Mackerras family did well; in fact Charles was slightly aggrieved when Catherine claimed to recognize all the tunes, for some were from little-known operas and 'even Alastair and Richard Merewether didn't know some'. He confided that the two 'mystery tunes on side 12 [of the recording] are *Princess Ida* — "We have learned the prickly cactus" etc — and end of *Di Ballo* overture . . . the only part not from a G & S score.'

Poll was later televised but though the music came through successfully the ballet itself lost much of its charm through being in black and white.

On the day that Charles was to finish recording Judy waited anxiously for him to come home. She knew that he would be paid in cash and that it would be, to them, an enormous sum, something like £100. As time passed and he did not appear she became very worried and when he was not back by midnight both she and Joyce Bell were sure there had been a disaster. Eventually Judy rang the police. She had meant to ask if there had been a breakdown on the Underground but when the telephone was answered she burst out pathetically, 'Could you help me please, my husband hasn't come home.'

There was a pause, then a frosty official said, 'Really, madam! This is Scotland Yard. We only handle international cases in this section. You should ring your local police.'

At that moment a cheerful voice was heard below in the road.

'Right! Well, goodnight then!' and up came Charles with his fortune.

He had been with two members of the Sadler's Wells financial section discussing *Poll*'s royalties. It had not occurred to him that he had any rights in the score, which he regarded as Sullivan's work, and because he had done the ballet for a fee he thought he could expect no more payment. After Chappell, the publishers, had explained to him that the copyright for the *arrangement* was his a contract was negotiated with Sadler's Wells and he received a modest royalty. This was unchanged for many years but in the early days, small as it was, it made a difference to Mackerras finances and many times *Poll* arrived just in time for the gas bill or to help with the housekeeping.

Pineapple Poll has been recorded six times, four times conducted by Charles. Recordings range from 78s made by the Sadler's Wells orchestra in 1951 to the latest digital stereo compact disc made by Decca. The first recording was made on 78s because EMI believed LPs were a flash in the pan and would not last. The Sadler's Wells record of *Poll* was so successful that Charles was asked by George Martin at Parlophone (later record producer for the Beatles) to do other ballets. The records were made but the quality of playing was less successful and they were never issued.

IX

Katya

WRITING TO CATHERINE in 1948, about the Prague Spring Festival, Charles had described the Janáček operas performed by the Brno Company and added, 'It is a terrible pity that these works are quite unknown outside this country. They are certainly in the front rank of modern opera and in my opinion the best works ever produced by a Czech. When I get back I shall do my utmost to persuade Sadler's Wells to perform one of them, though I don't suppose they will.'

Katya Kabanova was among the scores he had brought back to London and as soon as possible he showed it to Norman Tucker. Tucker, who was 'extra-receptive and one of the best opera directors ever' was interested, but Charles had only a vocal (piano) score and though he explained that Janáček's orchestration was 'a sort of mixture between Mussorgsky, Bartòk, Debussy, Sibelius and Mahler' he could give little idea of the actual sound, even to experts. It was not that Janáček was so particularly advanced in his composition methods — Schoenberg's *Pierrot Lunaire* had been written before *Katya* — but that he could express absolutely new ideas with apparently conventional means.

The BBC had in its vaults an old tape of a Brno performance of *Katya* and this was borrowed and played for Tucker and Desmond Shawe-Taylor, with Charles giving a running commentary on the action of the opera. After the audition both Tucker and Shawe-Taylor, who had heard a good deal about Janáček but little of his actual music, were deeply impressed, and Tucker decided to include the opera in the 1950–51 season. Since it would have to be given in English he engaged the Mackerras's Czech friend, Arnošt Propper, who spoke perfect English, to make a literal translation which he, Tucker, then rearranged to fit the composer's notes and rhythms. He became so enthusiastic about Janáček's work that eventually he presented other operas at Sadler's Wells, translating several of them himself.

The première of *Katya Kabanova* was to be 10 April 1951. The role of Katya was given to Amy Shuard, a strapping young Cockney soprano of great promise. She had been the star pupil of Dame Eva Turner, the Wagnerian singer, and later moved on to the Royal Opera House, Covent Garden. Dennis Arundell, who had done many Sadler's Wells productions, was to produce and Michael Mudie to conduct, while Charles taught the singers the opera and helped them with the unfamiliar Janáček idiom. Privately he was disappointed and slightly aggrieved. Not only had he made the suggestion about *Katya* and brought the score from Prague, he was the only one who had actually seen the opera performed and had discussed it with Talich, a Janáček authority; but Mudie was the regular conductor and though Charles had done an increasing number of operas he was after all a still unknown, rather new assistant.

The singers did not find the music easy. It was strange to them, based on the rhythm of Czech speech and the sounds of nature, and made even more difficult and peculiar with its new English words. Mudie was also in trouble. His illness had affected his eyes: he could manage familiar works but he could not study scores and (partly owing to Janáček's idiosyncratic way of writing) *Katya* was full of mistakes and wrong notes. He was also losing muscular control of his beat and increasingly Charles was called in to help. A week before the first night it became clear that Mudie could not go on and Charles would have to take over. With the dress rehearsal so close he asked for a special rehearsal, with orchestra alone, to sort out with them the many details that had not been clarified.

In the excitement of the emergency he was less worried than horribly nervous. He was taking on a tremendous responsibility and anticipated an ordeal. He had never before conducted a first night in London (apart from *Pineapple Poll*) let alone the British première of an almost unknown work; the critics knew of his part in introducing *Katya* and if the opera failed through his inadequate conducting he would be doubly to blame. There was also the uncomfortable realization that this great opportunity to prove himself had come through another's misfortune. It is not surprising that by opening night he was in a fair state of tension.

As he dressed for the performance he calmed himself by concentrating on the story of *Katya*, trying to achieve a suitable state of mind for tragedy. He was ready, in his tails, waiting to leave for the theatre when Judy, who had been trying to dress, rushed in with Fiona and thrust her into his arms. The *au pair* had not yet come home and the baby was in a state. She seemed to sense that her parents were planning to go out and leave her and, dumped on her father's knee, she picked up his tension and started to scream. According to Charles she also shat, though Judy denies it. Convinced that she did it on purpose Charles commanded her to shut up but she screamed louder and more fiercely than ever. By the time the *au pair* came in Fiona was mildly hysterical and Charles's hard-won calm had departed. With nerves on edge, in tails and long evening dress, the maestro and his wife set out. A taxi from Notting Hill Gate to Sadler's Wells was beyond their means. They took the Underground to Holborn, then a 19 or 38 bus to Rosebery Avenue.

Katya Kabanova is based on a Russian drama, *The Storm*, by Nikolai Ostrovsky. The heroine is a sensitive passionate creature whose dull husband does not understand her and who is completely dominated by his tyrannical mother. Katya falls in love with a rather spineless young man with whom she has an affair while her husband is away. Her lover has neither the money nor the courage to save her from her unhappy marriage and, torn by her guilty conscience, she breaks down during a terrifying storm and makes a public confession. Her lover has been sent away; she knows he will never be able to rescue her and in despair she drowns herself in the Volga.

The story, which is a comment on the narrowness and harshness of nineteenth-century Russian rural life, hinges largely on the Slav temperament; without an understanding of the mystical Russian soul Katya's behaviour seems extreme and the story over-melodramatic. The first night reviews were varied. There was general praise for the management's courage in presenting the opera but many commented on its 'Russian gloom'. Some found the music difficult; it was said to be strange and 'jagged'. The *Daily Telegraph* thought the performance 'lively . . . with animation and charm' but the 'vocal writing tiresome', and in the *Sunday Times* Ernest Newman damned with faint praise: 'Janáček is rather a scrap-by-scrap composer; finding it difficult to think consecutively for more than two or three minutes at a time; but there are enough good musical moments in his *Katya Kabanova* to keep the audience to the end.' He considered Amy Shuard's Katya 'rather more vociferous than the character calls for' and that the chief credit for the performance went to Charles and Dennis Arundell.

Charles himself suffered reaction and thought that nothing on that first night had been as good as it should have been. At the dress rehearsal when everyone had been so grateful to him for taking over and such tremendous efforts were made it had all been wonderful; now he was suddenly learning how it felt to conduct on a first night, how many things might not work as planned or rehearsed, how many forgotten details could go wrong for the first time.

Yet other important critics were enthusiastic. The perceptive ones accepted the story and those who had informed themselves about Janáček's work knew that the 'scrappy' 'jagged' music derived from the rhythm of Czech speech, an effect partly changed by the English translation. The *Manchester Guardian* considered that music-lovers should be grateful to Sadler's Wells for giving them the opportunity to see *Katya*, which the writer described as a masterpiece, a work of genius, a work of art unlike anything seen before in opera. He begged people to see it; he praised the performance, Norman Tucker's translation, Charles's conducting, Dennis Arundell's production. He felt that both Charles and Arundell had succeeded in making the cast familiar with Janáček's unusual idiom and that the whole company showed extraordinary response and dedication to the opera's demands. It was, he said, Sadler's Wells' most impressive and most courageous achievement since their production of *Peter Grimes* in 1945. And Lord Harewood in the *Daily Mail* called it ' . . . the most important operatic event of the London season. It is an achievement of a high order, and the performance seemed to me good enough to make the composer's points with certainty and sufficiency of style.' He praised Amy Shuard's sympathetic stage personality and the intensity of her very beautiful voice, and continued, 'I hope you will go and see the opera. . . . In fact I hope you will go twice . . . if you don't you will miss hearing a very remarkable work . . . much too good to be neglected in this country any longer.'

But people did not go twice and many did not go at all. *Katya* played to half-empty houses and despite the critics was a 'glorious failure'. It was breaking new ground; people were not yet ready for music that 'hits you between the eyes'. The opera was given two repeat performances in November and then dropped from the repertoire. By 1959, when it was revived, attitudes had changed and critics were writing of Janáček's music as thrilling, dramatic, passionate and realistic.

Charles was not given a Mozart opera until 1950 when he conducted *Così fan tutte* in Bristol on tour. In 1951 he conducted *Figaro* and by 1954 had increased his repertoire to fifteen operas: *Traviata, The Barber, Butterfly, Don Giovanni, Bohème, Cav and Pag, Figaro, Hansel and Gretel, Il seraglio, The Bartered Bride, Tosca, Carmen, Luisa Miller* and *Don Pasquale*.

But in 1951 he had not been at all sure that he would be at Sadler's Wells for another three years. He was growing discouraged. The honeymoon was over, the euphoria of *Poll* and *Katya* had faded. His

Left: 1928: Charlie aged three with his mother and brother Alastair

Below left: 1935: with his flute

Below right: *c.* 1935: Charlie as Ko-Ko, in *The Mikado*, with Alastair as a Maid from School

1946: Charlie conducting the Sydney orchestra, watched by Walter
Susskind

August 1947: the wedding at Cleeve Hill, *l.*: Judy; *r.*: Charlie

Prague, July 1948: Charles and Vaclav Talich

March 1951: Charles arranging music
for *Pineapple Poll*, in the flat at
Pembridge Crescent

1952: Judy and Charles at the Forth
Bridge

1927: Janáček in the garden of his house at Brno

1960: Charles with the composer Chlubna, at Hukvaldy, outside
the schoolhouse, Janáček's birthplace

Janáček's house in Hukvaldy

Above: 1960, Essex House: Fiona, Charles, Judy and Catherine

Left: 1962: Charles and Judy outside Essex House

Opposite above: 1960: Charles conducting in Sydney

Opposite below: 1963: on tour with the Queensland Symphony Orchestra

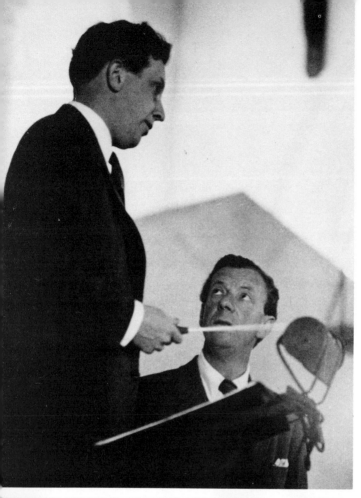

Left: 1959: rehearsing *Noyes Fludde* with Benjamin Britten

Below left: Martinů

Below right: Janáček in 1924

attitude to the company had changed, even to Michael Mudie, whom he had so liked and admired. Less than a month after the first night of *Katya* he was writing rather petulantly to his mother: 'Leo Quayle (whom you remember as my fellow assistant conductor at the Wells) has resigned . . . because of his dissatisfaction with his treatment. . . . They let him go without protest even though he is certainly the best operatic chorus-master in England, which shows you that they do not value good people who cross them. . . . I am rather expecting some squalls owing to the success of *Poll* and *Katya*. Mudie is a very jealous man and his conducting is now quite frightful owing to his illness. The only way he keeps his job is because everyone feels so sorry for him. It was a terrible blow to him when I had to take over *Katya* a week before the show because he didn't know it well enough. . . . I feel very strongly that I must greatly develop my outside connections . . . and try to leave the Wells within a year unless Mudie has to go and there is a lot of improvement in my position. But Leo's departure leaves only three conductors . . . and I believe they are not going to replace him (as a conductor). They MAY ask me to replace him as chorus-master which would be an improvement in salary . . . but personally I think they will not.'

Life at Pembridge Crescent was also uneasy: the flat was too small for two mobile babies. Judy had nowhere to put them while she did the chores and was exhausted with carrying them up 60 stairs each time she took them out. After she had dropped young Catherine, who rolled down twenty steps without damage, she was a nervous wreck and knew they would have to move. They began house-hunting, hampered by lack of capital, but Judy had £1000 from her father, Catherine arranged to release money from the family estate and at the beginning of 1952 they bought a suburban semi in Finchley. They chose the district because it was on the Northern Line, direct to Angel and Sadler's Wells, and the house in Templars Crescent because it had a tiny garden where the children could play in safety and four bedrooms, which meant they could take a resident *au pair*.

Once more there were painters and carpenters, bills to pay and a mortgage as well. A Dutch *au pair* girl moved in, the first of a series, later followed by Italians. Charles's letters at this time are those of a rather harassed young man, worried about money, one minute full of plans and confidence, the next in abysmal despair. Judy meanwhile stained floors, cooked, ran the house, coped with the children, cheered and encouraged Charlie when he was down. He was horribly thin and pale with dark circles under his eyes and was thought to have anaemia. When the doctor decided it was nothing more than overwork and fatigue she sent the babies and *au pair* off to her mother and took him to Cheltenham for a rest.

By now she had met more of Charles's family and come to know Alastair, who had been at Cambridge. To his parents' disappointment he had decided to teach and had taken a job at Christ's Hospital. Alan, a born teacher himself, felt that teaching was 'wasting one's brains' while Catherine referred to it ambiguously as 'an honourable profession'.

Alastair had become a favourite with Judy. He was considerate, easygoing, humorous and excellent company. When he came to stay he always brought some welcome contributions to the rather hard-up household. She was sorry when he went back to Sydney in 1954, but the following year Catherine arrived with Joan and Elizabeth for their introduction to Europe. They travelled about the Continent, went to operas, theatres, concerts and galleries and when Catherine sailed for home the girls stayed in England, Joan to study the violin, Elizabeth as a student at the Legat Ballet School in Tunbridge Wells. Two years later Alan came over. His main purpose was to persuade Elizabeth to return to Sydney with him but he also went to Scandinavia to look at yachts and talk to marine designers. He was planning to build a new boat and meant to design it himself.

Alan's first meeting with Judy was the start of a happy relationship. She pleased him in every way, her fresh-air appearance, her humour and intelligence, warmth and kindness, while she saw beyond the shy reserved manner to a lonely man who longed for affection but had become afraid to risk showing his need.

It was also a first encounter for Charles. When he and Judy dined at Alan's club he was astonished to find his father a charming attentive host who ordered an excellent meal and enjoyed with them a bottle of very good wine. He was so relaxed, so forthcoming and entertaining, so unlike the withdrawn silent character at Harpenden that Charles was astonished and admitted to Judy that he realized he had not known his father at all.

When Charles heard that the BBC intended to produce opera on television at Alexandra Palace he applied for the job of assistant to Eric Robinson, the resident musical director. The operas, sometimes cut and sometimes complete, were sung in English, in modern dress, and telecast live. There was a very good freelance orchestra and Charles was to work as coach and conduct the chorus.

Pagliacci was his first experience. At that time singers and cameras worked at one end of the studio with the orchestra at the other. Robinson conducted in headphones, watching the action on a monitor and Charles's job was to follow him and conduct the chorus, keeping out of sight of the viewers. It was a clumsy business and in the big chorus scenes the only way he could find a position from which he could see Robinson, while remaining invisible to the cameras himself, was to get right into the chorus. Since the singers were in ordinary street clothes he was able to mingle among them and give directions by jerking his head or raising his eyebrows. He could only hope they would understand his signals and that any viewers who noticed his behaviour would assume he was a singer with a nervous tic or St Vitus's Dance.

His next opera was *Rigoletto* and after that *Gay Rosalinda*, with Jack Buchanan as Eisenstein. Buchanan could never remember his music or words; there were idiot cards for prompting but he was lost if the boy was not quick enough in holding them up, and since the opera was telecast live the company was very nervous about him. The climax came when Eisenstein was obliged to explain why he had gone home from the carnival and left his friend Falke, dressed as a bat, in broad daylight. Buchanan began his speech but having said that Falke was terribly drunk he stopped dead. He could not see his idiot card and could not remember a word. There was a pause, then he made an effort and said, 'He was blind — ' and stopped again. Another terrible pause while the company held its breath, but the splendid old pro rallied. 'Blind — *as a bat!*' he ad libbed triumphantly.

Charles had a far wider knowledge of opera than Robinson and before long had replaced him. In the next few years, while still at Sadler's Wells, he conducted a great many television productions, some of them several times: *Carmen, Rigoletto, Tosca, Faust, Pagliacci, Gianni Schicchi, Cavalleria rusticana, Tales of Hoffman, Figaro, Bohème.* One performance of *Bohème* was a family affair with Fiona and young Catherine among the children in Act II and Judy as behind-scenes juvenile chorus nanny. By the early 1960s he had worked in seventeen operas and was the most experienced television operatic conductor in the country.

There had been another ballet collaboration with John Cranko, *The Lady and the Fool*, with music from unfamiliar Verdi operas. It was presented in 1954 at Sadler's Wells with Patricia Miller and Kenneth MacMillan, the future choreographer, and though its success was much quieter than that of *Pineapple Poll* the music was recorded and the following year Charles conducted it in a revised version at Covent Garden with Beryl Grey as The Lady.

He was taking as much work as he could get outside Sadler's Wells: television operas, conducting for an amateur music group at Colchester, with the Welsh National Opera and with the Dublin Grand Opera Society. This last was a semi-amateur group who performed with professional principals and conductors, usually from England, and the Radio Eireann Orchestra. Small parts and chorus were sung by amateurs and discipline was not very strict. The chorus members used to drink terribly during performances, they had a secret entrance from the stage-door into Neary's Bar where they soaked down pints of Guinness, still in their costumes, looking like the students drinking in *Tales of Hoffman* or *Faust*.

Unforeseen incidents occurred. One night, Marguerite (Ana Raquel Satre), singing of her love for Faust, went to the window to open it and lean out. It was stuck and could not be moved. Still singing, she pushed and pulled till a well-meaning stage hand came to her aid. He gingerly reached his arm round the scenery but since he could not see what he was doing his arm went up Marguerite's dress. Still struggling to open the window with one hand, while with the other she angrily slapped and brushed away the arm that was floundering about in her skirt, she sang on rapturously of her love.

An Irish journalist who came to watch rehearsals at this time described Charles as 'a red-haired young man with bright brown eyes and the dynamic energy that goes with the colouring. He smoked endlessly, pounded the piano, conducted and every so often took up one or other of the singers at a point, humming like a dragon-fly.' The journalist was 'amazed to find so much authority in so young a man . . . allied to vitality, scholarship and humour.'

By 1954 Michael Mudie was no longer at Sadler's Wells and when James Robertson left to take over an orchestra in New Zealand Charles decided it was time for him to go. Through his work in television opera and broadcasting he had become known to the BBC and had been offered the job of first full-time conductor of the BBC Concert Orchestra.

The prospect seemed full of possibilities. For all his wide experience in opera he had done very little symphonic work and was eager to conduct an orchestra of 45 players who were not just accompanying singers. He accepted the job but soon found to his disappointment that the repertoire he was to play was very much middle-of-the-road — music from Cole Porter to Bach via Edward German. The number of broadcasts made serious study impossible and the constant switching of musical styles from ballet to opera or light classics ruled out any

constructive thinking. He had been discussing Beethoven interpretation with Talich, in letters, but there was no longer time for such
subjects.

Before long he was suffering familiar feelings of frustration,
boredom and depression; he feared he had sold out to security, that
though he was earning a living he was making no artistic headway. He
held on for a year or so, conducting in London and the provinces and
taking an English-German programme to Munich, but it was not
good enough and at the end of 1955 he sent in his resignation.

Breaking the news to his mother he wrote: 'You will think I am mad
but . . . I feel that I have sufficient offers from here, there and
everywhere to earn as much money if not more as a freelance. . . . In
the BBC I was constantly being prevented from working outside, and
all the outside offers were always to do the type of music which I want
to do, such as opera, ballet and concerts etc. HMV have offered me
quite a lot of recording as the result of *The Lady and the Fool* record
being such a success. . . . In addition to this there is the English Opera
Group which pay very well and have asked me to become their
principal conductor. This will mean doing . . . performances of
Britten's new works all over the place. The BBC will also use me in
lots of different ways in both serious and light music . . . also some
conducting at Covent Garden and the Wells, and nearly every London
publisher has asked me to do arrangements for them *à la Pineapple
Poll*. . . . No doubt you will consider this move to be rather sudden
but I have considered it a lot and I definitely could not stand the pace of
the BBC job with about five broadcasts a week plus piles of office
work to do and always the same sort of hackneyed music except on
special occasions. . . . I am fed up with working like a slave and being
tired all the time and not even doing the type of work I want to do and
Judy has loudly applauded my decision.'

Perceiving the rather defiant, self-bolstering tone of the letter,
Catherine was not entirely convinced about the glowing future but,
like Judy, responded with encouragement and to outsiders showed
complete confidence. Only occasionally, to a close friend, would she
admit that she was concerned. She spoke uneasily about the danger of
versatility — a two-edged sword — and hoped that Charlie's
eagerness and enthusiasm would not betray him into shallow or facile
performances. She also wondered if the strain of freelance life might
not be even greater than churning out inferior music for broadcasts.

X

Freelancing

AT FIRST IT seemed that artistically life as a freelance had advantages but financially it was unpredictable and before long Charles's letters once more showed patches of gloom between the cheerful accounts of interesting engagements. He was over-working because he was afraid that if he refused an offer he would not be asked again. He needed the work but his good nature also made it hard for him to say No; finance apart, he liked to help and he liked to be liked, not to have to refuse or let people down. Because he was versatile and could do whatever was wanted, he was often asked, and always agreed, to turn out film scores, adaptations, orchestrations, occasional music for plays. He was known to be clever, quick, hard-working, reliable, always ready to come to the rescue. He believes that those years of freelancing had a permanent and negative effect on his life, that they made him incapable of refusing so that he still accepts work he no longer needs. Certainly they must have obstructed any attempt at self-searching or contemplation, any real discovery about himself or serious music.

It was not all hack-work. He had come to know the principal viola in the Sadler's Wells orchestra, a man named Quintin Ballardie, who acted as manager of a chamber orchestra, a group started in 1948 by Lawrence Leonard and the musicologist Arnold Goldsbrough, whose name it had taken. The Goldsbrough Orchestra specialized in the performance of eighteenth-century music, but Ballardie wanted to enlarge the repertoire with contemporary works. He was also in search of new talent. When Charles was asked if he was interested, he agreed to conduct a very difficult but successful programme of Kodaly, Ibert and Stravinsky's *Renard*.

The orchestra became a regular feature of the BBC Third Programme,* playing modern as well as early chamber music and

---

*In one of the broadcasts, in 1953, Charles conducted Arthur Sullivan's cello concerto with William Pleeth as soloist. The score and parts were later lost in a fire at Chappell, the music publisher, and the concerto was recently reconstructed by Charles,

Charles, who up till then had only broadcast light programmes, was delighted. He wrote to his mother that 'this of course is what I chiefly would like to do'. He continued to work with the group long after Arnold Goldsbrough died and it had become the English Chamber Orchestra, and he has always had for it a special affection.

Working with the Goldsbrough led to what he calls his 'semi-musicological career'. In Dublin, with the Grand Opera Society, he had spent his spare time in the library looking for Handel autographs and now he began to concentrate seriously on studying eighteenth-century performance practice. He was one of the first, if not *the* first, to ignore the convention that in the field of music, performers and scholars were always separate. The idea that discoveries, in music of all things, should not be put into practice seemed to him sterile and negative, particularly since with the Goldsbrough players he could try out the treasures he unearthed.

His researches into the performance of Mozart, Handel, Haydn, as well as lesser composers such as Bononcini and J. C. Bach, led to a series of concerts for the BBC Third Programme. Several were accompanied by a talk on some aspect of music of the period and there were soloists to illustrate examples of ornamentation. The talks were given by Fritz Spiegl, a flute player with the Liverpool Philharmonic who was also interested in musical history and unusual byways of music. Among the soloists Charles engaged were Jennifer Vyvyan and two Australians, Elsie Morison and Joan Sutherland, the guitarist Julian Bream and the horn-player Dennis Brain.

Joan Sutherland, who was then a young soprano at Covent Garden, had not yet begun her spectacular career but she was already training and studying with her husband and teacher, Richard Bonynge. So completely did Bonynge understand her voice that often, if she were not free, he would come to rehearsal in her place. Charles would explain what he wanted and so successfully would 'Ricky' pass on the instructions that when his wife herself came to rehearse she would sing everything perfectly, exactly as Charles had specified. The combination of Bonynge's remarkable musical intelligence and teaching with his wife's phenomenal voice eventually created an extraordinary singer.

Several programmes were devoted to Mozart's little-known arias,

---

with David Mackie, from a solo cello part. It was performed and recorded in 1986 with Charles conducting the London Symphony Orchestra and Julian Lloyd Webber as soloist.

decorated and sung as in his lifetime. Maurits Sillem, a young Dutchman who had lived all his life in England and who later conducted at Covent Garden, had played the harpsichord for Charles in many of these Mozart-Handel concerts and they had worked together on old music. From Sillem he had learnt of the library in the Fürstenberg Palace at Donaueschingen which contained great treasures of ancient German history, including the Nibelung Saga and much important source material. Mozart had stayed at Donaueschingen (the source of the Danube) when he was on tour with his father and done work there, and Sillem suggested that some of the manuscripts in the library might give clues to his performance practice.

Charles at once asked the BBC to subsidize a visit to Donaueschingen on the understanding that material found there would be used for the Third Programme. The BBC provided the money, also a gigantic photo-copier which weighed a ton and was the size of a suitcase. (On the way back, to Charles's horror, a drunk in the train was sick all over it.) He set out alone, but Sillem joined him there and they made some interesting discoveries. Charles wrote:

One can learn a great deal about the performance of this music by studying these parts. One reads in all 18th century books and memoirs that the soloists were expected to embellish the music but somehow it was a shock to find it being done to Mozart. However, we have proved that Mozart himself expected this to be done because there are extant versions of his arias embellished a little later by Mozart himself. When he was first attracted to Aloysia Weber he actually wrote all sorts of passages and cadenzas to help train her in the art of improvised embellishments — you remember, of course, that she was a great singer. It is also known that Mozart embellished his piano concertos too and there are a couple of examples in his letters of such embellishments written out. In fact, a study of these examples in his letters and all the examples I found at Donaueschingen written by 18th century singers proves that we are really quite wrong to perform Mozart exactly as written. This applied to Handel and earlier composers as well. Soloists were, in fact, judged on their ability to make embellishments and were criticised if they dared to perform the same variations twice. . . . Handel himself wrote various cadenzas for *Messiah* and it's beyond me why nobody ever sings them, except in 'cranky' performances which are put on from time to time in London and elsewhere. Surprisingly enough, this method of performance makes the music sound so different as to be almost unrecognisable . . .

. . . everybody knows that this was done in the 17th and 18th centuries but nobody dares to do it to masters like Mozart and Handel. We are shortly going to do two concerts of famous Mozart arias with ornamentation by 18th century singers and some by Mozart himself.*

These Mozart concerts, with Joan Sutherland and Dennis Brain, were particularly beautiful but there were other lovely programmes of eighteenth-century composers, of Haydn, arranged by H. Robbins Landon, the Haydn scholar, and played by the Boyd Neel orchestra; Gluck's opera *La Rencontre imprévue* and Charles's earliest piece of musicological discovery, Niccolo Piccinni's *La buona figliuola*, the score he had rescued so long ago from the rubbish tip in Sydney. It contained some charming airs and, sung by Elsie Morison and Joan Sutherland, was such an immense success that it was repeated several times. Richard Bonynge later included it in his wife's repertoire and she sang it in Vancouver, New York, Melbourne, Canberra and ironically, Sydney, at the Opera House, a stone's throw from the Conservatorium where Charles had found the score. The opera was presented as 'arranged by Richard Bonynge and Norman Ayrton' and as far as is known no reference has ever been made in programmes or publicity to the history of its re-discovery or to Mackerras's part in identifying it and bringing it back to the light after centuries of neglect.

Life as a freelance was not always grim, despite financial worries. In the days of the BBC Concert Orchestra Charles and Judy had made friends with a very talented young violinist. The girl, Pam Munks, had been intrigued by the conductor's passion for music, his remarkable knowledge and infectious enthusiasm. She liked his sense of humour and realized that he sometimes covered his insecurity with a little-too-obvious confidence.

After Charles left the orchestra they all remained friends. They were all hard-up and sometimes when Pam, who was also freelancing, was particularly broke she would move in with them to save rent and live as one of the family. When she had money she shared it. Judy was in charge of finances. Charlie, who lived on his nerves and never stopped smoking, had no idea of money. Judy allowed him a pound a week, which was very soon gone, mainly on cigarettes, and he would then try to touch Pam for a loan, if she had not first borrowed from him;

*C.M. Letter to his mother, 1957.

but no matter how low their joint funds they always managed to have a bottle of whisky in the house or at least enough to pay for a drink at the pub to cheer them when work was scarce. At such times Charlie would sink into Slavic gloom and the two girls would work to laugh him out of it; in fact, one way and another there always seemed to be laughing at Templars Crescent, even at bleak moments.

Pam, now married and living in Sydney, is still a very good violinist and is still conducted by Charles when he is in Australia.

One of his freelance jobs at this time was recording English music for the British section of Columbia and working as fill-in conductor for Walter Legge, the head of the International section. Legge, who was married to Elisabeth Schwarzkopf, was also the virtual owner of the Philharmonia Orchestra which he had founded and for which he hired conductors. Working with the Philharmonia was considered a very good job because of all the recordings involved and Charles had often been engaged to do substitute programmes when Klemperer, who was old and ill, or Giulini were not well enough to work. Recording in those days was a nerve-racking business demanding absolute perfection and sensitive artists sometimes could not stand the strain.

Charles had talked to Legge about his ideas and discoveries in Mozart performance practice and Legge had been interested. He did not make use of them in recordings but he agreed to let Schwarzkopf, a famous Mozart interpreter then at the height of her career, sing in a concert of eighteenth-century decorated music. It was held in the Royal Festival Hall on 16 January 1958. Schwarzkopf sang a scene from Haydn's *Berenice* and arias from *Figaro*, with ornamentation discovered by Fritz Spiegl. (The embellishments for 'Voi che sapete' had been written by Isaac Nathan's teacher, Domenico Corri, for his daughter.) The programme also included Mozart's Haffner Serenade and the original version of a 'lost' Haydn symphony, No. 63 in C major (La Roxelane), rediscovered by H. Robbins Landon, parts of which were being played for the first time since the composer's death.

Now that authentic performances are so fashionable it is difficult to realize the significance of this concert as an historical landmark; yet though it was a beautiful programme and an artistic success, well-attended, and broadcast, it was a commercial failure. Both Charles and the Australian impresario lost heavily, but the former, who had paid Schwarzkopf's fee himself, felt fully compensated by having a private recording of her singing 'Voi che sapete' while he conducted the orchestra. She became so attached to this decorated version that she often sang it as an encore in recitals.

Schwarzkopf, Thurston Dart and Dennis Vaughan had recorded a number of traditional songs for which Charles had made orchestral arrangements. Among them had been a rather soupy version of 'Silent Night' which Walter Legge had rejected as being far too pretentious for a serious classical singer. While Charles was rewriting it he consulted Robbins Landon about the original version and was surprised to find that the carol was not a traditional tune which Grüber had written down in the nineteenth century, but the organist's own composition. He also learnt that a miniature version of the score had been printed in Austria as a Christmas card and by sending for one he was able to prepare an arrangement in time for Schwarzkopf's recording. She sang it as a duet with herself by dubbing, taking both soprano and alto parts, while Charles conducted the orchestra.

Maria Callas was about to make a new stereophonic recording of *Lucia di Lammermoor* and Legge suggested that Charles write a cadenza for her, for flute and voice. Callas, however, had no intention of learning anything new, certainly not a cadenza by an unknown young man, and repeatedly refused to consider it. When Charles took the music to her at the Savoy to try and persuade her she was courteous and addressed him as *maestro* but declined to look at it. Legge was obliged to record the old cadenza and Charles was angry that Callas had wasted his time, for which he was not paid, though annoyance did not lessen his admiration for her as an artist.

In the late 1950s the Mackerras diaries began to show a mixture of cryptic entries, chiefly names of people, cities, operas — Pye, Schwarzkopf, *Screw*, Cantelo, Red House, Britten, Plaza Bar, Legge, Rob Landon, Aldeburgh, Goldsbrough, *Noyes*, Maurits, wedding anniversary, BBC, Badura-Skoda, Stratford, Fireworks. Charles conducted in Dublin, arranged and conducted for a musical, *Zuleika Dobson*, collaborating again with Cranko and Lancaster, and started working in ballet. Michael Frostick, the British representative of Sol Hurok, the American manager, had been asked by Robert Ponsonby, artistic director of the Edinburgh Festival, to form a small chamber ballet company for the 1958 Festival. There was to be a stage director, a ballet director and a musical director (Charles). The company of eight girls and four men, with about fourteen players in the orchestra, were to present twelve new works, each with a different choreographer, for which Charles was to make musical arrangements and conduct at performances. Maurits Sillem played the harpsichord for one of the ballets, *The Night and Silence*, suggested by Walter Gore and arranged from a Bach harpsichord and organ work.

Engagements had also come through Charlotte Nicholls, the Continental wife of a Harley Street specialist, a music-lover interested in organizing artists. Though not a full-time professional, she did publicity for Charles and introduced him to European performers and agents. Among them was Sander Gorlinsky, now Charles's manager but then an entrepreneur. In 1961 Gorlinsky engaged him to conduct the London Symphony Orchestra in a historic performance at the Royal Festival Hall. The concert, subsidized by a very rich man, featured the great violinist, Misha Elman. Though Elman was then in his seventies he was to play the Brahms and Mendelssohn concertos and three movements of Lalo's *Symphonie Espagnole*.

When Charles met him at the Savoy, Elman was very charming and apparently unperturbed by the conductor's youthful appearance. He did however say drily, 'I'm not exactly a beginner, you know, not entirely inexperienced!' to which Charles replied, 'I was brought up on your recordings of the Brahms and Tchaikowsky!' After this they got on extremely well. Charles, aware that it was a unique experience to work with such a distinguished virtuoso, did everything exactly as Elman wanted and enjoyed conducting the splendid orchestra. There was a slight contretemps with the opening of the Brahms concerto, the unison on D and G strings: Elman always started with an up bow, pushing it towards the violin, but he caught the tip between the two strings and had to stop and begin again. There were no other difficulties and he was very pleased with the concert.

In 1957, also through Charlotte Nicholls, Charles was engaged to tour with the Marquis de Cuevas Ballet in Spain, Switzerland, Germany and Austria. He joined the company in Madrid, a city which he found disappointing, apart from the Prado, but he was very happy in Germany, immensely impressed by its musical life and newly-built opera houses in which he longed to work. He travelled ahead of the company in order to rehearse the musicians who were to play for the performances and was fascinated to find himself conducting such famous and superb orchestras as the Vienna Philharmonic which, as he wrote to his mother ' . . . beats any I have ever worked with for beauty and magnificence of sound. . . . They have made a new ballet, for the Viennese première, to the Pathetique Symphony. This means that I will have conducted this work four times with the Vienna Philharmonic . . .'

When he arrived for his first orchestral rehearsal in Vienna he found that his music had been temporarily mislaid. He had only the score of *The Blue Danube* Waltz — part of *Le Beau Danube* ballet — the only music the orchestra did *not* need since they knew it, by heart.

He fell in love with Vienna, which he thought the most beautiful city he had ever seen, apart from Prague.

. . . Of course it is filled with my favourite kind of architecture, baroque. I think Austria must be the only place in the world where they still play orchestral Masses on Sunday. The work to be performed is advertised in all the papers and I heard a very impressive performance of Haydn's Nelson Mass in one of the churches. . . . It all fits in so beautifully with the surroundings. I was staying with an eminent musicologist friend, Robbins Landon, and he took me round and showed me all the places of musical interest of which there are literally hundreds. The orchestra was very nice to me and most complimentary, and I got a good press. This was especially gratifying, because ballet conductors rarely get noticed at all in the press. All in all the week in Vienna was one of the most enjoyable I have ever spent. . . . I was only sorry Judy could not come. . . .*

Judy had remained in London because her mother was very ill. On the day Charles arrived in Vienna Mrs Wilkins died, wasted away with cancer of the oesophagus. Apart from her grief, Judy, who had been very close to her mother, was now worried about her father. He was not well enough to live alone and had moved into Templars Crescent though the house was far too small. She was already searching for one big enough to hold them all, helped this time by the fact that Mr Wilkins had sold his own house and was sharing the cost of the new one.

The search ended at Southgate. Charles wrote to his mother that Essex House was

. . . quite extraordinarily beautiful . . . early 18th century with three rooms to a floor and three floors, also a tremendously spacious cellar, part of which can be used as a kids' play-room when it is properly furnished and warmed. . . . The previous owner has had the sense to centrally-heat it almost throughout and kitchen, bedroom etc have all mod cons. In addition, the top floor has already been converted into an entirely self-contained flat from which we hope to make some rent. We now have two houses of furniture so it will be quite easy to furnish the house and the flat with antiques. . . . An extremely large garage which used to be an old

*C.M. to his mother, 1957.

coach house . . . has a vast loft above it, which can be effectively converted into a marvellous studio flat . . . I don't know if you know Southgate at all. . . . Most of it is rather semi-detached and suburban but this one big village green is composed almost entirely of Georgian houses and Tudor pubs and the whole effect is very much like living in a country village. . . . It is a little further out from my usual working places round the West End but there are tubes and buses in profusion, so we are not isolated at all. . . . Judy . . . is very hectic at present. Unfortunately I had to leave her to make the move herself as I was away conducting . . . and at the time of writing I still have not spent a single night in our new house.

Charles was equally hectic, rushing about the country conducting, arranging, composing, orchestrating and preparing concerts for the BBC Third Programme. He had accepted an engagement in Southern Ireland for the Wexford Festival which specialized in unusual operas by great composers, sung in the original language. Though most of these works have now become familiar through recordings, at that time they were rarely seen.

The first opera that he conducted at Wexford, in 1958, was Donizetti's *Anna Bolena*, with Verdi's *Aroldo* the following year. It was also his first experience with an Italian cast and though he enjoyed their engaging charm he was astonished to find their behaviour completely unlike that of the co-operative, team-spirited singers at Sadler's Wells. Most of the cast had sung the opera before but in different versions so they all knew different cuts and Charles now found that once an Italian had thoroughly learnt a role he or she found it impossible to change. *Anna Bolena* was not well known, which meant there were no traditions, none of the customary concepts of interpretation, no appoggiaturas, and though he had his own theories about performance the singers, with one exception, were quite uninterested in trying them. Having mastered their roles they considered there was nothing more to learn, even though in ensembles they would all sing different sets of cuts.

The exception was a young mezzo, Fiorenza Cossotto, who was making her début outside Italy. She gave no trouble at all. She had not sung the part of Jane Seymour before and was willing to learn, to do what she was asked. She was also extremely musical and hard-working. Of her, and of Charles, a critic wrote:

The music . . . was given fullest importance by the vitality of the playing which Charles Mackerras drew from the Radio Eireann

Light Orchestra. To this conductor must go much of the credit for the great success of the performance. A perceptive artistic vision and variety were qualities of his direction which unified the whole performance and helped sustain interest from start to finish. Cossotto has a mezzo-soprano voice like some wonder of nature, beautiful and powerful. In addition she sings with extreme musicianship; her phrasing and expressiveness are wonderful, and it is obvious that she is one of the coming great singers.

Charles had also been discovering that German singers could be difficult. In 1958 he recorded a number of Mozart concert arias in Munich with Rita Streich, then a permanent member of the Vienna State Opera, accompanied by the Bavarian Radio Symphony Orchestra. These arias are among the most demanding of all the coloratura repertoire (one contains the highest note ever written for the human voice), and he had discussed them carefully with Streich, deciding how they should be handled. The soprano then went off for a season in South America, but when, on the appointed date, Charles, the producer and orchestra arrived in Munich she was not there. They waited for three days, endlessly rehearsing the arias, before she appeared, only to announce that the repertoire was wrong and the songs had not been agreed on. When eventually the recording was made it was done under stress, with everyone in a bad temper, for the work had to be crammed into a few days instead of the time originally allowed.

Patricia Foy, who had been an assistant stage manager at Sadler's Wells, had joined the BBC and become a television producer, specializing in opera and ballet features. She engaged Charles as resident conductor for a series called *Gala Performance* which ran for some years and in which famous artists were interviewed and presented in sections from their repertoires. (Charles also conducted for such other series as *Music in Camera* and *Profile in Music*.) The whole programme might be devoted to one performer or there might be scenes from a star's most successful operas, with supporting British artists. Margot Fonteyn, Rudolf Nureyev, Yehudi Menuhin, Tito Gobbi, Birgit Nilsson, Joan Sutherland, Mario del Monaco, Elisabeth Schwarzkopf were some of the celebrities who appeared in the series. Rehearsals were held in street clothes; when Schwarzkopf was rehearsing the first act of *Rosenkavalier*, stage hands, unfamiliar with the story, were fascinated to see a beefy German lady (Octavian) making apparently Lesbian love to Schwarzkopf (the Marschallin) in bed.

Most artists gave no trouble, others were difficult. For his programme, the tenor, Del Monaco, had chosen scenes from *Otello* and an extremely pretty model had been hired to lie on the bed as the dead Desdemona. This did not please Mrs del Monaco who was watching: she kept taking deep breaths all the time her husband was singing, rather as a nervous car-passenger puts a foot on an imaginary brake. She became extremely agitated when he began to kiss Desdemona and was almost beside herself as his enthusiasm increased and the kisses grew more passionate. There was nothing she could do, however; safe before the cameras Otello cried *Un bacio! Un bacio ancora!* and gathering the beautiful model up in his arms pressed his lips to hers.

Tito Gobbi's Gala Performance included excerpts from *Falstaff, Gianni Schicchi* and *Tosca*. He had recently had an immense success at La Scala and become a great star. It seemed to have gone to his head. Charles, who admired him very much, was astonished at his standoffishness, his high-and-mighty attitude to the other singers and shocked by his childish fits of temperament. In *Tosca* he made a great fuss over the firing of the cannon; the bass drum used as substitute sounded very loud in the small studio and Gobbi lost his temper, flew at Charles and was generally very unpleasant — disillusioning a young man who had not yet learnt that success may often have this effect on an artist.

There were no rows or temperament when Joan Sutherland came to sing the Mad Scene from *Lucia* but she was already so famous that she could make her own conditions, and she stipulated that Richard Bonynge should conduct her. In the past she had suffered from conductors who were impatient when she did not understand what they wanted. (Beecham had been particularly nasty. When she recorded *Messiah* with him he made a fool of her by taking one of her arias so appallingly slowly, smiling and stroking his beard and sniggering with the orchestra, that she withdrew and Jennifer Vyvyan took her place.)

The producer tried to persuade her to make an exception, since Charlie was not only an old friend but the resident conductor for the series, but she insisted. 'I'm sorry . . . with the best will in the world, but I must have Ricky. No one else knows how I do it.' The solution was for Bonynge to conduct while Charles's name appeared on the credits. He in fact was rather relieved for, whereas he would have had to rehearse and re-take, Bonynge knew exactly how his wife worked and they finished the scene in a few minutes.

XI

'Fireworks' and Britten

SINCE ONE OF his reasons for leaving Sadler's Wells had been to enlarge his experience of symphonic work, Charles was pleased to be offered a concert season in Cape Town in 1958. (At the time this orchestra was engaging guest conductors instead of a permanent head.) He left London in November and returned the following March. Catherine flew from Sydney to join him, their first meeting for several years. Apart from the colour question, Charles liked Cape Town; people were hospitable, he hired a car and joined a good dining-club, there were glorious beaches though 'not so good as Bondi or Palm Beach'. The scenery was wonderful, 'better than anything in Aussie of its type', the weather good, about the same as Sydney during January. Living was cheap and easy 'because . . . this is a semi-fascist country and the natives work for the whites for half-nothing. The colour thing here is unbelievable.'

He had not enlightened his Cape Town employers about his lack of symphonic experience, but, though in fact he was conducting much of the repertoire for the first time, reviews were very good and he was asked to return the following year. Critics wrote of his immense vitality and brilliance, his stylish Mozart, effortless and sensitive Schubert and memorable performances of the Mahler First and the Janáček *Sinfonietta*. It was the first time he had conducted the Janáček and he brought in extra brass for it from the army band at Simonstown Naval Base.

A soloist for the season was the Italian pianist Arturo Benedetto Michelangeli, a very great artist but a difficult man. He was so bad-tempered and moody and had such an outwardly forbidding approach that one of the local critics had nicknamed him the Unsmiling Pianist. He never showed emotion in playing and had an absolute obsession about artists achieving their effects through music alone yet, though he controlled his own facial and physical movements, his intense feeling and nervous tension were expressed involuntarily by tremendous sweating in his fingers, an unfortunate reaction for a pianist since it made the keys slippery. At rehearsals and on the concert platform he was given to sucking his moustache and muttering insulting remarks about the orchestra, but he seemed to like Charles and took down his London address, gave him an introduction to his own agent in Italy and requested him as conductor for all his concerts, which was gratifying but rather alarming at times.

Catherine, having enjoyed herself admiring the eighteenth-century Dutch architecture of old Cape Town and made the most of being alone with Charlie after so long, flew back to Sydney while he returned to London. Soon after his return, on 15 April 1959, he conducted the Goldsbrough Orchestra in an all-Handel concert in the Festival Hall. It was held to mark the 200th anniversary of the composer's death and the programme included an overture and decorated arias, an organ concerto, a harp concerto and — played for the first time — a *concerto a due cori* for strings and two choirs of oboes, horns and bassoons. Also on the programme was *Music for the Royal Fireworks*.

In 1749, to celebrate the peace of Aix la Chapelle, a huge fireworks display was planned in London. A fantastic pavilion was erected in Green Park (it took five months to build) and Handel's music, specially written for the occasion, was to be played by an enormous orchestra. Originally there were to be only 'martial instruments', although the composer had wanted strings. There was a public rehearsal in Vauxhall Gardens at which 12,000 people turned up, London Bridge was jammed for hours, many were crushed in the crowd, fights and brawls broke out. On the night itself it rained and the magnificent edifice in Green Park caught fire and was destroyed. The original version of the music had not been played since.

Charles had long been fascinated by the idea of reproducing it as it was first meant to be heard and had been trying to interest a recording company. When eventually Pye agreed to the proposition he spent months on research and preparing an edition that would give as closely as possible the original sound of the music. For practical reasons he decided to use a couple more oboes and bassoons than specified by Handel, for the recording would take three hours and the work made such tremendous demands on those instruments — they virtually never stop playing from beginning to end. The orchestra was finally composed of 12 first oboes, 8 seconds, 6 thirds; 14 bassoons, 4 contra-bassoons; 2 serpents, 9 horns, 9 trumpets, 3 pairs of timpani and 6 side drums and, since it was quite impossible to get all these players together in the ordinary way, the recording was made late at night, when musicians were free after concerts and opera. They assembled in St Gabriel's Church, Cricklewood, in North London and the session began at 11 p.m. on 13 April. It finished at 2.30 a.m. on 14 April, the actual 200th anniversary of Handel's death. (A tape had also been made for the BBC. (Appendix, see page 293.)

Describing the recording, Charles wrote:

It was amusing that night to see the motley costumes of the orchestra. Some turned up in white tie and tails, having come straight from concerts in the Albert Hall and Festival Hall, some in black ties from theatre orchestras, others in ordinary dress from broadcasts or recording sessions. The orchestra was 'led' by Terence MacDonagh and Sidney Sutcliffe and nearly every player of distinction came along to take part in this historic performance.

In the event the impressiveness of the sound surpassed my wildest dreams; and I was particularly delighted by the rich, almost organ-like sound of the orchestra, especially in the softer parts of the work. In the martial sections too the ringing sound of the horns and nine trumpets was an indescribable thrill.

My only slight fear was whether all this magnificence could be reproduced on a gramophone record. However, after the session the engineers worked all night on the tapes and the record was played at a party given by Pye that same night (14 April), in the Battersea Festival Gardens, to the accompaniment of actual fireworks. To my delight the music sounded even better in its recorded state, the tone being spacious and noble. On the published record, after the music is played 'straight' one of the movements is repeated with fireworks and cannon effects added, as spectacular as anything in the 1812 overture.

The performance was described as a landmark in stereophonic recording; it was certainly a landmark in Charles's career and helped to confirm his belief that re-orchestration and arrangement of music by Handel and others was completely unnecessary, 'as long as one is meticulous about obeying these old composers' instructions as to instrumentation and style of performance. . . . Georgian houses and churches which have not been "rearranged" are still obviously as beautiful as they always were, so why not *try* to play Georgian music as it was intended?'

The success of the *Fireworks* recording led to a special performance of the *Water Music*. This had first been played in July 1717, on barges moving up the Thames from Lambeth to Chelsea. The weather was perfect and King George I so delighted that he ordered it to be played three times. During the summer of 1959 Charles repeated the occasion with an orchestra playing on a houseboat at Hampton, also in perfect weather, but a later performance of both *Water* and *Fireworks Music* given in the docks area was a disaster. A high wind was blowing so strongly that despite a very large number of players no one could hear a note.

Sadler's Wells revived *Katya Kabanova* in November 1959 with Charles as guest conductor. The role of Katya, first sung by Amy Shuard, was played by Marie Collier, a handsome young Australian with a very fine voice. She was a splendid actress and this first performance with Charles was an artistic triumph. There were still empty seats in the theatre but people were beginning to show interest in Janáček and critics were enthusiastic. They wrote of Marie Collier's great gifts as an actress, 'her strong sympathetic understanding of Katya's dire emotional struggle' . . . 'her rich voice, passionate fervour and musical sensibility.' Charles was declared 'absolute master of the marvellous and intricate score', commended for his 'dynamic direction, strength and certainty', the 'passion, taste and insight' of his conducting, and said to have the music 'in his bones'.

This was the beginning of Marie Collier's career as a brilliant interpreter of Janáček roles and of a remarkable working partnership with Charles, at Sadler's Wells and later at Covent Garden. The *Katya* revival, like the *Fireworks* recording, the Cape Town engagement, the television programmes and musicological research were only part of an already crowded working life which since 1955 had also included conducting for the English Opera Group.

The English Opera Group grew up round the work of Benjamin Britten. After the sensational success of his first opera, *Peter Grimes*, at Sadler's Wells in 1945, Britten and a group of singers, musicians and writers formed the Glyndebourne English Opera Company. Their plan was to produce English works (old and new) of high artistic quality and small-scale operas with an orchestra of twelve to fifteen players. Their first production, Britten's *Rape of Lucretia*, was presented at Glyndebourne in 1946 and was followed in 1947 by *Albert Herring*. The company, renamed the English Opera Group, took both operas on tour in England and to festivals in Holland and Switzerland. It was during this tour that Peter Pears suggested creating their own festival at Aldeburgh, where he and Britten lived.

The first Aldeburgh Festival opened in June 1948 and lasted for nine days. By 1955 the E.O.G. had produced five works by Britten — *Let's Make an Opera, Billy Budd, Gloriana, The Turn of the Screw*, and his version of *The Beggar's Opera*. The Group's artistic standing was high, higher than their financial position, and when a deputy conductor was needed their manager, Basil Douglas, began looking for someone young and promising who would not expect a top salary. He engaged Charles to conduct a Christmas revival of *Let's Make an Opera* at the Scala Theatre in London. This 'entertainment for young people' which Britten is said to have written in a fortnight, had a small orchestra, and there were several songs which the conductor must teach the audience to sing. Though Charles was in agony from an impacted wisdom tooth he had been pleased at the opportunity to conduct Britten's music. The composer had liked his work and he had been engaged to conduct at the Aldeburgh Festival the following July.

For the next few years he was virtually the E.O.G.'s resident conductor at Aldeburgh, when Britten was not conducting. He also went on tour which meant 'rushing up and down the country in the car in order to fit everything in'. The Group, he told his mother, 'annoys many people because it is a bit arty-craft but it is . . . an excellent entree into various other things, both here and abroad. Also it is nice to be conducting the first performances of the only operas at present being written in this country!'

' . . . Our next season is in September. I am going to conduct Lennox Berkeley's new opera as well as Britten's *Turn of the Screw* . . . which is in my opinion his operatic masterpiece. Ben himself seems awfully taken with my work and already I have derived various benefits from his recommendations.'

Lennox Berkeley's new opera was *Ruth*, and other works not by Britten which Charles conducted were Poulenc's *Les Mamelles de Tirésias*, Gustav Holst's *Savitri* and the seventeenth-century *Venus and Adonis* by John Blow. He was happy at Aldeburgh, he liked the little town set between river and sea, the fishing boats, the countryside with its old churches. Festival audiences had grown and, as Aldeburgh then had no concert hall, performances were given in various buildings round the district, which added to the informal holiday atmosphere.

Charles, who had always respected Britten immensely as an artist, and as a musician and instrumentalist, enjoyed working with him and liked him as a person. Though at times he felt rather out of place in the somewhat precious atmosphere surrounding the composer, when it came to work Britten showed no hint of preciousness. At such times he was completely professional and wonderfully helpful, going out of his way to clarify and explain, which he did with great lucidity. He was always ready to go through his own work and had a genius for analysis, for getting to the heart of his music. It made his rehearsals memorable and Charles, who was deeply impressed, learnt a great deal by watching.

Yet for all his enthusiasm, his liking and admiration, his good-humoured worldly acceptance of homosexuals, unconsciously he must have felt some resentment. It surfaced in letters; he could not help making facetious and indiscreet remarks, even while admitting how much he owed to Britten.

> I did Britten's newest opera, *The Turn of the Screw* . . . a master-piece, based of course on the Henry James novel. No doubt the homosexual implication in the book has a great fascination for Ben. . . . We have had wonderful press notices . . . and Ben is at present very pleased with my conducting. . . . I regard my association with them [the E.O.G.] as the most important thing that has happened to me lately. . . . I really do enjoy the work with them very much despite their peculiarities and preciosity . . . Ben . . . suggested that I should conduct the première of his three-act ballet [*The Prince of the Pagodas*] at Covent Garden but they insisted that he do it himself.

In 1957 the Group was invited to take *The Turn of the Screw* to the Stratford, Ontario, Festival. They travelled across by ship and during the week at sea, and while they were staying in the same hotel, Charles had many long talks with Britten and Peter Pears. They were both extremely friendly and Britten, who was very interested in Janáček, questioned Charles about the composer's work. He wanted to learn as much as possible; he was, said Charles, 'one who drank in know-ledge', not only about music but about poetry, painting, the sea, people, natural wonders. He was exceptionally sensitive but could be humorous and amusing and told Charles plaintively that though he hated Brahms he could never escape him on library shelves because of their initials.

After the Festival and some sightseeing round the Great Lakes Charles spent a few days in New York. Though he had been born in New York State he had now decided to give up his dual citizenship and become a British subject.

The Group took *The Turn of the Screw* to Germany as part of the Berlin Festival and the following year, just before his thirty-second birthday, Charles was invited back to Canada to conduct the opera on television with Canadian singers and the CBC orchestra. When he returned to London Judy realized that for the first time in his life he was starting to put on weight. His appearance was changing, his face was rounder, his shoulders had broadened, he looked less like his father and more like his mother. It was almost as though Alan's genes which had dominated his physique in youth were giving way to Catherine's. Everything about him seemed more substantial, even his diaries, which from now on had better bindings, and it was no longer he but Judy, or even a secretary, who pasted in and annotated his press-cuttings.

He may also have put on weight because he no longer chain-smoked. The previous year he had broken the habit with the help of hypnosis. He had started the treatment in an effort to stop making faces — chewing his tongue — while he conducted; this Mackerras family peculiarity was a handicap in concert work, particularly on television. The hypnotist had not cured the tongue-chewing but had succeeded in stopping the smoking. (It was during these sessions that Charles was asked if he had ever been subjected to repetitive metallic sounds in his childhood — as of course he had, when at the age of three he had been aware of the hammering from across the water where riveters were working on the Sydney Harbour Bridge.)

Britten had been working on another entertainment for children, the story of Noah's Ark, inspired by one of the old Chester Miracle Plays. This was a new genre, a simple tale told with humour in a primitive way and performed mainly by amateurs. Apart from a professional string quintet, a recorder, a percussion player, two pianists and the organ, the orchestra was made up of children with recorders, bugles, handbells, drums, tambourine, cymbals and triangle, and for special effects, whips, gongs, Chinese blocks, wind machine, pieces of sandpaper rubbed together, and mugs hung on a rope and hit with a wooden spoon. There were also three sets of amateur violins which ranged from fairly capable children down to the most elementary players. Rehearsals were strenuous but enormous fun.

The only adults in the cast were Owen Brannigan and Gladys Parr as Mr and Mrs Noah, and Trevor Anthony as the Voice of God. The animals were played by children: lions, leopards, horses, oxen, swine, goats, sheep, camels, asses, buck and doe; dogs and cats, otters, foxes, polecats, hares, rats, mice; wolves, bears, ferrets, monkeys, squirrels; herons, owls, kites, cuckoos, doves, duck and drake, cock and hen, ravens, bittern, redshanks, peacocks.

In June 1958 at the Aldeburgh Festival Charles conducted the world première of *Noyes Fludde*. The performance opened with the congregation singing one of the popular hymns Britten had introduced into the score; then God's voice spake to Noah. The animals entered the Ark, singing *Kyrie Eleison* as they went; the storm came with wind, rain and thunder, and players and congregation sang *Eternal Father, Strong to Save*. The storm abated, it ceased and the animals left the Ark singing *Alleluia*. Then the rainbow appeared, the sun, moon and stars, and the Voice of God was heard blessing Noah.

The treatment of the story, the fresh, enchanting quality of the children were irresistible; critics were enthusiastic and Britten delighted.

He had seemed very pleased with Charles's work when he conducted *The Rape of Lucretia* at Aldeburgh and a television production of *The Turn of the Screw* in 1959, yet, the following year, when Charles returned from a concert season in Australia, he found the situation changed. Several other young conductors had been engaged in his place for the Aldeburgh Festival.

Although he was upset he was not really surprised; he knew he had risked offending Britten. During rehearsals for *Noyes Fludde* he had made a joking but indiscreet comment to John Cranko, whom he regarded as a friend, about Britten's fondness for writing parts for young boys. It was repeated back. It is also said that Charles had made outrageous remarks about fairies and queers one night when members of the company were drinking in an Aldeburgh pub. A German composer was there with his boy-friend and though Charles's companions had tried to stop him he had continued flouncing about and camping it up. It may have been alcohol releasing a hidden resentment but the story was repeated and Charles became one of what Lord Harewood has called Britten's Corpses.

He was distressed and ashamed that he had so thoughtlessly offended one who had been good to him and whom he revered as a musician. He knew he had only himself to blame. It was all very well to say he had meant no harm but he was well aware that Britten was supersensitive and hardly likely to take it as a joke. In fact Charles was not only offensive about the composer's private life, he was biting the hand that had fed him.

He still continued to conduct Britten's operas* and later even worked at Aldeburgh again, but the break had been made. It would probably have come anyway; though they had worked well together Charles had never really felt at home in Britten's circle, he was too

---

Peter Grimes at Sadler's Wells in 1965 and on tour in Europe; *Albert Herring* and *A Midsummer Night's Dream* in Germany; *Gloriana* in Munich (1972); in 1971 a revival of *Billy Budd* at Covent Garden and a concert version of *Gloriana* at the Albert Hall for Britten's sixtieth birthday.

direct, too unprecious and tactless. Sooner or later he would have upset someone, yet he still wishes it had not been Britten himself. Not even their rapprochement in 1966, their successful collaboration on the televised performance of *Billy Budd*, quite wiped out the regret.

XII

Flying Maestro

CHARLES HAD GONE to Australia in 1960 to tour for the Australian Broadcasting Commission. He was the first Australian to be invited to return as a 'celebrity' conductor for the Commission and his concerts were to be part of a summer festival. Judy and the two girls went with him. She had left her father at Essex House in the care of two of his sisters and had insisted on travelling by ship. It was the only way Charles would relax, though she knew he would work on scores during the voyage.

They arrived in Sydney at the end of January. Though Charles had seen most of his family in London he was pleased to find them all together again. The twins, who had been little boys of eight when he left, were now grown up and at the university. He amused them by asking which was which: Colin, tall and fair, Malcolm, roundfaced with red hair. Elizabeth, who had married Andrew Briger in 1957, now had a baby daughter, Joan was back in Sydney studying music and Italian at the university, Alastair was teaching at Sydney Grammar School and Neil was a barrister, married, with several children.

Both parents were well; Alan had left the Electricity Commission and was happier than he had ever been, lecturing at Sydney University, Catherine was doing research on her ancestor, Isaac Nathan, for a book she was writing. She gave a large reception at Harpenden at which friends and relations could meet Judy, Fiona and Catherine and marvel at Charles's changed appearance — *Charlie's got quite* FAT! Other people gave parties; he went to see old friends and even took Judy to visit his first violin teacher, Sister Mary Lawrence, who asked him what he did for a living. They went sailing in *Antares*, the beautiful boat Alan had designed himself. Alan was so proud of Judy that he took her to meet Uncle Willie Creagh to show her off and told his cousins that she was a gem. It was not only her warmth and humour that helped him relax with her but the feeling that she understood him and saw him as an individual in his own right, not a mere shadowy background to the family.

Catherine had arranged for Fiona and young Catherine to go to school at Loreto Convent, Normanhurst — also to have swimming lessons with an Olympic coach — while their parents were away on tour.

In Brisbane Judy met Ian Mackerras, who was Director of the Queensland Institute of Medical Research, his wife Jo, a Research Fellow, and their son, Charlie's cousin David, a university student; and there were old friends from Czechoslovakia — Eva Hustolesová now married to Frank Plodr, who after many vicissitudes had emigrated to Australia.

Touring in summer in Queensland was strenuous and exhausting but Charles enjoyed working with local musicians, particularly in Sydney where some of his former colleagues were still in the orchestra. These old friends did not know that he was conducting many works for the first time, but the concerts were a success, his performances were praised and no one realized the truth. The programmes were mainly of twentieth-century compositions and included Walton, Britten, Prokofieff, Bartók, Delius, Schoenberg, Hindemith, Stravinsky, Copland, Ravel, Richard Strauss and John Antill. The season ended with Bach's *St Matthew Passion* which had always been very much part of Mackerras family life at Easter, when friends were invited to Harpenden to hear the whole work on Alan's gramophone.

Charles flew back to London ahead of the family and stopped off in Rome to see Greti Ducci, the manager recommended by Michelangeli. The meeting brought concert engagements in Italy but in London there was bad news at Essex House. Judy's father had suddenly begun to go downhill and, from this time till his death in 1961, could not be left and needed constant attention. Judy returned to find her full-time job of running the house, looking after Charles and the girls, acting as chauffeuse, cook and secretary now included part-time nursing and finding and keeping suitable help for her father. For the next year or so she was under continual strain.

Charles was rarely at home during the summer of 1960. He had been engaged to take a series of concerts at a music festival in West Berlin* and had also accepted invitations from behind the Iron Curtain. In West Berlin he was to conduct an International Youth Orchestra drawn from the best members of the *Jeunesses Musicales* all over Europe and Canada. It was huge, with quadruple woodwinds and a vast array of strings.

*The concerts were under the aegis of Sir Robert Mayer, one of the founders of *Jeunesses Musicales* and of *Youth and Music* in England. He was also a great pioneer in children's school and educational concerts. He died in 1985, aged 106.

For two weeks before the Festival they rehearsed in a beautiful castle near Stuttgart, owned by the Hohenlohe-Langenbergs. The standard was very good indeed and although the players really needed plenty of rehearsal the final performances were extremely moving. The programme included Beethoven's Ninth Symphony; the chorus, which was also international, was trained by a German chorus-master in another *Schloss* about twenty miles away. There was a try-out performance in Bad Mergentheim, a spa town nearby, then they all travelled in buses through the Eastern Zone to Berlin.

Charles found the Eastern Zone in quite extraordinary contrast to the West, everything seemed broken down and ramshackle. They were not allowed to leave the autobahn and were rushed through places that he longed to see. At the border, officials were exceptionally difficult and the players were kept waiting there for five hours, for no apparent reason apart from the fact that there is always trouble when West Germans try to enter the Eastern Zone. The orchestra reached Berlin about midnight, four hours later than expected.

Though Charles was fascinated by the city he felt that life there must be like sitting on a time-bomb. It was startling to realize that being carried on in the tube or taking a wrong turn in the car could mean arrest. Crossing into the Eastern Zone, even by accident, was a very serious offence, especially for Germans.

The two youth concerts were a tremendous success and everyone was congratulated. There were 'fabulous notices in the press and . . . agents rushed about'. When it was over Charles went on to Vienna to do research on Janáček manuscripts. He was joined there by Judy, who had organized a nurse for her father and left the children in Holland with friends. They spent a few days' holiday with Christa Landon, the ex-wife of Charles's friend, the musicologist H. Robbins Landon, then they flew together to Budapest, where Charles had two concert engagements as part of Mahler Year.

In preparation for this he had begun to learn Hungarian by the subliminal method. It involved a large and cumbersome tape recorder with a loop cassette on which an Australian-Hungarian clarinettist friend had recorded twenty lessons from a Hungarian grammar. There was also a pillow-speaker so that the teaching could go on all night and seep into Charles's subconscious while he slept. The method was successful in that he learnt some Hungarian but the equipment made such a noise that it had to be left on the landing if Judy were not to be kept awake all night. Even so there was no escaping the loud repeated clicks and groans every time the loop came to the end and started its rounds again.

This was the first of a long line of gadgets and gear which were to become an ever-increasing part of Charles's life as his income grew and his travels exposed him to more and more duty-free airport shops full of electronic devices.

He wrote a very long letter to his mother describing his Iron Curtain visits.

It is quite an extraordinary feeling going behind the Iron Curtain. It's like going back twelve years when everybody bothered about currency restrictions, whether one had tea or coffee to bring in and all the old boring restrictions. We were treated perfectly politely but the Hungarians were taken into a Customs shed where every single article was looked at. . . . Near the border is a big television mast. You can pay a couple of forints to go up and have a look at Austria. Austria at this point consists of just a lot of fields and looks no different from Hungary but people go up just to look . . . the same television tower has machine guns at the top.

We were treated very well indeed by the Hungarians, although everything is so poor there that it is hardly credible. In our near-luxury hotel the door handles were falling off and the food, though beautifully cooked and served, was very unvaried and we got the impression of great want through the country. . . . Everything is in a fearfully ramshackle condition. Nothing seems to have had a coat of paint since before the war and many beautiful old baroque houses are falling to pieces. People still live in them of course because the housing shortage is very acute. Also one can see everywhere bullet holes from the 1956 'events' as they call them.

Budapest is very beautiful . . . and the State Orchestra is very good indeed, the Radio Symphony Orchestra less so, but the concerts were a great success . . . the orchestra were impressed that I spoke a little Hungarian, and in fact did most of my rehearsals in Hungarian, only reverting to German when I simply couldn't remember some complicated Hungarian word. The actual vocabulary is fiendishly difficult to remember because it has no resemblance to any other language and the grammar and construction of sentences is all backwards compared to other European languages. I don't know if I told you that I got Gabor Reeves to record twenty lessons out of my Hungarian Grammar on the tape-recorder. . . . I may say this method actually works because I could not possibly have learned so much in such a short time by the normal method. But it made an impression here and I have been invited back next year.

. . . We had a trip on Sunday to Esterhazy which is a most
gorgeous baroque castle. It is being renovated as a museum. . . .
There is still a lot of Haydniana left in Budapest. Esterhazy is right
on the border of Austria and Hungary and one has to get special
permission to go there . . .

In one of his last letters from Prague Charles had written, ' . . . this
city is lovely in the spring . . . we will be very sad to leave this
country and I do so much hope that we will return here some time
and have a holiday.' It had not seemed likely, nor had he managed to
go back and study with Talich, but suddenly an unexpected invitation had come. He and Judy were invited by the Czech State Musical
Foundation to spend a week in Prague, as guests, on their way home
from Budapest.

You can imagine how excited we were to get to Czechoslovakia
again . . . we were entertained in the best hotels and given all
kinds of modern Czech music and records. We were also taken to
the theatre every night and . . . for little trips in the country. I
can't imagine why they should pick on me to shower all this
bounty upon, but I am on visiting terms with the cultural people
at the Czech Embassy in London and I am known there as a bit of
a Czech and especially a Janáček fan. But it was all quite unbelievably wonderful having the red-carpet treatment to such an
extent. . . . We spent several days in Brno looking at Janáček MSS
and going for jaunts in the car and then we were driven to Prague
in the Foundation's car where we were put up in a marvellous
hotel. Prague is quite the opposite from Budapest, spick and
span* . . . they certainly have made the country into something
really good . . . and I think the life there can be very nice. . . . I
did a little bit of useful work though and actually discovered two
intermezzos in Janáček's *Katya Kabanova* which had been missing
(composed for a special occasion when the theatre had no quick
scene-changing equipment and written on the back of Janáček's
Sinfonietta). This created a sensation as Janáček is regarded by the
Czechs as something of a national hero. I think they were a little
peeved that their musicologists had not identified the intermezzos,
and although they expressed their delight they were just the tiniest
bit snooty about it, rather I suppose as we would be if some Czech
came over here and found another Enigma Variation.

*The situation is now rather the reverse.

The following April, 1961, he was back in Czechoslovakia for concerts in Prague. This was a three-week visit, though Judy stayed only eight days.

They welcomed me like a long-lost brother (or comrade), the red carpet was really laid out and I must say the orchestra responded marvellously and the actual performances went brilliantly. I also did some recordings for the radio (Britten's Purcell Variations and Walton's Second Symphony and *Portsmouth Point*) . . . being able to speak Czech and knowing so many people made it easier . . . various of our old friends were almost ecstatic with joy at seeing us again, especially Judy . . . Everything seems very prosperous, the Communists have really made a success, the country is working properly and appears like a paradise compared with Italy for example where there is quite striking riches and terrible poverty. . . . The British ambassador, Sir Cecil Parrott, with whom we became very friendly . . . is a very nice chap, a Slavophile who speaks several Slav languages, unlike most western diplomats, and he is also a very good amateur musician. The embassy is in one of the loveliest of all the old princely palaces, the Thun Palace where Mozart stayed for a while. Prague is really I think the most beautiful city in the world, except perhaps Rome. . . . I think I would rather be there than anywhere else in Europe and the musical level . . . is almost as high as anything in the West. They only lack the biggest solo singing stars and the best conductors. By the way, my dear old teacher Talich died, while I was there, aged 78. I had hoped to see him but he was too ill, more or less gaga and would not have recognised me. He had a huge state funeral. Although they had treated him like dirt when he was alive they certainly did him proud when he died. . . . I have been invited to the Prague Spring Festival next year . . .

At his first Prague concert of this visit he had conducted the Czech Radio Symphony Orchestra in Mahler's Sixth and Britten's *Sinfonia da Requiem* which was 'rapturously received'. He found that both Czech and Hungarian musicians had no difficulty in playing Britten and audiences enjoyed the music. He was impressed by the huge orchestras and the custom of having 'bags of rehearsals' and plenty of time to make recordings. Another surprise was the change in the Czech attitude to German music. During his student days it had been rarely heard and even the language had been hateful to the people who had suffered under the Occupation, but thirteen years had passed and now there was no restriction on Wagner or other German operas. The musical life of Prague was very impressive for a city of that size; there were three orchestras as well as opera and chamber orchestras, concerts every evening and two opera houses.

But his greatest excitement and one of the most wonderful moments of his career, after his years of research and work on Janáček, and having conducted the operas at Sadler's Wells, was to conduct *Katya* (with the two intermezzi), sung in Czech in the opera house at Brno, the city where Janáček had lived and taught, with an orchestra that took the composer's music and style for granted and to whom it presented no problems. Even in Prague, parts of Janáček's scores are re-orchestrated but the Brno tradition is to play the music as the composer intended it to be played.

Charles was the first non-Czech to conduct a Janáček opera in Czechoslovakia.

The Brno reviewers were very friendly: each one referred to Charles's student days in Prague, his knowledge of the language, his work in promoting the cause of Czech music, particularly of Janáček. The new intermezzi were mentioned. *Svobodné Slovo* said, 'He surprised us with augmentations to the entracte music, which is not customary among our own conductors' but 'enhanced the dramatic conflicts and with slower tempi made the lyrical passages more intense . . .' 'Mr Mackerras speaks Czech which enables him to penetrate more deeply into Janáček's style . . .' while *Lidová Demokracie* said, 'The performance of this musical drama by Janáček under the baton of Charles Mackerras was a profound experience. His fiery temperament and concentrated will to project himself into the drama sharply illuminate his approach to Janáček's score, which he safely masters down to the last detail. The music was unfolded in an immensely dazzling flow, tearing along with sharply passionate breath, with tense dramatic emotion . . . the appearance of the English conductor was vociferously acclaimed.'

Between his two visits to Czechoslovakia Charles went to Italy for concerts with Michelangeli. It was his first experience of Italian orchestras, in Rome with the 'Santa Cecilia' and in Florence at the 'Maggio Musicale'. Michelangeli was unpredictable, given to cancelling at the last minute, even failing to appear. In Florence, where he played the E flat Liszt piano concerto, he performed magnificently but it was a stormy occasion. Because Charles was the only foreigner, Michelangeli bypassed him at rehearsal and complained directly to the members of the orchestra who answered back. He was not satisfied with the triangle solo at the start of the scherzo and said so to the player. There was a fearful row, it almost came to blows; the whole orchestra joined in and in the end Michelangeli stormed out, swearing he would never play with them again.

At the concert for which he was booked with Charles in Milan he simply did not turn up. Charles however met an old friend:

. . . In Milan I saw quite a lot of Joan Sutherland and her husband who were staying at the same hotel as myself. She was making her début at the Scala, in *Lucia*. She is now among the most sought-after and one of the most highly-paid singers in the world as in fact she deserves to be. Apparently she now gets £stg 750 per concert, although I think the ABC have got her for a tour rather cheaper than that. That husband of hers entirely looks after her finances as well as teaching her everything. He is quite extraordinary. Everything that she is, he has made, like Pygmalion and Galatea. She has the voice and he produces the rest, as well as doing all her interviews, choosing her clothes, hair styles and everything. He decides the cuts in the opera which are to be made, and even has the tenor's name put in her contract. The other day, in a battle over cuts in a certain Bellini opera, the conductor got the sack because he wouldn't fall in with Joan's husband. It is extraordinary the influence he has over her, yet he seems very meek and mild . . .'

The fees for Charles's Italian engagements were ridiculously low, they barely covered travel expenses, which he had to pay himself. In Rome he could not afford an hotel and stayed with his friend, Ian Taylor; but it was all experience and he was learning. It was also a revelation of the difference between English and foreign orchestras and how incredibly casual and undisciplined the latter could be.

After the concerts in Hungary and Czechoslovakia invitations came from other countries in the Eastern Bloc, many of them with splendid orchestras crying out for western conductors who would accept their currencies. There was little material gain in such jobs since money was not transferable but as usual Charles saw them as experience. There was also the attraction of seeing new places, having adventures, mixing with all kinds of people.

The first engagement he accepted was in 1962 for concerts in East Berlin, with programmes that included *Petrushka*, Mozart Symphonies and the Beethoven Violin Concerto with Leonid Kogan, the distinguished Russian virtuoso. It was a good beginning: Charles was excited at conducting the great Berlin State Opera Orchestra, and the local reviewers liked his work. They wrote about his 'vivacious and precise' conducting, his 'brilliance of interpretation', called him 'extraordinarily gifted' and praised 'his sparkling interpretation of Stravinsky's *Petrushka*.'

Charles's admiration for the orchestra and interest in the opera house were so obvious that the Intendant asked if he would like to conduct an opera. He was already committed to a tour in Australia but he could not refuse such a chance to work in a theatre where Strauss, Leo Blech and Erich Kleiber had conducted. By cutting things fine he was able to fly to East Berlin during his 1962 Australian tour, conduct two operas (*Figaro* and *Fidelio*) and return to Australia in time to continue the tour.

The performance of *Fidelio* almost coincided with the anniversary of the building of the Berlin Wall, a time when the prisoners' chorus in the opera seemed particularly moving and apposite. Charles was warned to hurry on immediately after the chorus in case there should be a demonstration from the audience.

He was later to conduct many operas in East Berlin and when the famous old General Music Director, Franz Konwitschny, died the job was offered to Charles. He would have liked very much to accept but though the London musical press speculated about his having done so there were too many practical obstacles. He had no difficulty in entering or leaving East Berlin but his pay would be in East German marks which were non-transferable and no help to the expense of a growing family in England. It was better to make frequent visits for long periods. He took a room in the house of a woman who let accommodation to Staatsoper artists and Judy, whose father had died, joined him when she could. Artists (and sportsmen) were very well treated in East Berlin and she was able to buy their food at a special opera shop reserved for members of the company; the opera also had a very good canteen, much better than most city restaurants. Catering was more difficult in winter; eggs were scarce and the landlady, Frau Hoffert, usually had to boil six for breakfast if she wanted two that were edible.

Because his marks could not be taken out of the country Charles spent them on cameras, overcoats and records, but what he most valued was a whole series of orchestral parts of Brahms, Beethoven and Mozart symphonies from Breitkopf and Härterl of Leipzig, which he marked up with bowings and interpretation and which he still uses.

With Judy he often went over to West Berlin to read the Western news and buy such basic foods as rice and potatoes. At that time most inhabitants of the Eastern Zone wanted goods from the West and would have preferred to live there, yet Charles and Judy were both impressed by how much pleasanter the East Germans were than the people in the West. After the noise of West Berlin it was a relief to sleep in the East for there were few cars and the streets were quiet at night. Musically, everything was very good indeed, as it still is in the Communist countries; even so, a permanent tie with the East was impractical, nor could splendid museums and wonderful music compensate for the horrors of life for the East Berliners, the barbarities of the Wall, the shootings that took place almost daily.* As in Prague, it made a profound impression on Charles, opening his eyes to conditions as they were for so many less fortunate than himself, leading him to become an early supporter and campaigner for Amnesty International.

Charles went to Australia in 1962 for a series of Summer Festival concerts with the Melbourne Symphony Orchestra (now the Victorian Symphony) and the Sydney Symphony, and for a season as musical director for the Australian Elizabethan Theatre Trust Opera. He was to conduct *Ariadne auf Naxos, Don Giovanni, Traviata* and *Falstaff* and performances were to be in the old Elizabethan Theatre at Newtown, Sydney. Acoustics there were bad and the budget was very small but magnificent effects had been achieved by the producer, Stefan Haag, whom Charles admired and respected. (He still considers it a tragedy that Haag was ousted from the opera scene in Australia.) Several artists were being brought to Sydney for the season, including Rosina Raisbeck, Una Hale and Ana Raquel Satre, the soprano who in Dublin had featured in the incident with the stage-hand during *Faust.*

The opera company opened in Adelaide and moved on to Sydney, about 900 miles away, but Charles took a much longer route. Having agreed to conduct two operas in East Berlin he flew from Adelaide to London, crossed to Germany, and after *Fidelio* and *Figaro*, went on to Prague for the Spring Festival in May. From Prague he drove by car to the Polish border and crossed the bridge between Poland and Czechoslovakia. At the frontier a Polish Customs official, suspecting that the tubular case Charles carried might contain a weapon, opened it and held it up to the light, whereupon several batons slid down and hit him in the eye.

*Twenty-five years ago political horrors were less commonplace than today. Charles remembers the gasp that came from the boys at Sydney Grammar, when, giving a talk on East Berlin, he asked them to picture a wall completely dividing the city, from the school down to Circular Quay and which they could only cross at the risk of being shot.

From the border Charles was driven to Katowice, in south Poland, where he spent a pleasant couple of days making recordings with the Polish Radio Symphony Orchestra; he then walked back to Czechoslovakia across the bridge at a place called Těšin, was taken by car to the Moravian town of Moravská Ostrava and flew to Prague, where Judy joined him, then to Indonesia. In Djakarta they changed to a BOAC plane and continued on to Australia. Having made recordings on Saturday in Poland and having travelled from Adelaide to Sydney via Europe by various means, including walking, Charles started rehearsing the opera on Monday at the Elizabethan Theatre in Newtown.

Several months later he again worked with the Polish Radio Symphony Orchestra, this time at the 1962 Edinburgh Festival. Dmitri Shostakovich was to be Guest of Honour and Lord Harewood, the Festival Artistic Director, knowing Charles's special interest in Slav music, had engaged him to conduct the composer's Ninth Symphony. Since his teens, when he had first heard the Shostakovich Fifth Symphony, Charles had been drawn to the Russian's music; he relished the sardonic humour, the heroic quality (which he thought resembled Mahler), that balanced Slav resignation and despair. He was excited at the thought of working with one of the greatest composers of the twentieth century, whose work he not only venerated but for which he felt a particular affinity.

In Edinburgh Shostakovich came to rehearsals. He spoke no English and though Charles had begun to learn Russian he was not very advanced; however, he was fluent in Czech so they communicated with a mixture of Slavonic languages and a metronome. The composer was very friendly: he explained exactly how he wanted his symphony conducted and emphasized particularly that the slow movement should be played slightly rubato and not quite as originally written, but though Charles carried out the instructions so faithfully that Shostakovich was pleased, one critic complained that the slow movement had been played at the wrong tempo.

On Friday, 1 February 1963, Charles conducted the Oslo Philharmonic in Norway and on Tuesday, 5 February, rehearsed the Queensland Symphony Orchestra in Brisbane. In Sydney he and Judy stayed at Turramurra and once more there were parties and meetings with friends. The Mackerras family was well and busy: Catherine had finished her book about Isaac Nathan (*The Hebrew Melodist*) and published it that year. It had been launched with a party at Harpenden and she was now working on a biography of her grandfather, Sir

Normand MacLaurin and writing articles on religious and literary topics. She had lashed out with several new dresses for Charlie's concerts and was in excellent spirits. Alan was his usual self, still retiring at home but happy and relaxed with his university colleagues and students. His spare time was still devoted to his scientific interests, the sea and the stars were still his loves, his means of expressing the feeling for beauty that he could not put into words. He was still to be seen, alone, at Musica Viva chamber music concerts.

For four months Charles and Judy travelled round Australia, to capitals and country towns. In Sydney there were Summer Festival concerts, free lunch-hour concerts, school concerts, subscription concerts with visiting soloists — Lili Kraus, Julius Katchen, Nelli Shkolnikova, the Russian violinist (now living in Australia), a tour with the orchestra to north, south and west New South Wales and concerts in Adelaide, Melbourne and Brisbane. By the time he left Australia he had given 57 concerts and recorded music for a television opera. He was vastly overworked and much underpaid (£100 per concert, £50 for school concerts) but there had been a unique compensation.

For many years the Queensland Symphony Orchestra had been (and still is) making an annual tour to the far north of the State, giving concerts in halls and schools. When Charles was negotiating his Australian contract he suggested including this tour in his programme as a kind of working holiday. He had never been to the north of Australia and since the itinerary included Cairns it would allow him and Judy to see something of the Barrier Reef.

Announced by loudspeakers as THE QUEENSLAND SYMPATHY ORCHESTRA the players set off by night from the main Brisbane station. On board were also concert and orchestral managers, a soprano soloist (Rosalind Keene), radio staff and railway personnel, not to mention orchestral instruments. For two weeks, mainly in tropical heat, the travellers lived in five old sleeping cars and a luggage van. Charles and Judy shared an antiquated compartment, about 6 x 4 ft, in which there was nowhere to hang their clothes, so they slung a rope across the corridor outside the lavatory for Judy's evening dresses and Charles's tails and tuxedos.

The train had no restaurant; people cooked on primus stoves and Judy kept ice-boxes in the corridor for beer and fruit-juices. There were no showers so these were rushed at railway stations and hotels. Clothes were washed in hand-basins and hung out to dry on lines rigged across the platform when the train was in a station. Sometimes the carriages were hooked on to a passenger train, more often to a goods train carrying cattle, tractors, logs or cars. Most travelling was done by night, moving slowly on the narrow-gauge Queensland lines. (One goods train took ten hours to cover two hundred miles.) Sometimes the carriages were shunted into sidings to wait for transport, and shunting itself was a very slow process. One night as the players were dressing for a concert the warning came that they were about to be shunted and if they did not want to miss the performance they must get out at once. There was an immediate rush from the train with Charles in his white dinner-jacket and Judy and Rosalind Keene in long evening dresses clambering down the four-foot gap from the carriage door to the ground.

Sleep was difficult at first, sharp bends in the narrow lines caused lurches and shuddering jolts. 'We have often travelled in peculiar transport,' Charles said. 'But this was the most unusual train movement we'd ever encountered. You can see why people say that Queensland trains run on square wheels.'

Yet they were enchanted by the astonishing beauty of the scenery, the charm of the people. The train, with its huge sign, QUEENSLAND SYMPHONY ORCHESTRA ON TOUR, was greeted everywhere with shouts of delight from children, black and white, and adults overwhelmed the players with kindness and hospitality. They were entertained at each stop by townspeople and graziers, concerts were crowded, audiences wildly enthusiastic and afterwards Charles and the orchestra were inundated with presents of local products: rum 'straight from the vat' at Bundaberg, baskets of crabs and oysters at Rockhampton, a huge box of avocados at Mackay. As the train rumbled on through the night the happy travellers sang and caroused in compartments reeking of crab and rum, and shells were thrown out of the window.

Audiences were enthusiastic but neither ignorant nor lacking in discrimination. (In Bundaberg Charles met an old lady who had played in Dresden under Richard Strauss.) Most country music-lovers had excellent hi-fi equipment and were completely up-to-date with new releases. It often seemed that the more remote the district the better the equipment.

After Rockhampton, in the tropic of Capricorn, the pleasantly warm winter weather grew humid and hot. At Mackay the Macker-rases hired a plane to take them across the Whitsunday Passage to Lindeman Island, on the Barrier Reef, then the train set off inland, on a detour to Charters Towers, a whole day's journey. There had been no tour there for seven years and some of the children had never seen a live orchestra. A little girl who was asked what she knew about Brahms thought that he was a migrant from Europe.

North of Mackay the landscape became tropical, colours were startling with bright orange-red earth, the intense green of sugar plantations. Against the dark bunya pines were trees with brilliant flowers — mauve, orange, yellow, scarlet: grevillia, bauhinia, poinciana, tulip-trees and, among pawpaw and coconuts, bougainvillea in shocking-pink, gold, imperial purple. By the time the train reached Cairns the travellers felt they were on a South Sea Island. The air was heavy with the scent of frangipani, and the little town full of pawpaws and palms.

Charles and Judy spent their free weekend on the Barrier Reef at Green Island, eighteen miles from Cairns. They travelled there in a private boat with 21 baby crocodiles which were being taken across for the island aquarium. They had two perfect days of swimming and snorkelling and drifting about the reef in a glass-bottomed boat, marvelling at the tropical fish and coloured coral below them, enchanted by the curious calls of unfamiliar birds, the haunting mournful notes of the Torres Straits pigeons. Back in Cairns, conducting the Pastoral Symphony, Charles wondered how it would have sounded if Beethoven had written it in North Queensland.

From Cairns their train took them to the Atherton Tableland behind the town. Up there the air is cool and misty and the great rain-forests are inhabited by strange animals, insects and birds. It was cold enough for Charles to wear tails. Late at night, after the concert, they came back to Cairns hitched to a string of cattle trucks. Descending the slopes the drivers speeded up to 30 mph, the orchestra's last two carriages fell off and the train screeched to a stop. There was much shunting and crashing and bellowing from angry cattle before they were joined up again.

Cairns was the farthest point north for the tour. Going south again Charles was intrigued to find Innisfail, a sugar town, full of European migrants, and Italian widely spoken. At Townsville, before he and Judy left the train to fly back to Sydney, the orchestra gave their last concert in a hall full of sulphur fumes. The local bulk-sugar terminal had recently been burnt down, but the concert was a roaring success with an audience of fourteen hundred.

The tour had covered hundreds of miles and the orchestra had played in schools, a ramshackle School-of-Arts, ancient and modern halls with acoustics that ranged from frightful to excellent, and a cinema where the heavy instruments had to be hauled up to the stage by pulley. For the first time Charles and Judy had seen extraordinarily beautiful parts of Australia and met every kind of Australian. For them both it had been a unique interlude in their urban cosmopolitan lives and for Charles, the native, a more exotic experience than many he had encountered abroad.

Three days after leaving Australia he was rehearsing in Europe, at Cologne.

XIII

Figaro

AFTER 1963 CHARLES did not return to Australia until 1971; for the rest of the sixties his work was in England and Europe. There were concerts in London and the provinces with the New Philharmonia, the London Philharmonic, the Hallé, the English Chamber Orchestra; in Glasgow with the Scottish Orchestra and in Wales with the Liverpool Philharmonic. He conducted his first Prom and continued with Promenade Concerts through the sixties and seventies, missing only the seasons when he was in Australia. There were concerts in Romania ('Wonderful adventures with peasants in ramshackle trains, drinking brandy from flasks') and he enjoyed working with two excellent Scandinavian orchestras, the Gothenburg Symphony and Oslo Philharmonic, as well as engagements in Holland and Denmark.

In one of his 1963 Oslo concerts, before flying to Australia, Daniel Barenboim had been the soloist in the Brahms First Piano Concerto. He was then in his early twenties and Charles had been puzzled and concerned that a young man so gifted and bursting with energy, so clearly destined to be one of the world's outstanding pianists, should have such a great fear of being alone. He seemed constantly to crave company, someone to talk to, even comparative strangers like Charles. For all his immense talent he appeared to need encouragement and friendly advice. He could not sleep — he even rang Charles in the middle of the night to ask him to come for a walk — and was in a very bad state of nerves. He frequently said he felt that he would not live long. Perhaps because he had been a child prodigy he somehow linked himself with Mozart and feared that, like that most wonderful prodigy of all, he would die young.

Charles's own life was now all travel and overwork. Judy worried that he had no time for reflection, even for relaxation; if he sat down at all it was to study a score. During 1961 he had given a very interesting series of broadcast talks on *Style in Orchestration*, illustrated with examples played by the BBC Northern Orchestra. In these he had shown how a composer's style was inherent not only in music but in orchestration, for instance, how Mozart's orchestration of *Messiah* was more Mozart than Handel, Tchaikovsky's *Mozartiana* more Tchaikovsky than Mozart, and so on. He had been asked by a publisher to write a book on the subject, had accepted with his usual eagerness and even begun work, but constant movement had made it impossible to continue and to Judy's regret the project had been abandoned.

In February 1964 he was in London for the English première of *The Makropulos Case*, by Janáček, at Sadler's Wells. Norman Tucker had made an English translation and Charles had agreed to be guest conductor, also to work on the score. He was fascinated by the story of the opera with its alchemists and strange magical happenings but editing was long and difficult, owing to the eccentric and often indecipherable way Janáček wrote down his music, and in order to finish the work in time an engagement in the USSR had to be postponed. The orchestra and most of the cast found the idiom peculiar, even those few who had performed Janáček's music before, but problems were overcome and the opera was a success.

Gregory Dempsey played Albert Gregor, Raimund Herincx was Jaroslav Prus and Marie Collier gave an electrifying performance as Emilia Marty, the opera singer who has taken the Elixir of Life. She had made her name as a tragic Janáček heroine in *Katya Kabanova* but many, including Charles, consider Emilia Marty her greatest role. He still speaks of her astonishing acting as the woman who has lived so long and experienced so much that she is totally burnt out, no longer able to feel emotion. The extraordinary mystery she emanated, her beauty and arrogance, her power to chill the blood remain one of the most powerful memories of his operatic career.

In the thirteen years since the first Sadler's Wells production of *Katya Kabanova* had been played to almost empty houses the climate had changed. There were still critics who disliked the Janáček cult but those who appreciated his work were enthusiastic about the opera, about Marie Collier and about Charles as a 'Janáček specialist'.

In the autumn of 1964 the BBC broadcast a new edition of Rameau's *Castor and Pollux*, on which Charles had worked with Basil Lam of the BBC Old Music department. Recreating certain features of early eighteenth-century French baroque style had involved much research and, though he had enjoyed doing it and thought the music very beautiful, the singers found it all very difficult and unfamiliar. It was a pleasant surprise when the broadcast, which Charles conducted, received very good notices.

Judy had been making improvements and alterations at Essex

House and though Charles had had little time to enjoy them he had managed to start laying down a cellar. Fiona and Catherine were growing up, they were Beatle-mad and the walls of their rumpus room were plastered with posters and pin-ups. There were plenty of visitors; travel restrictions were being released in Iron Curtain countries, people could go abroad, but since they could not take out currency, friends from Czechoslovakia, even the friends of friends, kept arriving at Essex House in search of free beds. At times a special Iron Curtain tent was set up in the garden for the overflow.

There was coming and going between Australia and London; Charles's letters to his mother ask her to entertain Edward Downes, the conductor and Alfred Deller, the counter-tenor, who were going to Sydney to work. The Mackerras twins were in England. Colin, a Sinologist, had been at Cambridge since 1961 and, when he married in 1963, Malcolm came over to be his best man. The bride was Alyce Brazier, a pretty Australian scholar of Japanese, and the wedding was from Essex House. Both Colin and Alyce were Catholic converts and were married by Monsignor Gilbey, a friend of Alastair and a chaplain at Cambridge. Charles reported to Sydney:

> Both wedding and reception were a huge success and Colin, despite his usual vagueness, did manage to engage the most splendid firm to do the catering. We did however have to spruce him up a bit and Malcolm insisted on his buying some decent shoes. This turned out to have been most essential, as of course the ONLY part of his clothing visible during the entire nuptial mass was the soles of his shoes! Alyce looked very beautiful in her bridal frock. . . . On the last night before the wedding, the house was crammed from top to bottom with our family, plus Marie Hill, plus some undergraduate friends of Colin's so you can imagine the pandemonium. Unfortunately the resident parish priest was rather disagreeable and unhelpful . . . he was blind drunk most of the time . . .

On 14 October 1964, after concerts in Sweden, Charles met Judy in Copenhagen and they flew together to Moscow. He was to conduct two concerts in Leningrad, two in Riga and two in Moscow but due to the peculiarities of Soviet concert management he had no idea which orchestras he would work with or what they would play. Not till almost the last moment did he learn that in Leningrad the orchestra would be the Leningrad Philharmonic, in Moscow the new Radio Orchestra and the programmes were to be mainly of British works. In Riga, an all-British programme had been arranged for British Week, but the Walton Symphony did not arrive in time and was replaced by the very unBritish Dvořák Eighth.

In Leningrad Charles and Judy stayed at the old Europa Hotel, just off the Nevsky Prospekt. The city was beautiful with its autumn mists and pastel buildings, its little canals and bridges, and spires across the Neva. It was already cold and Charles bought his first fur hat, which soon fell to pieces. Newspapers had vanished — even foreign language publications — and it was not until they reached Moscow that they learnt Krushchev had been deposed and Labour had won the UK elections.

One morning, at breakfast in the hotel with their interpreter, Nina Pulova (later head of the USSR Gosconcert Agency), Charles remarked that Shostakovich was sitting at a table across the room. Nina assured him that he was mistaken but he was convinced and taking her with him to interpret went over to speak to the composer. Shostakovich, who remembered him from Edinburgh, seemed pleased to see him and very willing to help with information about his opera *Katerina Ismailova*, which Charles was to conduct at Covent Garden in December that year. During the production there in 1963 the composer had come to rehearsals and explained his wishes about tempi to the conductor, Edward Downes, but he had also given Charles a recording of *Katerina* in which the tempi were different again. He agreed to meet Charles in Moscow for discussions in the rooms of the Society of Composers — the Composers' Guild.

Since the meeting was unexpected Charles had not brought a score of the opera to Russia but a solo cellist who taught at the Moscow Conservatoire offered to borrow one from the library.

Katerina Ismailova (Lady Macbeth of the Mtsensk District) had first been performed in 1934 and had been very successful until denounced by Stalin as musically and morally unacceptable. It was banned and Shostakovich fell into disgrace and, though he cut and changed the opera, it was not performed in Moscow for many years. When the helpful cellist-professor tried to borrow the revised score for Charles he discovered that not a single copy remained; the only score to be found in any of the libraries was the original banned version. With this he had to make do.

Shostakovich was not surprised to hear the story, regarding it as typical of his country. He was very thin and though friendly seemed nervous, almost chronically apprehensive, peering shortsightedly through his thick glasses, chain-smoking, yet still eager to help with the interpretation of his opera. He answered all Charles's questions, discussed tempi, also talked about his Fifth Symphony, which Charles had conducted several times, giving advice, explaining the ideas and feelings he had tried to express in the music.

Katerina Ismailova, on 8 December 1964, was Charles's first operatic engagement at Covent Garden. Marie Collier was a wonderful Katerina, supported by Charles Craig and Otakar Kraus. Desmond Shawe-Taylor wrote in the *Sunday Times* that Shostakovich's score had found 'a new and outstanding interpreter in Charles Mackerras, whose decisive and dramatic reading fully deserved the ovation he received.' Other reviewers spoke of his 'elegant and sensitive conducting', his 'power, verve and feeling for detail', his 'joyous vitality and obvious sympathy for Slav composers'.

He had agreed to be guest conductor for several operas at Sadler's Wells for the 1965 season and afterwards to tour with the company in Europe. His London performances were to be revivals of *The Makropulos Case*, *Figaro* and *Peter Grimes*, with the Australian tenor Ronald Dowd in the part of the fisherman. Charles, who had often worked with Dowd, believes that Peter Grimes is one of the tenor's greatest roles, that Dowd's earthy interpretation is far more in keeping with the character than that of Peter Pears, for whom the role was written but who was really more at home in poetic parts.

The production was a spectacular success; both Dowd and Charles received enthusiastic reviews and the critic of *Opera* magazine (Harold Rosenthal) wrote that ' . . . we now have another outstanding British operatic conductor in our midst.'

All Sadler's Wells's productions did not achieve such heights. In the dialogue version of *Carmen* the title role was sung by a Yorkshire lass named Joyce Blackham who had changed her north-country accent for a very upper-class one. Don José, however, the magnificent Australian tenor, Donald Smith, had kept to his native speech, so since the extremely refined gypsy and the very Strine Spanish officer were performing in English their dialogue was somewhat unusual. '*What are yew dewing, soldiah?*' '*Oym myking a chyne.*' '*Well, mayke a chayne for may hart!*'

Ever since his visit to the Fürstenberg Library at Donaueschingen Charles had been thinking, talking and writing about the discoveries he had made there. He had published articles in musical journals explaining and defending the use of ornamentation in Mozart opera and had argued with musicologists who disagreed with his theories. He had quoted contemporary authorities and given examples from early scores he had studied, not only at Donaueschingen but in the State Library in East Berlin and the *Istituto Musicale* in Florence, but he had not been able to put any of his discoveries into practice. When he was engaged by Norman Tucker for *Figaro* in 1965 it was as a good Mozartian who had conducted the opera a number of times, but for Charles it was a chance to demonstrate his beliefs. He made the suggestion to Tucker, his 'artistic godfather', and, as with *Katya Kabanova*, Tucker was interested and gave his approval.

It was a litle more difficult for Charles to persuade the artists to accept his proposals but once he had convinced them that they would be performing the opera as it was done in Mozart's day the majority were converted and became his keenest supporters. Since most of the cast were singing their parts for the first time they did not have to re-learn the music, but rehearsals, which were usually held outside the Director's office, took rather longer than usual. As they progressed Tucker's interest and enthusiasm increased. Hearing some new cadenza or variant that Charles had found in Vienna, Florence or Donaueschingen he would rush out in excitement demanding, 'Where did you get that?' and not be satisfied till he knew the source.

When the rumour spread that this was to be an unusual *Figaro* there was comment among musicologists; decorated performances were not to everyone's taste and were even viewed with suspicion but Tucker and Charles remained unperturbed. Shortly before the first night *Opera* magazine published an article — *What Mozart Really Meant** — in which Charles discussed the problems of correctly presenting Mozart operas when the composer's intentions were not always clear. He concluded, 'Composers' second thoughts can certainly baffle us, even today. And in the specific case of *Le Nozze di Figaro*, the problems referred to in this article have been freshly considered in our preparation of the new Sadler's Wells production of the opera this month.'

The cast on that historic first night of 9 April were Donald McIntyre — Figaro; Raimund Herincx — the Count; Ava June — the Countess; Elizabeth Harwood — Susanna; Margaret Neville —Cherubino; Rita Hunter — Marcellina; Jean Bonhomme — Don Basilio. The opera was produced by John Blatchley, with Vivienne Kermot as designer. Charles conducted the orchestra and played the continuo for the recitatives.

Now that decorated performances have become so familiar it is hard to understand why this 1965 Figaro was considered controversial, even revolutionary. As expected, adverse opinions were freely expressed, even with indignation. Other writers seemed faintly

*See Appendix, page 275.

uneasy about 'a too-fancy Figaro', questioning whether the revival of ornamentation was a step forward or back, wondering if the restoration of Marcellina's aria and the switching of Susanna's and the Countess's lines in the ensembles was an improvement or a mistake; however, such critics as Arthur Jacobs, Desmond Shawe-Taylor and Edmund Tracey were generous with their enthusiasm, praising Charles's scholarship, his understanding and natural sympathy for Mozart, the loving way in which he gave value to every phrase.

Perhaps the reaction of the majority was best summed up in *Stereo Review*:

For anyone thoroughly familiar with this wonderful opera it was an utterly fascinating and at times slightly disturbing experience. Yet it is a tribute to the strength of Mackerras's case and to the remarkable skill with which he put his ideas into practice (every single embellishment to the vocal line came from some contemporary source), not to mention his effervescent conducting and the delightful way in which he accompanied the recitatives . . . that the half-expected protests never got off the ground. For my part I am convinced that this *Figaro* was a step in the right direction; to judge from the evident joy with which most critics and the public greeted Sadler's Wells' brave try, its lesson is not likely to be ignored.

XIV

Background to 'Figaro'

IN 1947, WHEN Charles first joined the Sadler's Wells Company, the musical director had been James Robertson, a former repetiteur at Glyndebourne. Robertson venerated Fritz Busch's interpretation of Mozart and through working with him on the operas Charles had acquired a thorough grounding in the type of Germanic Mozart interpretation then prevalent in Europe. He became particularly familiar with the Busch *Figaro* and though he admitted that the performance had sparkle, both from Robertson's orchestra and on stage from such singers as Rose Hill, Anna Pollak and Arnold Matters, he felt it had little freedom and a somewhat exaggerated insistence on small unimportant details in the score.

He has never known exactly what made him rebel against this way of presenting Mozart, though it would seem to stem from his interest in the autograph scores of the great composers. Careful study of original material and accounts of contemporary performances suggested to him that many of the details on which later interpreters set so much store could have been, in fact often were, the result of a completely non-musical factor such as a page turn or cut or even a blot. There were also the circumstances in which the music was written. For Mozart, these were often a matter of great speed and tremendous pressure, as for instance the overture to *Don Giovanni* which he wrote down only the night before the performance.

It appeared that at times even the greatest composers — Bach, Handel — could be offhand about where they put *forte* and *piano* or grace-notes, perhaps because they did not think it important, that there was not much difference anyhow. If a genius like Mozart could be inconsistent in writing the length of notes (the most famous example of all is the opening of *Don Giovanni*), it may have been because he did not regard it as worth worrying about or that it was not then the custom for players to hold minims and crotchets as modern musicians are trained to do. Indeed, the practice of holding notes their full length is comparatively recent — 80 years or so.

Charles studied Quantz's treatise on the flute (1752), Leopold Mozart on the violin (1769), Tosi on singing (*c.* 1730) and C. P. E. Bach on the clavier. These works not only discuss the techniques of production but contain fascinating chapters on interpretation, rhythm, notation, improvisation, ornamentation and many other subjects, including *Affekt*, the varying of expression to suit the style and mood of the music.

The realization that the performance of eighteenth-century musicians differed on almost every point from that of present-day players stimulated his research. His visit to Donaueschingen had revealed many interesting details about Mozart's works. The Fürsten- berg library contains copies of the five most famous operas, apparently made from the original score or from the very first manuscript copies, and in studying the Donaueschingen score of *Figaro* Charles found that in all the ensembles the Countess sings the upper line and Susanna the lower, as in Mozart's autograph, before he changed them round. As Charles told his mother at the time, the biggest revelation for him came from a study of the individual part-books which had actually been used by those singers at Donaueschingen in the 1780s and 90s. All the arias were heavily ornamented and at every *fermata* lavish cadenzas had been inserted. He was shaken to realize that Mozart's operas had been treated in this way by contemporaries; it gave him a completely different view of eighteenth-century performance interpretation in general, one quite unlike the strict way in which his generation of musicians had been trained to regard the great baroque and classical composers.

The Donaueschingen copies led him to make a thorough study of old performance material and during his travels as a conductor he continued his search in the great libraries of Florence, Prague, Paris, Vienna, Hamburg and Berlin.

At this time the well-known Austrian pianist, Paul Badura-Skoda, was also studying the same subject in relation to piano music and in England Fritz Spiegl was researching ornamentation from the point of view of eighteenth-century barrel-organs and other musical automata. More importantly, Spiegl, who had spent much time in the British Museum Library (now the British Library) looking for musical curiosities, had come upon an aria by Johann Christian Bach from his London opera *Adriano in Siria* which Mozart had ornamented for the singer Aloysia Weber. Other examples, of Mozart's own music, ornamented for Aloysia Weber were found scattered in various libraries in Paris, Salzburg and Hanover.

In 1958 came the two concerts for the BBC Third Programme with Jennifer Vyvyan and Alexander Young as soloists and the then Goldsbrough Orchestra, with commentary by Fritz Spiegl. They included the material from Donaueschingen and as much of the original Mozart as had been discovered at that time. The broadcasts created a stir in London musical circles and led eventually to the concert in which Elisabeth Schwarzkopf sang two Mozart arias, with ornamentation (see page 106). In the programme notes for this occasion Fritz Spiegl wrote:

> This short example is taken from an aria in *Lucio Silla* (K.135) with decorations he wrote out some years later, probably as part of a singing lesson he gave to Aloysia Weber. It is taken from a manuscript in the Mozarteum. Mozart's embellishments are here written underneath his original melody:

One can easily imagine the outcry that such additions might produce nowadays had *Lucio Silla* become as well-known as *Figaro* and the aria in question as firm a favourite as 'Voi che sapete'.

Our trouble is that we have heard so much 18th century music performed in a 19th century manner that we are now bound to be suspicious of the real thing. (For this we must blame the great prima donna conductors, now dying out, who never read anything except scores, who take the printed note as gospel, and to whom the word 'autograph' means only the thing admirers ask for.) What then are we to do? It is useless to try to put the clock back in the search for absolute authenticity: if we use convex bows we must also have short-necked fiddles and one-keyed flutes,[*] and from there it is but a short step to powdered wigs, candles and primitive sanitation. Old music should be robust and virile, and if anything kills it it is preciousness. But the human voice is almost the only musical instrument that has not changed over the centuries and it is only in vocal music that we can be sure of reproducing the sounds composers intended. Heaven forbid that we should ask present-day singers to improve on Mozart but they *should* be expected to be able to interpret at least the most elementary and very necessary minor ornaments such as appoggiaturas (especially in recitatives) and cadential pauses in accordance with the explicit instructions that survive.

Between 1958 and 1959 Charles had continued his studies of Mozart's autographs and copies of his contemporaries, trying to establish the truth of how much or how little ornamentation Mozart might have wanted, or whether he might have put in an appoggiatura *here* and not *there*. When Norman Tucker approved the idea of presenting *Figaro* in a really different way Charles had scoured all the late eighteenth-century and early nineteenth-century sources he could find for signs of appoggiaturas and embellishments in the vocal line. He had also restored Mozart's earliest version of Act II in which the Countess, not Susanna, sings the top line in the ensembles. This makes much better dramatic sense, particularly in the trio, where the Countess is made to soar defiantly up to top C.

The opera was given entirely without cuts, it is said for the first time in London, and Rita Hunter's performance of Marcellina's brilliant aria in Act IV, and Jean Bonhomme's of the rather odd aria for Don Basilio (both usually cut) were among the highlights of the evening.

The new methods of interpretation were also applied to the orchestral parts, with many passages double-dotted, minims and crotchets shortened and trills starting on the upper note. Tempi, especially Mozart's typical *Andante alla breve*, were re-thought, although here Charles did not quite go to the extreme he adopted some ten years later, when he even used eighteenth-century bowing techniques and baroque timpani. He now admits that in his

[*]Since this was written these predictions have come about, with the emergence of ensembles specializing in 'authentic' instruments and style of performance, such as those of Christopher Hogwood and Trevor Pinnock.

enthusiasm for change he went rather too far in some of the ornamentation, particularly when he included a Rossinian double cadenza by Sir Henry Bishop (1819) at the end of the Letter Duet in Act III!

The performance was so successful and so widely hailed as a major advance in interpretation that he expected the record companies to take up the idea, but to his amazement no one outside Sadler's Wells circles seemed very interested. (Recording the Mozart operas under ideal studio conditions still remains one of his very few unfulfilled ambitions.) Although moves were being made towards more authentic interpretation of baroque composers such as Bach and Handel, Mozart was still locked into the Viennese school of interpretation of Böhm and Karajan. The smallest change from tradition was regarded with intense suspicion and no doubt the Sadler's Wells 'Figaro from a clean slate' earned a few black marks through being in an English translation. The industry continued to record Mozart operas in the same way as before, each interpretation indistinguishable from the other, until the 1980s, when Nicholas Harnoncourt's Zurich performance of Idomeneo was recorded by Telefunken. In Charles's view the phrasing and dynamics of both singers and orchestra are exemplary in this performance though the many problems of the vocal line remain unsolved.

Later, during his years in repertory opera in Hamburg, Charles found it quite impossible to make any changes in Mozart performance; even the odd appoggiatura had to be dragged from the singers because they were not used to them.

On the other hand, in major revivals or new productions of eighteenth-century works in German, such as Così fan tutte and Il Matrimonio segreto in Hamburg in 1967/8 and Die Zauberflöte in West Berlin in 1978 the singers were very ready to accept new and interesting ideas and took great trouble in carrying them out. Resistance to change came from the orchestras and critics. Even when Charles presented the musicians with a set of carefully marked parts they still played them as they had always done and referred to 'mistakes' in his orchestral material, while most of the critics harked back to the 'great days' of Bruno Walter, Klemperer and Kleiber, apparently unaware that Charles was aiming at a style completely different from that of his distinguished predecessors. One eminent Berlin critic even castigated him for trying to turn The Magic Flute into a baroque opera.

Critics may have been infected by a feeling of unease emanating from the pit, due to the orchestra's lack of sympathy with Charles's ideas. The conductor's art, after all, is to persuade the musicians to adopt his interpretation willingly and if they refuse he has failed to some extent. Charles also experienced audience hostility to appoggiaturas and ornamentation in Mozart operas in France as well as Germany, possibly because so many music-lovers learn their operas from recordings, which are almost unanimous in rejecting these very important facets of eighteenth-century style.

Comparing the enthusiastic reception given to the 1965 Sadler's Wells *Figaro* with the prejudiced, often ignorant reaction to anything untraditional by French, Italian and German audiences and critics (not to mention the Austrians, the most hidebound of all) has impressed upon Charles how enlightened the British public and critics were at that time.

He has continued to perform Mozart's music in the style in which he believes, and in 1984 was rewarded with a wonderfully committed presentation of *Don Giovanni* by singers and orchestra of the Welsh National Opera. Unfortunately on that occasion the cohesion of the musical performance, combining as it did all his credos of Mozartian interpretation, was to be severely damaged by the 'symbolic' and 'socially relevant' production of the East German director, Ruth Berghaus.

XV

Hamburg

AT THE END of the 1965 London season Charles left with the Sadler's
Wells Company for a Continental tour that included Amsterdam,
Geneva, Lausanne, Prague, Vienna and Hamburg. The repertoire
comprised three English-language operas — the Gilbert and Sullivan
Iolanthe and Britten's *Peter Grimes*, both to be conducted by Charles,
and the Stravinsky/Auden *The Rake's Progress*, which Colin Davis was
to conduct.

Despite the success and critical acclaim of *Figaro* Charles was restless
and disheartened. He was dissatisfied with life as a freelance artist and
hankered after jobs abroad. When Sadler's Wells reached Hamburg he
called on Rolf Liebermann, the Intendant of the State Opera House, to
enquire about openings for guest conducting. He was disappointed to
find there were no vacancies, but soon after the interview Liebermann
came to a performance of *Peter Grimes* and was so impressed with
Charles's work that he invited him to join the Hamburg Opera as
Erster-Kapellmeister or principal conductor, the position second only to
the musical director. (It is said that Dr Liebermann was also influenced
by learning that Charles was the orchestrator of *Pineapple Poll*.) Before
the engagement was confirmed he was asked to return to Hamburg
for an *Informationsgastspiel* or trial run.

The previous year, cruising with Judy in the Mediterranean, the
ship had called at Portoferraio, on the island of Elba. They had both
been so charmed by the little sea-town, the coloured houses and
harbour and fishing boats, that they had decided to return there for a
holiday in 1965. They stayed in the coastal village of Marciana Marina
and hired a car, also a boat, so that they could explore the coast and
secluded beaches inaccessible from the land as well as the hill-towns
and villages. It was summer; in the *macchia* that covered the steep
slopes yellow broom, scarlet and yellow poppies, coloured daisies,
pink, white and yellow cistus grew wild, with lavender, borage,
rosemary. All over the island were beautiful trees — cypresses,
umbrella pines, forests of chestnuts.

From the hill behind Porto Azzurro, on the south-west coast, Charles and Judy looked out on fantastic views, across Elba to Italy, the whole sweep of the Mediterranean with its islands: Monte Cristo, a ghostly mountain peak rising out of the sea, Pianosa and, in the distance, the great shape of Corsica. Above them was Capoliveri, a hill-town of pink houses cascading down from a church tower and ahead, beyond a blue bay, a great line of mountains against the sky.

They decided they must have a house on the island where they could come for holidays, where Charles could work at his scores but also relax and swim and sail as he had done in Sydney. They found an old peasant's cottage that faced across the bay to the mountains and began to plan how to buy and convert it.

For his Hamburg *Informationsgastspiel* Charles conducted three operas of different types, in each case after one rehearsal (with solo singers only) the night before the performance. The first opera was *Trovatore*, sung in German and, a few weeks later, *Fidelio* and *Così fan tutte* on alternate nights. He had conducted *Fidelio* a number of times in East Berlin and he liked the Hamburg production of *Così*, but he was worried by the lack of rehearsal, the rushed atmosphere of the tests; the feeling of improvisation made him uneasy about his own performance. Liebermann, however, was satisfied and confirmed the appointment for three years. Charles, who was the first Englishman to hold such a position in Germany, decided to let Essex House and move his family to Hamburg.

In October 1965 he was again guest conductor at Sadler's Wells for the English première of Janáček's *From the House of the Dead*. This opera, which he edited and which he had already conducted in a BBC broadcast, is based on Dostoevsky's experiences as a prisoner in Siberia (the novel, *From the House of the Dead*). It had been slightly altered by pupils of Janáček to give it a somewhat less grim ending, but Sadler's Wells used the original version. Reviews were extremely good and the *Sunday Times*, having described Charles as 'a superb Janáček conductor' who 'brought out all the force and tenderness of the score', concluded, 'How sad, and how disgraceful that London should have lost him to Hamburg.'

He was not to start work in Hamburg until September 1966 but in May he spent several weeks there at Liebermann's request, rehearsing a new production of Britten's *Albert Herring*. The visit, which would enable him to find a house for his family, was to be combined with work in Belgium: he had prepared an edition of Handel's *Agrippina* for a joint BBC-Belgian Radio broadcast, and Judy, who was already

packing up for the move, arranged to meet him in Brussels with the
car and drive him on to Germany.

On the day of the broadcast she packed her Vauxhall with personal
possessions and piles of scores and set off for Dover, listening to the
broadcast on the way. She crossed by the night ferry, arrived at
Ostend at 4 a.m. in bright moonlight and drove on to Brussels,
reaching Charles's hotel extremely tired about two hours later. She
collected the key from the night porter and went upstairs to their room
where Charles was dead to the world. Without waking him she
climbed into the twin bed and fell asleep. At about half-past eight
Charles woke and realized with horror that there was an unidentified
female form under the covers in the other bed. There had been a late
party in his room the night before and it seemed that, with Judy about
to arrive at any minute, he would have to make some explanation.

Before moving to Hamburg Charles conducted two television operas,
Otello and Britten's *Billy Budd*, which the composer had agreed to
supervise. Production methods had changed since the days when he —
Charles — ran about among the chorus, winking and jerking his head,
but many operas were still produced in the studio. This had certain
advantages over telecasts made direct from the theatre: film techniques could be used, there was greater mobility in shooting, and the
restricted rectangular view from the auditorium was avoided. On the
other hand, in the opera house, where singers faced the audience, they
had the conductor clearly in view in the pit, whereas in the studio, if
the action took place in different dimensions, obliging them to face in
any direction, they did not know where to turn in order to see him.

The problem had been solved by separating conductor and
orchestra from the singers and putting them in another studio. They
were able to watch each other on monitors and a projection screen and
the music was synchronized through loudspeakers. The conductor,
who needed to be constantly alert to the needs of the singers, was
helped by an assistant in the singers' studio who followed and
duplicated his movements on the projection screen, beating time, also
prompting and calling in off-stage effects. Perfect rapport was
essential between conductor and assistant but though it was a clumsy
arrangement and made great demands on both, musically the result
was often very good.

When Britten came to the studios to supervise *Billy Budd* he was
completely bewildered by these processes and horrified by the
inartistic way the work was done — the crowds of people in the
studio, the scenes shot out of order or rushed through because

technicians were packing up for their next job — but he gave Charles all possible help and advice. It was their first meeting since the rift* but apparently all rancour had been set aside and he and Peter Pears were prepared to forgive and forget. The opera had an exceptional cast with Peter Pears, Robert Tear, Peter Glossop, Michael Langdon, Geraint Evans and John Shirley-Quirk, and Britten was delighted with the final result, which won the Television Opera Award for that year.

Charles realized one of his ambitions in 1966 when he recorded *Messiah* for His Master's Voice. This was a fresh edition which Basil Lam and he had prepared several years before from the autograph score. They had often worked together, Lam doing the groundwork and Charles putting the findings into professional musicians' form. At that time players were not used to the 'new' baroque style and everything had to be indicated in the parts to clarify the meaning (see Appendix, page 294).

The Lam-Mackerras *Messiah*, which had been broadcast by the BBC at Christmas 1963 and performed a number of times by the English Chamber Orchestra and the Ambrosian Singers, had roused interest and criticism. Many of the details of eighteenth-century performance practice were still unfamiliar and as with the decorated *Figaro* some musicologists complained that there was too much ornamentation, that it was incorrect or not stylish.

It had taken a very long time for Charles to persuade EMI to record this *Messiah*; in fact they had hesitated so long that when they finally made the decision they found that Colin Davis was conducting another version for Philips. Both recordings were released almost simultaneously.

Charles did not always agree with Basil Lam on how the work should be sung but he had ensured the recording's success by choosing outstanding artists — Janet Baker, Elizabeth Harwood, Paul Esswood, Robert Tear, Raimund Herincx. There were those who felt that liberties had been taken and others whose researches had led to different conclusions objected on various grounds, but most critics were enthusiastic. *The Gramophone* admired 'the spirit and integrity' of the conducting and described it as 'a most alive and fascinating performance with splendid orchestral playing, soloists who all seem at the very top of their form and excellent recording quality'; *Records and*

---

*Though they had already been in touch the previous year: Britten had written to congratulate Charles on his Hamburg appointment and later again about *Peter Grimes*: ' . . . I hear on all sides how wonderfully you do the work. Thank you so much for the time and trouble you have taken over it. . . .'

Recording considered it ' . . . superb — scholarly and idiomatic in concept, deeply considered in interpretation, brilliant in execution and entirely satisfying as a musical experience . . . unlikely to be bettered for a considerable time . . .', while *Music and Musicians* declared it to be ' . . . very nearly an ideal interpretation'.

The record was nominated for the 1967 Grammy Award.

In September 1966 Charles and Judy loaded their Volkswagen microbus and set out for Hamburg with young Catherine. Fiona was to join them when she had finished a typing course in London. Their route, via Harwich and Bremerhaven, was to become very familiar to Judy but not to Charles who was in the air far more often than on the road.

In Hamburg they had rented a pleasant house in the suburb of Othmarschen, near the river Elbe and not far from the International School where Catherine was to be a pupil for the next two years. Essex House had been let to Canadian diplomats and, for taxation reasons, the Mackerrases had become German residents. Since this meant that they must never stay in their own house during the period of their UK tax exemption, when they came to London they rented rooms from Judy's friend and former fellow-student, the clarinettist Thea King, or relied on friends for beds.

Hamburg *Staatsoper* is a repertory house, performing about 60 operas and ballets, including eight new productions, each year. It is financed by the town and *Land* (state) and at the time Charles joined it had changed from a purely German to an International opera house. With constantly rising artists' fees and union demands, money was always short and economies had to be made; possibly it was for this reason that there were no changes in established productions which were never 're-thought' as in England where new ideas on well-established works might be tried out each season. While Charles was rehearsing *Albert Herring* in May he had also conducted performances of repertory operas, usually in German, a couple of times a week, thus saving the administration his rehearsal fee since he was paid for conducting.

He had had several weeks of preparation for *Herring* and a very good cast, including Tatiana Troyanos, Edith Lang and two very distinguished character artists, the tenor Erwin Wohlfahrt (Albert) and Martha Mödl (Mrs Herring). The appearance of Martha Mödl, who had come out of partial retirement for the occasion, was considered rather a *coup* for Hamburg for she had been famous at Bayreuth with Furtwängler. To Charles, the opera seemed odd sung in German, as it has been in each of the many times he has since conducted it, but all the artists were excellent and the production was very good indeed. He was more doubtful about the next Britten work — *A Midsummer Night's Dream* — which he conducted in Hamburg: he felt the composer would not have been happy to hear Oberon sung by a character-tenor instead of a counter-tenor.

Albert Herring had been well rehearsed because it was a new production but this was by no means normal. For works already in the repertoire there was only a brief run-through, just with soloists, the night before the performance and often not even that. An artist who was playing a new role would be given production rehearsals with piano, usually alone although sometimes with other members of the cast. Otherwise, though cast and orchestra changed constantly and performances seemed to come round very frequently, there were no rehearsals. There were over three hundred performances in the season of some 50 different works. The opera house closed only on Easter Monday. On Christmas Eve and New Year's Eve the opera was *Fledermaus*. On Christmas Day Charles conducted *Don Giovanni*!

When Charles first began to work regularly at the *Staatsoper* he felt he had been thrown in at the deep end. He was used to the *stagione* system at Sadler's Wells where an opera would be repeated a number of times in a season and then taken on tour, where there were always plenty of rehearsals and the conductor worked with the same singers and orchestra. He adapted to the system but always with a feeling of strain and before very long had taken up smoking again. He found the chamber operas that he so often conducted — *Albert Herring*, *Il Matrimonio segreto*, *The Rake's Progress* — particularly trying. Being written for small orchestras they are noticeably affected by constantly changing personnel, yet the main orchestra was also so overworked that often players were not available for an opera they had learnt and new ones had to be taught; in fact it was necessary to train several orchestras for one opera. Charles also conducted ballets, which were usually unfamiliar and more or less unrehearsed.

Of the works to be performed, Leopold Ludwig, the general musical director, had first choice of the operas, and Charles or a guest conductor would take what was left. When Nello Santi, the regular conductor for Italian operas, was away Charles deputized for him and took over many other works in the repertoire. This involved constant study for there were different operas every week, often with no time between them; for instance, after the opening of *Don Pasquale*, on which he had been concentrating for weeks, he conducted *Arabella* the very next night. This opera had not been performed for months and since he had never done it before he had to re-learn it in one day. Having switched his thoughts from the Donizetti comic opera to the intricacies of Richard Strauss he then returned the following night to *Don Pasquale*.

Normally he was given a reasonable time to study a work he did not know but though he had two weeks to prepare for *Boris Godunov* there was only one rehearsal with the soloists and none at all with chorus or orchestra, both so important in this opera. It also transpired that the tenor engaged for the part of the false Dmitri had not read his contract and had assumed that he was to sing Rimsky-Korsakov's version of *Boris* when in fact it was the Shostakovich arrangement. Since he was not aware that another version existed he naturally did not know the music he had been hired to sing and for two consecutive nights Charles and the prompter had to steer him through his role, calling him in when he missed his cue, stopping him when he came in at the wrong places. Somehow they staggered through it, hoping the audience did not know the opera well enough to notice the mistakes.

Yet the opera house itself was most efficiently run with performances moving on a conveyor belt night after night, though artists frequently did not meet before performances or even see the stage and sets they would work in. Judy remembers Amy Shuard, the English soprano, interrupting a conversation in her dressing-room before *Die Walküre* to say, 'Just a minute while I go on stage and see where the Rock is.' Another night, at supper after *Don Giovanni*, Donna Anna was introduced for the first time to the Don (Theo Adam) who had sung with her all evening. She was pleased to find him as handsome in life as on stage.

Despite his worries Charles, like his family, enjoyed living in Hamburg. They all look back on it as a very happy time. Judy was busy but there was a sense of freedom in being away from her own house, her familiar routine and responsibilities. When Fiona arrived from London she and Judy enrolled at the Berlitz for German lessons and for three months went to school every day. Fiona soon acquired a German boy-friend which greatly increased her fluency, while Catherine passed her A levels with top marks in German, French and English.

Fiona, who had already left school, spent less time in Hamburg than Catherine. She came and went from London where she was doing various courses and sometimes taking jobs. As the only daughter at home, Catherine was included in much of her parents' social life and was able to develop a rather special relationship with her father. She amused him by her juvenile attempts at joining in adult conversation, he gave her confidence by discussing artistic matters with her, by asking her advice and taking it seriously. He was proud of her talent for languages and pleased that she was interested in opera production.

They all made good and lasting friendships through the opera, the school and the Hamburg Players, an amateur drama group run by an Englishman. Judy and the girls all had parts in their first production (*The Summer of the Seventeenth Doll*) and, even after Fiona and Catherine had left Germany, Judy stayed on with the group and enjoyed playing leading parts. Social life was lively, people from England and Czechoslovakia came to stay. Jiřinka Kadainková took over for a month while Judy was away and devoted herself to spoiling Charles. The British Council representative, Dennis Clark, was friendly; there were many parties for distinguished visitors who included Barbirolli, Benjamin Britten and Peter Pears, and the Mackerrases often entertained in their own house where they could talk informally to interesting artists. The only part of the family that did not care for Hamburg was the Vauxhall car. Despite, or perhaps because of being registered in Germany it was always breaking down and giving trouble.

Judy spent much time driving Charles to and from the airport to see him off or welcome him back. He was commuting between Germany and England to rehearse and conduct at Sadler's Wells and Covent Garden. It was rather like going to the office; he left by the 8.30 plane and came home in the evening. In 1966 the BBC made a film (*Allegro Vivace*) which gave some idea of his life, showing glimpses of his work in Hamburg, Scandinavia and England. He had concerts in London, Prague, Helsinki and Florence and made trips to Vienna to record early music. For Vanguard he conducted the Italian version of Gluck's *Orfeo*, with Maureen Forrester and the Vienna Volksoper Orchestra, and for DGG Cavalieri's *Rappresentazione di anima e di corpo* (his only known work), which was played in a baroque palace on authentic instruments, probably one of the very first recordings of early music made in this way. In England he recorded Purcell's *Ode on St Cecilia's Day*, with English choir and singers, for Deutsche Grammophon Archiv, with whom he had a contract, and in Germany there was a somewhat decorated edition of the same composer's *Dido and Aeneas* with Tatiana Troyanos, the Hamburg Radio Orchestra and a wonderful Hamburg choir; also, for L'Oiseau-Lyre, Purcell's *Indian Queen*, with April Cantelo, Robert Tear, the ECO and the St Anthony Singers.

Whenever there was time he continued his researches into early music. In the Hamburg Library he had found a contemporary French score of Cimarosa's *Il Matrimonio segreto* and, although he had not seen the composer's autograph, had revised and corrected it and conducted it many times at the *Staatsoper*. Normally there was no chance to try his ideas of ornamentation. Occasionally, as in *The Magic Flute*, he could introduce a few appoggiaturas, but the general feeling was against decoration. There was little point in trying, with the repertory system of a different opera each night; few artists were prepared to learn a completely new way of singing for a few performances just to please a conductor and, even if they were, the next conductor would very likely change it. It was as hopeless as trying to shape an orchestra with musicians who continually came and went.

He was often frustrated and impatient with this unrelenting closed mind to the interpretation of Mozart and at times felt fed up with the whole Hamburg system yet, apart from the strain, working without rehearsal was extremely valuable experience. It was helping him to develop the power of emanation, the mysterious process of projection by which a conductor galvanizes an orchestra into giving a quite different performance of the same work on different nights (see Appendix, page 326). In his early days at Sadler's Wells, when he took over the orchestra after Mudie or Robertson had rehearsed an opera, he had had to depend on emanation to a certain extent, but at Hamburg the demands were far greater. At first he did not know if he could meet them, he had not fully realized just how much he must get a grip on a work in his own mind before it could be projected successfully upon the orchestra. He felt that his early performances were often too flaccid but he knew he must persevere and improve, it would be impossible otherwise to work without rehearsals and with constantly changing singers and players. He watched and learnt much from Nello Santi, the Italian conductor, who had so mastered the art of emanation that he always gave a completely fresh performance of the same work on different nights; but for Charles by far the most valuable experience and important part of learning was practising it himself on the orchestra.

From time to time Charles had conducted the Symphony Orchestra of the Norddeutscher Rundfunk and one day he received a telephone call from the head of the Light Music Section. Rudolf Friml, the Czech operetta and film composer, was looking for a conductor to record some of his 'serious works'. Would Charles be interested?

He agreed to look at the music and went with the NDR representative to meet the composer. Friml was very affable and produced a number of symphonies, suites and concertos which were all in piano arrangements. When Charles asked about orchestral scores he found that there were none, and to his enquiry as to how the orchestra could perform without them Friml replied airily that the musicians would be given piano arrangements and the conductor would tell each instrument what it was to play.

Charles was staggered. He said, 'But you can't do that!'

Friml was very surprised. 'Why not?'

'Because there must be an orchestral score with parts for the instruments.'

Friml, who clearly thought him an incompetent idiot, shrugged this off as nonsense. He had never needed orchestral scores and if there was going to be so much fuss he would have the music recorded in Czechoslovakia where apparently they knew how to do it. To the astonishment of Charles and the NDR official, the composer had not only never orchestrated anything himself, he did not seem to know that orchestral parts were necessary.

When the *Staatsoper* was invited to Canada in 1967 to perform at Expo '67 they took a company of several hundreds and a large well-rehearsed repertoire including four newly-commissioned works, two from Germany and two from the United States. From Montreal they were to go to New York for a two weeks' season at the Metropolitan.

Rolf Liebermann, who wanted an impressive name for the occasion, had engaged Hans Schmidt-Isserstedt, the distinguished conductor of the Norddeutscher Rundfunk. He was to conduct the first night of Hindemith's *Mathis der Maler* and then hand over the opera to Charles, but Schmidt-Isserstedt, 'a charming, amusing old boy', had the only orchestral score and was so reluctant to give it up that Charles did not see it at all until after the first performance, and then only after great efforts. He had no chance to study the work except from a piano score. Not only was the opera completely new to him, enormous cuts had been made and the time reduced from four hours to two, partly for the tour, partly because of overtime costs at the Met. The singers knew the cuts because they had learnt the reduced version, but for Charles the performance was a nightmare of trying to keep up with the cast, feverishly turning the pages to find his way through the butchered remains of the score.

At the Met in New York he conducted *The Rake's Progress* and the following year, when Hamburg gave a two weeks' season in Rome, he conducted it again. This was an easier tour, with only two works.

Leopold Ludwig conducted the other opera, Strauss's *Die Frau ohne Schatten* (*The Woman without a Shadow*), and there was time between performances for the singers to go by train with Charles to Piombino and across to Elba to join Judy at Villa Mackerras.

Earlier that year Catherine, whom Charles's daughters called Austra, had come to Europe. She stayed at Norwich with Joan, who had married and was living in England, then flew to Prague where Charles was conducting. The temperature was 10 degrees below zero but she enjoyed herself. She was enchanted by the beautiful city under snow, by seeing Janáček's *The Cunning Little Vixen*, by Mass in splendid baroque churches but was disappointed by a bad performance of *Figaro* in the theatre where *Don Giovanni* was first performed.

After spending time with the family in Hamburg she returned to Australia to give approving reports of the way life was going for Charlie. She had found him, at 43, quite surprisingly solid. It seemed his metabolism had completely changed: he smoked, worked harder than ever, burned up energy yet continued to put on weight. He had now quite lost the lean aquiline resemblance to Alan's family, yet he was not like Catherine. Despite his sandy colouring, in photographs where his eyes appeared black he looked Jewish, as though Isaac Nathan were emerging from his Celtic descendant. He enjoyed life, loved good food and wine and long convivial meals. Left to himself he would never have kept to a diet if Judy had not concerned herself with his health. He rarely took a holiday on Elba. The plan to buy and convert the peasant's cottage had been abandoned and they had built a villa to their own design. It was simple, charming, comfortable, unfussy with white walls, coloured glazed floors, a terrace with vines, a sweeping view of mountains and sea and an annexe for friends and grandchildren. They swam from the rocks at the foot of their land or from the beach where Charles launched his sailing boat, *Emilia Marty*. It was perfect, except that there seemed no time to enjoy it.

He was still accepting too many engagements outside his regular job but he was enjoying himself. He liked conducting at Covent Garden and he liked working with distinguished artists in the international atmosphere of Hamburg and other European opera houses. At the *Staatsoper* famous singers — Pavarotti, Fischer-Dieskau, Mirella Freni, Teresa Berganza, Tito Gobbi — often appeared for one or two performances with the resident company. Gobbi, once so haughty with the young unknown television conductor, had mellowed with age and was now very friendly to Charles. They worked together happily on a number of performances, including *Otello*, though younger artists sometimes behaved as Gobbi had done in the past. When Pavarotti and Mirella Freni sang in *La Bohème* there were only two rehearsals, both on the day before the performance. Because of an airline strike, Charles, who had been working in Paris, had trouble returning in time to conduct. Trains were crowded, he could not get a sleeper and sat up all night, arriving extremely tired to find the two stars had failed to appear for the first rehearsal. They came to the second but though Freni was easy to work with Pavarotti threw his considerable weight about and exasperated Charles by telling him how to conduct 'Che gelida manina'. Despite their differences the tenor's performance was a triumph and with time and assurance he became more reasonable and co-operative.

A number of very interesting new artists were starting to emerge at Hamburg, most of them young inexperienced discoveries of Liebermann. Placido Domingo, Richard Cassily, Tatiana Troyanos, Arlene Saunders were all to become famous. Charles often conducted Domingo, whom he admired as an actor, singer and musician. They always worked together on Italian-type operas, in which the tenor excelled, though early in his career Liebermann had made one mistake and cast him as Lohengrin, a role for which he was quite unsuited. With his immense charm and talent he overcame this first failure and went on almost immediately to huge successes.

Sometimes members of the 'old guard' would come in to sing a role they had made famous. Charles conducted *Pagliacci* with the tenor Hans Hopf as a somewhat faded Canio, a rather uneasy *Otello* with the Viennese Hans Beirer (a once-renowned Florestan and Siegfried), and a *Don Carlos* with the old Wagnerian, Hans Hotter, who had more or less retired, in the role of the Grand Inquisitor. These performances were often not very good but were usually received with tumultuous applause for old times' sake.

In 1966, the year in which Charles went to Hamburg, his former 'artistic godfather', Norman Tucker, had resigned from Sadler's Wells and Stephen Arlen, Tucker's business manager, had become sole managing director. Arlen felt that the time had come to leave Rosebery Avenue. The company's work deserved better facilities and a wider audience, and a larger, more central theatre might also help solve the financial difficulties that had overtaken Sadler's Wells. There had been the possible project of an opera house on the South Bank as part of the National Theatre complex but this had failed to materialize and in 1967 Arlen decided to move to the West End. The old Coliseum music hall, built in 1904, with 2,500 seats, was about to become available. It had been used for Cinerama for years but could be converted for opera. By 1968 finance had been raised, mainly from the Arts Council, then headed by Lord Goodman, and alterations had begun. They were to be finished by August that year and the New Sadler's Wells Opera was to open with a performance of *Don Giovanni*. Charles was invited to prepare an edition and conduct on the first night. John Gielgud was to produce the opera and Derek Jarman, a young painter who had not previously done operatic work, was chosen as designer.

After studying as many editions of *Don Giovanni* as possible Charles decided to make the performance less elaborate than the 1965 *Figaro*, while keeping as close to the score as Mozart would have wanted. Feeling far from confident about producer and designer he gave Gielgud a copy of the original stage directions and went back to Germany to work on the score.

The move, the remodelled Coliseum, the future of Sadler's Wells had roused popular interest and sympathy and Gielgud's name attracted further publicity. Newspapers published articles and pictures of progress in rebuilding, Gielgud was photographed taking rehearsals, he and Derek Jarman were interviewed and expounded their theories about production. In Germany, Charles kept his misgivings to himself and concentrated on preparing his orchestral parts.

At the end of July he went with Judy, the two girls and their boy-friends to Elba. They had been there only a few days when he woke very early one morning with a sudden acute pain. Judy immediately thought of appendicitis and when he was no better by six a.m. she drove him down to the doctor at Porto Azzurro. The doctor made a few tests and decided the pain came from a colonic spasm. He prescribed rest and a liquid diet but Judy was still uneasy and insisted he give her a letter to the hospital at Portoferraio in case of emergencies.

For two days Charles lay about looking and feeling miserable. He was not in great pain but considerable discomfort and Judy's concern increased. She was extremely worried by the time their friend Inge Henderson arrived to stay. Inge, who is a leading practitioner of the Alexander Technique, had had medical training. She took one look at Charles in his deck-chair on the terrace and said, 'If he hasn't got appendicitis he's got an intestinal block, I can see by the way he's sitting. If they don't get him open quickly he'll die!'

She at once rang a friend, Barbara Ingham, who lived in a neighbouring villa and had also had medical training. Mrs Ingham said emphatically that Charles must not go to hospital at Portoferraio, even if they operated successfully the after-care would be inadequate; he must go immediately to Livorno where there was a very good teaching hospital and where she knew the specialist, Dr Spinelli. He lived near the hospital and they could stop at his house on the way.

Mr Ingham rushed down to the port for ferry tickets and within an hour, with Charles lying prone on the back seat of the Inghams' car, they set off for Porto Azzurro. On the ferry they were allowed to park with the back of the car in the open so that the patient could have air; then came a very hot two-hour drive to Livorno where they found that Dr Spinelli was away from home. They drove straight on to the hospital and once Judy had explained that the maestro was fully insured (since Italians prefer not to act till they know they will be paid), he was put on a stretcher and wheeled away to the theatre.

As Judy had feared, it was the appendix, and it took an hour to get it out; it was not only twisted round behind other organs but gangrenous and there was also extensive peritonitis. When Charles was wheeled from the theatre festooned with tubes and drips he looked as though he had died but, being very difficult to sedate, he was already coming out of the anaesthetic. For a week he was very ill indeed, needing constant care and antibiotics (the nun turned her head away as she injected them into his behind). Judy was put in a double room with him and told to watch the drip and that he must have a teaspoonful of mineral water every hour. She was terrified; if he didn't move she thought he had died, if he made a noise she thought something was wrong. She dared not close her eyes and sat on the edge of the bed all night watching him. After a night without sleep she announced that she would be on duty from 8 a.m. to 8 p.m., would wash the patient, give him his teaspoonfuls of water and anything else he needed but she must have sleep and she must have a male nurse to help with the lifting. The nurse was provided and Judy took a room in a house across the street with a most sympathetic landlady. All the Italians were very kind. The landlady visited Charles and took him a packet of biscuits, which he could not eat, and the male nurses at the hospital sang opera choruses for his benefit as they worked.

Charles was not a good patient, he moaned and groaned and was sure he was going to die, as he very nearly did. Not till the sixth day was he allowed a meal, a small helping of chicken and spinach, but when he saw there was also a tiny carafe of white wine on his tray he took heart and decided to live. Once he began to complain Judy knew he was out of danger and she could go back to Elba to fetch the family. Her landlady had agreed to let a room to Fiona and Catherine but thought it improper for their boy-friends to stay in the same house.

After a fortnight in hospital Judy took the patient back to the island where Barbara Ingham had invited them to stay for a week at her house. This was a great blessing for which they were both grateful for Mrs Ingham knew how to dress Charles's wound. He convalesced for another six weeks in Hamburg and started work very cautiously with small chamber operas. He had been warned that strenuous arm movements could reopen the scar or result in lesions.

The news of his illness had caused a sensation at the Coliseum and frantic efforts were being made to secure a substitute for the opening night. Mario Bernardi, one of the company's two conductors, was to take over *Don Giovanni* from Charles, but he was on holiday and could not be reached. He had driven to Venice and left his car with an uncle while he went on a Mediterranean cruise. He was believed to be sailing somewhere along the Yugoslav coast but no one knew when or where he might land. Telegrams were sent to the uncle, who did not speak English and had to refer them to a relation some distance away, but they continued to arrive, with telephone calls, till Bernardi returned to Venice and rang the Coliseum himself. He rushed back to England in time to rehearse and conduct on the opening night.

During his convalescence Charles, who had lost many pounds in weight, had been very depressed. He had missed not only the opening of the Coliseum but the Wieland Wagner production of *The Flying Dutchman* which he was to conduct for the Hamburg Opera at the Edinburgh Festival, and other engagements which included a Promenade concert. However, when the reviews of *Don Giovanni* arrived he wondered if after all he had not had a lucky escape. Some critics tried hard to be kind but others did not disguise their disappointment. It was said that Gielgud's production was 'diffused and unfocussed'; several reviews were facetious, the Jarman sets were described as 'low-grade panto' with the Don living 'in the Strand Palace'. There were 'trees like green triffids out to get the chorus' and scenes set on what looked like a golf-course 'with pennants hinting at a marina nearby'. Don Giovanni himself, dressed in striped poncho, was 'like a Mexican bandit' or 'a second-hand horse dealer from some poor corner of the Argentine'. Though most of the musical press had wished the new opera house well, there was no hiding the fact that the Gielgud–Jarman production had not been a success.

Towards the end of 1968 Stephen Arlen came to Hamburg and spent a few days with Judy and Charles. He told them that he had decided to abolish the old Sadler's Wells system of two conductors and appoint a musical director. He wanted to know if Charles was interested in the job.

Charles needed considerable thought and discussion before he could make up his mind. During his years at Hamburg he had moved away from opera in English and singers who worked as a team. His outlook had become completely international and he was accustomed to star-studded casts; on the other hand he had never broken his ties with Sadler's Wells and it was tempting to think of helping to mould a company, of having a chance to carry out his own ideas of performance and repertoire.

For the family, a move back to England was practical. Both girls were to continue their education there: Fiona was already at the Froebel College in London, and Catherine, also in London, had taken a job at Cranks in Carnaby Street, while she waited to do an Honours degree in French and Drama at Birmingham University. They had all been very happy in Germany but Judy now felt it was time to go home. When Arlen made his proposal it seemed to be well timed.

XVI

The Coliseum

BY THE SUMMER of 1969 the Mackerras family was back in England. Charles, who was not due to start at the Coliseum until January 1970, spent the rest of the year flying to Hamburg, and rehearsing, arranging and conducting for Sadler's Wells in London, Liverpool and Manchester, and at the Royal Opera House, Covent Garden. He also conducted a BBC broadcast of Janáček's *The Adventures of Mr Brouček* and an opera season in the USA, and prepared an edition of Donizetti's *Roberto Devereux* for a concert performance of the opera which he conducted in 1970 at Drury Lane with Monserrat Caballé, Tatiana Troyanos, the Ambrosian Singers and the Royal Philharmonic Orchestra, and for a recording of the same work with Beverley Sills.

While they were still in Hamburg he and Judy had reluctantly come to the conclusion that they must leave Essex House. Beautiful as it was, and much as they all loved it, it would be too big with Judy's father no longer there and both girls living away from home. It was also too far from the Coliseum.

A new house was found almost by accident; in fact, as Judy said, the whole operation hung on a pair of braces. In May 1969 Charles had come to London for a concert. As he and Judy drove down Hamilton Terrace on their way to the Royal Festival Hall he realized that he had forgotten the braces he wears with tails. Philip Jones, of the Philip Jones Brass Ensemble, who was to play at the concert in the Janáček *Sinfonietta*, lives at number 14 so they stopped there to borrow a pair.

The next day, when Charles had gone back to Hamburg, Judy returned the braces and learnt from the Joneses that number 10 Hamilton Terrace was about to come up for sale. After the generous Georgian proportions of Essex House the building seemed rather high and narrow but it was very graceful, with long sash windows and a delicate staircase. At the back, French windows opened upon a terrace with steps leading down to the garden. There were shrubs, a willow tree, urns and flagged areas for tables and chairs and at the far end of the lawn a garage and studio. It was peaceful yet close to the West End, the EMI studios in Abbey Road and far more convenient than Southgate.

When Charles saw number 10 on his next trip to London he was so charmed by the then quiet street with its trees and elegant Regency houses, said to have been built for royal mistresses, that he announced at once that they must live there.

They moved in with their Georgian and Regency furniture, their books, discs, tapes, stereos and cassette players, pianos and antique musical instruments. There was room for the 1778 Kirckman harpsichord, the eighteenth-century barrel organ encased in an elegant escritoire, the krumhorns, kortholts, cornetto and gems horns, oboes and clarinets but not for the spinet and 1800 square piano which were lent to friends, nor for Charles's immense bundles of orchestral parts which were kept in the garden studio with his monumental albums of press-cuttings.

On 24 September 1969 Judy, with the help of Jiřinka Kadainková and Jana Skuhravá, coped with the move while Charles was in Liverpool with the Sadler's Wells company rehearsing *The Rake's Progress* by day and conducting *The Magic Flute* at night. Two days later he returned to London, sorted some of his belongings, conducted a BBC Gala Performance, flew to Hamburg for three operas and on Sunday, 5 October arrived in San Francisco to start rehearsing at the Opera there. While he waited for Judy to join him he set up house in an apartment with what she calls his Mackerras Fallout — a collection of patent pencils, pens, watches, hair-combs, tapes, earphones, little packets of instant coffee and artificial sweetener, tiny notebooks and small cakes of soap — and made bachelor shopping lists in his diary among his rehearsal dates: paper plates, bottle-opener, laundry, kettle.

The season opened in October with a very good production of *The Magic Flute*. The English cast included Margaret Price, Geraint Evans, Stuart Burrows and David Ward. *La Cenerentola*, which followed on 5 November, with Teresa Berganza, was a great success. It was the beginning of a connection with San Francisco Opera that Charles has continued to enjoy.

When he learnt that Giorgio Tozzi, the Italo-American bass at the opera, was an amateur hypnotist who had successfully hypnotized his wife during childbirth he asked if Tozzi could help him break the smoking habit revived by working in Hamburg. Though their first sessions were not successful and Charles had a brief relapse he soon found that he no longer wanted to smoke and has not done so since.

★

On 1 January 1970, Charles moved into his office at the Coliseum and started work as musical director. That night he conducted a festive inaugural performance of *The Magic Flute* but there was really little cause for festivity. Stephen Arlen's brave move to the West End had created serious problems. Sadler's Wells had been operating as two companies for some years, one going on tour and one working in London but the London company, with an orchestra of 45 and a chorus of 30, was now hopelessly inadequate in the huge new opera house and singers who had been chosen for the old, far smaller theatre, where their voices were perfect, were now quite unsuitable. The regular Sadler's Wells audiences had not yet adapted to the move (they did not come to the West End), and new patrons had not yet appeared. Arlen was at his wits' end to know how to keep afloat.

At Hamburg Charles had had no need to worry about finance but now it became a constant preoccupation. Arlen had hoped that the move to a bigger theatre would bring bigger audiences but this had not happened and most of the time the house was nearly empty. Performances were sometimes given to very small audiences indeed; the public simply did not come. Various inducements were tried: theatre-party concessions, tickets that included dinner; a Friends of the Coliseum was formed, opera-pantomimes were put on by the company, even musicals such as *Kiss Me Kate*. They were not successful — opera singers are not suited to musicals, their whole approach is different. Malcolm Williamson's pantomime, *Lucky Peter's Journey*, played to a handful of people. A new production of Berlioz' *The Damnation of Faust* with unusual effects by Michael Geliot was a commercial failure. The situation was serious and ways of economizing had to be found.

One way was to cut rehearsals. Hamburg might have had too few but Sadler's Wells had always had too many. Since, by contract, the chorus and orchestra could only work a certain number of hours it was a matter of determining how many should be used for performances, which brought in revenue, and how many for rehearsals, which did not. It was also decided that new works, which needed more preparation, should take priority in rehearsals over familiar revivals, and that the two companies should be amalgamated. (The fact that Arlen had replaced the two former conductors with an overall musical director suggests that he already had this in mind). The whole company was now to remain in London, then would go on tour between seasons. It would split into two unequal parts, the larger with a repertoire suitable for big theatres in cities like Manchester and Liverpool, the smaller to play chamber operas needing fewer chorus and orchestra in towns with appropriate theatres. At the old Sadler's Wells there had been performances all the year round but henceforth the Coliseum was to be let for musicals and Christmas pantomimes while the company went on tour.

When Charles accepted Arlen's offer he had looked forward to putting his operatic ideas into practice and presenting fresh and unusual works, but it was clear that the public was not going to flock to new unpopular operas, no matter how artistic or beautifully performed. What people wanted was something they knew, old favourites with familiar tunes they could 'go away whistling'. To attract and build up an audience the Coliseum announced a whole run of really popular operas in grand new productions — *Carmen*, *The Barber*, *Bohème*, *Fledermaus*, Gilbert and Sullivan — which could be done with a minimum of rehearsal.

The public responded and audiences began to improve. Gradually, as business increased, less well-known works could be added to the repertoire from time to time: for Beethoven's bicentenary in 1970 his only opera was produced in both versions, *Leonore* in March, and *Fidelio* in November; and in October Handel's *Semele* was performed in an edition which Charles had prepared.

The original libretto of this work, by Congreve, was written for an earlier composer but Handel adapted it for a secular oratorio which may also be sung as an opera. For this new Coliseum production Charles engaged a distinguished soprano (Elizabeth Harwood) for the title role and, as designer and producer, Filippo Sanjust, an aristocratic Italian with whom he had worked very happily in Hamburg on Mozart operas.

Semele was a beautiful production and should have been a great success but it seemed to be dogged by bad luck. Sanjust was upset by the constant industrial troubles at the theatre and the first night was a disaster. Elizabeth Harwood, having completed all the rehearsals, collapsed at the end of the first act. She was in great pain but managed to sing her aria — 'Endless pleasure, Endless love, Semele enjoys above!' — before she fainted. The curtain came down and there was a very long interval while the star, still in full eighteenth-century costume with immense wig and a beauty spot, was wheeled out of the stage door on a stretcher and into the Charing Cross Hospital next door. Urgent telephone calls were made to the understudy. The curtain went up for a scene with Juno and came down for another long interval, giving time for Lois McDonall to rush in from Hendon, dress and take over. Elizabeth Harwood did not return to the cast; she was ill for weeks and by the time she recovered Lois McDonall was established in the role.

A week after the opening night Charles flew to Chicago at very short notice. He had been asked to conduct a replacement concert (Sir John Barbirolli had just died suddenly) and though he knew it meant missing performances of *Semele* he saw no reason to refuse. The opera had been well rehearsed, there was an assistant conductor who could take over and in Europe he had been used to people filling in in this way. It was a bad mistake. What was acceptable common practice in Europe was not good enough for London; audiences were annoyed and Charles was severely criticized.

He was also in trouble with his managing director; they were not getting on at all well. Stephen Arlen was a superb man of the theatre, brilliant, adventurous, almost inspired at times, with great experience, vision and courage. He was tireless in surmounting incredible obstacles and finding financial solutions but his field was straight drama, he did not like opera, a fact he never concealed. Judy remembers sitting on his knee at a party while he said loudly, with drunken persistence, 'I hate opera and I hate Charlie!' During Norman Tucker's time at Sadler's Wells this antipathy had been controlled but with Tucker gone, Arlen, who had been instrumental in removing him, was in sole charge of artistic as well as financial affairs. His prejudice against opera made it difficult to work with him in an opera house. Singers sensed he was out of sympathy with them, they tended to dislike him, feeling he did not value or appreciate their efforts, and Charles clashed with him constantly. Arlen preferred to engage straight drama producers who did not always understand operatic requirements and Charles, who was concerned about the singers, was not backward in saying what he thought. He sometimes wondered why Stephen had been so anxious for him to join the Coliseum since their ideas were so completely opposed. It seemed that the very qualifications that had recommended him for the job, his wide knowledge and feeling for opera, his international experience, were the cause of many of their disagreements.

Sadler's Wells had always been a people's theatre: it was a company without stars, singers did not even take individual curtain calls at the end of an act, and operas had always been sung in English. Charles was ambitious for change: he was still rather star-struck from Hamburg and wanted to build up stars within the company and hire big names from outside; he wanted operas to be sung in their original languages, was in favour of adapting the German repertory system and talked of giving Covent Garden a run for its money; in fact his outlook and experience were more suited to Covent Garden than to Sadler's Wells and Arlen thought his ideas élitist.

Each was aware of the other's good qualities but they were temperamentally unsuited to working together; hostility was so great that it almost became 'him or me'. Charles complained to the Board but the members made it clear that while they could see his point, if it came to a showdown they would support Arlen because of the tremendous work he had done for the company.

By 1971 Charles was already thinking of resigning but in January 1972 Arlen, who had never been known to be ill, went into hospital. He was found to have cancer and died in a very short time. His death was a tremendous shock for the company and for the theatre world. A memorial concert was held at which artists, including Charles, performed and Laurence Olivier, in his eulogy, spoke of 'the realm where grief will soon be swallowed in gratitude'. For Charles there was remorse. He knew he had behaved churlishly to Arlen and was ashamed of having made efforts to have him removed.

Arlen's death came only a few weeks after another great loss to the company and to the operatic stage. On 8 December 1971, Marie Collier fell to her death from a window. She had been unsurpassed in passionate tragic roles — a great Tosca, a great Katya, a great Katerina Ismailova, a magnificent Emilia Marty. This last had been her most extraordinary performance of all. Charles, who had worked with her since her arrival from Australia, still considers her one of the most superb singing actresses he has ever known.

The one man in England whom Charles felt would be ideal as the new managing director for the Coliseum was George Lascelles, Earl of Harewood. He had been an opera enthusiast all his life, starting very young with gramophone records, and had acquired a vast experience and knowledge of artists and performances. (He claims much of this resulted from reading Grove as a prisoner of war.) He had been a founder and co-editor of *Opera*, had revised and edited Kobbé's *Complete Opera Book*, had been on the staff of Covent Garden for seven years as assistant to Sir David Webster, the General Administrator, and as Controller of Programme Planning. He had been Artistic Director of the Edinburgh Festival for five years, was Artistic Director of Leeds Festival, Artistic Adviser to the New Philharmonia and a member of the Royal Opera House Board.

Charles had known Lady Harewood since their student days at Sydney Conservatorium but his first real awareness of Lord Harewood had been in 1951, when the latter wrote his enthusiastic and appreciative review of *Katya Kabanova* in the *Daily Mail*. They had met occasionally while Charles was working with the English Opera

Group and again in 1962 when Harewood engaged him for the Edinburgh Festival, and when Charles had conducted orchestral concerts with the New Philharmonia.

After the Mackerrases moved to St John's Wood they saw more of the Harewoods who lived near, at one time in, Hamilton Terrace. Later, when Charles conducted Handel's *Israel in Egypt* and *Saul* for the Leeds Festival he and Judy stayed at Harewood House; the Harewoods spent holidays on Elba.

It was not only that Lord Harewood's great knowledge and love for opera would benefit the Coliseum, he and Charles shared so many operatic tastes and ideas that they would make good working partners. The suggestion was put to Harewood and he agreed to apply when the job was advertised. His application, of one line, was conspicuous among those listing qualifications and curricula vitae, but he was the best and most suitable man for the position. He was appointed and almost simultaneously resigned from the Board of the Royal Opera House. He had always been so much part of the international world of original-language opera that Charles sometimes wondered if the move to the Coliseum had not been rather a culture shock, if Harewood had quite realized how important finance was there, and how much of his time and attention it would take. The R.O.H. was also dependent on the Arts Council, but its grants had always been far bigger than those for Sadler's Wells. The former member of Covent Garden staff was now in charge of a slightly down-market opera house where for the first time he had a taste of watching the budget very carefully.

Though he was officially managing director he had much to contribute artistically and he and Charles worked out programmes together, subject to the Board's approval. Harewood did not seem disconcerted by financial problems. He not only knew a great deal about opera and singers, he was good at finding and handling rich benefactors to sponsor productions, enabling the company to engage stars it could not have otherwise afforded. Both he and Charles were determined to raise the standards while maintaining old traditions. Like Arlen, Harewood's idea was to continue performances in English, to keep the Coliseum a theatre for the people where they could learn to regard opera as a part of life, and audiences could come straight from their jobs in jeans or working clothes. Charles, who by now had modified his original ideas, agreed that there was room in London for two good opera houses and that the public should be able to choose whether they wanted to hear an opera in its original language or their own.

Before very long performances at the Coliseum had improved so noticeably that, though the company still bore the rather plebeian stigma of singing opera in English (the only language believed to be understood by the masses), for the first time in its history it seemed that it might become a serious rival to Covent Garden. Singers with bigger voices had been engaged and bigger operas were being produced.

Between 1970 and 1973 there were successful performances of Wagner operas including *Lohengrin*, *The Mastersingers*, *The Valkyrie* and *The Twilight of the Gods*. In 1973 the first complete *Ring* cycle was produced and in 1976 it was repeated seven times — three times in London and once each in Leeds, Birmingham, Manchester and Glasgow. Although the 1973 cycle had become associated with Reginald Goodall's name, Charles later conducted a number of performances at the Coliseum and on tour. (His love for Wagner, which dated from childhood, had not prevented him from appreciating Anna Russell's interpretation of *The Ring*. After conducting her performance with the London Philharmonic Orchestra, in the Royal Festival Hall, he told the press, 'I don't think I've ever enjoyed myself so much.') The cycles, produced by Glen Byam Shaw and John Blatchley, were an outstanding success. The casts included Rita Hunter, Margaret Curphey, Alberto Remedios, Jon Weaving, Norman Bailey and Raimund Herincx, and the critics hailed the venture as a tremendous achievement for the company.

For Charles, the six years he and Harewood worked together at the Coliseum were exciting and happy. Both were devoted to opera and prepared to give and take; they agreed about engaging guest stars and presenting new works. Charles sympathized with his managing director's frustration when the marketing department, to whom contemporary works meant financial disaster, insisted on playing safe with old favourites. Impatient himself, he was greatly impressed by Harewood's reasonable attitude, even when disappointed, and his philosophical and realistic acceptance that popular revivals helped to pay for new uncommercial productions.

To the staff the new managing director was a very approachable man who was always ready to give them a hearing but at first he met a few rebuffs. The secretary of NATTKE* was also named Lascelles, but pronounced with the accent on the second syllable. At their first meeting when Lord Harewood said politely, 'I think Mr Las*celles* that we have a name in common,' the secretary replied shortly, 'That's all we do have in common.'

*National Association of Theatrical Television and Kine Employees.

One of Harewood's very early suggestions had been to change the name of the company to something appropriate and easier to remember. *Sadler's Wells at the Coliseum* was far too cumbersome and *Sadler's Wells* alone was misleading, people sometimes went to Islington by mistake. It was not easy to find a suitable replacement and the final choice, *English National Opera*, ran into difficulties. The company was government sponsored, which meant the name needed official approval and there were objections to the use of the word *National*. It was some time before it was settled and the company could give its first performance under its new name — a revival of *Traviata* with Valerie Masterson as Violetta, on 3 August 1974.

Gradually Charles and Harewood realized more of their ambitions — the production of new and interesting works, the development and emergence of distinguished singers from the old team system, the introduction of guest artists. Programmes during 1972–3 included Prokofieff's *War and Peace*, Bartók's *Bluebeard's Castle*, Stravinsky's *Oedipus Rex*, Janáček's *Katya Kabanova*, as well as *Rhinegold, Siegfried, The Seraglio, Così fan tutte, Lohengrin, Figaro* and favourites like *Carmen* and *Il trovatore*. Some were new productions, some were revivals.

Life at the Coliseum was also made easier for Charles by other members of the staff. There was his orchestral manager, Charles Coverman who had been with Sadler's Wells for a number of years and upon whom he was able to place complete reliance; there was also his assistant musical director, David Lloyd-Jones (now musical director of Opera North), with whom he had worked in television opera; and Noel Davies, staff conductor at the ENO, who shared Charles's interest and views on eighteenth-century performance practice. Together they worked on editing two Handel operas and became close and greatly valued friends.

The most important event of the 1970s was the beginning of Dame Janet Baker's association with the Coliseum. She had worked with Charles on the Lam-Mackerras *Messiah* and his whole-hearted admiration for her had increased with time. He believed she would be brilliant in certain operatic roles and had been hoping for an opportunity to make the suggestion. Though her repertoire included works in French, Italian and German he knew that unlike many famous stars she was quite unsnobbish and unprejudiced about opera in English. He approached her and found she was willing to sing at the Coliseum; a sponsor was found to guarantee her fees and in the 1971–2 season she appeared as Marguerite in a revival of *The Damnation of Faust*, the Geliot production that had failed earlier. It was not a big part but she enjoyed it and the following year agreed to sing in Donizetti's *Maria Stuarda*.

It was not definitely known if this opera had ever been sung in English before: it is so extremely Italian in character that there were fears that it might fail in translation, but Charles was determined. He was convinced that Janet Baker was perfect for the part of Mary, Queen of Scots, because of her particular personality and the sincerity that is one of her chief features. Not only is she a very great singer and actress but she radiates a rare quality of dedication.

His confidence was more than justified; the opera was transformed by the star's performance. The production by John Copley was sensitive and imaginative and the first night, 13 December 1973, was an enormous success. William Mann wrote in *The Times*, 'The final scene is almost a solo recital. . . . Miss Baker held attention throughout by sheer musicianship, command over words and intonation, rhythm and phrasing . . . it is a lovely impersonation in a genre of music that she will adorn, I hope, again and again.'

Martin Cooper, in the *Daily Telegraph*, said that Janet Baker invested Mary's last message to her rival with a 'superbly personal individual eloquence which stood out sharply against the more conventional music', and Philip Hope-Wallace of the *Guardian* wrote, 'Miss Baker did everything with such artistry and in the later and deeply affecting scenes, before going to the block, so touchingly that the house was gripped. . . . It was a most beautiful performance.'

It was also an historic occasion, the first of a series of wonderful collaborations between Dame Janet and Charles.

The Harewoods liked staying on Elba. They enjoyed the swimming, sunbathing and sailing, the long walks and expeditions round the island. With Charles and Judy they explored the little hill-towns and climbed up Monte Giove to the church of the Madonna del Monte and the abandoned hermitage where Napoleon had received Marie Waleska. Elba was still largely unspoilt and free of tourists, apart from the camper-vans of Germans and Scandinavians.

Life at the villa was relaxed. Everyone was on holiday and chores were shared. The ENO's managing director swept the terrace conscientiously and put out the ice for the pre-lunch drinks. Living was kept as simple as possible and equipment to a minimum. When Harewood looked round the lunch table and asked, 'Where's my cheese knife?' Judy took the knife he had just used, wiped it on a paper napkin and handed it back.

'There's your cheese knife, George.'

'Just like prisoner-of-war camp,' he rumbled.

During the afternoon they all separated, the maestro to study his scores and Harewood, with Charles's little old portable, to work on Kobbé, which he was revising and editing.

He and Charles talked constantly about opera, in amicable agreement but for one famous exception. They had planned a new production of Verdi's *Don Carlos* for the 1974 season, with Margaret Curphey, Katherine Pring and Gwynne Howell, but at almost the last moment the tenor singing the title role dropped out, causing great confusion. There were disagreements about who should take over; Harewood felt it should be a member of the company but Charles was afraid that the singer suggested was not up to the role. Discussions started in London and continued on Elba while the Harewoods were at the villa, and since neither side would give way arguments became quite acrimonious, almost to the point of spoiling the holiday atmosphere. It was a relief when news came from Brian McMaster, then assistant director at the Coliseum (soon to be general administrator of the Welsh National Opera), of a South African, Joseph Gabriels, living in Milan, who could be suitable for the part. He was coloured and thus might not be affected by Equity's ban on South Africans.

Charles rang Gabriels and invited him to Elba for an audition. The local cinema at Portoferraio was hired and when the tenor arrived with his wife he sang well and made a favourable impression. He was available and pleased to accept the offer.

Charles and Harewood were unaware that Gabriels was no actor and by the time they found out it was too late. His performance was so poor and reviews so cool that he had to be withdrawn. He was replaced by the tenor Harewood had originally suggested, but meanwhile *Private Eye* had heard of the incident and was demanding to know what Charles and Lord Harewood were doing — if they were out to destroy ENO and why they were engaging singers they had picked up and auditioned on the beach at Elba when there were excellent tenors in the company.

Charles was at the Edinburgh Festival conducting the Sydney Symphony Orchestra when he heard of the article. He was unhappy about the dubious publicity but his friends were more amused than concerned and there were facetious congratulations on having achieved *Private Eye*. 'Charlie,' said Barry Tuckwell. 'You've made it!'

For some years industrial trouble had been simmering at the Coliseum and in 1974 it came to a climax with a prolonged strike. The details of the affair are so complex, and involve so many conflicting viewpoints, that they cannot be discussed here. It need only be said that on 30 October

1974 the curtain came down during a performance of *The Bassarids*, by Hans Werner Henze, which the composer was conducting, and the theatre remained closed for five weeks. After official enquiries into the dispute the ENO eventually re-opened with a performance of *The Mastersingers* on New Year's Eve, 1974.

During the troubles, while Charles was making himself unpopular by expressing his views in no uncertain terms and giving provocative statements to the press, Harewood was being criticized for indecisive action. His patience, his mild and sympathetic attitude to the strikers had astonished Charles who regards anything that deliberately injures music as the sin against the Holy Ghost. He was staggered when, having decided to move on, the Coliseum chief trouble-maker asked the managing director for a reference and was given one.

The loss and disruption caused by the strike resulted in one great artistic benefit. The ENO's first production of *Rosenkavalier* had been planned for January 1975 and, because the opera was new to most of the orchestra, Charles had scheduled a large number of rehearsals. Owing to the strike musicians and cast had plenty of time to learn the work. For five weeks Charles could concentrate on the orchestra, holding rehearsals for violins alone, for cellos alone, woodwinds alone, brasses alone. No opera at the ENO had ever been so well prepared and the performance was given a 'rapturous welcome'. One paper claimed that standards had never been higher; another said that the orchestral playing under Charles was 'absolutely glorious'; and Desmond Shawe-Taylor in the *Sunday Times* called it 'an outstanding achievement. Nothing dragged; nothing was rushed. The sweetest pages were given their full due, but not over-caressed, the grand climaxes lacked nothing in power but allowed the singers a fair chance to project tone and words. . . .'

Everything and everyone was praised, John Copley, the producer; the designer, David Walker; the cast — Anne Evans (the Marschallin), Josephine Barstow (Octavian), Valerie Masterson (Sophie) and, as Baron Ochs, Neil Warren-Smith, brought from Sydney for the role at Charles's instigation. Having worked with this singer in Australia at the Elizabethan Opera, Charles had been so impressed by his voice and talent for comedy that he had invited him to London and battled with immigration and labour laws for a permit to allow him to sing in *Rosenkavalier*. The role of the Baron is very difficult, demanding a subtle mixture of nobility and vulgarity for though Ochs is low-minded he is also high-born. Charles was astonished by Warren-Smith's interpretation. He could not imagine where a young former butcher who had never before been outside Australia could have learnt

the refinements of eighteenth-century Viennese manners and manner-
isms. He did not know that, long before the invitation to London,
Warren-Smith's old singing teacher and his wife, both from Vienna,
had decided the young bass-baritone would make an ideal Baron Ochs
and had been coaching and grooming him for the part for years,
hoping his chance would come.

Despite their financial difficulties and industrial troubles, in the next
few years the ENO produced a number of new works, as well as
revivals and fresh productions of old ones. There was more Wagner,
more Janáček, more Mozart, more Verdi as well as Britten, Puccini,
Rossini, Bizet, Massenet, Strauss, Mussorgsky, Smetana, Offenbach,
Donizetti, Bartók, Handel and Sullivan.

In September 1972 the company had taken Britten's *Gloriana* to
Munich during the Olympic Games. The German reviews were half-
hearted. Performances were good but the work seemed dated. When
it was first produced in 1953 for the coronation of Queen Elizabeth II it
had been bitterly criticized and a failure with the first night audience,
and though it had had a better reception in later revivals at Sadler's
Wells and on tour, it was not considered suitable for performance
abroad. Yet it did very well when the ENO presented it at the
Volksoper for the Vienna Festival of 1975.

Even more successful was John Cox's production of *Patience* at the
Theater an der Wien during the same tour. Charles had suggested
changing Wilde's aesthetes to hippies and flower-people and though
these were now slightly dated the audience appreciated the satire. Far
more Viennese are familiar with English humour than audiences in
England are with Viennese.

When Charles was appointed Chief Guest Conductor of the BBC
Symphony Orchestra in 1976, he was charmed and touched by a letter
from one of the first musicians to befriend him in England. Sir Adrian
Boult was now a very old man but still generous to younger artists.

For years Charles had been anxious to conduct Smetana's *Dalibor*,
which he and Judy had first seen so long ago in Brno while they were
hitch-hiking through Slovakia. It had been hard to find a tenor who
could sing the title role, which is extremely difficult, very high, heroic
and exhausting, but by 1976 the Coliseum was able to stage the opera
with John Mitchinson as a very good Dalibor. It was a successful
production and even did well at the box-office; but the highlight of
these years, and one of the ENO's greatest and most memorable
triumphs, was the new production in March 1977 of Massenet's
Werther, with Janet Baker. Though Charles has never been able to

decide which of her performances was the finest he feels that in *Werther* she reached really extraordinary heights. The way that she, a mature woman, presented herself and entered into the character of an innocent young girl with tremendous desires was astonishing and profoundly moving.

All ENO performances were not on this level. The previous year there had been a most harassing revival of Mozart's *Idomeneo*. Anne Evans, who was playing Ilia, had been taken ill and neither of the understudies was available. The opera was to be broadcast and it was essential to find a good singer, but none was free. Telephone calls were made to Lucia Popp, the Czech soprano, who was recording in Cologne and she agreed to come to the rescue. She knew the part of Ilia but only in a different version and only in Italian. This meant that in the famous Act III quartet Rita Hunter would have to sing with the music; however, as she was very large and dressed in voluminous black, by standing at the back of the group she managed to look down at her score discreetly without being noticed. The theatre audience and those listening to the broadcast may have been puzzled that Ilia's part was sung in Italian while the rest of the cast were singing in English.

Far worse had been a performance of *Figaro* at Wolverhampton in the early 1970s, particularly since the audience included an MP who believed that government money should be spent on repatriating West Indians rather than subsidizing the arts. Due to a fault in the scenery, or the rake of the stage, when Geoffrey Chard, as the Count, came on to demand why his wife's door was locked he found it wide open and impossible to keep shut. Though it continued to gape he carried on with his lines, 'Why is this door locked? Why will it not open? . . .' etc., and though the key was not only visible but immovably stuck in the lock, 'Where is the key? I must get tools to force the lock!' To the producer's despair and the delight of the baffled audience, the door swung open again as he stormed off.

While Charles was caught up with the Coliseum and engagements abroad his family were busy with their own lives. Young Catherine had spent a year at Lyons University as part of her four year honours course and after graduating was up in Shropshire forming the Telford Community Arts with her former drama tutor, Graham Woodruff. Fiona, who had qualified for her Certificate of Education in 1971 and B.Ed. the following year had been teaching in Germany, first in Würzburg, then in Hamburg. She was now taking a further diploma in English for Overseas Students at Manchester University, while Judy, as well as her overtime job of wife-housekeeper-secretary-chauffeuse-accountant-confidante-critic-adviser-encourager had up book-binding and was binding Charles's scores. She had also taken a holiday. In 1973 she and Inge Henderson set out for Nepal and a long trek in the Himalayas with their stores and their sherpas. She was not worried about leaving Charles, who was working in London; she felt he was in good hands. The girl she had hired to come in each day to look after him had a bag with JESUS LIVES on it.

As his fiftieth birthday approached in 1975 she began to plan a surprise. She had found a copy of *Marsyas*, the cantata Charles wrote at the age of thirteen, with libretto by his mother, and had decided to present the work at a party at Australia House. It was all kept secret from Charles. She was helped by Geoffrey Chard and Noel Davies, who was to conduct and also play the harpsichord. The cast was to be Janet Baker as First Muse, Felicity Palmer as Other Muse, Pauline Stevens (Chloe), Alexander Young (Marsyas) and Geoffrey Chard (Apollo). Fritz Spiegl was to give a talk on eighteenth-century ornamentation, John Amis was to be compère, George Harewood toastmaster, and other friends were to play in the orchestra, including Lady Harewood, who had seen the original *Marsyas*. The performance was to be announced as the première of a work not yet known in Britain, but when most of the preparations had been made Charles found out what was happening. He was upset and asked Judy to call it off; he did not want *Marsyas* revived, he said it would be too embarrassing. It was a great disappointment but he was adamant and in the end Judy and Lord Harewood hired the Colosseo Restaurant in May's Court, near the theatre, and gave a party there. The patron co-operated by painting on the window COMPLIMENTI MAESTRO and providing an excellent supper. The party was held after a performance of *The Makropulos Case* and all the cast and management came and as many friends as could fit in. There was only room for about sixty so a second party was held at Hamilton Terrace.

There was another ghost from the past several years later when Charles and Judy were on a musical cruise in the Caribbean. Other artists were Lili Kraus, James Galway, Moura Lympany, Henryk Szeryng. Charles conducted and Judy played the clarinet when needed. (On board also was Benny Goodman with his clarinet but 'nobody asked him to play' and he left the ship feeling rather hurt.) After a concert in Miami Charles was visited by the widow of his cousin, John Creagh, who had sung Apollo in the first performance of *Marsyas* and who had died as a result of POW experiences. She gave Charles a recording made in the 1940s of himself playing oboe obbligato while John sang *Jesu, Joy of Man's Desiring*.

XVII

Lightning Conductor

THE NIGHT AFTER his inaugural performance at the Coliseum in 1970, Charles conducted *Coq d'Or* at Covent Garden; the next day he flew to Hamburg for *Il Matrimonio segreto*, then to Cincinnati for concerts. Such ceaseless activity was to be the pattern of his life for the next seven years.

When he joined the Coliseum he had chosen to accept a much lower salary than he could have demanded; in this way he felt freer, less guilty about taking outside engagements. After Lord Harewood became managing director he had tried to persuade Charles to spend less time away from the company, had offered a higher salary, even sought Judy's help but Charles, who now feels that Harewood was right, continued to conduct as much abroad as in England, moving about at such a rate that one London newspaper named him the Lightning Conductor.*

He was like a car that has become jammed in top gear or someone whose system is flooded with adrenalin. He was known to love his work but people asked, Why go at it so hard when he did not need the money? It was not greed; he was notorious for taking obscure, inconvenient jobs because the work interested him. What was he trying to prove? He already had recognition in most parts of the world; if it were only a huge ego-trip he would certainly not be so ready to fill in or take over for others who had had first refusal.

Workaholic is a glib and convenient term about which everyone has a theory. Carlyle believed people were driven to work by guilt but Charles's guilt is more result than cause, a matter of knowing he should be getting on with the job if it is to be finished in time, aggravated by irritation at his own fatal habit of accepting too much at once. Others say workaholics lack commitment to life or hope to escape from the world, yet for Charles work and music are synonymous, and music, to which he is committed, *is* life; and why should he

*A quotation, no doubt from Norman Tucker's translation of the Storm Scene in *Katya*.

want to escape from a world that has always treated him well? He himself often says the compulsion to overwork dates from the material insecurity of his freelance days but others who know him well have sometimes wondered if unconsciously he is not moved by a quite different insecurity, despite years of achievement: the always unattainable goal that recedes as one moves.

For several years he worked as both musical director at the Coliseum and as guest conductor at the Royal Opera House. It was a delicate situation: although the two companies always tried to avoid duplication they were often rivals for repertoire. Charles sometimes wondered if it was quite seemly for him to conduct in both houses during the same season — the fact that he could and did says something for British tolerance as well as for the open-mindedness of Georg Solti, Covent Garden's musical director. Solti's generosity to the younger man was not confined to the ROH but also led to engagements at the Paris Opera and with the Chicago Symphony Orchestra. Charles, well aware of the beneficial influence Solti has had on his career, has always been grateful to his distinguished colleague.

He had started to work at the ROH in the early 1960s when Joan Ingpen, a former agent, was the casting and programme director and planner. She knew Charles's work, his special interest in Slav music and when an English version of *Katerina Ismailova* was being planned for 1964 she had recommended him to Solti.

After the success of *Katerina*, Solti invited Charles back in January 1966 for *Turandot*, with the Finnish soprano, Anita Välkki and Charles Craig, and again in May the same year, not long before he moved to Hamburg, for a revival with Amy Shuard as Turandot and Franco Corelli as Calaf.

This was the first time Charles had conducted an opera with such a large orchestra and his first experience, apart from television productions, of working with really famous stars. Corelli, who was then one of the most highly-paid singers in the world, is a sensitive artist but was spoilt and extremely temperamental. He tended to behave in a childish manner, he could not read music and he made little attempt to act. (When the slave girl Liù, who had been tortured for his sake, fell dead at his feet in Act III he simply walked off and left her.) His over-protective wife constantly interfered, giving orders to conductor and producer. Charles, who felt himself on trial, had made a point of being very careful with the orchestra but Corelli insisted it was too loud and told his wife to see that it was kept down. By the end of Act I he had worked himself into such a state that when the moment came for Calaf to give the signal that he would answer Turandot's three riddles he struck the painted gong on the backcloth so savagely that the fabric tore open, revealing the stage carpentry and a shirt-sleeved percussionist beating a real gong behind the scenes.

Charles was again engaged for *Turandot* the following year, 1967, in January, with Birgit Nilsson and James McCracken and in February with Nilsson and James King. He developed immense respect and admiration for Nilsson, and for her musicianship; he found her easy to work with, although she stipulated in her contract that she would only rehearse for a certain number of days before a performance, in this case only one dress rehearsal. She also had a habit of being late and, when she did arrive, would not sing out: even in dress rehearsal she 'marked' (singing at half voice) which made it difficult for Charles to find a balance with the orchestra. It was not till the opening night that he heard her really sing for the first time and he still speaks of his excitement at hearing that warm, tremendous voice filling the theatre, accompanied by a huge orchestra and chorus.

By now he was living in Hamburg and flying across for rehearsals and performances in London. He had been engaged for several seasons of *Carmen*, with Josephine Veasey, Peter Glossop and, one year, Jon Vickers, a very famous Don José. The recitatives by Bizet's friend, Guiraud, were to be used, and Charles had restored parts of the opera that were usually cut. The atmosphere was not friendly: Vickers objected to the restored cuts which he felt made the performance too long and he also disliked Charles who was inclined to stand up to him. Charles, who admired Vickers as an artist, was irritated by his insistence on being the centre of attention. The years at Sadler's Wells, where singers had worked as a team and never expected special treatment, had made him impatient with stars who felt they should be privileged above ordinary mortals. The performance with Vickers was not a success; the critics agreed with the tenor about the length and complained that the restored cuts spun the opera out for nearly four hours. They thought the patched-up version nothing more than an interesting historical experiment, were lukewarm about Charles's conducting and made comments on the cast that varied from facetious to acid.

Charles and Vickers were to clash again at Covent Garden in 1977. In the meantime they had managed to work together peacefully in *Aida*, an opera they both knew well (they got on best when there was no need to rehearse); but in *Jenůfa* they nearly came to blows. Vickers was a week late for rehearsal and when he arrived did not know the role properly. He was the only one in the cast new to the opera (Wendy Fine, Gregory Dempsey, Patricia Johnson had all sung it before), and he needed a great deal of rehearsing and help, but he had no intention of being told how to sing his role by a conductor younger than himself whom he regarded as an upstart, even one reputed to be a Janáček specialist. Charles for his part did not mean to let Vickers tell him how to conduct Janáček and his blunt remarks infuriated the tenor who declared that he would never again sing in an opera conducted by Mackerras. It is said that the mere name is enough to enrage him; yet though he had never sung the role of Laca before, he gave one of the best interpretations that Charles has ever seen, a fact he freely admits.

Until Charles returned to London to live he continued to commute between Hamburg and Covent Garden. In March 1968 he came over for *Tosca*, with Geraint Evans as Scarpia, Franco Tagliavini as Cavaradossi and Sena Jurinac, a 'very Viennese-orientated Yugoslav', as the most distinguished Tosca he had ever conducted; and, during the summer, he took over several performances of *Così fan tutte*. It was the opera's first performance at Covent Garden; Solti conducted, with Pilar Lorengar as Fiordiligi, Josephine Veasey as Dorabella, Lucia Popp as Despina and Luigi Alva as Ferrando. John Copley was the producer and it was a mildly decorated performance with appoggiaturas which Charles and Maurits Sillem had prepared at Solti's request.

The strain of working in Hamburg and constantly flying about had built up in Charles a state of chronic tension and he and Judy had both become students of the Alexander Technique of relaxation through correct posture. Inge Henderson was their teacher; she worked with many singers and actors and one night while Charles was conducting *Così fan tutte* she came to the theatre to help him relax before the performance. They had just finished the lesson when Sir David Webster, Chief Administrator at Covent Garden, appeared in the doorway. Webster was a charming and cultivated man but so shy that even his own friends sometimes found it hard to communicate with him. Charles had never been quite at ease with him, he felt that his own direct manner was a further obstacle between them, yet on this night Webster had taken the trouble to climb several flights of stairs to speak to him, perhaps about something important. He had clearly not expected to find the maestro half undressed, with his fly undone, in the company of a woman; even worse, they had turned out the light because of the glare in Charles's eyes as he lay on the table.

Though he and Inge were embarrassed they could see the humour of the situation but Webster was not amused. Charles's sheepish explanation that Mrs Henderson was helping him to relax sounded horribly inept, even suggestive, and Webster departed in haste, without revealing why he had come. It seemed a trivial incident but Charles has never ceased to believe that it influenced his future at Covent Garden.

His later performances of *Così* were very happy. He was conducting it in his own right, with a cast that included Elisabeth Söderstrom, Yvonne Minton and Lucia Popp. It was his first experience with Söderstrom, who enchanted him with the beauty of her acting and ensemble singing.

During 1969 he flew to London for a revival of *Aida*, with Grace Bumbry, Martina Arroyo and Charles Craig and for Tito Gobbi's production of *Simone Boccanegra*, with Peter Glossop and Carlo Cossutta, with whom he had done performances of *Otello* in Hamburg; but by the following May (1970), when *Tosca* was revived, with Gobbi as Scarpia, Gabriella Tucci as Tosca and Ermanno Mauro as Cavaradossi, Charles was already living in London again and a member of the rival opera house. (*Coq d'Or* had overlapped from December 1969 to January 1970.)

Nevertheless, in January 1971 he was at Covent Garden for his fifth *Turandot* with Nilsson and James King and during the summer, after a tour of Australia, for Gluck's *Orfeo ed Euridice*. Solti had invited him to prepare an edition for Yvonne Minton, who was singing the title role with Elizabeth Vaughan as Euridice. The original opera is very short, lasting barely half an evening, but Gluck had added ballets to lengthen it for Paris audiences. In this version, the one most often heard, which contains some of his best-loved music (The Dance of the Blessed Spirits) the part of Orfeo was written for a high tenor but since the days of Pauline Viardot it has always been sung by a mezzo. Charles had also arranged to relieve Solti for six performances but after the fifth he began to feel very ill and, to his astonishment, was found to have malaria, probably contracted in Kenya on the way back from Sydney. He and Judy had broken their journey to spend a short holiday with Judy's cousin, Bill Hindley, and visit a game reserve. Charles missed the last performance and did not conduct the opera again until its revival the following May, with Shirley Verrett as a magnificent Orfeo — a triumphant occasion for both singer and conductor.

His last engagement that year at Covent Garden was *Billy Budd*, in December (1971).

When *Jenůfa* was revived in 1972, with two different casts, Amy Shuard, who had been Charles's first Katya at Sadler's Wells and one of his earliest Turandots at Covent Garden, sang the part of the Kostelnička each time. He enjoyed working with her again but neither he nor she were to know that when she sang on the night of 10 June he was conducting their last performance together at Covent Garden. Still young she died suddenly of a heart attack.

In March 1973 Charles conducted *Aida* with Leontyne Price. The cast included Ludovic Spiess, Gian-Piero Mastromei and the young Kiri te Kanawa.* The opera was repeated in April, with Carlo Bergonzi and the Mexican singer Gilda Cruz-Romo, then with Grace Bumbry, Charles Craig and Martina Arroyo. In May there was *Il trovatore*, with Martina Arroyo, Carlo Cossutta and Fiorenza Cossotto, the mezzo Charles had first encountered making her foreign debut at Wexford.

At this time a London musical magazine published a conversation between two opera-goers, both enthusing about *Trovatore* and Charles as a 'magnificent' Verdi conductor; but whereas one was praising the Covent Garden performance, with Fiorenza Cossotto as Azucena, the other had seen the opera in Paris. There, Charles had been asked to take over, at short notice, for Riccardo Muti at the Opéra, where Shirley Verrett was appearing with Carlo Cossutta, Piero Cappucilli and Oriana Santunione. Since he was also committed to *Trovatore* for the ENO, in Liverpool, he conducted it three times with three different casts and in three different places within a very short period.

His engagements at Covent Garden for 1974 were Britten's *A Midsummer Night's Dream*, *Otello* and *Tosca*; however, he was suddenly asked to take over John Copley's production of *Faust* — a somewhat nerve-racking experience: there was no rehearsal and the opera was being broadcast at its first performance. The cast included Kiri te Kanawa, Stuart Burrows and the great American bass, Norman Treigle, as Mephistopheles.

But the high point of that year at Covent Garden, and indeed in Charles's career as a Verdi conductor, was *Otello* in May, with Cossutta as Otello, Piero Cappucilli as Iago and Kiri te Kanawa as Desdemona. The performance has been described as one of the great events of the last thirty years in the history of the Royal Opera House. Reviewers raved about te Kanawa's voice and youthful beauty, Cossutta's richness and eloquence, Cappucilli's faultless intonation and flexibility, and under the headline, BLAZING VITALITY OF MACKER-

---

*She had come several times to audition for Sadler's Wells Company at the Coliseum while she was a student at the London Opera Centre. The management felt she showed very great promise but was not yet quite ready. While they were deciding to take her on as an apprentice singer she auditioned at Covent Garden and was engaged at once by Colin Davis.

RAS OTELLO Martin Cooper, the *Daily Telegraph* critic, wrote, 'Charles Mackerras's handling of the score combined the most refined sensibility in phrasing and dynamic nuance with a blazing vitality of sound at the emotional climaxes.' The *Sunday Telegraph* applauded the singers and concluded, 'But it was really Charles Mackerras's conducting, taut but never unyielding, that gave this performance the unmistakable stamp of greatness'; and Philip Hope-Wallace, in the *Guardian*, had 'no hesitation in calling [Charles] our best Verdian conductor'.

The list of Charles's foreign engagements during his years with the Coliseum becomes tedious, the concerts and operas in Berlin, Vienna, Prague, Brno, Paris, Florence and Rome, in Switzerland, Holland, Scandinavia, his dashes to the USA, even a couple of times to Australia.

After Rolf Liebermann had left Hamburg and joined the Paris Opera Charles was often engaged, through Joan Ingpen, to conduct there. There was *Tosca* in 1974, with Santunione and Cossutta, and Gabriel Bacquier as Scarpia, and in 1975 he took over *Don Giovanni* from Solti. He was later engaged for a performance of *Die Entführung aus dem Serail* but Karl Böhm heard of the project and made it known that he wished to do it. So great was Böhm's standing that Paris asked Charles if he would accept Strauss's *Elektra* and let Böhm have *Die Entführung*. Charles agreed, in fact he was pleased; he had conducted *Die Entführung* many times but never the Strauss opera, which he saw as a challenge. He greatly enjoyed the revival, in which Ursula Schröder-Feinen sang the title role, Astrid Varnay was Klytemnestra, Arlene Saunders was Chrysothemis and Hans Sotin sang Orestes.

He made his Paris début, as distinct from taking over or coming to the rescue, in 1976 in *Faust*. Musically it was a superb occasion, with a magnificent cast: Mirella Freni (Marguerite), Nicolai Gedda* (Faust), Nicolai Ghiaurov (Mephistopheles) and Tom Krause (Valentine) but for Charles the opera was visually destroyed by the work of Jorge Lavelli, the South American producer. Lavelli, who claimed, perhaps rightly, that Gounod's music was far more expressive of late nineteenth-century France than Goethe's medieval Germany, had changed the period, costumes and scenery. Characters were dressed as

---

*Nicolai Gedda, singer, actor and musician, could not only sing in almost any style in the tenor repertoire but was a brilliant linguist who spoke eight languages. The son of a Swedish mother and Russian father, in Paris he spoke Italian to Freni, English to Charles, Swedish to Tom Krause, Spanish to Lavelli, French to others in the company, as well as Russian, German and Czech when needed.

late nineteenth-century Parisians instead of medieval Germans and Mephistopheles wore a top hat, although in the text he quite distinctly describes himself as wearing a sword by his side and a feathered cap on his head. Charles felt that if a producer intends to disobey the libretto's specific directions he should also change the words, as Jean-Louis Barrault did at the Met, New York. For that Gounod-period production, at Pierre Monteux's insistence, *la plume au chapeau* became *le plus haut chapeau*.

Some of Lavelli's sets made the scenes quite ludicrous. Gounod, who saw *Faust* with the eyes of a romantic nineteenth-century Frenchman, wrote beautiful luscious music for the garden scene in which Faust and Marguerite declare their love, but Lavelli's lovers sang their melodious duet in a humble back-yard with Marguerite's neighbour hanging out the washing, to Charles's mind a drab setting that completely contradicted the music.

He protested that Lavelli had also made nonsense of the scene in which Mephisto interrupts the drunken songs of the students and soldiers, promising that he will produce for them a better wine. When Gounod's Mephisto struck at the tap, to everyone's astonishment wine gushed out but despite the devil's magical powers and despite the music describing wine pouring forth, Lavelli had decided that revellers and audience should only *think* they saw it. Other moments became quite pointless: when the devout Crusader soldiers should have held up their swords like crosses to frighten Mephisto (who cannot tolerate any Christian symbol), they held up nineteenth-century sabres which are not at all like crucifixes; nor did the triumphant music of the soldiers' chorus accord with the dejected and battered troops who limped in as though on their last legs.

The whole opera was produced in such a way as to make Charles wonder if Lavelli had actually understood what Gounod, and originally Goethe, was saying. He found it intensely irritating, as did the singers. Though they were obliged to obey the producer's directions they avoided giving their roles the particular reading he wanted and performed according to Gounod's original directions, as they had always done, though the whole staging contradicted their interpretation.

The Mozart operas which Charles conducted in Paris were less traumatic: *Figaro, Don Giovanni, Die Entführung*, the Ponelle production of *Così fan tutte*. In *Figaro* Mirella Freni or Lucia Popp sang Susanna, Margaret Price was usually the Countess, Tom Krause or Gabriel Bacquier sang the Count, José van Dam was Figaro and Frederika von Stade or Teresa Berganza played Cherubino. At that time Berganza was full of high spirits and one night brought Margaret Price very near to breaking up. For Cherubino's attempted love scene with the Countess she had the bright idea of putting two tangerine oranges and a banana inside her breeches. In *Die Entführung* Constanze was sung by Valerie Masterson, then starting to make an international career. In *Don Giovanni*, José van Dam or Geraint Evans sang Leporello, Stuart Burrows was Don Ottavio, Margaret Price or Edda Moser played Donna Anna, Kiri te Kanawa was Donna Elvira and Ruggiero Raimondi the Don. Edda Moser, te Kanawa and Raimondi sang the same roles in the Joseph Losey film of the opera.

During the summer, in France, various parts of Provence break out in festivals: at Orange, Avignon, Nîmes, Aix there are performances in theatres, halls or amphitheatres and in the smaller towns plays are put on in castle courtyards, paintings hung in the Mairie, ceramics displayed on trestles along the streets. People come from miles around, shops sell out, hotels and pensions are full and there is nowhere for the locals to park their cars. There is great competition and artists engaged by one festival must sign a contract agreeing not to appear at another, unless arranged by the town who hired them and certainly not at one close enough to be considered a rival. When Charles conducted *Messiah* in the *Théâtre Antique* at Orange in 1975 it was exclusive to that town.

Usually the weather is hot and still and the nights are beautiful, with lights on Roman walls and fountains playing, but there is always a chance of the Mistral. It rose while Charles was rehearsing the Philharmonia Chorus and the National Radio Orchestra at Orange and blew the music all over the arena, and when the pages were picked up they were so out of order the players and singers could not find their parts. The evening of the concert was perfect, but when a German company arrived for a one-night performance of *Die Walküre*, for which enormous preparations had been made, the Mistral raged the whole time, scattering the orchestral music and turning the performance into a disaster.

By doing a certain amount of commuting and manoeuvring of other engagements Charles managed to conduct at Aix-en-Provence for two consecutive festivals. In 1977 he was engaged for a series of concerts with the English Chamber Orchestra and performances of *Così fan tutte*. Because he was to be there on and off for nearly two months, Judy arranged through an agency to exchange houses with a French family. Number 10 Hamilton Terrace was spring-cleaned, she emptied cupboards and drawers and left Teresa, her splendid Catalan helper, to look after the visitors. At Aix she found a huge seventeenth-century château with high ceilings and enormous salons; it was beautifully cool and there was plenty of room for friends to come and stay, which they did in force, but everything was frightfully dirty and falling to pieces: mattresses were covered with sinister stains, rails fell down when clothes were hung on them, one night at dinner a chair collapsed under Alastair, but no one minded and they all enjoyed themselves. Meanwhile the French family were making themselves unpopular in Hamilton Terrace by playing pop music full blast on Charles's hi-fi at all hours.

Between rehearsals for the Festival Charles flew to London and other cities for concerts, operas and recordings. Several times he and the ECO were farmed out by Aix to other non-competitive Provençal towns round the district, and one weekend they were all off-loaded to Corsica.

They were to give one concert down in St Florent and another at the property of an extremely rich baron, a left-wing millionaire who had written a biography of Mahler and lived in a castle that had once been a monastery. The concert was to be held in his garden and the baron had provided a magnificent lunch, with lashings of pastis and superb wines. The singers and orchestra tucked in and before long were all in a state of euphoria; then rain began and was soon so heavy that the concert could not be held out of doors. It was decided to move it to the local church, which meant taking everything, chairs, instruments, music-stands down to the town. They were all just setting off when the audience, unaware of changed arrangements, began to arrive, roaring up in their cars. The two lots of traffic met, in pouring rain on a narrow road; it was a shambles, a chaos of people, vehicles, furniture, musical instruments.

The members of the orchestra, who were the first to reach the church, went into the town and continued to drink till the others arrived, then everyone squeezed into the building for the concert. There was so little room that the soloists were standing almost on the feet of the first row. They were late starting so the programme had to be cut, for the orchestra had to return by bus to St Florent, but Charles and Judy went back to the castle where they slept in the monks' refectory.

Così fan tutte at Aix turned out to be a constant source of trouble. Jean Mercure, the producer, had very definite theories, most of which Charles found hard to accept. To give the effect of the sea in Act I a gauze curtain with moving waves was hung over the pit. It hid the orchestra and cast from each other, deadened the music and made it almost impossible for the conductor to keep things together. Charles used every persuasion to have it removed but the producer was adamant and when Charles became too insistent threatened him with legal action.

There was a very good cast which included Valerie Masterson and Gabriel Bacquier, but Mercure had decided, from his experience of eighteenth-century French comedy, that in plots depending on disguise and mistaken identity, as in *Così*, it was always the women who were clever and the men who were made to look fools. He thought it inconceivable that the sisters, Fiordiligi and Dorabella, would not have recognized their lovers in disguise and insisted that the girls were not deceived when the two young men appeared dressed as Albanians.

This made absolute nonsense of the entire second act, since the whole development of the plot, as written by Da Ponte and Mozart, depends on both girls being duped. Though Dorabella falls easily and is soon ready to be unfaithful with her new suitor, Fiordiligi goes through much heart-searching and agonizing before she finally gives way. Mercure may have been correct in his theory that *Così* is unique in showing women outwitted by men but to change a story against libretto was quite ridiculous.

To Charles's astonishment, however, none of the reviewers seemed to realize what the producer was doing, that his intention was to change the meaning of da Ponte's libretto. Some liked the production and reviewed it favourably, others merely thought the girls were acting in a peculiar way. He could only assume that modern critics have become so immune to strange and outrageous productions that they are prepared to accept anything, even when the producer's concepts are so abstruse that the performers themselves do not understand them.

XVIII

The Seventies in America

A FEW MONTHS after the Aix Festival Charles was writing to Judy from Houston, Texas: 'I bought some lovely presents for the girls and you for Christmas. There is a Mexican shop just up the road . . . I also went to Nieman-Marcus where they have the most delightful things to buy. Apart from presents for you and some clothes for myself . . . I got an electric pencil-sharpener, like one I saw at Solti's place. What will they think of next!'

He had been flying to and from the USA since 1970. He had made his American début that year in the depth of winter, conducting the Cincinnati and Dallas Symphony orchestras and in May had gone to Chicago, at Solti's invitation, for an all Janáček programme with the Chicago Symphony. These first experiences with American orchestras had been a revelation. In Cincinnati it was the wonderful string players, many of them of Slavonic, Hungarian or Ukrainian Jewish blood, that impressed him so profoundly; in Chicago it was the general excellence of the orchestra. The Janáček programme had included the *Sinfonietta*, the suite from *The Cunning Little Vixen* and the *Glagolitic Mass*. The *Sinfonietta* is notoriously difficult, particularly the third movement, even for good European orchestras, but to Charles's amazement the Chicago Symphony had sight-read it all without hesitation. It was the same with the *Glagolitic Mass*. Some years later a famous Rome orchestra behaved so badly over this music, refusing to take it seriously and implying that Charles did not know what he was doing, that he decided never to conduct them again, but in Chicago he had had no problems at all.

The orchestra was the most disciplined he had ever encountered. He had expected it to be good, but could not have imagined such extraordinary precision and virtuosity, such efficiency and quick response, so unlike those in Europe where players are often inclined to lounge about and lack interest. All the players were superb, particularly the strings, and the collective intelligence was staggering.

Orchestras in America are supported by private sponsorship, government subsidies being almost non-existent. The sponsors or Board of Directors appoint a general manager who runs the orchestra, handles difficulties between Board and players and when necessary deals with the very powerful Musicians' Union which is always ready to fight on behalf of its members. Union rules for work periods are very strictly observed (2½ hours as against 3 hours in the UK and Australia). Players stop on the dot, but they also start on the dot and work hard with complete concentration. Charles found them co-operative and eager to do their best.

After his first experience in Chicago he had returned there later in October 1970 (when he missed performances of *Semele* and annoyed the Coliseum patrons). The programme had included the Shostakovich Ninth Symphony, the work he had conducted at the 1962 Edinburgh Festival and, as at Edinburgh, one of the critics complained about his interpretation of the slow movement, the very movement in which he had been coached by the composer himself.

Early in 1971, on his way to Australia, he again conducted the Cincinnati and Dallas orchestras. In October, returning from the Australian tour, he broke his journey in San Francisco for *Eugene Onegin* and *Un ballo in maschera* at the Opera. *Onegin* was sung in English, with an outstanding cast led by Evelyn Lear and Thomas Stewart, a husband and wife who had worked together in Germany for years. Charles wrote to Judy, who was in France visiting young Catherine at Lyons University: 'Paul Hager, the producer of *Onegin*, I find really marvellous. He is just ideal for this sort of piece. . . . Tom Stewart (Onegin) and Stuart Burrows (Lensky) are absolutely splendid. Evelyn Lear finds Tatiana a bit heavy for her, however it is all a huge success and I am already well into rehearsals of *Ballo*.'

The magnificent Martina Arroyo was singing Amelia in *Ballo*, Helen Donath was Oscar and Riccardo was played by Luciano Pavarotti, 'who although he has a gorgeous voice is TERRIBLY difficult to manage. He doesn't know the music very well and gets rather touchy if you correct him. . . . He seems to have no sense of rhythm at all and jumps beats and gets the music wrong continually. But the rest of the cast is VG, especially Martina Arroyo and it's a great experience conducting this marvellous piece. It is being done in the Boston version, with Red Indians at the beginning, playing homage to Riccardo, Earl of Warwick.'

As rehearsals went on Pavarotti became more difficult. He was singing the role for the first time (though he had already recorded it), he was young and perhaps insecure despite his quite recent tremendous success. He continued to ignore the producer's directions and refused to sing out at rehearsals so that it was impossible to hear him. He also made a fuss about the length of notes, wanting other singers to stop and let him sing alone. This led to words with Charles, who though ravished by the tenor's 'God-given' voice did not intend to allow anyone to mess about with Verdi's music.

The climax came in Act II, the scene in the witch's cave, when Pavarotti insisted that Charles stop the rest of the ensemble so that his last note became a prolonged solo. He kept referring to the quintet as *my aria* and when it was pointed out that others were also singing, said, Yes, but they were just accompanying him; they must stop and let his last high note be heard. 'But Verdi wrote the note to be two bars,' said Charles. 'Never mind, you must make them stop!' Charles refused. Pavarotti was furious. He declared, 'You obviously don't know the traditions!' 'I do know the traditions,' said Charles. 'But I don't intend to observe them. Traditions have gone far enough. It's Verdi's music we're dealing with.'

Though a San Francisco critic wrote that Pavarotti looked like a preposterously overstuffed Kewpie doll and his notions of acting were, to put it kindly, quaint ('But how he sings!'), Charles was able to tell Judy that *Ballo* 'had its first performance to cheering and clapping for Pavarotti, who I must say has a GORGEOUS voice.'

Charles was enjoying himself in San Francisco where he had made a number of friends, all very hospitable. He had not yet begun using the telephone instead of writing, and when Judy was not with him he kept in touch faithfully with scrawled aerogrammes or barely legible letters on hotel stationery. In these hasty scrambled reports of work past, present and future, among the requests and instructions were scattered little messages of affection and a docile desire to please, strange in one so determined in many ways. From San Francisco he reported, at first hopefully, then somewhat plaintively on his progress in the campaign Judy was trying to wage for his health and relaxation. ' . . . I have bought all the various health food products from round the corner. . . . I have bought the Adelle Davis books . . . please tell me if I should buy further copies . . .' and later, from Texas, ' . . . T.M.' (transcendental meditation) 'is going well . . . on the whole I am keeping fairly strictly to it. . . . However . . . I find that although I do it religiously twice a day I am not able to concentrate on it any better as I progress, in fact that I am not progressing at all. I still find my mind wandering all the time . . . it's difficult to get it back onto the mantra. However, perhaps it will improve. . . . I wish I were coming back to you sooner as I am getting fed up with living alone. I miss you terribly and I am decided I shall never go on such a long trip without you again. All my love and kisses to you, my darling. Tons of love . . .'

From San Francisco he had gone to Texas to conduct *Fidelio* for the Dallas Civic Opera. The tenor singing with Helga Dernesch was Jon Vickers with whom he had clashed more than once, but this time there were no difficulties and Vickers gave a very fine performance as Florestan, a role in which he was famous. Whether it was the relaxing atmosphere of a smaller provincial city or the mellowing of age, he even agreed to include some of Charles's appoggiaturas in Florestan's aria.

America was becoming a part of Charles's life: in 1972 there was Gluck's *Orfeo*, with Marilyn Horne at the New York Metropolitan, an experience that should have been wonderful but was in fact disappointing. Gluck's original score had been mixed with the Paris version and choreographed as a ballet. The chorus was down in the pit, there were only three soloists and everything that should have been done by the chorus was left to the ballet. To Charles, it was all completely against the style and feeling of the music but he had good reviews, though some critics considered he took the music too fast. The production in general was panned and Marilyn Horne was said to seem tired and not at her best (discouraged perhaps by the situation in which she found herself) but, for Charles, working with her only confirmed his belief that she is the finest singer of her kind, a superb artist with immense virtuosity and a voice of extraordinary beauty and range. He was profoundly impressed by her intelligence and musicianship, the fact that he could discuss work with her without having to cope with tantrums or lack of comprehension, and it seemed that she could sing anything. During the Thanksgiving holiday, at her house, he heard for the first time her new recording of Lieder by Hugo Wolf, a fresh revelation to him of her tremendous artistry and versatility.

In 1976 Charles conducted a Mozart concert in New York at Avery Fisher Hall and a concert with the Chicago Symphony Orchestra; he then went to Houston to conduct *The Barber of Seville* with Hermann Prey and Maria Ewing at the Houston Grand Opera. The next year he was back in Houston for Strauss's *Arabella* with Kiri te Kanawa, Ashley Putnam and Thomas Stewart; te Kanawa, who had sung the title role at Covent Garden, was an immense success with her voice, beauty and charm.

When Charles returned to America in 1979 he was again on his way back from Australia. He broke his journey to work once more with Marilyn Horne in Meyerbeer's *Le Prophète* at the Metropolitan. Horne was magnificent as Fides, the role created by Pauline Viardot, but

Charles felt the opera was less successful than it should have been because the French tenor, Guy Chauvet, was unable to master the complexities of the score.

During this visit Charles substituted for Rafael Kubelik in a concert with the New York Philharmonic. The programme included Janáček's *Taras Bulba*, but though he was known as a Janáček specialist he had not been approached immediately because he was already engaged at the Met. When eventually he was asked to take over he agreed to help, though he would have to conduct the concert after the Saturday matinée at the opera.

The New York Philharmonic had never heard of him, but knowing that others had refused the engagement they had concluded that he must be of little account. When an orchestra feels a conductor is not their equal they show it; the New York Philharmonic behaved in a very offhand manner, Charles was angry that he, an established artist, should be treated as a nobody and the result was a performance which, though not bad, was far less good than it should have been with so famous an orchestra. It took concerts with the Milwaukee Symphony to restore Charles's good spirits; yet his respect and admiration for the great American orchestras and his enjoyment of working with them remained unimpaired. As he continued to return for concerts and opera on into the 1980s, he often wished that his commitments allowed him to spend more time in the USA.

XIX

Guest Conductor

As far back as 1971 Charles had been thinking of leaving the Coliseum; his letters to Judy from San Francisco were full of uncertainty as to whether he should stay or go. At first it was Arlen, then, when Harewood replaced Arlen and all seemed to be going so well, there were industrial troubles. ENO had survived the five-week strike but unrest continued, breaking out occasionally in the sort of incidents he found so exasperating. During a performance of *The Magic Flute* the chorus, who were paid to sing but sometimes expected to dance, worked to rule so that the Moors who should have been set dancing by Papageno's magic chimes sang but did not move, making nonsense of the scene; and in *The Twilight of the Gods* the man who should have moved the dead Siegfried's hand at the end, so that Hagen would not get the Ring, was prevented by union rule from rehearsing, so failed to lift the arm at the right time and the whole point of the Ring cycle was lost.

Charles was fed up with industrial wrangles that kept him from what he considered to be his real work. He had been a union member all his working life and was well aware of how conditions had been improved for musicians by united effort, but he could not accept actions that intruded on artistic matters. He never hesitated to say so and had, more than once, been in trouble by publicly expressing the fear that opera in Britain would be killed by militant unions who regarded it as an élitist entertainment and were out to destroy it by slowing down or restricting work, as though fighting a class war against capitalism.

To make matters worse, it seemed to him that opera houses everywhere were also struggling with constantly growing costs and astronomical artists' fees. They were becoming weighted down by top-heavy administration, management was often bigger than the work force, more and more staff were needed to handle union demands, artists' agents, marketing. The only way to avoid administrative and industrial headaches was to work as a guest, free to concentrate on preparing and giving a good performance which, to his mind, was a conductor's proper job.

In 1973 he gave notice of his intention to resign from the Coliseum but agreed to stay on until the end of 1977 and then to act as the ENO's Principal Guest Conductor. The last opera that he conducted as musical director was Janáček's *From the House of the Dead*, in December 1977. He was given a farewell dinner by the Chairman of the Board of the ENO, Lord Goodman, at one of the city livery halls and presented with a beautifully-bound score of *Salome*. At his final appearance as a member of the company, Lord Harewood, interrupted by cheers and applause, referred to him as ' . . . the best Janáček conductor we've ever heard . . . the most skilful and most practical of all Mozart scholars, the most indefatigable of operatic performers and he knows more about this business . . . than anybody else in this building.' He described Charles as having a unique versatility and wider breadth and range of taste than any music director of the post-war period . . . who had done everything from *The House of the Dead* to *Fledermaus*, from *The Ring* to Gilbert and Sullivan . . . an esteemed and highly-regarded colleague and much-loved friend.

In his reply, Charles, very moved, reminded the company that he had been associated with Sadler's Wells–ENO for thirty years and though it might seem rash to suggest he continue for another thirty he certainly meant to try.

'A chief guest conductor is an ideal thing to be,' he told an interviewer, enlarging on how happy he was to be free of administrative worries but, though he could now concentrate on the musical side of opera neither the pressure nor volume of work was reduced. Shortly after his last appearance at the Coliseum he was in West Berlin conducting *Don Carlos* and *The Magic Flute*. He has always enjoyed working for the *Deutsche Oper* with its continuous supply of great singers (many of them from communist countries) who are never heard in the West, but his second season at Aix-en-Provence that summer was less agreeable.

He was to conduct *Messiah*, a revival of *Così fan tutte* and the Scottish Opera production of Purcell's *Dido and Aeneas* with Janet Baker, John Shirley-Quirk and the Scottish Opera chorus, but in *Così* the troubles of the previous year were renewed. The stage was again muffled behind the gauze curtain and when he tried to have it removed he was told that if he did not conduct the opera as produced he would be sued. There was also trouble with *Dido and Aeneas*. It was quite exceptional for Janet Baker to be singing at Aix (she does not care for working abroad) but, having agreed to sing at the Festival, she was shocked to find herself booed at one of the early performances. It had never happened to her before and though the cause was national rather than musical or artistic, and only one person was responsible, she was so upset that her work was affected for the rest of the season. Charles was beside himself with rage, not only on Janet Baker's behalf but because he regards this barbarous practice, which is particularly prevalent in France, as a form of terrorism in the theatre.

After concerts in London, Hungary, Australia and Chicago and *Un Ballo in Maschera* at Covent Garden, with José Carreras, Vicente Sardinero, Sylvia Sass and Patricia Payne, he returned to the ENO as guest conductor for a Janáček opera, *The Adventures of Mr Brouček*. He had been wanting for a long time to present it in London but had hesitated because of its 'minority appeal'. (The first act is about 'Bohemian' Bohemians, the second about the Hussite wars.) Rehearsals were held under dreadful conditions, the weather was freezing and when the cast arrived at the hall where they were to rehearse one Monday morning they found the heating had been turned off for the weekend and it was so cold that the musicians could not play. Nevertheless, much to Charles's surprise and delight, *Mr Brouček* was a success. It was revived in 1983–4 and became one of the ENO's most popular Janáček operas. The production, by Colin Graham, was good and the two Australian singers, Gregory Dempsey and Geoffrey Chard, and Lorna Haywood were all excellent. After the première in December 1978, the 50th anniversary of the composer's death, Lord Harewood came on stage to introduce the Czech ambassador, Dr Černík, who presented Charles with the Janáček medal for services to Czech music.

He had already been awarded the CBE in 1974, and in the 1979 New Year's Honours List he received a knighthood. He was abroad at the time when he should have gone to the Palace, and when he returned to London the Queen was in the Middle East and the Prince of Wales was taking her place. Having missed his proper turn, Charles had been put in ahead of a fresh batch of awards and, being the first, had no chance to see how the others coped with the bowing and kneeling. When the Prince of Wales, perhaps to put him at his ease, remarked how pleasant it was to be giving recognition for services to opera, Charles replied how pleasant it had been for him to see His Royal Highness in the royal box the other night at Covent Garden. At this, the prince said impulsively, 'Oh, good lord, was that you conducting?' The conversation then became slightly uneasy, for both were well aware that the one thing visible from the royal box is the conductor.

★

Charles had not seen very much of his daughters since they had begun living away from home. There was affection between them all and the girls were happy about his successes, but they were absorbed in their own lives and work, and he was often abroad. As children they had grown so accustomed to his absences that when he went out to post a letter one day Fiona had asked if Daddy had gone to Australia.

Charles knew that Fiona and Catherine had both had boy-friends and long-standing affairs but Judy was the one who had always been there to listen to confidences, so he was somewhat taken by surprise when Fiona asked if he had a free weekend because she was marrying Christopher Janaway and would like him to be at the wedding. Catherine then announced that she and Peter Templeton had also decided to marry and wanted his next free date.

Wedding photographs of 6 July and 15 December show Charles, expansively smiling, escorting Fiona, then Catherine, against a background of cheerful and happy guests; then personal affairs gave way to work again, the family man was submerged in the guest conductor.

For some years he had hoped to conduct Janet Baker in Handel opera and she had now agreed to sing in that composer's *Julius Caesar*. The title role had been written for and sung by a castrato, as were most of Handel's male characters (see Appendix III), but Janet Baker's voice was much higher than the singer for whom the part was designed* and to make it possible for her to perform it Charles had really to 'take the bull by the horns and do a big adaptation job'. He did so without compunction for tailoring roles for singers was an accepted eighteenth-century practice. He also added decorations to some of the arias and, with the help of Noel Davies, edited the opera, cutting it by about half an hour.

Musicologists had not always agreed with his views on Handel performance, but though he had edited and conducted a number of oratorios since the Lam-Mackerras *Messiah* none had roused great controversy. When his edition of *Julius Caesar* was produced by the ENO in December 1979 there were a few musicological mutterings, but audiences and most critics were enthusiastic. Janet Baker's dramatic acting and virtuoso singing were magnificent and Harold Rosenthal, editor of *Opera* magazine, described it as 'the most exciting Handel singing heard on the London operatic stage for many years'.

---

*It is said that Cleopatra's arias in *Julius Caesar* are written in E major because the first singer of the role had the most beautiful note E ever heard and that the part of Caesar was written so low because the original performer, a castrato, was famous for his low notes.

It was not till the opera was revived in 1981 that a voice was raised very loudly in protest. The musicologist, Winton Dean, who had missed the 1979 performance, was invited to review the revival for *Opera*. Dean, who had published works on Handel and had himself edited *Julius Caesar*, was shocked by the Coliseum production. He wrote a scathing and hostile review, sparing nothing and no one. He complained that there was no drama, the performance was slack, painfully slow, sentimental; the cuts had disrupted the design, more arias should have been included, the treatment of *da capos* was tasteless and Mackerras's ornaments were appalling: they careered wildly over the stylistic spectrum, undermining the emotional impact of the arias, cluttering them up with appoggiaturas, distorting Handel's melodic line. He had, he said, sat through the opera wondering at every moment what horror would come next. The cast, even Janet Baker, were harshly criticized, as were costumes, producer and designer, but the arch-criminal was the editor and conductor. Though the editor of *Opera* had toned down some of the most vituperative comments the message was clearly that Charles Mackerras might be a good conductor in certain areas but he should leave Handel's operas to someone who had given more study to their style.

Charles, who is no good at rows in his private life, does not hesitate to attack when music is involved and at such times his tactlessness is almost inspired. He published a letter in *Opera*, defending his work and accusing Dean of sour grapes because ENO had not used his edition, also of axe-grinding where Handelian criticism was concerned. Dean replied, charging Charles with being disingenuous; the correspondence became heated. Readers wrote and took sides — '*Is it a private fight between Charles Mackerras and Winton Dean or can anyone join in?*' Some called Dean a philistine, others defended him. The battle continued in other journals, and in *Opera* until the editor stopped it by announcing that the correspondence was closed; meanwhile the production had won the Evening Standard Opera Award for 1979 and theatres in Switzerland and the USA were anxious to produce it. In May 1982 Charles conducted the ENO production with the San Francisco Opera and later with the Geneva Opera.

As the 1970s moved into the 1980s life for Charles became ever more crowded with work and travel. He moved from concerts in the Queen Elizabeth Hall and the Royal Festival Hall, with the English Chamber Orchestra, the Royal Philharmonic, the BBC Symphony Orchestra, to concerts in Munich, Vienna, Czechoslovakia, Switzerland, Holland, Scandinavia and Italy. There were Proms in the Albert Hall, oratorio at Leeds, in Barcelona and Geneva; performances at the

Royal Opera House, the ENO, with the Scottish National Opera, the Welsh National Opera, and opera in Paris, Cologne, Geneva, Zurich.

In March 1980, in Zurich, he conducted *Tosca* produced by Tito Gobbi, who had now retired from singing, with the Bulgarian soprano Anna Tomova Sintov as a brilliant Tosca. Gobbi, who had sung the part of Scarpia more than a thousand times, had an intimate knowledge and understanding of the opera and Charles, who enjoyed working with him, thought his production excellent.

At the end of that year he went again to Zurich to conduct the Delius opera, *A Village Romeo and Juliet*. Although it is based on a novel by Gottfried Keller, the most famous author from German Switzerland, it had never been produced there before. Because Delius rarely heard his operas performed he tended to over-orchestrate, blotting out the voices on stage, and though Beecham had edited the score Charles still had great problems balancing the orchestra and singers.

Nevertheless, the production was a huge success, for the story is familiar to all Swiss and the beautiful romantic music of Delius suited it perfectly. The cast, which was excellent, included a wonderful Swedish tenor, Gösta Winbergh, who has since become very eminent, but the German critics did not agree about the opera or about Charles. One reviewer said that he 'proved a sympathetic interpreter of the work . . . [that] the orchestra [was] directed with such care that every nuance and detail was clear and all directed towards the emotional impact', but another disliked almost everything about the production and specially loathed 'Sir Charles Mackerras's coarse and overblown rendering of Delius' score'. However, in the *Sunday Times*, Felix Aprahamian, who had been Beecham's assistant, wrote, 'From the Zurich players Charles Mackerras coaxed heartrendingly lovely nuances in the Beecham tradition.'

For his part, Charles considered the opera worth all the trouble. It was one of his happiest performances in Europe, made even happier when Judy, with their great friends, Dr and Mrs Nicholson, flew out to join him for Christmas, which they spent in a mountain hotel.

The Delius opera was a longstanding engagement, but Charles had been suddenly asked to conduct a new production of Flotow's *Martha* in Cologne at the same time. He had refused, for it seemed impossible to fit in, but the management of the Cologne Opera had persuaded him that the production of an Anglo-German opera really needed an English conductor. For Charles this meant making seventeen journeys between Zurich and Cologne in the depth of winter, mainly by rail, but he enlivened the journeys by telephoning

Judy from the train, commenting on the scenery— '*We're just passing the Lorelei rock . . . We're just going into a tunnel*' — as he travelled along the Rhine.

Unlike the Delius, which had been so successful, *Martha* was a failure. The German producer, who had previously worked so well with Charles on *The Girl of the Golden West*, disliked Flotow's sentimental story, the reviews were bad and one critic, after taking the production to pieces, said, 'Even the conductor, Sir Charles Mackerras, could not rescue it . . . indeed he appeared to have given up altogether!'

During rehearsal Charles encountered the mercenary attitude common to many orchestral musicians of any nationality. The music of *Martha* is light and frothy but brassily and heavily orchestrated and again he had great trouble in keeping the orchestra, particularly the brass, quiet enough for the singers to be heard. At the first rehearsal the players did their best to keep down but the balance was still far from satisfactory. After the rehearsal the three trombones came to him and suggested that if they could play on the little narrow-bore trombones used for Mozart and other old music they could blow normally but the sound would be soft. It seemed a good idea and Charles agreed. Next came the trumpet players who said that if the trombones were going to change their instruments would it not be better if instead of big trumpets they used narrow bore cornets, which were also easier to play? Again Charles agreed. Next came the tuba player who said that in order to fit in with the others, would it not be better if he played the baritone, which had much the same range as the tuba but, having a very narrow bore, made a much less massive sound.

'Yes,' said Charles. 'Excellent! Please all bring these instruments to the next rehearsal,' but then to his dismay the orchestral manager now appeared and demanded 'Do you realize what you're doing? You've just committed us to over half a million marks . . . our entire budget for the whole season to cover illness, extra musicians, etc. We can't possibly afford it, you must cancel the arrangements.'

Charles agreed to try to persuade the musicians but he feared that if they were now refused the special instruments (which meant extra pay) they would simply play extra loud. This is exactly what happened; the sound was deafening so there was nothing for it but to let them use the instruments they wanted, which undoubtedly improved the performance, as well as teaching Charles a lesson.

At the end of 1981 and again in April the following year Charles conducted two special performances for Janet Baker. She was approaching her fiftieth birthday and though she was still at the height of her powers had decided to retire from the operatic stage. She would continue singing in concert and oratorio but felt it absurd for mature women to go on too long playing the parts of young girls. Her farewells were made at the three opera houses in which she had sung her famous roles — at Glyndebourne in Gluck's *Orfeo*, conducted by Raymond Leppard, in Gluck's *Alceste* at Covent Garden and, at the ENO, in Donizetti's *Maria Stuarda*, the two last conducted by Charles.

He had prepared a special edition of *Alceste* for Janet Baker. She had originally found the music rather too high but, by a certain amount of transposing and arranging, he produced a version that suited her voice very well. The performances and the final curtain calls were emotional, for artists and audience. Describing her Coliseum farewell Dame Janet wrote: 'I am literally snowed under with daffodils. . . . Lord Harewood comes on to make a delightful, charming and utterly appropriate speech. This is the hard moment; I hold on to Charles. He knows what I am feeling and I know that passing through his mind are the many, many moments of marvellous triumph we have shared together on this stage. How much I owe these men, what their vision and faith in me have given to me in terms of my development as a performer and achievement as an artist.'*

It had been a wonderful period for everyone concerned. Janet Baker's work with the ENO had been one of its greatest glories; her performances had raised the standards of opera in English and helped to set the company on its way to success.

Charles had left the Coliseum saying how happy he was to be free of administrative work and that his only wish was to be a guest conductor, yet in 1982 when speculation began about a successor to Colin Davis at the ROH he found he was not so sure. Though he did not want to return to the problems and strains of a full-time job in an opera house, he felt he should have been given a chance to refuse.

The opportunity did not arise. Unsuccessful advances were made by the Board to various European conductors but not to Charles, which was puzzling and frustrating, for in the late 1960s he had been considered as a 'powerful possibility' to succeed Georg Solti, had he not already been committed to rejoin Sadler's Wells as musical director. (Lord Drogheda, the then Chairman of the Board, has since admitted privately that he was mistaken in not making the appointment.) Many people were astonished; some were indignant and said

Full Circle, by Janet Baker. London, Julia Macrae. 1982.

so in print, in some cases so strongly that it has even been suggested they unwittingly did more harm than good. Alan Blyth, in the *Daily Telegraph*, incurred the Board's displeasure by an outspoken article headed *The Right Man*: ' . . . Nobody to whom I have spoken in the world of opera doubts that he is the best man for the job. . . . Let us first look at Sir Charles's attributes for the post. Nobody, and I mean nobody, conducting opera today has such a wide range of works in his repertory, or such a catholicity of taste, nor such a great experience of exercising his talents in the opera house, both here and abroad. . . . Can anyone show just cause why such a comprehensively equipped musician should be passed over. . . ?'

Charles appreciated and was grateful to Blyth for his championing; he did not believe that support worked against him for he felt the 'passing over' was far more likely to be a matter of personalities than of his qualifications and ability. He knew that these were beyond question but that, as the *Sunday Times* tactfully put it, he was 'notably forceful in character'. He had worked very happily at Covent Garden with Solti but apart from George Harewood, a former member of the Board and assistant to Sir David Webster, he had had few personal contacts with the administrative side and had never felt a true rapport with the management. With his naive belief that artists are valued according to their ability he had always neglected to cultivate those who could advance his career unless he found them congenial.

He also believed, and still does, that the ludicrous incident in his dressing-room with Inge Henderson and David Webster had not helped his image. Like those who know him well — Judy, the Harewoods, Richard Merewether — he is aware of his own lack of diplomacy, his fatal inability to suffer fools gladly, his incurable habit of expressing blunt and ill-timed opinions when he feels truth is at stake. Friends see it as honesty, distaste for dissembling; others see it differently.

'Charlie is bone-honest,' says Lady Harewood; but another old friend remembers the days when Charlie offended people because he knew everything — and worse, was usually right.

XX

Recording Janáček

THOUGH CHARLES HAS had some of his worst reviews and nastiest moments with the notorious Viennese critics, in November 1979 they were kind for his first concert and studio recording with the Vienna Philharmonic Orchestra. This was a very beautiful performance of Janáček's *Sinfonietta*, Dvořák's Fifth Symphony and Mahler's *Des Knaben Wunderhorn*, with Christa Ludwig as soloist; but whatever the critical reception he has always loved this city which has become for him almost a home from home. He has many friends there, including his Czech mother-figure, Zdeňka Podhajská, to whom he is devoted; there is the Vienna Philharmonic and the Opera House where he has conducted so many splendid singers, both from Iron Curtain countries and the West — Nicolai Ghiaurov, Piero Cappuccilli, José Carreras, Francisco Araiza and sopranos ranging from the young Bulgarian, Ghena Dimitrova to the celebrated Sena Jurinac, who had been his Tosca at Covent Garden in 1968. She was a member of the Vienna Opera for many years and when he conducted *Jenůfa* there in 1982 he was delighted to find her, no longer young but still beautiful, singing the part of the Kostelnička.

In the summer of 1981 he took a two-week master course on Mozart Opera at the Vienna Conservatorium. Among the fifteen students, selected from forty applicants from all over the world, were Martin Fischer-Dieskau, Dmitri Dmitriadis and an Australian, Brian Stacey, who was to become resident conductor of the Victorian State Opera. The Romanian chamber orchestra engaged for the students to practice on came from Braşov, which has a large German minority, but though some of the players knew German most spoke only Romanian. This was excellent for training the young conductors to communicate by gesture and demeanour; not only could they not talk to the orchestra except through an interpreter, the musicians, though good professionals, had never played Mozart opera before and did not know the music.

The course, which involved teaching the technical side of conducting and the handling of recitative, gave Charles an opportunity to explain his ideas on interpretation and he enjoyed it so much that he agreed to give one on the different versions of Beethoven's *Fidelio*, though it would be some years before he could fit it in.

In 1982, Lorin Maazel, then at the Vienna Opera, asked him to conduct a Christmas performance of *Der Rosenkavalier*. There was a splendid cast with Gundula Janowitz as the Marschallin, Agnes Baltsa (Octavian), Manfred Jungwirth (Baron Ochs) and Patricia Wise (Sophie), but Maazel's rule allowed only two rehearsals with orchestra. Charles felt this was not enough to be really effective and when the two were cut to one, with no singers, it seemed hardly worth rehearsing at all. He consulted friends in the Vienna Philharmonic and found that they agreed with him; they believed that the members of the orchestra, who knew the opera inside out, would pay more attention to him and tend to be less relaxed at the performance if he did not rehearse with them.

There was no rehearsal and on the night they behaved as predicted. The performance was superb. For Charles it was an immensely exhilarating experience to conduct this wonderfully sensitive orchestra, without rehearsal, in a work its players knew so perfectly. The music was in their blood; Strauss himself was not Viennese but in *Der Rosenkavalier* he has so perfectly captured the spirit of Vienna that the people have taken the opera to their hearts.

It is not only exciting for Charles to conduct the Vienna Philharmonic, one of the greatest orchestras in the world: he admires the musicians' wholehearted attitude to their work and finds endearing their genuine love and enjoyment of playing. They work exceptionally hard. It is quite usual for them to rehearse in the morning, record in the afternoon and play for the opera or a symphony concert at night, yet despite heavy commitments they always strive to give the best possible performance.

It is an enormous orchestra, with a pool of nearly two hundred, and it is self-governing. The players elect a management committee or a manager from their ranks and they/he combines administrative work with playing. Because the members make their own conditions and the orchestra is their own concern they feel responsible. They know it depends on them whether or not their work is good and they take pride in making sure that it is. This enthusiasm and pride in keeping high standards puts them in a different category from clock-watching orchestras to whom playing is a job to be done during specified hours.

The Philharmonic's traditions go back to the mid-nineteenth century; past conductors have included Nikisch, Furtwängler,

Weingartner, Bruno Walter. It is in some ways an orchestra of the old European school, with marvellous string sections, without the absolutely military precision of the Chicago Symphony. Charles finds that he must work to get this quality from them, as he works to produce from the Chicago players the wonderfully loving sound so much a feature of the VPO. The two orchestras cannot be compared. Equally magnificent, they are entirely different. This was brought home to Charles when, immediately after recording *The Makropulos Case* in Vienna, he flew to America and conducted the *Makropulos* overture in a programme with the Chicago Symphony. Both orchestras played it superbly but each with its own unique sound.

Charles's most important work with the VPO began in 1976 when they and he embarked on their famous Janáček recordings. The project is described by James Mallinson who was then Artists' Manager for Decca:

> Discussions on the project began in the early seventies. I had seen all the Sadler's Wells productions, most of them several times and felt that, as one of the great opera composers, Janáček should feature in the catalogue of a company such as Decca which is famous for its opera recordings. The progress from good idea to actual project came about because of the conjunction of a number of happy accidents.
>
> Georg Solti . . . went to hear *The Makropulos Case* at the ENO, was fascinated by it and talked seriously to Decca about recording it. Ultimately he decided that he would not have time to learn the piece and the idea of his conducting it was dropped, but his interest and enthusiasm were important in persuading Decca to take the project seriously.
>
> At about the same time as all this was going on David Rickerby* was appointed Marketing Manager at Decca. He is a fellow Janáček nut and embraced with enthusiasm the idea of recording the operas, and has been one of its most enthusiastic champions ever since. Also at about the same time Ray Minshull, who was then Manager of Classical Artists and Repertoire at Decca, had a meeting with Lord Harewood about entirely different matters. During the course of this meeting Harewood, who is another Janáček enthusiast, did a quite independent promotional job on Minshull on behalf of

*Sadly, David Rickerby died on 19 January 1987.

Janáček and of the ENO's music director, Charles Mackerras, as conductor for any recordings which might take place.

Things might well have stopped there had there not been yet another fortunate occurrence. At that time Decca had a contract with the Vienna Philharmonic which guaranteed the orchestra a minimum number of recording sessions per year. The minimum had to be paid for even if the sessions were not used and Decca was having great difficulty in finding the conductors and repertoire to fulfil the commitment. Thus faced with the prospect of having to pay for sessions which would not be used the idea of recording Janáček in Vienna suddenly became rather attractive and it was decided to go ahead with *Katya Kabanova*.

The casting of *Katya* was in theory simple and in practice very complicated. The choice of Charles Mackerras as conductor was really quite obvious and he rapidly and rightly became the linchpin of the whole project. Complications arose from the decision to ask Elisabeth Söderström to sing the title role and to use native Czech singers for nearly all the other parts. The Czech musical authorities didn't appreciate the idea of an outsider singing the title role, in an opera they considered very much their own, while their own people sang supporting parts. Negotiations with the Czech authorities were byzantine in their complexity and became more rather than less so as the project progressed. Interestingly the one person the Czechs never complained about was Charles Mackerras whom they obviously considered to be an adoptive Czech quaintly masquerading as an Australian.

The fact that Elisabeth Söderström was the only non-Czech was less serious than might seem for she had not only sung *Katya* before, she has a Slavonic background with a Swedish father but a Russian mother and speaks both these languages perfectly: Russian grammar is very similar to Czech. Charles had conducted her only once before, in *Così fan tutte* at Covent Garden, but he knew her to be an immensely intelligent and gifted artist, capable of identifying herself with almost any role, and a wonderful ensemble singer. During the Janáček recordings they worked so well together that he believes the project could not have succeeded as it did without her splendid co-operation.

He had also worked before with Naděžda Kniplová, who sang Kabanicha, with Libuše Marová (Varvara) and other Czechs in the cast, but the tenor was a new discovery. There had been trouble finding one for the part of Boris, Katya's lover, and a singer had still not been found when Charles, who was in Milan, heard of a Slovak

named Petr Dvorský who might possibly do for the part. He
arranged to hear the young man in a studio at La Scala but though
Dvorský had a beautiful voice the arias he sang were all from his *bel
canto* repertoire and gave no idea of how he would cope with
Janáček's idiosyncratic music. Charles explained that for this audition he must be heard in something in Czech in which the words
came fast. Dvorský knew nothing suitable but offered to sing an aria
from *Rigoletto* in Slovak. It was an odd mixture but it was enough to
show that he could manage Boris; in fact he did much more than
manage, he was a genuine find. He not only sang the music beautifully but interpreted the character with great sensitivity and understanding.

Charles was excited and pleased with the recording, he knew it
was excellent but he was also uneasy, worried that if it did not sell
the other operas would be cancelled. In fact, *Katya* was acclaimed: it
won the 1977 *Gramophone* Award for the *Best Opera Recording*.

Decca had meant to follow *Katya* with *Jenůfa* but there were
difficulties of casting, in securing artists and orchestra at the same
time. *Jenůfa* was postponed and replaced with *The Makropulos Case* in
1978, again with Söderstrom, who was magnificent as Emilia Marty.
This recording was also greeted with rave reviews.

From the House of the Dead, which has an all-male cast, was
recorded in 1979 at a time when no women singers were available.
For Charles it was a total immersion in Janáček for he was also
conducting *Jenůfa* at the Vienna Opera. Musicians and singers who
were engaged for both operas would work on recording all day in
the Sofiensaal and in the evening play in *Jenůfa* at the Opera House.

This was Charles's operatic début in Vienna and though it was an
ordinary repertory performance it received an ecstatic review in *Der
Merker*, the opera-lovers' magazine. The writer, Sieglinde Pfabigan,
hailed him as a new discovery, described the enormous enthusiasm
and interest he had generated by his performance and concluded by
declaring that he must be brought back more often to Vienna. His
operatic engagements there, past and future, include three Verdi
operas, three Puccini, one Wagner, one Strauss and a new production of Gluck's *Iphigénie en Aulide*.

From the House of the Dead was greeted with quite extraordinary
enthusiasm. It won for Decca the 1980 *Gramophone Record of the Year*
Award and the 1981 Grammy *Best Opera Record of the Year*. The
critic of the *Gramophone* wrote, 'Sir Charles has long known and
understood this music. . . . Together with Kubelik, no conductor
has done more to establish Janáček in this country. . . . Scholarship

and creative understanding go hand in hand . . . not only a superb performance of a masterpiece but a real contribution to knowledge.'

The Cunning Little Vixen was recorded in 1980, with Lucia Popp as the Vixen. She was an ideal choice; apart from her brilliant performance she comes from the very district in Moravia in which the opera is set. The local dialect and pronunciation were familiar to her and she was able to teach and correct the accents of Czechs from other areas. *The Cunning Little Vixen* won the 1983 Deutscher Schallplattenpreis and the *Gramophone Best Opera Recording* and was nominated for a Grammy.

The last of the series was the long-postponed *Jenůfa*, recorded in 1981 with Elisabeth Söderström as Jenůfa and Eva Randová as the Kostelnička. Petr Dvorský sang the part of Steva, Wieslaw Ochman was Laca and Karolka was sung by Lucia Popp.

Reviewing this performance, which won the 1984 *Gramophone Best Opera Recording*, the *Scotsman* described it as, 'The best and most beautiful, as well as most important recording of 1983 . . .' and spoke of its 'authority, conviction, devotion' — its musicological accuracy and lyrical fervour. Other reviews were equally enthusiastic and at the end of the series the critic of the *Sunday Telegraph* considered that few projects had reflected greater glory on the recording industry in recent years, for which 'the ultimate praise must go to the affectionate sweep of Sir Charles Mackerras whose thirty-five year campaign for Janáček here achieves its culmination'.

For Charles, the recordings had been a tremendous achievement, exciting, absorbing and satisfying. Despite the VPO's reputation for being traditional and hide-bound he had no difficulties with them over the Janáček music; he found they could do whatever he asked, immediately, without fuss, he needed only explain once, and they understood and could follow.

To the rapport with the orchestra, many of whom have Czech blood, was added the marvellous partnership with Söderström and Decca's recording technicians. In the past, because of Janáček's peculiar orchestration, certain passages of the operas would have had to be rewritten or touched-up but the Viennese orchestra, the Sofiensaal acoustics and the engineers were all so good that no such measures were needed. The use of digital recording allowed more licence in balance, as in the concert hall; in the old days this was always a problem — brass too loud etcetera — but now sound could be modified and balanced, so that faking became unnecessary.

Editing was also simplified, tapes did not have to be cut. For instance, during *Jenůfa*, Eva Randová as the Kostelnička recorded a beautiful solo but the harp accompaniment was not quite perfect. It would have been far too expensive to re-record it entirely so the Kostelnička solo was played and the new harp recorded over it. There was no loss of quality.

The relationship between Charles and the orchestra is summed up in Mallinson's account of the first day's recording:

When everyone assembled in Vienna for the first session on December 1st, 1976 there were three main concerns: one, would the Czech singers turn up? Two, how would the VPO react to an Australian conductor they had never met and, being the provincial bunch they are, probably never even heard of; and three, would he be able to teach them how to play Janáček? The session went very well with Charles directing operations in various different languages but mainly in German and Czech. The following morning shortly before the second session I was approached by a delegation from the VPO committee: could they have a private word. I took them into the control room with a sinking feeling. The VPO is well known for devouring conductors for breakfast.

'This Mackerras, tell us about him, he is not really English, is he?'

'Well as a matter of fact no he isn't.'

'That's what we thought, he certainly has a Czech parent or grandparent?'

'As it happens none of those, he's Australian.'

They looked at each other in a bemused manner clearly wanting to know where in the world Australia is, but rather too polite to ask and then shuffled off to play the session with only one further comment . . . 'unglaublich . . . incredible.' From then onwards they took Charles to their hearts and have continued to do so ever since.

XXI

A Day in the Life of the Maestro

CONDUCTORS IN HOLLYWOOD films are often very grand and very temperamental. They live in palatial mansions with glamorous wives or mistresses who are permanently *en grande tenue*, drink champagne like water and lead what the newspapers call a glittering life.

Life at 10 Hamilton Terrace is rather different. If the maestro is not abroad, hurtling through space with a score on his knees and earphones on his head, or up in Abbey Road recording, or rehearsing at the Coliseum or the ROH, he is poring over Handel scores or listening to tapes or dictating to his secretary, while the maestro's wife may well be gardening or in the kitchen making yoghurt, entertaining her grandson or packing her husband's clothes for his next flight tomorrow.

Journalists who come for interviews hoping to write a piece called *A Typical Day in the Life of* . . . find there is no such thing; no one day is typical except that the telephone never stops ringing and if the maestro is home there is music from early morning to late at night.

His day starts any time after 7 a.m., unless he has had a concert or opera the night before. After a performance he is exhausted and often does not sleep easily, particularly if he has a quite different work to conduct the next day. When he has been on a high it is hard to unwind, he lies awake going over the performance, though he knows he should be thinking about tomorrow's work. Often when Judy drives him home after a beautiful programme he will put on a tape for the next night's concert and when she protests that she does not want to hear it he says he must wipe out the last performance to prepare for the next.

Today he has woken before five. He takes off his eye mask and lies for a few minutes thinking of work ahead. On the bedside table is a life of Mozart (in German), a book about Sullivan and a thriller which he would like to read but it is too dark and he does not want to wake Judy by putting on the light. He reaches for his Walkman, adjusts the earphones, replaces his eye mask, lies back and switches on.

At six o'clock a fearful crash outside announces the arrival of building materials for the house being renovated next door. The workmen's transistor begins and will play pop music full blast all day. Judy wakes, disturbed by the noise but not surprised by the space-age figure lying beside her.

While she takes her shower the maestro gets up and consults his bio-rhythm calculator, one of his toys from a duty-free airport shop. It claims to tell what form he will be in for the day but its predictions are based on the hour of birth and since he is using it in London but was born in New York State there could be a margin of error. Judy has pointed out the time difference but he is not discouraged. She cannot see the advantage of being told in advance that you are going to feel low when you need to be at your best but Charles, who takes his bio-rhythm calculator as seriously as Schumann took the Leipzig psycho-meter, believes it is better to be forewarned in order to be prepared.

He is about to take his shower when he remembers something and goes down to the study to fetch it. Once there, he has a fresh thought, puts on a tape and stands listening intently. The long room is lined with shelves of scores, discs and albums, transistors, cassettes, record-players. It is becoming crowded with objects recently acquired — a beautiful Georgian table, a patent typist's chair waiting for washers before it can be assembled, a colourful plastic bio-clock which is powered by fruit or plants and a pen that theoretically turns into a torch or a screw-driver. It does not work and is waiting to go back to the mail-order house from whence it came. Beyond the french windows the sunny garden is green and sparkling and full of birds but the maestro is absorbed and oblivious.

The secretary arrives, uncovers the typewriter and attends to the answering service. Already the telephone calls have started. With Europe one hour ahead and the United States five hours behind, business calls come in from 8.30 a.m. to 9 o'clock at night. There are five floors in the house and extensions on each, as well as inter-coms and a cordless telephone for the garden.

*The Mass of Life** surges fortissimo through the house. The front doorbell rings. Concentrating on Delius the maestro has forgotten his early appointment but courteously, in his dressing-gown, with half-spectacles on the end of his nose, welcomes the visitor who has come to ask his advice.

Music pours from the maestro's bathroom, drowning the sound of the shower. It will also pour forth when he takes a shower late at night. In his dressing-room he puts on a sock and stands listening critically to

*Which he conducted at the Edinburgh Festival in 1985.

a phrase. The telephone rings in the bedroom next door; the inter-com on the landing buzzes: breakfast is ready. House-guests patter down the stairs, a strange man wanders up. Meeting him on the landing the maestro says, 'Good morning,' in his pleasant abstracted way. 'Did you want to see me?' 'Morning sir,' says the handyman, proceeding on to the attic to fix a window.

Breakfast is set in the kitchen; Handel has spread from the study to the dining-room and orchestral parts are strewn all over the table. Judy deals out her home-made yoghurt, fruit, honey, cereal, toast and tea. Letters are piled on the table to be answered or queried or filed. Already there have been calls from Europe and now the extension rings in the kitchen.

It is a beautiful summer day. The maestro's wife would like to be trekking in the Himalayas or relaxing on Elba or taking her grandson to the Zoo, perhaps binding a score or playing her clarinet; instead she is going to deal with mail, talk on the telephone, make appointments, do household chores, work out a menu for tomorrow night's dinner-party, take clothes to the cleaner, cook, shop, interview a Caribbean girl who is coming to help Teresa. She will go next door to complain to the builders about the noise and the mess they leave in front of Number 10, the plumber is coming to mend the sink garbage-disposal unit and she herself is going to try to fix the basement door which is stuck and which the handyman has overlooked. She must take something up to the EMI studios in Abbey Road where the maestro is recording and be back in time to prepare supper for him and Marilyn Horne who is coming to rehearse the decorations he has written for her. With luck everyone will get to bed about midnight if there are not too many late international telephone calls, but Judy is thankful she does not have to dress up and go out this evening.

The maestro has eaten his health-giving breakfast and taken his vitamins. There is something very disarming about this large man, so erudite and distinguished, obediently swallowing his pills, a touch of the schoolboy as he takes the lunch-box Judy has packed and the thermos of fresh juice so he need not eat canteen food. This charming docility is an offshoot of extreme preoccupation. With his mind entirely on music he leaves his physical well-being in her hands. How much of his immense energy would there be without her care, feeding, managing, without her to study his interests and needs and relieve him of material worries? He knows it and he is grateful.

Teresa has arrived and is washing up. She is depressed because she has lost one of the maestro's recordings. He and Judy promise they will give her another. Teresa describes her decision to work at

Hamilton Terrace: 'There was another job, very good also but when I found this was Mackerras I chose because I love his music.'

Mackerras is about to leave for the studios when the secretary announces that Marilyn Horne's manager has rung to say she is still in Italy and will not be coming tonight. Charles is concerned that there will not be another chance to rehearse with her before their performance in New York. Appointments have been postponed and rearranged to fit in with the star and it is too late to change them back. There are more telephone calls, more messages and rearrangements.

Up at Abbey Road the orchestra is in the recording studio, cynical older players, bearded young men, a baroque cellist with long streaming hair and unworldly expression, a violinist who unstraps a baby from her back and hands it to her husband to mind while she works. Soloists arrive. The maestro is ready, the red light shows above the door. Over and over again the orchestra plays, over and over again the soloists sing their arias and duets. To listeners in the studio it all sounds perfect but each time there is something wrong: the orchestra is right but a singer is flat, the singer is perfect but the orchestra is not; both are perfect but there is a technical flaw. *We'll take it again*; and again, yet no one complains or makes a scene. To an outsider the patience of these artists is extraordinary, they seem more concerned with the music than their own comfort, the necessity to get it right overcomes fatigue and irritation. How can they keep on dredging up the necessary feeling when they are constantly interrupted and made to repeat?

From time to time soloists and conductor go to the control room to hear a take, then back to resume and repeat. There is a break for lunch, people go out or to the canteen; then it starts again. New soloists arrive, Janet Baker with her husband Keith Shelley, Valerie Masterson, Della Jones, Sarah Walker. At close quarters the women are prettier, smaller and slighter than they appear on the stage. In the studio the beautiful voices seem drowned by the orchestra, but in the control room they come through perfectly. The maestro conducts with ruffled hair and glasses on the end of his nose. The music is so lovely, surely this time it is perfect, but the telephone on his desk rings and he stops them. Over and over, repeating, interrupted, repeating, repeating. Then tea time; starting again; and so it will go on till he comes home for a very late dinner.

Yesterday he worked at home in the afternoon, marking orchestra parts. Wearing his patent acupuncture sandals that resemble a bed of nails he sat in the garden with his score on the table and headphones on ears, oblivious of observers, conducting, humming under his breath, silently whistling, chewing his tongue, lifting his shoulders for emphasis, busy, peaceful, absorbed. From time to time came the faint purring sound of his electric rubber, the whizz of his battery-operated pencil-sharpener, the almost inaudible *beep* of his wrist watch marking the hour. Indoors there would be a background of chinks and clicks as timers, alarms and clocks go off.

Last night when people came to dinner they sat in the garden having drinks. The maestro is a genial host, relaxed, amusing, a good raconteur. He keeps the glasses filled and enjoys himself. After dinner he showed his visitors his eighteenth-century barrel-organ and speculated on its origin. He told how he and Judy found it in the Portobello Road, how they waited for several years to be able to buy it (with the price going up every year) till at last they knew they must plunge. It is almost his dearest possession. As the frail mechanical tunes tinkle out he stands listening with an expression of childlike enchantment.

He enjoys seeing friends, but towards the end of the evening he becomes tired and, unless the subject is music, a familiar absent look appears. Though he seems to be genuinely sorry when it is time for people to leave, the minute the front door shuts behind them, if it is not too late, he is in the study, putting on a cassette, 'just running through this before bed'.

Tomorrow they are making a video film of *Julius Ceasar* down in Limehouse at Canary Wharf, West India Docks. This is an old warehouse where cargo was stored, now converted to television studios. A video film in production is a fearsome sight to see: wires, flexes, headphone leads, cameras (some hanging from the ceiling), lights, overhead microphones, microphones on the end of booms, cranes, effects, monitors, musical instruments, directors, endless technicians and hangers-on. Charles and the orchestra are away in another studio; Noel Davies, his assistant, is conducting the singers and playing the harpsichord for recitatives. There are problems of communication: people call, 'Can you hear me?' 'Yes, yes I hear you . . .' Something goes wrong and private rather acid comments are broadcast to everyone, including the object of criticism. The dry-ice machine plays up. People stand round the monitors blocking the view. It is all very much as it looked in BBC television studios thirty years ago.

There are more amplified calls from maestro to assistant conductor, then they are ready. Cleopatra (Valerie Masterson) in her eighteenth-century costume and wig takes her place with Ptolemy

(James Bowman). The lights move closer, the music starts. It stops. Pause. Delays. Repeat. Start again. A break, and lights are turned off. Caesar (Janet Baker) and his Roman sailors lie on the deserted shore while the wreckage of their ship is arranged round them. A signal is given, the dry-ice machine cranks and clatters and belches out clouds of mist. Shouts and yells . . . someone is standing in front of the monitor. The assistant rushes to the harpsichord to play for the recitative and finds a fat man sitting there eating. Outside the studio Keith Shelley is encountered carefully carrying a cup and saucer and slice of cake for Caesar. 'The poor girl deserves her tea.'

Filming will go on till quite late and all will be exhausted. The maestro will be too tired to sleep and will lie awake going over all the things he thinks went wrong. In the morning he has a rehearsal at Covent Garden. Judy will cut sandwiches — he won't have time for lunch — and possibly drive him in. In the afternoon there is more recording and a concert at night. The following day he goes off to Vienna and Prague. This will be really hectic, everyone mobilized to get him to the airport in time. Judy will have done his packing but there will be last-minute panic, he will still be checking orchestral parts when the hire-car comes. Scores are collected, telephone calls dealt with, letters signed. Judy, Teresa, the secretary and any odd friends who are present stand in the hall handing him coat, cabin bag, ticket, passport. His luggage, almost too heavy to lift, is carried to the car. *'What's in it? Iron bars?'* No; he has just filled it with scores. *'Have you got your. . . ?'* *'Have you put in my. . . ?'* *'Yes yes, it's all there . . .'* *'Goodbye . . . goodbye.'* The car drives off, the door shuts, the women limp to the kitchen for coffee as once more the telephone starts to ring.

One day when Judy went to collect the maestro's tails from the dry cleaner the man in the shop said, 'Is your husband a conjuror then?'

About to say No, she thought of Charles who that night would go into the silent pit at the theatre and by waving a wand cause musicians and singers to create a work of art.

'I suppose he is really,' she said.

XXII

Chief Conductor, Sydney Symphony Orchestra

CHARLES HAD SEEN members of his family in Europe, but he had not been back to Australia for nearly eight years. When he returned there in 1971 to conduct for the ABC, there had been changes among the Mackerrases. After Joan's marriage Harpenden had been sold and Catherine and Alan had moved back to Balvaig, the house where Catherine grew up. During the 1930s it had been turned into two large flats and Elizabeth and Andrew Briger had lived in the upper one since their marriage. Catherine redecorated the lower apartment, added a study for herself and resumed work on the biography of her grandfather, Sir Normand MacLaurin, which she had started some years before. Alan was still at the university, happy among his colleagues and students.

Alastair, who was now headmaster of The Sydney Grammar School, had married a young widow with four children; Elizabeth and Andrew had a son and three daughters. Elizabeth had become an interior designer and Andrew, an architect, had gone into local politics and was a city alderman. Neil was a very successful barrister with nine children and both the twins were working in Canberra — Colin, now with a family, as a Sinologist at the Australian National University, Malcolm a political commentator and psephologist.

Judy and Charles stayed with Alastair and his wife Sue, at Mosman, on the north side of the harbour. It was a cheerful but hectic time with orchestral concerts in all States, including Tasmania. In Sydney, conducting Janáček's Glagolitic Mass, Charles encountered a friend from the past. Singing in the Philharmonia Choir, with her husband Vince, was Dulcie Bormann, daughter of Ernest Bormann, the neighbour at Turramurra on whose harmonium Charles had improvised as a boy.

He was taken over the Sydney Opera House, at last approaching the final stages of construction, and expressed concern about its limitations. He was dubious about the prospects for large-scale productions, though it was now too late for major alterations. He had already agreed to conduct there on the opening night in 1973.

Between the concerts and touring there were many parties, dinners, interviews, a Guest of Honour broadcast, a civic reception at Sydney Town Hall attended by all available Mackerrases. Neil and his wife Elizabeth gave an enormous welcome-home at their mansion in Wahroonga, to which they invited brothers, sisters, cousins, all with husbands and wives, old friends, musicians, academics, lawyers, medicos, civic figures. It was the last time the family was all together, prosperous, healthy and full of high spirits.

The following year Alan, so active and slim, so moderate and abstemious, had first one stroke, then another. By Christmas Eve Catherine was writing to Judy, ' . . . poor Alan. Almost overnight he has been transformed into a very old white-haired man, limping badly and tremulous; when tired his speech can barely be understood. He seems to me to grow worse every day but the specialist describes him as holding his own.' Specialists notwithstanding, Alan continued to decline, though struggling to keep going, even sailing with friends, lashed into the cockpit of his beloved *Antares*. A few weeks before Charles and Judy arrived in 1973 for what should have been a very happy occasion, his two years of terrible suffering came to an end.

Fiona and young Catherine had both graduated that year and Charles had given them a trip round the world so they could be in Sydney for the Opera House celebrations. Their grandmother was glad to see them but she was in a low state, emotionally worn down by the prolonged spectacle of Alan's cruel fate and stunned because in his extremity he had turned away from her. Elizabeth had taken her place, and she had been unable to help him except by her prayers for a happy death. She was a warm-hearted woman and, for all the long silence between them, his rejection had been a great shock. She also felt irrational guilt and remorse that through her conversion she had created the gulf between them.

She pulled herself together and went to the Opera House where Charles was conducting an inaugural concert with Birgit Nilsson, who sang magnificently; and later *The Magic Flute* in the presence of the Queen. The production was enlivened by several incidents. To the amusement of some and disapproval of others John Copley, the producer, had replaced the wild beasts which Tamino charms with his flute by little Australian animals, possums, koalas, wallabies, platypus played by small boys from Sydney Grammar Junior School. One child, swamped in his costume, was quite blind and made straight for the footlights. Charles signalled to warn him but he could not see and continued on till it seemed he would fall into the pit and be badly hurt. The audience, which had been holding its breath, gave a burst of laughter when a shirt-sleeved stage-hand appeared and rescued him.

After the first act the company lined up to be presented to the Queen, who was leaving to drive to the airport. The cast were arranged in order of their appearance with conductor, set designer, producer etcetera, but to the embarrassment of Edward Downes, the musical director, the Queen came in at the wrong end of the line and, rather baffled, met first all the characters who had not yet appeared in the opera.

Charles left for London worried by his mother's condition and saddened by Alan's unhappy end. He felt that he had never given his father a chance, in a sense, had not taken the trouble to know him until far too late, and without Judy even this might never have happened.

In London he was soon absorbed in the famous *Maria Stuarda* performances with Janet Baker at the Coliseum and it was nearly five years before he returned to Australia. Meanwhile, in 1974, the Sydney Symphony Orchestra came to Europe and he toured with them to Vienna, Stockholm, Montreux, Basle and the Edinburgh Festival. When he flew to Sydney in 1978 for his fifth season with the ABC there had been another great change in the family. This time it was Catherine who was missing.

After Alan's death she had continued her work on 'Grandfather's Biography' but it had gradually become too much and she had put it aside. She still read voraciously but had grown rather prone to melancholy reflections; she had always been very conscious of mortality and now spoke of Alan more kindly than she had done during his life. Her religion was a great consolation. As time passed she went out less, mainly to church and to concerts when Alastair could take her. She spent much time in her long white sitting-room, moving only to leave her armchair for the meal table, then back to the chair, always with a book in her hand. Walking had become difficult. The doctor, who had dared tell her she needed more exercise, had been taken aback when she replied firmly, almost proudly, that she never took exercise, lived a very sedentary life and had no intention of changing. Her body was becoming a burden but she still enjoyed food and wine and the little cigars she had taken to smoking. She spoke in a dismissive way of her arteries as a nuisance invented by the doctor to interfere with her pleasures, but she really felt that extreme old age was a great humiliation and hoped to be released in a suitable manner before she reached it.

She very much wanted to see Joan again, and the new grandchildren born in England, but hesitated to travel alone. In 1975 Alastair's wife, Sue, took her to London. They stayed in a hotel, for the stairs at

Hamilton Terrace were now beyond her, and she visited Joan and her family at Norwich; but it was clear to everyone that she had gone downhill physically and when she left for home Charles knew he would never see her again.

Early one morning in February 1977 Alastair rang from Sydney to say that she had died peacefully in her sleep. The night before, after a good dinner with him, a glass of red wine and an animated conversation about Moses, she had gone to bed with a book (*Queen Victoria and her Ministers*, by Phillip Guedalla). In the morning she woke early to read, dozed off, and was found a couple of hours later with her glasses on her nose and the book on her chest. She was buried in the family vault at Waverley cemetery on a perfect summer day. The blue sky, the sweeping view of the Pacific from the mausoleum, the stately manner of her disposal, would have pleased her. It was not a sad occasion; it was even felt that with her taste for gothic romance she would have enjoyed her funeral.

Charles had been away from her for many years but she had always been a tremendous influence in his life, his champion, friend, adviser and confidante. Though Judy had long played these roles no one would ever quite replace Catherine.

Eventually the long-entailed MacLaurin estate was wound up and in order that Balvaig should remain in the family Charles bought the lower flat for use during his Australian visits. Once more the apartment was repainted and decorated, though much of Catherine's furniture remained, her rugs, books and china; and Alastair, who was now a widower, moved in as permanent occupant with his vast collection of books, tapes and records.

There was quite a family atmosphere at Balvaig in 1978 with Charles and Judy and Alastair downstairs, and Elizabeth and Andrew and their children up above. Charles had come out to conduct a concert season for the ABC, programmes of Prokofieff, Schubert, Rachmaninov, Debussy, Delius, Liszt, with Michele Campanella as soloist, and Mahler's *Song of the Earth*, with Lauris Elms and Anthony Roden. The next year he was back for *Jenůfa* and *Simone Boccanegra* for the Australian Opera at the Sydney Opera House and Janáček's *Glagolitic Mass* with the Philharmonia Choir.

He was greatly surprised to find himself the centre of a *This Is Your Life* television programme. It was the culmination of most complex and ingenious arrangements. For months the television channel had been secretly working with Judy, making furtive telephone calls to London when Charles was away from the house, and his astonishment was genuine as the members of his family appeared in turn —

Alastair, Neil, Elizabeth, Colin (now Professor of Asian Studies in Queensland), Malcolm and Uncle Ian from Canberra, Joan, flown out from England — and old friends, Neville Amadio from Charles's early days in the Sydney Orchestra, Pam Munks and most incredible of all, Jiřinka Kadainková, brought from Prague through Judy's diplomatic genius.

It was on his way home from this Australian season that he broke his journey in New York for the revival of *Le Prophète* with Marilyn Horne. Due to the peculiarities of the international date-line he was able to conduct *Jenůfa* in Sydney on Saturday night and be in the pit of the Met on Monday morning to rehearse the Meyerbeer opera.

By the 1980s Charles had a foot on each side of the world. His home was in London and his work in the northern hemisphere but his own family were in Australia; he loved Sydney, the harbour, the sailing, he enjoyed working with his old orchestra, he liked the way he was treated when he returned. At times when the winter sun was warm and the view from Balvaig was at its best with white sails and blue water, he even talked vaguely of coming back there to retire. He would weigh up the attractions against the warnings of those who had already returned to live after years abroad — the distance, the feeling of being cut off, the growing elements of complacency and 'Gumnut Nationalism' — but it was never a serious project; he was not likely to retire or cut down his career by settling in Sydney. In any case there was Judy to be considered. For her the situation was clear-cut; she was English, her roots, family, friends, interests were in England and Europe. She was happy to come to Australia but not to migrate.

For Charles the trouble was that he really did not know where he belonged, he had become *déraciné*, he was not even quite sure what he was. In England he was constantly labelled *Australian*, in certain circles his Mackerras directness and impatience with humbug were seen as rather crudely 'colonial', yet in Australia he was often regarded as a 'bloody Pommie'. To the British his accent was almost 'ocker' yet in his own country his voice was referred to as 'plummy British'. He was too cosmopolitan now to belong completely anywhere.

In 1980, when the ABC offered him the position of Chief Conductor of the Sydney Symphony Orchestra, it seemed the perfect solution. (At this time the Sydney Symphony Orchestra was administered by the Australian Broadcasting Corporation.) He would spend several months a year in Australia and be free the rest of the time for international engagements; he would be able to shape the orchestra, develop repertoires, work with singers he knew and respected — Joan Carden, Marilyn Richardson, Beverley Bergen, Lauris Elms,

Margreta Elkins and the two great basses, Bruce Martin and Donald Shanks. When he accepted the offer he became the first Australian to be appointed Chief Conductor.

The engagement, for three years, was to start in 1982 but he was in Sydney again in 1981 as guest conductor. There were concert performances in Melbourne of *Die Walküre*, with Rita Hunter, Donald Shanks, Raymond Myers and Lauris Elms and in Sydney of *Götterdämmerung*, with Rita Hunter again, Bruce Martin, Robert Alman, Jon Weaving, Margaretta Elkins and Lauris Elms. The tour also included five orchestral concerts with the Sydney Symphony and nine performances of Verdi's *Macbeth* at the Sydney Opera House.

His first season as Chief Conductor was again a combination of orchestral programmes and a concert version of Wagner. In Sydney and Melbourne he conducted *Tristan and Isolde* (Rita Hunter and Alberto Remedios), and with the SSO a repertoire that ranged from Mozart to Stravinsky, from Haydn to Mahler's *Des Knaben Wunderhorn* with Birgit Finnilä and Håkan Hagegård as soloists.

By the time he returned to Sydney for the 1983 season he had conducted his own edition of *Semele* at Covent Garden, revivals of *Werther* at the ENO, *Rosenkavalier* and *Jenůfa* in Vienna, and concerts in Rome, Switzerland, London and Leeds, a Handel oratorio, a Mozart Mass, and was beginning to realize that regular flights to and from Sydney might be more demanding than he had anticipated. The four months he spent in Australia in 1983 were interrupted when he flew to Switzerland to conduct *Julius Caesar*, sung in Italian, at the *Grand Théâtre de Genève* with Tatiana Troyanos, a former colleague from Hamburg, as a magnificent Caesar. He returned to Australia, finished the season and moved on to Vienna for *Il Trovatore*. After concerts with the Welsh National Opera he then set out with 40 members of the English Chamber Orchestra for the United States.

It was a punishing itinerary with seventeen concerts in three weeks. The tour began in New York at Carnegie Hall and went on to Washington, Milwaukee, Detroit, Ann Arbor, Chicago, Omaha, Kansas City, Tucson, San Francisco, Los Angeles, Santa Barbara, New York again and Boston. With a concert in a different town almost every evening there was never time for the players to wash clothes or have suits cleaned. Only once, in Chicago, were they not travelling all day with a performance at night. To reach Tucson, Arizona they had to leave Houston, Texas at 7 a.m., fly up to Denver, then down to Phoenix and take a bus to Tucson, arriving there late, to find a new pianist just arrived from New York. He was waiting to rehearse the Mozart concerto for that night and the piano was out of tune.

1970: Charles and Fiona in San Gimignano

Nepal, 1973: the maestro's wife recharges herself

1962: Edinburgh Festival. Shostakovich advises Charles on
conducting his Ninth Symphony

Rome, 1968: Charles and Tatiana Troyanos. Visit of
Hamburg State Opera

1961: Charles rehearsing with Mischa Elman

Behind the scenes with *Tristan*. The dying Tristan (a super); television technician; Birgit Nilsson (Isolde); Patricia Foy, producer; Charles Mackerras, conductor

Left: Number 10 Hamilton Terrace

Below: 1975: Charles and Judy at The Coliseum

Below: Elba: Charles sailing *Emilia Marty* into Zuccale Bay

1984: Charles on Sydney Harbour, Opera House in background

1982: Charles with daughters Fiona and Catherine and grandchildren
Nicholas and Alice

1982: Judy and Charles with their two eldest grandchildren

1985, Australia House: double birthday party for Charles (60) and
Catherine (35). Alice helps cut the cake.

1986: Judy and Charles at 14,000 feet on the continental divide, Colorado, USA

1984: Charles with Janet Baker

Although the orchestra had been given a great reception wherever it went, by the time it reached New York for the final concert at Lincoln Centre, the players were quite worn out and Charles was also exhausted.

The year ended, the next one began in the same frantic way: opera at the ENO, concerts in Prague, Verdi's *Attila* at the Vienna Staatsoper, Australia again, the Edinburgh Festival, *Tosca* at Covent Garden, *Don Giovanni* with the WNO, interspersed with concerts in different parts of the country; and, always ahead, the long flight, the strenuous months in Australia.

To Judy's delight, she and Charles had become grandparents in 1980. When the news came he was at the Paris Opera conducting *Jenůfa* and she was at Hamilton Terrace recording for him an ENO broadcast of *Così fan tutte*. She spent an uneasy evening between telephone and tape recorder till she heard that all was well and a son, Nicholas, had been born to Fiona and Christopher on 11 October. Young Catherine's daughter, Alice, arrived in the summer of 1981 while Charles and Judy were on Elba.

As the children started to walk and talk Charles found them very intriguing. Judy was amused when he remarked naively how strange it was that grandchildren were so much more interesting than one's own children had been; he seemed not to realize why he was more relaxed with them than he had been as an overworked, often worried young father. Grandchildren were not one's responsibility in the same demanding way as daughters, there was not the constant threat of serious interruption to one's work; they had parents to cope if they were naughty or ill and could be sent home at the end of a visit. One saw them by choice, and for as long or short a time as one liked, so could give them full attention and affection.

Nicholas, who was handsome and very intelligent, lived in London and could come easily to Hamilton Terrace; Alice lived in Shropshire and did not see her grandfather so often, yet she had quickly established with him a special rapport rather as her mother had done. Both children had endeared themselves to him by showing definite musical awareness: though Alice was not yet two she could sing in tune and often supply a missing note if he stopped playing, while Nicholas had already shown that he preferred classical music to pop.

Alice had always been a lively and outgoing child but she suddenly began to cause concern. Young Catherine was expecting her second baby when the little girl's pallor and listlessness became so alarming that she was taken to hospital for tests. She was two and three quarter years old when her parents were told that leukaemia had been diagnosed. The date was 23 February, Handel's birthday.

Judy had been preparing for the annual Australian visit but had become so anxious that she had gone to join Catherine and her husband Pete at the Birmingham hospital. She immediately rang Charles and cancelled her flight to Sydney. Charles was in Vienna conducting Verdi's *Attila*, with Nicolai Ghiaurov, Maria Chiara and Piero Cappuccilli. They had given four performances but he at once withdrew from the next and flew home to London. It was the first time in his life that he had allowed anything other than his own serious illness to come before a musical obligation. He was soon to leave for Australia but he rushed to Birmingham to talk to the doctors, to make sure that everything possible should be done and no expense spared. The specialist spent a long time with him explaining the treatment, trying to assure him that in very young children the chance of recovery was high, but Charles was not much comforted; he was going to the other side of the world with little hope of getting back quickly if there were a sudden emergency.

Before leaving for Australia he found time to tape *Peter and the Wolf* and other children's favourites for Alice to amuse her in hospital, and in San Francisco he consulted a specialist about the case and rang Judy to pass on information. For the whole of his Sydney season he was in a state of anxiety. At Balvaig, Neil's daughter Susie came in to look after him and he had the company of Alastair, Elizabeth and Andrew, but he was miserable.

In the past, on long trips, when all went well he was absorbed in his work, or Judy had been with him to discuss and reassure. Now there was no one really to share the anguish of helplessness in quite the same way, no matter how affectionate and understanding others were. He needed to be in constant touch, to hear the news direct, in Judy's voice. The telephone became his lifeline. He rang her in London, Shropshire, Elba when she finally went there for a break. By the time he left Australia the bill for his long-distance calls was so huge that Telecom rang to enquire if it could be a mistake.

A month almost to the day after the bad news Pete Templeton rang to say that Catherine's second daughter, Chloe, had arrived on 24 March. The news about Alice was good, she was responding to treatment, taking it well, apparently unperturbed by hospital or the fact that her hair had fallen out. It would grow again and there was every reason to hope for complete recovery. Nevertheless Charles had been badly shaken: 23 February, which for him had meant only Handel's birthday, now had a new and terrible significance. Not only had little Alice penetrated his protective wall of abstraction, for the first time he had really understood what distance meant. Most Australians grow up to take distance for granted but now he knew how terrible it was to be far away and helpless at such a time, how inadequate telephones and airlines really were.

His original contract with the ABC was about to expire and he had been asked to extend it. For some time he had been undecided. When he accepted the appointment with such enthusiasm he had really believed the arrangement would work; he had not realized the effort, time and exhaustion involved in making the long flights each year, the amount of high-pressure work demanded in a short time, the problems and strain of fitting his European commitments round an annual absence and the fact that he now lived the whole year in winter. When he could have been taking a summer holiday on Elba he was in Australia and when he went home it was winter again and colder than ever. He was uneasy about the future of the orchestra, the philistine attitude to the arts in official circles, the rumours of trouble within the ABC. In England, a four months' absence from the scene each year was too much, people assumed he had gone back to Sydney to live and Judy was often asked how long she would be in London 'this trip'.

He had wanted to go on with his plans for the orchestra, the repertoires he had chosen and worked on; there were also his own family ties. He had hesitated, but the trauma of Alice's illness made him realize what he must do. He did not renew his contract but agreed to return for a season in 1985 and again in 1988, for the Australian bicentenary.

Before leaving the country he conducted members of the Sydney Symphony and the Australian Opera Orchestras in a concert at Sydney University. It took place in the MacLaurin Hall, named after his great-grandfather, and was held to raise funds for the Malcolm Sargent Cancer Fund for Children.

This was not quite the last of his Australian engagements for 1984. He had not been long back in London when the Australian Youth Orchestra arrived for a concert tour of Europe. The players, aged from sixteen to twenty-three, had all made the journey at their own expense. They travelled about, performing at summer festivals and in various cities on the Continent. Sometimes, to advertise their concerts, they played in streets, in market squares, on barges moving down canals, and everywhere people gathered, drawn by the music, the freshness and youth of the players. They made a good impression wherever they appeared and Charles, who conducted them at the

Edinburgh Festival and in London, was enthusiastic about their talent and general excellence.

He conducted their last London concert, a Prom in the Albert Hall. A colossal balloon in the shape of a kangaroo almost as high as the building was anchored outside the main doors and inside, to a crowded house, the Youth Orchestra played the Stravinsky Suite from *Petrushka* and the Strauss Second Horn Concerto, with Barry Tuckwell. At the end of the concerto, as the middle-aged soloist and conductor shook hands Lady Harewood, in the audience, murmured, 'Two little boys playing on the shores of Sydney Harbour.'

XXIII

Producers and Singers

THE WELSH NATIONAL Opera was one of the first companies, outside Sadler's Wells, that Charles had conducted and ever since the 1950's he had taken an interest in its work and often accepted engagements with it. Though small, unstarry and short of money he considers it in many ways the most interesting opera company in Great Britain; and since Brian McMaster became Managing Director it has gone from strength to strength. It engages excellent young singers, has one of the best opera orchestras in the country and a superb chorus, certainly one of the best in the United Kingdom, perhaps even the world. When Charles was invited to become its Musical Director, to start in 1987, he had no hesitation in accepting.

One of the company's most successful productions, which he conducted in March 1981, was *The Greek Passion* by Bohuslav Martinů. Though this composer was Czech he lived much of his life abroad and the opera, which was written in the United States, is in English. The Czech company Supraphon were anxious to record the work, but since they had no English-speaking soloists a group of WNO principals went with Charles to Czechoslovakia during the summer of that year, to make the recording. It was done at Brno, with the Brno Philharmonic Orchestra and the Czech Philharmonia Choir whose members had learnt to sing in English for the occasion. After performing in Beethoven's Ninth Symphony the night before, the choir rose at dawn and came down to Brno from Prague by bus, sang all day, recording the entire chorus parts, then returned in their bus to the capital for a concert that night.

In October 1984, after conducting *Tosca* in September at the Royal Opera House, with the impressive young soprano Mara Zampieri, Charles went to Cardiff for the WNO's new production of *Don Giovanni*. The producer was to be Ruth Berghaus from the (East) Berliner Ensemble, a group noted for its new and original interpretations, particularly of Brecht. Brian McMaster is keenly interested in unusual and innovative stagings of operas and the WNO has engaged more continental producers, mainly from Eastern Europe, than any other British company. The policy has often proved very successful and has brought this provincial company much acclaim in the operatic centres of the world.

It has also caused considerable controversy, which in itself is no bad thing, among those musicians, singers and critics, not to mention the public, who believe that the producer's function is to stage the opera as the composer wrote it and not use the music as a vehicle for some notional 'concept' of his own. From the very beginning there was an uneasy atmosphere of suspicion between Charles and Ruth Berghaus for he had realized from the designs of Marie-Louise Strandt that the production was going to be contrary to all his beliefs about opera production, particularly as they applied to Mozart. Contemporary productions of Brecht's works are not out of place, for he is after all a near contemporary, but with such classical operas as *Don Giovanni* they can be disastrous. In Charles's view, changing or disregarding the meaning of composer and librettist, taking apart the words of the text and introducing symbols for each phrase, detracts from the power of the music (which after all is the main *raison d'être* for opera), and replaces it with the personality, opinions or beliefs of the producer.

Ruth Berghaus used every incident in *Don Giovanni* as an opportunity to present, through the use of symbols, what, in her opinion, was the inner meaning of the opera. For instance, after the Don's attempt to seduce Zerlina the poor girl was obliged to limp for the rest of the opera because on one foot she wore a peasant's clog and on the other an elegant lady's shoe. This symbolized the fact that, though basically a peasant in love with Masetto, whom she was to marry, she also had ambitions above her station and was extremely flattered by Don Giovanni's advances. There were countless other instances of this kind and the production was like a surrealist painting that fitted ill with Mozart's essentially classical music.

After the first night in Cardiff the singers and musicians were cheered by the audience, but producer and designer were heavily booed, an extremely rare occurrence with the WNO in its home city. Reviews praised performers and music, but damned the production; however, after touring in various other cities the opera was taken to London where it was again booed on the first night, though cheered on the second. The London performance was reviewed only by *drama* critics, who praised it highly, and it became a huge success, despite the terrible notices given in Cardiff by the *music* critics. Notorious and controversial performances appear to draw large audiences. It may be that when people cannot understand the language and cannot follow the story they search for something to divert the eye, and end by becoming fascinated by the strange activities invented by the producer.

There have been other equally controversial productions at the WNO, which Charles himself has not conducted, but he was delighted when Brian McMaster's faith in the West German producer, Peter Stein, was vindicated by his magnificent staging of Verdi's *Otello*, which brought unanimous praise from audience and critics of all persuasions. Though so often critical of the domination of producers in opera, Charles found the production a perfect fusion of music and drama.

There is a basic difference in the way conductors and singers see an opera, and the way producers regard it. Conductors and most singers strive to express the composer's meaning while producers are trying to express their own 'concept'. Whereas musicians are concerned with interpretation, producers frequently see opera as a challenge, an opportunity to create something from bare bones, and will often go to incredible lengths to distance their own ideas from the original, sometimes successfully, more often not. In Germany, a country which tends to lead the way in operatic taste, the cult of the experimental producer at first caused great enthusiasm among audiences but is now showing signs of rebounding, with unfortunate consequences where subscriptions and audience attendance are concerned. The difference in attitude between musicians and producers has led to great conflict. In a battle, the strongest wins. If a conductor hopes to succeed he must make sure he is on the same wave-length as his producer, but sometimes, as happened with Berghaus at the WNO, the producer refuses to reveal his concept of a work to the conductor until it is too late to make changes.

Occasionally a producer will err through ignorance; the real culprits are those who are musically knowledgeable but deliberately contradict the composer's wishes. In either case they are now immensely powerful. Most singers are easily overawed and cowed: they do not protest enough when told to sing in impossible or precarious positions on the stage. They have come to regard the producer's word as law. Choruses are often placed in positions where they cannot see the conductor and cannot be heard. Charles, conducting a performance of *Fidelio* in Cologne, was staggered to see the curtain lowered *during* the final chorus, a producer's whim which ruined Beethoven's noble musical climax.

It is not strange that he, who is so concerned with loyalty to composers, should resent what he calls 'the Dictatorship of the Producer'. He cites photographs of Carl Ebert's beautiful and faithful pre-war productions at Glyndebourne as evidence of the increasing wilfulness of the modern producer. He also objects to the present custom of referring to an opera by the producer's name rather than that of the composer: Peter Hall's *Ring* instead of Wagner's, Ponelle's *Macbeth* instead of Verdi's, not to mention Shakespeare's.

When Verdi and Wagner were writing their operas, producers, as we know them now, did not exist. The cast created the production through their acting and singing and any scenic effects required by the stage directions were arranged by the stage manager, usually working with stock scenery and costumes. It is true that in the past, as far back as the Renaissance and Monteverdi, and on through the baroque period and Handel to nineteenth-century grand opera, there was great emphasis on spectacle — magic effects with transformations and exciting happenings on stage — but a producer with a particular concept or theory of an opera's interpretation neither existed nor was thought necessary. This may have been because composers expected performances and productions to be seen for what they were; the more realistic the stage action the better. Wagner, who was more concerned about the correct interpretation of his music than with achieving his almost unobtainable stage effects, nevertheless expected his directions to be followed to the letter, and tailored his music to express what was happening on the stage. In *The Ring* one has only to read a few of his stage directions to realize they are quite beyond achieving, even with all the most modern stage machinery at Bayreuth. The production there of *The Ring* by Sir Peter Hall, which set out to be entirely realistic, seems to have failed partly because so many of the directions could not be carried out.

In the twentieth century much drama production has become less realistic and either more symbolic or impressionistic. A producer favouring the former approach studies the period and setting of the work, then uses symbols to represent scenery and action, even moods, to bring out *his* interpretation of the meaning underlying the author's words. Impressionism in theatrical production no doubt results partly from the impoverished condition of theatres at the end of World War II and the need to find new economical ways of staging without elaborate scenery. Wieland Wagner, the composer's grandson, was a great pioneer of this method. In his productions at Bayreuth he made no attempt to follow his grandfather's instructions, particularly with *The Ring*; impressions of action were achieved with lighting, light and shade used to create illusion rather than realistic effects.

He set the example for many producers, particularly in Germany, and his experiments were the start of the present era in which producers tend to ignore stage directions, even the original meaning of the text, replacing them with a completely new concept. This sometimes succeeds in straight theatre where there are only words to be considered, but in opera the composer has designed his music to evoke a certain atmosphere and, if a producer or designer opposes or ignores it, he produces a contradiction which affects not only the music but the singers who are interpreting it through their roles.

A besetting sin of contemporary operatic production is changing the period either to modern times, or to the period of the composer, something Charles has encountered so often in his career that he begins to wonder if he is ever to see an opera in the setting the composer intended. Ever since Jean-Louis Barrault set Gounod's *Faust* in Gounod's period instead of the Middle Ages (see p. 188) the practice has flooded the opera world, suggesting that producers regard it as wildly original. After suffering it for forty years, Charles feels that the time has come for new ideas.

Rossini's *Moses* set as the Six Day War; Verdi's *Aida* at the time of the Suez Canal opening, or in a modern museum of Egyptology, with the administrator as Radames, and Aida as the office cleaner; Wagner's *Flying Dutchman* set in a Victorian drawing-room with Senta as a Women's Libber; Handel's *Julius Caesar* with Caesar as Ronald Reagan; Tchaikowsky's beautiful romantic music for *Mazeppa* set in a brutal Soviet milieu; *Il trovatore* set during the *Risorgimento* (were witches still burnt at the stake in the nineteenth century?); Busoni's *Doktor Faust* set in the 1920's; Wagner's *Rienzi* in Fascist Italy; Handel's *Xerxes* in Vauxhall Gardens in the eighteenth century; and a mafioso *Rigoletto* set in New York of the 1950's. Strangely enough, these last two were immensely successful with audiences and critics, and Jonathan Miller's mafioso *Rigoletto* was so popular that it was distributed on video all over the world.

It is an interesting fact that many of the most wilful producers can also, when they choose, be faithful to composer and music. David Pountney's productions of the Janáček operas and his film productions of Gilbert and Sullivan hardly prepare one for his extraordinary treatment of *Pelléas and Mélisande*, *The Queen of Spades*, and, above all, Dvořák's *Rusalka*. This fairy tale of a mermaid falling in love with a mortal prince was interpreted as the awakening of a young girl's erotic fantasies and set in a nursery, which completely contradicted Dvořák's atmospheric music, so descriptive of nature and 'Bohemia's meadows and forests'.

Jean Mercure's distortion of *Così fan tutte* at Aix has already been mentioned (see pp. 190–91), as has Lavelli's nineteenth-century *Faust* at the Paris Opéra. Since then Lavelli has gone even further, and his recent production of *Salome* was set in a period after the nuclear holocaust. Strauss's reaction to this may well be imagined; he had been in favour of filming his own ideal productions of his operas to serve as models for future generations.

Charles does not believe that all operas should be produced in the old traditional way and is the first to agree that a too rigid conventional attitude to production leads to stultified and uninteresting performances. After all, the theatre lives on new ideas. His objections are to productions that quarrel with the music rather than enhance it. He is far from being hostile to all producers. In his early days at Sadler's Wells he worked well with Dennis Arundell, who produced the first *Katya*, and he has always regretted that there was not more opportunity to collaborate with him. When, in the 1960's, Charles returned to the Wells as guest conductor there was already a new management and production was mainly in the hands of John Blatchley and Glen Byam Shaw. Two memorable Blatchley-Mackerras operas were *The Makropulos Case* in 1964 and the famous 1965 *Marriage of Figaro*. He also worked very closely with a number of other producers at the Coliseum on some of the company's greatest successes.

He has enormous admiration and respect for the work of John Copley, who was very active with the ENO and at the Royal Opera House. Copley made his début young, in *Peter Grimes*, as the boy apprentice. His operatic experience and his professionalism, his wide understanding of opera make him, in Charles's opinion, one of the most competent of all English producers. Whenever he has engaged Copley he has known that all the characters would be expertly delineated and all their feelings and inter-relationships clearly presented on stage. Operas on which Charles and Copley worked include *Carmen, Traviata, Werther, Julius Caesar, Maria Stuarda* at the ENO, and at Covent Garden, *Così fan tutte, Orfeo, Alceste* and *Semele*.

He has also enjoyed working with John Cox, the present director of Scottish Opera (at one time Director of Productions at Glyndebourne); with Anthony Besch and Colin Graham and, among non-British producers, with Gian-Carlo Menotti, Filippo Sanjust and Claus-Helmut Drese. Such men know their job and fulfil what he regards as essential in opera production: that the composer's music be fully expressed and the plot clearly presented. This is not always easy to do, particularly with opera in a language that the audience does not understand. There may also be ensembles in which all the characters sing different words, expressing different feelings at the same time. In such instances the producer must make it quite clear to the audience what is going on; not only may they be unable to identify and disentangle the individual words of each singer, but quite often singers with the best voices have the worst diction.

Unfortunately, producers whose work Charles and other conductors regard as ideal are frequently the least highly regarded by the public, even by the critics, because their faithful interpretations are not sensational.

One of the most puzzling styles of opera for a producer is the Handelian *opera seria* style which consists entirely of recitatives and arias with almost no ensembles. The problem is knowing how to present such operas, though in fact they are perfectly viable on the stage if treated with imagination. The present interest in the authentic performance of old music has led to a belief that they should be produced as closely as possible to the performance of their own day, but interesting and significant as these experiments are from an historical point of view, they tend not to produce a living theatrical performance.

The Handel Year of 1985, during which Charles conducted five of this composer's operas, offered a good opportunity to see various styles of baroque production. (These performances have been described elsewhere.) The production on which he most enjoyed working and which he considered excellent was *Xerxes*, staged by Nicholas Hytner, with David Fielding as designer; yet Charles had intensely disliked not only Hytner's up-dated *Rienzi*, done for the ENO, and his very un-Brittenish *Turn of the Screw*, but also Fielding's designs for the notorious ENO *Mazeppa* and *Moses*.

Though Charles is looking forward to confronting the difficult marriage of music and drama in his work with the Welsh National Opera, there are times when it does seem to him and to other musicians that the only place where opera is still safe is in the recording studio.

In the past it was not unusual for singers with beautiful voices to have very little musical education; in fact, though this is now far less common among younger artists, there are still a number of famous stars who cannot read music properly.

Lack of musical knowledge in a singer increases difficulties and can lead to disagreements with the conductor, as does a tendency to dwell on high notes, drawing them out to impress the audience. A long high note sung by a great voice may produce a physical thrill for the listener but may interrupt a performance and annoy the singer's colleagues on stage or in the orchestral pit. Another problem, often encountered in Italian artists, is a reluctance to sing out at rehearsal, to save themselves by 'marking' (singing at half-voice) so that it is impossible for the conductor to find the right balance between voices and orchestra. (They assume that he knows by instinct how loud the orchestra should play.) This is particularly frustrating in the operas of such composers as Bellini and Donizetti who tend so to over-orchestrate simple primitive accompaniments that it is very hard for singers to project their voices through the thick orchestral sound.

There is also the Italians' resistance to any changes in the interpretation of a role once they have mastered it. Even if a singer does occasionally agree to try, and masters the changes perfectly at rehearsal, he frequently forgets them at the performance and goes back to his old way. There are honourable exceptions, however. One of the most remarkable and unusual occurred at the Royal Opera House in 1974 during rehearsals for *Otello*. At Covent Garden the great ensemble in Act III is always sung complete but the baritone, Piero Cappuccilli, knew only the cut version. To Charles's astonishment and admiration he agreed to learn the extremely complicated part and did so in one day. On the other hand it is not unknown for famous singers to insist in their contracts that they be not asked to make any changes. Charles has occasionally refused to conduct operas in which these conditions are made.

Singers are often given to rivalry, even in quite humble repertory companies. There are many ways of advancing a career at the expense of colleagues. One very popular method is the 'psychosomatic' illness. Towards the end of rehearsals one of the principals develops throat trouble and at once all attention swings to him or her and away from the rest of the cast. There are concerned enquiries: 'How are you, my dear?' . . . 'Are you any better today?' Everyone wonders if the star will sing or if the cover must be ready. The repetiteur makes special efforts to train the understudy in time. The star, who does not come to rehearsals or if he/she does, does not sing out at all or sings an octave lower, is saving the voice while all the others are singing their heads off. Conductors have to allow 'marking' at rehearsal but modern producers do not spare singers. They demand the artists use their full resources at all rehearsals. By the time of the première most of the cast are too exhausted to do their best, but the star, who has saved his/her voice by 'coasting' through rehearsals or missing them altogether, remains fresh for the performance and gets the best reviews . . . although more often than not critics devote most of their space to the production, the cast having been reduced to hoarse puppets by a megalomaniac producer.

Some singers become very difficult once they achieve success. They ride roughshod over their colleagues, repetiteurs, dressmakers, wigmakers and prop men, regarding them as pawns whose sole purpose is to contribute to their glory. They demand all attention for themselves at rehearsal, become unreliable, walk out of rehearsals, cancel at the last minute or fail to turn up at all.

Yet the singer's time of glory is short compared to the length of a conductor's career. Since Charles began in the opera world he has worked with four or five generations of artists. Most of those who were starting when he was young are now ending their professional lives or have already retired. Too many famous singers overspend their voices; without the right training they are soon finished. Constant travelling in air-conditioned pressurized planes, living in air-conditioned hotels are further hazards for the vocal chords. There are exceptional cases: the most remarkable is Joan Sutherland. She came to London soon after Charles, they worked together in their youth and she is still singing splendidly, long after others have given up. Her voice has lasted because (partly through her husband's tuition) she knows exactly how to treat it, how to use and conserve it. Recently, when she recorded *Norma* with Montserrat Caballé, who started her career ten to fifteen years after Sutherland, she sang everything in one take while Caballé did not find it so straight-forward.

The singer is really the most vulnerable of all musicians. If a violinist loses his violin he can buy another but a singer's instrument cannot be replaced and because it is within the body it is dependent on bodily health. The greatest singer in the world cannot sing at all with laryngitis. Singers are so conscious of this that they often get 'psychosomatic throats' out of sheer nerves. There are, in fact, some great stars who seem to be always indisposed. One famous mezzo invariably cancels the first night, then does all the rest of the performances.

Charles finds it very encouraging that there are now so many good younger singers. In the past, England was never regarded as a country that produced a great number but there is now a most impressive list of young British artists. Apart from good voices, one of their great advantages is their adaptability. They are prepared to be flexible and are musically educated. Among brilliant UK artists Charles has worked with and watched with interest are Thomas Allen, now one of the greatest Mozart baritones in the world; the sopranos Felicity Lott and Valerie Masterson, the mezzos Anne Murray, Anne Howells, Sarah Walker; Handelian and Mozart tenors Anthony Rolf-Johnson and Philip Langridge; basses John Tomlinson and Robert Lloyd; the

Welsh mezzo Della Jones and Welsh sopranos Margaret Price and Anne Evans and the Scottish sopranos Margaret Marshall and Marie McLaughlin.

Because of his interest in Handel's music Charles has probably worked more than most conductors with English counter-tenors (normal male voices trained to sing high in falsetto, often taking castrato roles, a type of singing developed from the Anglican church). He has worked with Alfred Deller and more recently with James Bowman, Paul Esswood and the splendid young singer and actor Christopher Robson.

Australia still produces marvellous young singers. The most recent to succeed in England and to be allowed to remain and work were Yvonne Kenny and Jonathan Summers. It is one of Charles's greatest grievances and frustrations that in 1972 the Home Office made it impossible for young Australian artists to work in the UK unless they have 'patriality', (at least one parent or grandparent born in the country), unlike the days when they were the mainstay of opera at Sadler's Wells and often at Covent Garden.

XXIV

Handel Year

HANDEL YEAR, THE third centenary of the composer's birth, was celebrated in 1985 but for Charles it began in 1984. During the summer the ENO production of *Julius Caesar* was recorded and filmed for video* and in November he went to New York for a concert performance of *Orlando* at Carnegie Hall, with Marilyn Horne, for whom he had prepared an ornamented version, and an Anglo-American cast.

On the composer's birthday, 23 February of the anniversary year, he conducted the first night of *Xerxes*, Handel's only comic opera, at the Coliseum. It had been edited by Charles and Noel Davies and was produced by Nicholas Hytner; the young Irish mezzo, Anne Murray, sang Xerxes, and Valerie Masterson, Romilda, his beloved. This is an extremely difficult work but it was an instant success. Because it was common practice in Handel's time to wear contemporary dress for productions set in earlier periods, Hytner had created a clever eighteenth-century English view of ancient Persia and Persian history, or non-history, which perfectly fitted the concept of baroque opera. Apart from a few quirky touches Charles considered it the most successful Handel production on which he had ever worked.

The critics were as enthusiastic as the public, describing it as a delight from beginning to end, and complimenting singers, orchestra and Hytner's imaginative treatment and witty sets. Of Charles's edition, one critic wrote, 'No praise is too high for his creative coloraturas, cadenzas . . . the light, airy buoyant orchestral texture.' This did not prevent others from commenting on the amount of over-decoration, to Charles's amusement, since there is very little ornamentation in *Xerxes*.

By March he was in Venice rehearsing *Orlando* at La Fenice, again with Marilyn Horne, and a mainly Italian cast. Horne was superb, the beautiful eighteenth-century theatre was perfect, the orchestra

*With Janet Baker, Valerie Masterson, Della Jones, Sarah Walker and James Bowman.

friendly and co-operative. The musicians behaved with surprising discipline during rehearsals and were very receptive to Charles's ideas and suggestions. The producer, Virginio Puecher, created splendid effects, using moving screens for scene-changes in the eighteenth-century manner, and critics and audiences were happy. Charles had found a flat in a palazzo very near the Fenice, with plenty of room for friends and relations to stay, and Judy, for once, had time to explore and enjoy her surroundings.

A beautiful baroque concert was held in San Marco before an enormous audience. Charles conducted the Bach Magnificat and the complete Handel *Water Music* (he referred to the programme as 'a high-water mark' in his career), and though he had been worried about the bad echo at the brief rehearsal, the sound became luminous and clear when the building was packed to the doors, and music and Byzantine splendour merged in perfect harmony.

At the end of the six-week season Charles and Judy spent a fortnight on Elba before she returned to London to prepare for the flight to Australia, and he moved on to Paris to conduct Handel's *Rinaldo*, with Teresa Berganza. 'It is a little bizarre, all these middle-aged ladies playing the parts of legendary heroes originally sung by castrati,' he wrote to a friend. 'But I suppose it's better than not doing Handel opera at all, or worse still, with baritones in the main roles.' He had written decorations for Berganza's arias, which she had learnt perfectly, and great preparations had been made at the Châtelet Theatre for Pier Luigi Pizzi's production.

Unfortunately Berganza mistook the date and arrived in Paris far too early. She was annoyed at being kept waiting for the rest of the cast and when rehearsals began was even more upset to find she was to sing from a high wooden horse. She complained that there were not enough rehearsals and, two weeks before the opening night, she walked out. Since she was well known for cancelling, covers had already been engaged and Eva Podles, a Polish mezzo, took over her role in the first three performances and the Israeli singer, Zehava Gal, in the final one. The critics seemed to find the opera rather dull though they were much taken with Pizzi's production, which was spectacular and original. The singers, in gorgeous costumes, were mounted on chariots, horses and boats and pushed round the stage like great toys.

Judy came over from London for the opening night and spent a week in the flat which Charles had taken in the Marais district. He rehearsed at the Châtelet, flew up to Switzerland to conduct *Belshaz-zar* at the Lausanne Festival, and returned for *Rinaldo* rehearsals and performances. Despite his holiday on Elba he was feeling very tired and run down. Without Judy to look after him he did not bother to cook, and when not dining out ate at small fish restaurants where the food was good but the hygiene perhaps rather suspect. He took his shirts to the *blanchisserie* but washed his smalls and hung them out of the window to dry.

On 21 June he flew to London and left for Australia the same day for his final season as Chief Conductor, Sydney Symphony Orchestra — an absurd situation caused by his accepting a concert with the Orchestre de Paris on 20 June. He was looking forward to conducting a number of important works in Sydney, including Berlioz' *The Damnation of Faust* and since it was Handel Year, the oratorio *Saul* with the Philharmonia Choir. On his way home he was to conduct *Orlando* yet again with Marilyn Horne at the San Francisco Opera.

In London Judy had packed for him and herself and was ready to leave, but on their way to Heathrow discovered her Australian visa had expired. She said goodbye to Charles and went home for a sleep. When Australia House opened after the weekend she renewed her visa and bought herself three pairs of shoes before flying to Sydney. It was the first time for months that she had been able to shop for herself.

Charles had also been shopping: at Singapore airport he had found a smaller-than-ever cassette player with its own built-in copier. When he rang London to announce his safe arrival he asked Judy to be sure to buy him another one at the Singapore duty-free shop; but though pleased to have it he appeared untypically low and depressed, and appalled by his heavy programme. There were to be only five free days in two months of non-stop rehearsals, orchestral and choral performances and he was already exhausted. Leaving the Opera House after his opening concert he was heard to groan, 'And this is just the beginning.'

The next day Judy went down with a short vicious form of influenza that was raging in Sydney. She was far from well when Charles began to feel ill. He conducted his second concert, but half-way through the third he thought he was going to collapse. He was sent to bed with a high temperature and when, after a few days, he turned a bright yellow it was not influenza that was diagnosed but hepatitis, a legacy perhaps of the meals in the little fish restaurants of Paris.

Faced with a six-weeks' illness and a long convalescence he lay in bed feeling miserable. The gloom of his ailment was suicidal enough without the acute disappointment of missing his last season as Chief Conductor and of not completing the works so carefully prepared for the orchestra. People tried to cheer him by saying a forced rest was a blessing in disguise, that he had been overworking for years and at least he was in the best place, in his own house, with Judy to nurse him and his brother and sister nearby, but his depression did not lift.

A dietician/homeopath was found and gradually Charles began to improve. The first sign of recovery was his revived interest in the little cassette player from Singapore. He lay in bed in his headphones and when he was allowed up removed them only for meals. At weekends when Alastair was at home the two brothers spent the day each in his own private world of music.

'Look at them!' said Judy, glad to see Charles returning to normal. 'It's like living with zombies. It's no good speaking to them, you won't get an answer.' A visitor one day waited fifteen minutes to get into Balvaig. Charles and Alastair were both visible through the glass doors but so shut off by their headphones that no one could make them hear.

At the end of six weeks Charles was considered well enough to travel. He was no longer yellow, but was very thin with dark circles under his eyes. He was still in low spirits, further depressed by the plight of music in Sydney, which seemed even worse than during the previous year. The ABC was rent by dissension and muddle, decisions could not be made, musicians were confused and demoralized by their uncertain future. The orchestra was overworked by a system that treated artists like machines. The members rehearsed and performed with no time to rest or recharge themselves, or for conductors to study new music. They frequently played a programme one night, next morning rehearsed quite different works, and the same night repeated the first programme. No allowance was made for the nervous strain of this constant switching of focus; an annual holiday, suitable for office staff, was inadequate for musicians. Many had moved to other States or left the orchestra to work as teachers. The Opera was in disarray and under attack from philistines. There was no shortage of talent, of beautiful voices and good musicians; what was so disheartening and frustrating was the dead hand, the complacent ignorance and provincial mentality of many in positions of power and a largely apathetic public, a section of whom regarded music as an élitist luxury far less important than sport.

By the time Charles left for the USA he was still unsure whether he would be well enough to conduct *Orlando* at San Francisco. He had very little strength or vitality; a farewell visit to the orchestra and a couple of interviews had left him exhausted. On the last day at Balvaig people came to say goodbye while Judy finished the packing. Luggage stood about in the sitting-room, the dining table was littered with cassettes, books, papers, among them Charles's little nylon zip-bag of Lilliputian tools: a tiny hook for tapes that get stuck, a minute tuning fork, a midget screw-driver, microscopic batteries and a miniature jewel-case to hold them.

When the last bag had been closed and sat on, the family gathered upstairs for drinks and dinner: Charles and Judy; Neil, down from the country with his daughter Susie; Graeme Hall, Joan's husband, out from England; Alastair, Elizabeth and Andrew, their son Alex and daughter Gabrielle; a couple of family friends. Dinner was cheerful and noisy with all Mackerrases talking at once. Charles, though very pale and drinking only Perrier, enjoyed himself till he was called to the telephone. It was the Welsh National Opera ringing from Cardiff to talk about work.

Next morning, 16 August, he and Judy flew to Tahiti, arriving, owing to the international date-line, the day before they had left. They spent a week of peace and beauty on Moorea where it was warm enough to swim and paddle about in an outrigger, which they capsized. When they flew on to San Francisco they were both optimistic. They had taken a flat where Judy could cook, for Charles was still on a strict diet; rehearsals and performances went well and reviews for *Orlando* were good. Critics said *Magnificent Marilyn Horne . . . Peerless Marilyn Horne . . . Smashing tunes . . . Imaginative and vivid theatre.* Charles, they wrote, had prepared and conducted a stylish performance that respected Handel by 'honouring the original simple orchestration . . . making only negligible cuts and creating exciting embellishments for the singers.'

He was to stay in California till October for four performances of Handel's *Solomon* but Judy could not be away from home so long. When she flew on to London she felt Charles was well enough to be left though he still tired very easily; but he had been warned to expect this.

He began to rehearse the oratorio with the San Francisco Symphony Orchestra and chorus but instead of feeling stronger with time he found his fatigue increasing and before long had developed a pain in his side which was aggravated when he moved his arms to conduct. He tried to ignore it, dismissing it as another aftermath of his illness, but it persisted and grew so acute that after two performances of *Solomon* he was forced to withdraw and let the chorus-master take over.

He was not well when he flew home in time for the Leeds Festival. As the new Musical Director of the Leeds Philharmonic Society he was to conduct the Beethoven *Missa Solemnis*, for which the Philharmonic Choir was augmented by the Festival Choir, also a Christmas performance of the Handel-Mozart *Messiah*. The Beethoven, with the main rehearsal held on the same day as the performance, proved too strenuous for him, and the pain had become so intense that he knew it could not be a mere post-hepatitis symptom. When it was in fact found to be caused by a hernia he agreed to cancel his engagements and go into hospital the day after his sixtieth birthday.

Ten years earlier he had been upset by Judy's plan to produce *Marsyas*, but for this anniversary he not only co-operated but suggested the form the celebration should take. It was to be a charity concert with a party to follow, and the big reception hall at Australia House had already been booked, caterers engaged, crates of wine ordered and invitations sent out. In all these arrangements Judy had been enormously helped by Morris Barr of the Australian Music Association, Tom Higgins of the ENO orchestra and Sylvia Darley of the Malcolm Sargent Cancer Fund for Children. Charles signed some 200 personal invitations.

The event was a communal effort: everyone in the family helped with preparations. Catherine lettered the programmes in handsome italic script; at rehearsal, Neil's daughter, Judy, put out the music stands and acted as orchestral manager; Tina Briger, Elizabeth's daughter, made tea and Judy supplied refreshments for the players. Fiona and Catherine, with husbands and children, were among the 160 friends, artists and other colleagues who came to the party. Those who could not come sent donations.

It was, Judy said afterwards, like a lovely eighteenth-century musical evening: the programme, the stately marble hall, the elegant guests. Anne Murray, Valerie Masterson, Philip Langridge, John Tomlinson and Christopher Robson sang duets and arias from *Xerxes*, *Orlando*, *Samson*, *Julius Caesar*, *Semele* and *Messiah*, accompanied by about twenty players from the ENO orchestra. (It was said that the rest of the orchestra were hurt at not being included.) Voices and music sounded thrilling and beautiful, Charles was a genial and witty compère-conductor and gave a brief introduction to each of the items. When, at the end of the concert, he invited the audience to supper and told them how much had been raised for the Fund there were cheers and a chorus of *Happy Birthday*, though some friends were concerned that he looked so exhausted by what was, for him, a very light performance.

The caterers had produced an excellent supper from the archaic kitchens under Australia House, splendid Australian wines flowed, old and new friends mingled and people were there from different parts of the world. Watching little Alice eating her way through a large slice of Black Forest cake, and remembering that terrible birthday of Handel's in 1984, Charles and Judy marvelled and were grateful.

'We had an absolutely fabulous evening,' Charles wrote to a friend in Rome. 'All the singers sang magnificently and it was a most nostalgic party as many people hadn't seen each other for many years. We made an overall profit for the charity of nearly £4000.* Grandson Nicholas (5) and granddaughter Alice (4), the latter the main inspiration behind the whole idea, attended and were the life and soul of the party.'

The next day he went into the Humana Hospital Wellington in St John's Wood for his operation. Never one to do things by halves he was found to have not one but three hernias, partly as a consequence of his 1968 emergency appendectomy in Livorno.

When he was wheeled from the theatre after surgery the nurse on duty was astonished to find he was wearing his headphones. In view of his recent hepatitis the doctors had decided to give him an epidural, but this had proved impossible to administer and had been replaced by a general anaesthetic. His Walkman, which he had taken to keep him occupied during the operation under an epidural, had not been turned off and he had drifted away to sleep listening to Rossini's *Stabat Mater*. The hospital was not perturbed by the fact that an unsterile cassette player had invaded the operating theatre, but Charles was incensed to find it had been left on and the battery had run down.

A few weeks later, convalescing at home, he was delighted to find, among his Christmas presents, a compact disc Walkman even smaller and more ingenious than any he had yet seen.

---

*15 per cent of the takings went to the Australian Musical Association, which had been so helpful with arrangements.

XXV

The Maestro at Sixty

SINCE HIS ILLNESS Charles is rather less solid than he was during the last few years; his red hair has faded to sandy-grey but is still curly and plentiful. Though his eyes sometimes look out over half-moon glasses they are as alert as ever. His smile is as cheerful, his voice as far-carrying, his sense of humour as keen and dry. He speaks in an oddly measured, almost formal way but now and then breaks into a very poor imitation of ocker Australian which confuses those who take it seriously.

He dresses well, likes clothes and enjoys shopping for them, but otherwise seems without personal vanity. He describes himself as 'a not very interesting person' and discusses his own shortcomings with the same candour and bluntness he is said to apply to others. He is a *bon vivant*, genial, witty, hospitable, also withdrawn, given to solitary scholarship; his mother's full-blooded enjoyment of life is for ever at odds, in him, with his father's austere obsessive passion for work.

He is heart and soul in the classical eighteenth century yet drawn to nineteenth-century romantics, to the world of opera. He is erudite, has a first-rate intellect yet is credulous, superstitious, fascinated by the occult, the mystical. He is fair game for soothsayers, hypnotists, astrologers, though with a faint sense of shame. Writing to his mother to ask, rather sheepishly, for the exact hour of his birth (needed for casting his horoscope), he reminded her that the early popes relied on priest-astrologers. He has no orthodox religion and sees himself, if anything, as a pantheist with Buddhist leanings. Like Janáček, he cannot believe until he 'sees for himself': only if he could get in touch with Mozart and Handel would he be convinced of survival after death. He is deeply religious in his feeling for music, the source of his spiritual strength.

A Swiss interviewer describes him at sixty as, '*Un être bouillant capable d'irradier cette force qui le conduit d'un continent à l'autre, baguette en poche, pour exprimer la musique . . . l'éclairement d'un art qui fait partie de lui-même . . .*'. Other journalists, he says plaintively, often write of him as 'cheerful' and 'burly', words that imply directness, energy, optimism but also heartiness, bluffness, lack of subtlety, even of depth. The old-fashioned romantic image of the thin, pale, preferably starving and consumptive musician still lingers, though neither Bach nor Gluck was exactly sylphlike, nor was Handel, and one could hardly say their music lacked sensitivity.

Charles is eager to act, yet a hopeless procrastinator. One side of his nature is positive — it is this that responds to Handel's sanity, nobility, honesty, humour, his vitality, as well as his serenity and depth, his 'gorgeous tunes' — yet underneath is a strong Celtic strain of melancholy: the affable manner hides a deep reserve, a shyness and need for privacy. Searching personal questions give him a sense of invasion, an instinct to retreat; there is an inherited resistance to verbal self-revelation, to 'giving away', though he lashes out impulsively in indignation. His father had been like the character who, if he saw emotion approaching, smiled painfully and hoped it would pass, but, unlike Alan, who had become too inhibited to express his emotion, Charles has the outlet of music. Music is safer than speech, which may be misunderstood or laughed at: music allows expression of feelings too deep and fragile to be put into words, and acts as a screen protecting the vulnerable inner being from the world. He is embarrassed by emotional display in public, even by the last night of the Proms when the audience gives itself up to cheerful patriotic fervour. He tries but cannot join in wholeheartedly, covers up with a slight air of tongue-in-cheek which some resent and see as superiority. He explains that it is because he is 'really a rather serious musician' who dislikes turning himself into a variety act, but it is the same self-consciousness that makes him reluctant to speak a foreign language until he has mastered it.

He is said to be abrasive, opinionated, impatient and tactless, also friendly, unpretentious, infectiously enthusiastic, easy-going, generous to those seeking his help in his special fields of music. He spends hours replying to letters from young conductors and patiently answers their questions when they besiege him after a concert. He is said to browbeat and bully singers and players at rehearsal yet to be unequalled in his understanding and consideration for them during performance; to shout at orchestras, lecture them, call the players *you*, yet charged, he is stricken at having caused hurt feelings. (*But can't they understand it's not personal?*) It is said by some artists that he is inhuman, never satisfied, ungrateful, too quick to leap into criticism after performances, too reluctant to praise; yet others who have worked with him have expressed only gratitude, affection and respect. Neil

Warren Smith wrote of him as one of the two conductors he loved most dearly as men, and believed that a less forbidding, more helpful man would be hard to find, while Janet Baker makes no bones about the warmth of her regard for a conductor who treats her like 'a valued ally', 'a respected equal rather than an unintelligent cog in the wheel'.* These singers understand that Charles's one concern is trying to achieve the very best.

He is fascinated by eighteenth-century autograph scores, also by electronic toys; he collects antique musical instruments and the most advanced reproducing equipment, he buys rare editions but also gimmicky do-it-yourself acupuncture kits and home blood-pressure monitors. He loves spending; alone in an airport duty-free shop, with a wallet full of credit cards, he is happily fair game for anyone and is an ideal target for mail-order merchants and shysters, yet in other ways he seems not to care about money, is more concerned with the interest of work than its fee, leaves finances to Judy; even asked her to make out his Will and signed without reading it. In matters concerning music he is independent, self-sufficient, decisive, practical, in other ways he turns to her, as he once turned to Catherine, for advice, support, encouragement; to her intense amusement he once even rang her long-distance to say he could not open his suitcase. He knows nothing about the inside of cars and claims he cannot open a tin, yet he skilfully handles delicate electronic devices. His life has been a tale of success and good fortune yet he often seeks reassurance, though he no longer needs to cover or bolster himself up as he did in his youth. His oldfashioned idea, less arrogant than naive, that an artist's ability should be recognized without distasteful efforts on his part, makes him rather a trial to his manager, S. A. Gorlinsky. What can you do with a maestro who is likely to walk to his hotel after a concert, pulling a little suitcase on wheels, like a child with a wooden horse? He is too honest, has too keen a sense of the ridiculous, is too impatient with pretension to co-operate in self-promotion, an attitude bred in him since birth, and insists that he is a musician, not a showman. For all his ambition he is neither competitive nor ruthless. His manager reproaches him for his unremarkable way of life, would like him to show more newsworthy evidence of his success and plaintively holds up the example of a once-impecunious artist who has moved on from a humble Škoda to a silver Mercedes. It is not enough that Charles could have several silver Mercedes; they need to be seen. Though he revels in the colour, flamboyance and drama of opera, his private life is

*Full Circle.

too stable and normal, too devoid of sensation and theatricality to interest the press; in fact there is really nothing but just getting on with the music, and Judy is not one to try and change her husband. Success and a cosmopolitan life have left her completely unspoilt, her values unimpaired.

There are those who feel diffident about engaging Charles in conversation, who see him as cold and aloof, elusive and hard to know. It is not that he is at all forbidding or unco-operative, but often he has a slightly distrait air. He is willing enough, disarmingly so, yet this very willingness is almost a kind of dismissal: *If I agree nicely to it all they might leave me alone to get on with what's really important.*

'Charlie! You're not listening!' his mother would say, exasperated by glazed eyes and absent expression.

'Yes I am, I am. I heard every word.'

'You did not! I can tell. You're *conducting!*'

This abstraction is baffling, frustrating because it is difficult to know how to cope with it. No matter how friendly, it is hard to get through to someone who is not there. You are not cut off or asked to shut up, but though outwardly he remains courteous he is not with you. He replies to questions in an absent way or seems to 'come back', recalled from his private world, yet because of an amiable disposition he shows no resentment. In these moments even his normally quick response to humour is slightly uncertain; he is eager to laugh though in fact he really has not heard the joke. Sometimes while answering a question it seems that a section of his mind has detached itself and wandered away from the part that is talking. Pauses occur, speech slows and grows less incisive; he hesitates over words or draws them out as though almost forgetting what comes next. Unconsciously he may repeat himself; then he either snaps out of it and goes on more briskly or begins to look restive.

'Yes, yes . . .' biting the end of his glasses, his mind on the tape he is copying in the next room. There is a faint click; he gets up looking worried and vanishes. To protests he replies with mild surprise, 'Yes, but you see I have to fix this tape . . .' He returns and continues the conversation, again very ready to co-operate and again after a few minutes there is the distrait air, the listening, the sound of the click . . . 'Excuse me . . . I must just . . .' Or politely, even apologetically but with underlying determination, 'I wonder would you mind frightfully if we continued this some other time . . . there's something I have to do now.' It is said with such compunction but also such certain expectation of agreement that one cannot object and may even feel slightly guilty. This is infuriating when it occurs in the middle of an important or interesting or even convivial conversation.

He is an interpreter not a creator, a performer not a contemplative; his absorption is not a poetic dreaminess, it is total and has been responsible for much of the tactlessness and apparent lack of appreciation of which he is sometimes accused. In the same way the abrasiveness, impatience and ill-timed criticism that have caused offence derive from his dedication to truth in music. Since the days when, as a little boy, he went through *Messiah* to see that it had been correctly played he has spoken up in defence of music if he feels it has not been properly served. One could say that he has never really bridged the gap between music and ordinary living; circumstances have protected him from life and, in a sense, he has never grown up. He has never had to struggle, never had to make sacrifices, has always been allowed to put music first, to let it stand between him and people. He has more than once been declared 'the most selfish man I ever met'; he describes himself as self-centred, yet no true egoist could so faithfully serve others as he dedicates himself to the composers he reveres. The centre is not the ego but the Cause with which he is so identified that he and it have become one. It was said of Mahler that he was utterly self-centred yet never thought of himself, only his work. The same might be said of Charles.

'He thinks of nothing but music,' says Judy. 'He eats, sleeps, breathes music; it is his whole life. It's the thing he loves best in the world.' If this is accepted his life and behaviour make sense, otherwise there will be misunderstanding, hurt feelings and constant exasperation. He is well aware of his good fortune in having a wife intelligent enough to understand and generous enough to make allowances.

As an individual he has mellowed with age; those who share his life behind the scenes know him as affectionate, compassionate, vulnerable and lovable, yet sometimes he says glumly that he has no friends. There are plenty of colleagues, acquaintances, good companions shared with Judy but, apart from her, no one like the two Richards.* Yet the Richards were exceptional, they not only shared his obsession with music, they were part of his early life, they grew up with him and were almost like family for whom no effort needed be made. He has moved too quickly for others to know him well or for him to know them, even to know himself. He is aware of this, it disturbs him; he means to do something about it, to give time to cultivating friends, to finding out who he is, to serious thought; yet he still lets his diary fill up for years ahead.

*Both Richard Farrell and Richard Merewether were killed in accidents.

Judy recharges herself and finds solace in music, through contact with nature, the mountains, the countryside; for him, music is still too closely connected with work and though, like his father, his feeling for nature is expressed in his love of the sea he rarely gives himself time to enjoy it. It is a question of time rather than lack of interest, there is never time to watch, to contemplate what is going on around him. On Elba, idle for once, with time to spare he astonished his friends by growing absorbed in a family of fly-catchers that had nested out on the terrace over a group of lights. He declared the switch out of bounds lest the heat became too much for the eggs, then the baby birds, and when they hatched he spent hours watching them through binoculars, completely fascinated. He called them A, B and C and showed great concern about C who was rather weak and did not get enough to eat. Such apparently uncharacteristic behaviour could never have occurred in the course of his normal life.

'Charlie is wild,' says his sister Elizabeth. 'He's not like the rest of the family.' She is not referring to the wildness of his early days, she means the restless spirit; yet after 40 years of marriage Judy can say, 'He really is the most peaceable, even-tempered man, particularly when one considers the strains he puts on himself.' In fact, like most human beings he is a mass of contradictions.

One of the strangest is that someone so essentially easy-going should always have been so driven. On Elba, if asked, he goes, cheerfully obedient, down to the village with his shopping list and instructions; at home, when not submerged in work, he wanders about like an absent-minded professor, exuding good-natured vagueness, headphones on ears, half-glasses on nose, patent pencils strung round his neck like crucifixes. Interrupted in listening to tapes or discs he shows no resentment or irritation, is almost apologetic as he turns in his chair and lifts an earphone to hear what is said. Called to meals he may say, 'Good, but I must just finish this . . .' and put back the earphone but if it is made clear that he must come *now* he switches off and comes downstairs with no sign of annoyance.

Yet the life of this peace-loving man who never fights has been dominated by ceaseless, even aggressive action. Whenever the forward movement has paused there has been restlessness, dissatisfaction. Perhaps it derives from a conflict between ambitious nature and restraining upbringing, perhaps from far-back strains of Slav and Jew mixed with Celt. Whatever the cause it is the grain of sand in the oyster and will never leave him in peace; he will never willingly retire. Like Ulysses he must always go on exploring, further into music, led by something just out of sight. ★

'I would like to urge any young musician who contemplates this most arduous and responsible of careers to make his watchwords *integrity* and *sincerity* (to yourself) and *loyalty* (to the man whose music you are seeking to interpret). Never think, "What can I *make* of this piece," but try to discover what the composer meant to say. . . . Performances that are made merely a vehicle for indulging the vanity of a personality, however talented that personality, can only lead us away from that which should be the goal of all true musicians: Service to that great art which it is our privilege to serve.'

These words of Sir John Barbirolli also express the aims and ideals of Charles Mackerras.

ENVOI

Just before going to print the very sad news came that Sir Charles's lovely grand-daughter, Alice, who has featured a lot in this book, died on 19 June 1987 following a relapse of leukemia earlier in the year.

APPENDICES

by

CHARLES MACKERRAS

APPENDIX I

*The Appoggiatura**

As HAS BEEN told by Nancy Phelan, my interest in reviving more authentic performance practices in eighteenth-century music started in the 1950's when I studied early Mozartian sources in Donaueschingen and conducted concerts, putting some of my ideas into practice.

I also wrote articles for various musical magazines, some of which are reprinted here. These days, when so many of my recommendations *are* practised, it should not be forgotten that in the 1950's and 60's the use of the appoggiatura was absolutely exceptional and ornamentation not practised at all. I have had second thoughts on some of the opinions expressed in the following pages. In certain matters I have become more moderate, in others more radical.

★

Among all the embellishments in the Art of Singing, there is none so easy for the Master to teach, or less difficult for the Scholar to learn, than the *Appoggiatura*. This, besides its Beauty, has obtained the sole privilege of being heard often without tiring, provided it does not go beyond the Limits prescrib'd by Professors of good Taste.

Pier Francesco Tosi (1646–1732)
(1752 English translation by J. E. Galliard)

More† and more often, and particularly during the past year or so, critics in *Opera* and elsewhere have castigated conductors for neglecting, or omitting or being inconsistent in, the use of *appoggiature* in their performances of older operas. The public has every right to be bewildered, since the matter is not usually argued but stated dogmatically. Properly, however, the subject demands patient historical elucidation and the weighing of evidence.

*Reprinted from *Opera*, Oct. 1963 and *Records & Recording*, Feb. 1965 from † onwards.

The definition of the term provides an initial stumbling block. Every home pianist knows the appoggiatura as it occurs, for example, at the beginning of Mozart's *Rondo alla turca* and in countless other compositions of the period: an auxiliary note printed in smaller type which takes half the value of the following main note. The instrumental appoggiatura is thus a written convention which the performer has to learn only to recognize at sight and to interpret. The vocal appoggiatura, however, on which the current controversy turns, only occasionally took written form; at other times it had to be supplied by the performer, who replaced a written note of the composer's by a different note. In doing so, he was not defying or improving on the composer but doing what the composer himself expected and intended. As a simple illustration, in Act IV of *Le Nozze di Figaro*, the final syllables of recitative (accent on the *con*) before Susanna's aria were written as Example 1a but sung as Example 1b.

Ex. 1

Yet performances today mistakenly often give us Example 1a instead. How has this practice arisen? Composers of the last 100 years or so have written their music exactly as it is to be performed and conductors and repetiteurs all over the operatic world have drummed into singers that they are interpreting the composer's wishes only if they sing his works exactly as written. Performers are now so conditioned to this exactness that they tend to apply the principle to all music. Because Wagner, Strauss, Puccini and Britten write precisely, they expect the same of Mozart, Beethoven and Handel. Thus a number of unwritten traditions in opera have become thrown out or forgotten. Conductors, anxious to expunge all the excessive ornamentation in which nineteenth-century singers indulged, threw out the baby with the bath-water and got rid of the appoggiatura as well, forgetting that it is not just an optional embellishment but forms an essential part of the melodic style of all vocal music of the eighteenth and early nineteenth centuries, particularly the recitatives.

Appoggiaturas gave graceful and natural expression to words of more than one syllable, making song imitate the natural intonation

and flow of speech. Instructive works of music, for example C. P. E.
Bach's celebrated treatise (1753) on clavier-playing, treat the appog-
giatura as an essential of musical language. The treatise by the famous
Italian castrato, Pier Franceso Tosi (1646–1732), as translated into
English (1752) by the composer J. E. Galliard, contains the following:

> Appoggiatura as a word to which the *English* Language has not an
> Equivalent; it is a Note added by the Singer, for the arriving more
> gracefully to the following Note, either in rising or falling. . . . The
> Word *Appoggiatura* is derived from *Appoggiare*, to lean on. In this
> Sense, you lean on the first to arrive at the Note intended, rising or
> falling; and you dwell longer on the Preparation, than the Note for
> which the Preparation is made, and according to the Value of the
> Note.

The appoggiatura as an expressive device — a strong syllable as a
discord, falling (or, less often, rising) to a weak syllable as a concord —
was part of the musical language of opera for about two hundred years
and was used by every vocal composer from Purcell to Wagner (for
example in Wolfram's two arias in *Tannhäuser*) and in Italian opera
even later: many may be found in the Prologue to *Pagliacci* (1892). But
whereas Verdi, Wagner and later composers wrote out their vocal
appoggiaturas, Mozart, Handel and Rossini did *not*.

The modern performer, however, need not be in any doubt as to the
correct performance of these unwritten appoggiaturas. Contemporary sources give detailed instructions as to how and when they are to
be sung. It is interesting that *all* authors agree that appoggiaturas are
essential, though conventions of performance and notation undergo
historical changes. Let us begin with the period of Handel. Tosi, in the
treatise already quoted, gave an extremely detailed description of
every case in which the appoggiatura may be used, and then attacked
composers who even at that time tried to limit the scope of the singer
by writing out the appoggiatura in full:

> If the Scholar be well instructed in this, the *Appoggiatura*'s [sic] will
> become so familiar to him by continual Practice, that by the Time
> he has come out of his first Lessons, he will laugh at those
> Composers that mark them, with a Design either to be thought
> Modern, or to shew that they understand the Art of Singing better
> than the Singers. . . . Poor *Italy!* pray tell me; do not the Singers
> now-a-days know where the *Appoggiatura's* are to be made, unless
> they are pointed at with a Finger?

Another teacher of the Italian style, Giambattista Mancini, re-marked in his *Riflessioni pratiche sul canto* (1774 edition):

> All the excellence of the recitative depends on the knowledge of the proper use of the appoggiatura, or the musical accent, as it is generally called. This precious accent, in which is contained all the grace of a *cantilena*, consists, in short, of one note a tone higher than that written, and this is practised especially when a word of several syllables is written with notes of the same pitch.

In 1757 J. F. Agricola, a pupil of Bach, published a German translation of Tosi's treatise, in which he added several illuminating passages of his own. After giving his own explanation of the need for appoggiaturas, such as a better joining of the notes, and giving the melody more vivacity, he remarks that certain notes in recitatives are always changed and gives the following examples:

Ex. 2

It will be noticed that not only 'feminine endings' (i.e. a strong followed by weak syllable, as in Ex. 2a) but also masculine endings (i.e. a strong final syllable, as in Ex. 2b) were made to receive an appoggiatura. Agricola also gives several examples of embellished recitative-endings in which the appoggiaturas become even more complicated.

In the earlier part of the eighteenth century, appoggiaturas could be placed in almost any degree above or below the main note, but as time went on music tended to settle down to the more or less stereotyped appoggiatura starting from above. Two famous violinists of the eighteenth century, Leopold Mozart and Tartini, both condemned upward appoggiaturas as unnatural and not in accordance with musical grammar. Such upward appoggiaturas, nevertheless continued to be sung and played, but were less frequent than the descending variety. In the works of composers who wrote out most of their appoggiaturas, such as Cimarosa,* Bellini and Verdi, there are about ten times as many descending appoggiaturas as ascending.

It was not only in the Italian style that appoggiaturas were widely used. In 1725 Telemann published a number of cantatas under the title *Harmonischer Gottesdienst* and in the preface gave precise instructions about appoggiaturas. Not only does he show how to sing conventional recitative cadences, which exactly correspond to the examples of Agricola and others, but he actually writes out a passage from his own work, in which not only is every ending both masculine and feminine notated with appoggiaturas, but all intermediate two-syllable words as well.

Ex. 3

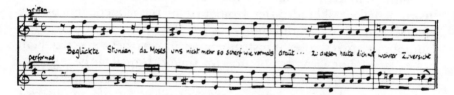

This melody is typical of the German religious recitative and strongly resembles many recitatives and arioso passages in Bach's Cantatas and Passions, which should probably be sung in this manner. Bach only occasionally notates appoggiaturas as they are to be performed; Handel never does. When all Bach and Handel's contemporaries agree on the necessity of performing appoggiaturas, though unwritten, and on their interpretation, can anyone today imagine that these two great men considered themselves outside the conventions of their time?

Teachers and composers who have written on this subject never say that appoggiaturas *may* be sung at will, but only that they *are* or *must*. For instance Vincenzo Manfredini in his *Regole armoniche* put the matter quite plainly:

Whereas an instrumentalist is not strictly required to perform appoggiaturas not indicated by the composer, this is not the same

*In the Ricordi edition of Cimarosa's *Il Matrimonio segreto* there are 695 appoggiaturas in the recitatives alone; in Bellini's *Norma* about 500. In both the above-mentioned operas, the incidence of appoggiaturas is over 99 per cent of all possible.

for the singer, who (especially in recitative) whenever he sees two notes of the same value and pitch, must consider the first of these as an appoggiatura from above; that is, particularly on a strong beat, he must perform it a tone or a semitone higher, according to the key in which the notes are written.

Manfredini goes on to discuss the treatment of such Italian words as *mai* and *Dei*: 'Poets sometimes treat these as monosyllables and therefore composers set them as one single note. Notwithstanding this, the singer must always treat them as disyllables and sing them with an appoggiatura from above, as already described.' This, written in 1775, the year of Mozart's *La finta giardiniera*, leaves no room for doubt that appoggiaturas were regarded as part of the musical language — not merely, as some modern singers like to suppose, only at choice in order to heighten the expression of certain words.

Manfredini seems to suggest that the treatment of grace notes by instrumentalists should differ from that of the singer, and by the second half of the eighteenth century this was indeed the case. Composers often wrote for instruments exactly as they expected them to be played, but accurate notation for singers lagged far behind. No doubt, an accurate system of notation was less urgent for singers, who learned their roles from memory under the direction of composer or Kapellmeister, than for the orchestral player, who was continually reading his part without memorizing. But it seems that musical notation had become a hopeless muddle about the time when Mozart, Haydn, and the young Beethoven were composing.

Domenico Corri (1746–1825), an Italian singing-teacher who emigrated to England, complains bitterly:

When a person has purchased a book, would it not appear very extraordinary, if he should be under the necessity of applying to a master of language to correct the orthography, and to distinguish the members of every sentence by proper stops, in order to render the author's meaning intelligible? Just such an absurdity appears in written music, vocal music in particular; for, notwithstanding the many alterations that are daily making, the manner of noting it, which remains nearly the same as it was in the infancy of the art, is quite insufficient to express the meaning, spirit, and peculiar delicacy of the composition.

Later he writes:

We do find our mode of noting, not only deficient but erroneous, for . . . such a mode of noting has been used, as might necessarily lead the singer if guided by it alone, into positive error. . . . Indeed, either an air or a recitative sung exactly as it is commonly noted, would be a very inexpressive, nay uncouth performance; for not only the respective duration of the notes is scarcely hinted at, but one note is frequently marked instead of another, as is the case when a note is repeated, instead of that note with its proper appoggiatura or grace . . . in consequence of which the singer is misled, by being made to sing a wrong note.

Corri gives precise examples of the use of appoggiaturas. Here is one from Gluck's *Orfeo*:

Ex. 4

Urbani, another eighteenth-century Italian singing teacher, who published *The Singer's Guide* in London, gives these examples (this time in the English language.

Ex. 5

Example of Comic Recc.ᵗᵒ

Ex. 6

Example of Sacred Recc.ᵗᵒ Accompanied.

It will be noticed from these examples that some people added appoggiaturas also to words of *one* syllable and even to the *first* word of a phrase, as well as to the intermediary and final words. These kinds of appoggiaturas went out of fashion earlier than the downward two-syllable variety, which became the general rule at the ends of phrases in vocal music.

The practice extended right into the nineteenth century. Perhaps the most interesting link with earlier tradition is Manuel Garcia's *Traité complet de l'art du chant* (1847), which contains page after page on the proper use of the appoggiatura. Garcia, let it be remembered, was the son of the tenor who was Rossini's first Almaviva, and his sisters were Pauline Viardot and Maria Malibran, so he was in a position to span the practice of singing from Mozart to Donizetti. He wrote (translation by Ross Reimueller, who has given particular study to this question):

> The appoggiatura is also found in recitatives, not as an ornament, but as an elevation of the voice for the purpose of expressing the tonic accent of two and three-syllable words followed by a rest. This elevation always occurs on the first of the two or three equal notes, depending on the type of word involved. Within a phrase one often fills out the appoggiatura with a prolongation of sound. In the latter case the stressed syllable should have at least double the value of the shorter syllables . . .
>
> Two repeated notes followed by a rest are never sung as written. In the serious recitative, just as in those of comic nature, the necessity of accentuation demands that one change the first of the two notes into an appoggiatura from above or below, according to the dictates of good taste. In fact, if one were to sing scrupulously, note for note, the recitative which begins the scene 'Sposa! Euridice!' from *Orfeo** or Donna Anna with her dying father, or the scene of Sara, 'Chi per pietà mi dice', from *Il Sacrificio d'Abramo* these three masterpieces of declamation would become unbearable at the end of several bars . . .

It was also felt that the French language with its even accentuation required the appoggiatura less often than the Italian in which the difference between strong and weak syllables is much more marked. This is mentioned by Lablache and Garcia, although French recitatives (e.g. Guiraud's for Bizet's *Carmen*) show appoggiaturas on most phrase-ends. In the Italian language, though, *all* writers are in agreement about the use of the appoggiatura at the end of a phrase.

Garcia says: 'In Italian vocal music, the appoggiatura can hardly be considered an ornament, for it is required by the prosodical accent.'

Or again, Sieber, mid-nineteenth century: 'The appoggiaturas in recitative are of special significance; they must always be introduced

*q.v. Corri's Ex. 4.

whenever two repeated notes are followed by a rest — even if the composer did not write them. It then remains to the singer to decide whether the appoggiatura should be made from above or from below. The former is more common — the latter imparts a particular emphasis.'

Mannstein in his *Grosse Italienische Gesangschule* (1848): 'But even where the melody has been more richly filled out by the composer, one usually finds only harmonic tones on the strong beats of cadences. The singer must alter the first of these by raising it a half or a whole-tone, a third, or a fourth etc.'

Peter Lichtenthal in his *Dizionario* (1826): 'The appoggiatura from above is the most frequently used ornament and is indispensable in recitatives. It serves to decrease the severity of certain intervals, such as the descending third. The Italian school has made the singers so familiar with these appoggiaturas that composers refrain from notating them in the recitatives.'

These examples can be used as models for the correct performance of similar passages in the works of composers such as Mozart, Rossini and Donizetti, who only notated the appoggiaturas when they wanted to make sure of them being performed in a certain way.

But *why* — the modern performer or listener may reasonably ask — did composers write one thing if they meant another? The main reason is probably that the extra note of the appoggiatura is often grammatically 'wrong' (forming an unprepared discord) according to the old rules of harmony, and composers preferred to write 'correctly' even though the performance would have departed from 'correctness'. A second reason is practical: an accompanying continuo-player would find it difficult to choose the right chords when faced with a note 'foreign' to the chord at every change of harmony. I know from experience that it is easier to accompany *secco* recitatives from appoggiatura-less 'Urtext' editions than from certain modern ones where the appoggiaturas have been printed at their true pitch. When the practice of continuo became extinct, composers soon took to writing out the appoggiaturas.

A third reason for inaccuracy in notation is mentioned in Leopold Mozart's *Treatise on the Fundamentals of Violin Playing*, 1756 (English translation by E. Knocker, OUP):

It is true that all the descending appoggiaturas could be set down in large print and divided up within the bar. But if a violinist, who knows not that the appoggiatura is written out, or who is already accustomed to befrill every note, happens on such, how will it fare with melody as well as with harmony? I will wager that such a violinist will add yet another long appoggiatura. . . .

This dictum would apply even more to singers than to players. At all events we know that the anomaly existed, and that many musicians found it annoying and strove to devise a more accurate way of writing music. From the second half of the eighteenth century onwards we find composers trying to be more accurate, but none were consistent and they all chose different ways of attaining the same end. Even the most accurate composers often slip back into the old traditional notation. Verdi, who in his fair copies always wrote everything exactly, used the old convention in his sketches. (In Rigoletto, for example, at least two recitatives are sketched in the old manner, with appoggiaturas not written out but left as if the singer would put them in.) He was the first Italian composer of distinction to write out appoggiaturas in normal-sized notes. In Verdi, appoggiaturas on disyllabic words are in the overwhelming majority. For instance, out of several hundred feminine endings in the last act of *La Traviata*, fewer than ten are treated as repeated notes (most of these during Violetta's last dying utterances); the others have the initial note altered, making an appoggiatura. To Verdi, a lack of appoggiaturas always suggests something sinister, and during a conspiratorial recitative between Sparafucile and Rigoletto he goes so far as to write expressly that 'This recitative should be sung without the *usual* appoggiaturas' (my italics). This is to prevent singers automatically translating Verdi's simple notes on the chord of D major into the customary appoggiatura-ornamented recitatives. Even in as late an opera as *Otello*, Verdi writes *senza appoggiature* over one passage.

There were authors on singing who protested against over-ornamentation, but their strictures apply not to appoggiaturas, which all agree are demanded by the natural accent, but to the practice of introducing a cadenza or flourish on any word, however unsuitable. Verdi gives us an example of the *tasteful* use of such a flourish in *La Traviata*, in Violetta's famous recitative. The flourish is, suitably, on the word *gioia* and the phrase ends with an ordinary appoggiatura:

Ex. 7

I think we would all agree that Mozart was the greatest operatic composer of his time. The fact that his melodies have such a distinctive quality sometimes creates doubt as to whether we should regard them as so untypical and in advance of most eighteenth-century writing as to ignore the contemporary practice of ornamentation.

Musicians of Mozart's time treated his music like that of any other composer. Arrangements of his operas for piano, wind band, string quartet etc., all show that the convention of the appoggiatura applied as much to his music as to anyone else's. Two examples taken from early piano arrangements of *Figaro* show appoggiaturas added (marked with a cross), in places where Mozart himself did *not* write them:

Ex. 8

These and hundreds of similar examples go to show that, whether he was in full agreement or not, this was the way his music was performed. In most eighteenth-century operatic arrangements of his works one finds very few ornaments *other* than appoggiaturas and these are used only where one would expect, i.e., just where the authors on vocal interpretation agree they should be.

It has been suggested that in *Don Giovanni*, Donna Anna's aria expresses more vigour and determination if the word 'l'onore' is sung *without* appoggiatura,* but Kuchař (see page 284), who played in the very first performances of the opera, wrote out the aria like this:

*See Garcia's remarks on this aria (page 263).

Ex. 9

(The observant will notice a copyist's error in bar 1.) Presumably the appoggiaturas in bars 3 and 5 are intended to be performed in the manner described by Haydn, viz. — that the three notes

are to be sung as   and not

This confusing convention of notation meant that when Mozart *wanted* the three notes actually sung he was obliged to write them out, as in the aria 'Ah, lo veggio', from *Così fan tutte*:

Ex. 10

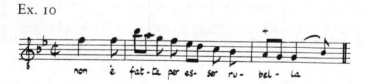

non è fat-ta per es- ser ru- bel- la

In general he follows the principle of only notating the appoggiatura when it would give rise to misinterpretation. In the Agnus Dei of the *Coronation Mass* (which is substantially the same melody as 'Dove sono' in *Figaro*), his embellishments were spelt out for an inexperienced singer; and in *The Magic Flute*, in Pamina's 'Ach, ich fühl's' there are so many different kinds of appoggiaturas on both one and two syllable words, upward and downward, single and double that he had to write them all out if he wanted to make sure the aria would be sung exactly as he imagined it. The single word 'Sehnen' ('longing') is treated with three different kinds of appoggiaturas, none of them the conventional one. Indeed, the part of Pamina throughout the opera has the appoggiaturas written out — perhaps because Mozart knew the part was to be sung by a seventeen-year-old girl. The other principal parts in *The Magic Flute* are mostly left to be treated in the conventional way. Surely it is not logical or musical for only one part to be sung with appoggiaturas?

Although Mozart never wrote any instructions on the use of appoggiaturas, we do find him carefully notating them whenever he wanted to show a particular singer the true method of interpretation.

Here are parts of his aria 'Non so d'onde viene', K. 294, as he wrote it first and as he embellished it later for his beloved Aloysia Weber. (The embellished autograph is in the City Archives, Brunswick.) In the examples the original version appears above and Mozart's own performing version underneath. Every ending has an appoggiatura inserted:

Ex. 11

Ex. 12

Although Mozart wrote out so few appoggiaturas in full, obviously singers should insert them after the above model.

In general he wrote out appoggiaturas in big or small notes when he felt that there might be some doubt as to the *kind* of appoggiatura to be employed. He wrote out the appoggiatura, for example, in this

passage from *Don Giovanni* (sung by Don Giovanni himself), in order
to avoid an equally possible but, here, undesired interpretation, or
even the omission of the appoggiatura altogether.

Ex. 13

Unlike his predecessors, Mozart also always wrote the appoggiatura of the descending fourth in normal-sized notation. Haydn did
not, however, as the following examples, respectively from *Don
Giovanni* and Haydn's *Scena di Berenice* show:

Ex. 14

Otherwise Mozart leaves it to the singer, whom he presumes will have
the education to know the traditions. If he *had* wanted to go against
tradition and leave out the appoggiaturas, he would have had to make
this obvious, but nowhere in the whole of Mozart's known correspondence does he ever mention it. I feel that he expected his music to
be performed according to the accepted conventions of his time. He
frequently supervised performances of his operas and could give direct
verbal instructions. Would that we had a recording of one of his
rehearsals!

The *secco* recitatives in Mozart surely provide no doubt at all as to
performance. Their shape is extremely similar to those of other
eighteenth-century composers, such as Cimarosa, in whose published
works the appoggiaturas are written out. They should certainly be

performed with appoggiaturas in accordance with the examples given here. As regards the dramatic, orchestral, recitatives, there are many instrumental arrangements pointing to the current interpretation of Mozart's time.

Selections from Mozart's popular operas were made for various combinations of instruments during his lifetime. As instrumentalists did not adopt the convention of the unwritten appoggiatura, these had to be written out for them, and they give us a perfect picture of the procedure of the period. Take for example, an arrangement by Kuchař of *Don Giovanni* for string quartet. The copy is in the Prague National Museum.

Ex. 15

Such parallels may be found over and over again, and comparison of the un-literal vocal part with the exactly notated instrumental part can often reveal composers' intentions. In *Così fan tutte* we may note a passage from the opening trio where instruments and voices obviously should proceed in unison but the vocal part at the word 'spada' still follows the old tradition.

Ex. 16

The same case occurs in Fiordiligi's aria 'Per pietà' at the words 'mancò di fede'.

There is yet another convention of notation which composers adopted towards the end of the eighteenth century, in an attempt at greater clarity, when writing the appoggiatura as a *small note*. From H. C. Robbins Landon's collected Haydn correspondence we learn of Haydn's instructions to a monastery about the interpretation of his *Applausus* cantata: he sets out the correct and incorrect interpretations of a certain passage, as follows:

Ex. 17

This valuable piece of information shows us exactly how to interpret hundreds of identical cases, of which I quote a few well-known examples, showing the original, the suggested interpretation, the incorrect interpretation and, where relevant, the accompaniment.

Ex. 18   Ex. 19

Ex. 20   Ex. 21

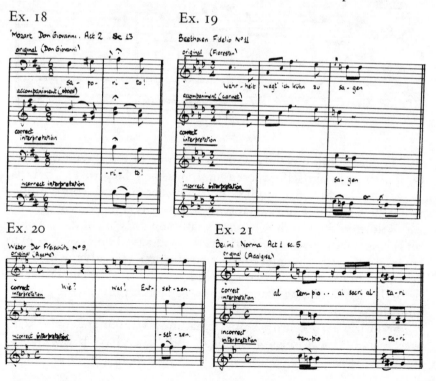

A familiar example from a Schubert song is at the words 'Er hat den Knaben' in *Erlkönig*. Of all the ways of writing the appoggiatura, this one (with the small note) is the most often misinterpreted. Schubert and Beethoven come in for the worst treatment, simply because interpreters feel such reverence for their works that they dare not change a single note, even when demanded by tradition. Beethoven is inconsistent, sometimes writing the appoggiatura out fully, in normal-sized notes as in Ex. 13 below, sometimes in small notes as in the example from Florestan's aria (Ex. 21 above), and sometimes not indicating them at all. Beethoven was composing at a time when notational conventions were in flux and he even adopts several methods in the course of one piece. In Leonore's aria it is inconceivable that an appoggiatura should be sung only *once* (as written) out of four times on, of all words, 'Liebe'! All four points should properly receive their appoggiaturas. In Florestan's great recitative, appoggiaturas are rarely sung in modern performances, but they are positively demanded by good taste in the following two cases:

Ex. 22

Ex. 22 corresponds exactly with an example of interpretation given by Beethoven himself (quoted in Ignaz von Siegfried's analysis, 1832, of Beethoven's studies in counterpoint and composition) where he wrote out such an appoggiatura. It is equally clear that the bass soloist in the Ninth Symphony, at the words 'nicht diese Töne!' must sing a falling appoggiatura (not two identical notes on Töne) to correspond with the preceding instrumental recitative where the appoggiatura is fully written out. Indeed any musical singer would naturally use an appoggiatura here were he not prevented by ignorant prima donna conductors!

For nearly two centuries appoggiaturas, written and unwritten, were part of vocal musical language. Why then have performances with unwritten appoggiaturas been so rare in recent times? From about the end of the nineteenth century, the 'prima donna' conductor sought ascendancy over the 'prima donna' type of singer, and everything not written down by the composer was dismissed as a typical 'singer's excess'. A proper reverence for great composers' wishes brought an improper reverence for their written notes and a misunderstanding of the conventions in notation adopted by great and mediocre alike. Mahler, as a conductor, expunged many a bad tradition from the Vienna State Opera. Many conductors of his school, whose performances are in every other respect magnificent, remain obdurate on the question of unwritten appoggiaturas. Yet Erwin Stein once told me that he actually heard Mahler ask a tenor to sing the traditional appoggiaturas in Tamino's Portrait Aria.

The revival of interest in careful and devoted interpretations of operas by Mozart, Rossini and Donizetti unfortunately did not bring with it the necessary interest in finding out how these works were performed in their own day. Literature on musical performance of other ages was not so readily available as it is now, so I suppose conductors and singers could once be excused for not even knowing that all these authors existed! Yet how can one forgive those conductors who permit performances in which some singers perform the unwritten appoggiaturas and others do not? These are quite common in this age of the guest star and jet travel. One would expect it to be a matter of concern to a reputable conductor as to what notes, what *tune* is sung at his performances, but I have been actually present at recording sessions of operas in which every singer adopted a different style and the word 'appoggiatura' was never once mentioned by either conductor or producer or leading singers.

I have found modern singers of all nationalities take naturally to singing appoggiaturas and soon feel the lack of them to be *insupportable*, as Garcia did over 100 years ago. As his friend and pupil, Hermann Klein, wrote: ' . . . in music of a date earlier than Rossini's one has still to deal with the old custom that gives a loop-hole for wrong treatment to the ignorant, the ill-informed, or the bigoted, or to those who imagine that every note written by the old masters, in recitative or elsewhere, should be literally sung as it appears on the printed page; who imagine that because Bach does not require (nor should he receive), the usual Italian interpretation of the appoggiatura, the same strict law must perforce apply to Mozart.'

One final quotation from a great opera-composer:

Nowadays music is written pretty nearly as it should be executed; in the old days it was otherwise, and conventional signs were used which had to be translated. Performing old music as it is written is comparable to speaking a foreign language one does not know how to pronounce. The greatest difficulty, apparently, is the appoggiatura which is no longer in use in our time. Everybody interprets it in his own fashion according to his taste. Now this is not a matter of taste, but of erudition. It is not a question of knowing what one prefers, but what the composers intended to write. Saint-Saëns (quoted in *Composers on Music*, ed. Sam Morgenstern).

APPENDIX II

Mozart

---

1. *What Mozart Really Meant: 'Figaro'**

OPERA IS SUCH a complicated form, it is understandable that composers have tended to make alternative versions and extensive revisions of their operas rather more often than of their instrumental works. Even Mozart, whose music seemed to pour out of him like a magic torrent, and who hardly revised a single note of his symphonies or chamber music, made different versions of his operas and altered ensembles and arias to suit a particular singer, or the circumstances of a particular performance. He re-arranged the part of Idamante in *Idomeneo* for tenor instead of soprano. He made extensive cuts in several of the arias in *Die Entführung aus dem Serail* (the lengthy 'Martern aller Arten' was originally even longer than in its present form!).† In *Così fan tutte* Mozart and Da Ponte, having decided that one of Guglielmo's arias was too long, substituted the less pretentious but equally beautiful 'Non siate ritrosi'; and in *Don Giovanni* Mozart made even more extensive changes for the second production in Vienna.

The question which arises today for performers, conductors, and especially producers, when preparing one of the famous masterpieces of opera is, should we adopt the alterations made by the composers themselves or respect their first intentions? For example, should we omit the many wonderful passages in *Ariadne auf Naxos*, which Strauss cut out of his second version? Should we perform the Paris version of *Tannhäuser*, in which the music, although superbly dramatic, and in many ways an improvement on Wagner's earlier composition, is in such a different style from the rest of the opera that it hardly seems to have come from the same composer? Should we perform Verdi's *Don Carlos* in four acts or five? (The revised four-act version omits the prologue, yet still contains reminiscences of its themes, notably the Love Duet.) Should we perform Bizet's *Carmen* as

---

*Reprinted from *Opera*, April 1965.

†Recent research has yielded the theory that these cuts were not made by Mozart but by someone else.

an *opéra comique* with dialogue, or should we, in the absence of singers able to speak as well as they can sing, stick to Guiraud's recitative version? What should we do when, as with *Les Contes d'Hoffmann*, no definitive version was left by the composer? Is not much of Beethoven's *Leonore* just as beautiful, if not *more* so, than the revised *Fidelio*?

Even such a perfectly shaped masterpiece as Mozart's *Le Nozze di Figaro* bristles with problems when one comes to study the various revisions Mozart himself made. Consider, first, the two extra arias which Mozart wrote for the soprano Adriana Ferrarese del Bene, who sang the part of Susanna in the second Vienna production of the opera in 1789. She was destined also to be Mozart's first Fiordiligi in *Così fan tutte* and was an entirely different type of singer from Nancy Storace who had created the role of Susanna (also in Vienna) three years previously. Storace seems, by all accounts, to have been more of a singing actress than Ferrarese del Bene, and her two arias, 'Venite inginocchiatevi' in Act II and 'Deh vieni non tardar' in Act IV, must have been perfect vehicles for her talents. But Mozart, who always took great care to compose arias to suit particular singers, wrote more conventional, *bravura* arias for Susanna — 'Un moto di gioia' and 'Al desio' — when the role was taken over by a more 'operatic' type of singer.

The simple, unaffected beauty of Susanna's two original arias appeal to us today as being much more in keeping with the dramatic situations set out in the opera, and no doubt appeared so to Mozart when conceiving the role with Nancy Storace in mind. But it seems that eighteenth-century taste preferred the two substituted arias. It could even be argued that, in the hands of certain singers, the aria 'Al desio' is *more* suitable to the dramatic situation of the nocturnal rendezvous, with its dark colours of basset-horns and bassoons, and its intensely chromatic and, later, rather florid vocal line. The former esteem given to this aria is shown by the fact that, in many eighteenth-century scores, it appears not, as is the practice today, simply in the appendix to the score, but in its proper order (as No. 27 in Act IV).

Mozart made many other changes to the part of Susanna, as can be seen from his own corrections to his autograph score (now in the State Library, East Berlin). As mentioned elsewhere (page 147), he had first intended the Countess always to have the higher line in the ensembles and Susanna the lower line. Later in the process of composition he altered almost every ensemble in which these two characters take part so as to make Susanna always sing the line *above* the Countess. These changes might have been made before the first production; but the possibility that they were made (like the addition of new arias) for the second production, with Ferrarese del Bene as Susanna, is suggested by the fact that the earliest known manuscript copy of the score (in the Fürstenberg Library at Donaueschingen) still allocates the higher line to the Countess.*

From the ensembles in Act II of *Figaro*, as Mozart first wrote them, it seems that the Countess was intended to be the big singing role of the opera and Susanna more of a singing actress's role. Furthermore, the part of Susanna as originally conceived by Mozart matches that of Figaro in the ensembles, while the Countess's music has a quite different character: it contains those soaring, grandiose, but slightly hysterical passages which Mozart so often gave to his aristocratic heroines. When he later interchanged the two soprano lines he sometimes — as we shall see — disturbed this dramatic contrast between the Countess and Susanna.

Admittedly, in many parts of the ensembles, where all the characters sing similar music, it hardly matters which character sings which line, as in the scene with Antonio which forms part of the Finale of Act II. But further on in the Finale the question of whether Susanna, or the Countess should sing the higher line starts to matter considerably. For instance, in the long 6/8 section in which (before the entrance of Marcellina, Bartolo and Basilio) Figaro finally succeeds in outwitting the Count, Mozart's original plan gave the main melody to Susanna and Figaro together — while the Countess sang a particularly characteristic kind of phrase soaring *above* with a long-held note F for several bars. Mozart's later interchanging of these parts hardly makes good dramatic sense.

Later, the differentiation made by Mozart between the two characters is even more marked: the Countess (aside) has her own phrase passionate, wide-spanning, later florid — while Figaro and Susanna answer each other in low, broken-up phrases.

Ex. 23

(Other vocal and orchestral parts omitted)

*The pros and cons of the chronology and authenticity of the various versions of *Figaro* are still (1986) being researched and Dr Alan Tyson has recently discovered more new details about the whole matter.

Here again the original version (the Countess taking the upper line) makes the better dramatic sense. At such moments we recognize how much more subtle Mozart is than other composers of his time, who hardly ever pursued musical characterization beyond the juxtaposition of a 'patter' phrase for the comic role against a slow, lyrical tune for the 'romantic' soprano or tenor. In *Figaro* Mozart further depicts the differences between Susanna and the Countess very cleverly in the finale to Act IV, and those between Susanna and Marcellina in the Act III Sextet. When Susanna is angry with Figaro (having seen him embrace Marcellina), she copies the jerky dotted style of the Count as if siding with him, for once! (See Ex. 24.) But as soon as her anger is dispelled on learning the truth, she joins the blissful *legato* of Marcellina, Figaro and Bartolo, *against* the Count who rages on under his breath with Don Curzio. (Note that the Countess is not taking part in this ensemble.)

Whether one would be justified, in the finale of Act II, in re-establishing Mozart's original distribution of parts must depend on one's view of Mozart's corrections and when they were made. But he himself did not interchange the lines *throughout* the ensembles. In the trio of Act II ('Susanna, or via sortite'), he saw that it would be nonsense for Susanna to sing a brilliant coloratura flourish (going up to high C) when she is supposed to be in hiding, and accordingly left this and several other passages as he had originally intended, i.e. for the Countess to sing. Throughout this trio, one can see evidence of Mozart's alterations (by the abbreviations *Sus,* and *La Con.* in his handwriting) — but *not* at the point where the coloratura passages occur. Scores which allot these passages to Susanna are false to the autograph score. Mozart evidently always intended that these should be sung fortissimo, proudly and defiantly by the Countess, and *not* in the arch, pretty manner which modern interpreters of Susanna are forced to adopt when this music is (wrongly) allotted to them and they must vainly try to make sense of this dramatic situation and the music at the same time.

It follows, then, that one is in duty bound to perform this trio in accordance with Mozart's autograph in order not to make nonsense of the dramatic situation.

All this is typical of Mozart's amazing gifts of musical characterization throughout his ensemble writing. (One has but to think of the differentiation made in *Don Giovanni* between the female characters in the sextet in Act II, or in the trio of the maskers in Act I.) The Count in *Figaro*, too, has, on the whole, a very different kind of melody in the ensembles from that given to the socially inferior Figaro or Bartolo.

Ex. 24

(Other orchestral parts omitted)

Because the Count is frequently sung by a fairly high baritone and Bartolo by a basso-buffo, it is now generally thought appropriate for these two characters to exchange lines in the finale of Act II — where Mozart has written particularly low-lying music for the Count, though the Count has virtually a second tenor part in the finale of Act IV! It is indeed difficult to imagine exactly the kind of voice which Mozart had in mind for this character. He may well have changed his mind during the course of composition of the opera when he found that the particular singer available, Mandini, had a high bass voice (what we should today call a baritone).

A further point requiring some thought is the order of events in Act III, which many people have noticed to be less logical in their sequence than the rest of this brilliantly constructed plot. How could Susanna have obtained from the Countess a large sum of money with which to pay off Marcellina without already having explained to the Countess about her proposed assignation — explaining, in other words, the events we have just seen taking place on the stage between Susanna and the Count? But there is no time for her to have done so. And how could a whole trial have taken place (as it must have done) on such an important matter as Figaro's liability either to pay up or to marry Marcellina, since the Count (who would presumably have presided at the trial, as he does in Beaumarchais' play) has for the whole time been on stage singing his aria ('Vedrò, mentr'io sospiro')? Furthermore, it is extremely unusual for a character to remain on the stage after singing a bravura aria of this nature, as the Count is here called on to do.

All these problems would disappear if the Countess were to sing her recitative and aria 'E Susanna non vien . . . Dove sono . . .' (together with the preceding recitative which introduces Barbarina with Cherubino) *before* the sextet in which it transpires that Figaro is the son of Marcellina and therefore cannot marry her. This would have the added advantage of contrasting the characters of the Count and Countess in consecutive arias, as well as of introducing the new character of Barbarina much earlier in the act. The sequence of keys, so important in Mozart's operas, is not in any way disturbed by these changes. In fact it could be argued that 'Dove sono' in C major followed by the sextet in F major and then the letter duet in B flat major makes a better and more typically Mozartian key sequence than the existing one.

Unfortunately there is no concrete evidence in the autograph of *Figaro* or early prints of the libretto that Mozart ever envisaged this very logical order of Act III.

A possible explanation has been put forward by Robert Moberly and Christopher Raeburn. In the original production, the parts of Dr Bartolo and Antonio were played by the same singer (Francesco Bussani) who needed time to change his costume — provided, at this point, by the Countess's aria. When the two roles are performed by two different artists, as today, this necessity disappears. There would seem a case, therefore, for adopting the order that makes more dramatic sense, viz: the Count's aria ('Vedrò mentr'io sospiro'); Recitative, Barbarina and Cherubino ('Andiam, bel paggio'); the Countess's aria ('Dove sono'); Recitative and Sextet ('È decisa la lite'); Recitative, Count and Antonio ('Io vi dico, Signor') . . . afterwards continuing as usual.

With Act III still in mind, it is worth mentioning the various versions of the Count's aria which were extant at the end of the eighteenth century. The passage of triplets near the end of this aria is almost unsingable, and attempts were made to simplify it. Two of these solutions are so typically Mozartian in their melodic contour and orchestration that they must almost certainly stem from Mozart himself. Morever, in a most interesting score of the second version of *Figaro* in the Istituto Musicale in Florence, the Count's part has been altered to include an extremely high tessitura. As this role is usually sung today by a high baritone, modern performers might do well to adopt this version, which seems to have been generally performed during the last decade of the eighteenth century. The Countess's aria

'Dove sono', was likewise subjected to several variants, one of which is highly Mozartian in its rather chromatic vocal line. It exists in several old scores of *Figaro*.

Old copies of Mozart's operas make fascinating reading, because they often show us the style of interpretation then in vogue. For example, the first English version of the opera, arranged by Sir Henry Bishop and performed in 1819, alters both music and plot to such an extent that it is certainly a travesty of the opera we know and love so well. The study of such a score, however, does help the modern performer, because Bishop indicates where all the appoggiaturas and embellishments were, in his view, required — and not only in recitative! (Here he bears out the writings of late eighteenth-century singing teachers.) We produce the original printing of the end of the Letter Duet:

Ex. 25

Further searches into old material and orchestral parts sometimes may bring other discoveries no less astonishing. Perhaps the most surprising revelation is that in the famous, supposedly Masonic, chords played by the priests' trumpets in *Die Zauberflöte*, most old scores and parts show that two of the notes were *tied*, so that each chord would have been sounded not three times (semi-quaver, minim, minim) but only twice.

So, similarly, when these chords are announced in the middle of the overture (see the illustration below). This would indeed agree rhythmically with the opening of the overture as we know it today.

Ex. 26

Such mysteries in the works of the great composers of the past can never be solved with complete certainty. The musician can only use his good taste and feeling for history. Even today, with the gramophone at our disposal, we cannot be sure of composers' wishes! The famous trumpet note during the Presentation of the Rose in *Der Rosenkavalier* is a case in point. An old trumpet player whom I met while conducting in East Berlin told me that Strauss asked him to play

E flat whereas an elderly conductor colleague, who had been a repetiteur under Strauss in Dresden, assured me that the composer wanted E natural! Shostakovich supervised and approved the performance of *Katerina Ismailova* at Covent Garden in 1963 — but he gave me a magnificent Russian recording of the opera in which orchestration, vocal line and text are all considerably altered. Composers' second thoughts can certainly baffle us, even today.

★

2. *'Parlando and Nearly All Improvised'*: Thoughts on a performing version of *'Don Giovanni'**

MOZART WROTE *Don Giovanni* in response to a commission from Prague, as a follow-up to *Figaro*'s immense success there. This in itself is important. Artistically, he felt at home in Prague; the people loved him and understood his music. *Figaro* had been unpopular in the aristocratic court opera of Vienna. Prague was a provincial town in the Austrian Empire, although nominally still the capital of Bohemia, and the opera was a municipal affair, supported by a group of citizens and merchants as well as enlightened aristocrats. *Figaro*'s liberalism, its topicality contributed to its success in Prague instead of impeding it, as it had in Vienna. When *Don Giovanni* was brought to Vienna, Mozart reworked it. He added an aria for Donna Elvira ('Mi tradì') and one for Don Ottavio ('Dalla sua pace'), both of which have since become famous; also a comic duet between Zerlina and Leporello which, although a rather amusing piece of slapstick, is not really up to the general high level of the rest of the opera. In order to accommodate these additions one other very beautiful piece for Don Ottavio had to be sacrificed ('Il mio tesoro') and some of the final scene was cut. Mozart probably sanctioned a Vienna production without the epilogue but including the somewhat vulgar duet between Zerlina and Leporello in the second act. Thus, the opera ended with Don Giovanni's final downfall, carried off to hell by demons.

Already in 1788, the Age of Reason was giving way to Romanticism and during the nineteenth century the merry little moral epilogue was customarily omitted. Even Tomaschek,[†] a contemporary of Beethoven, who had seen early performances in Prague, applauded the excision. The Epilogue had to wait for our more realistic, practical twentieth century for its reinstatement. Mozart's *Don Giovanni* was the third opera on this subject performed in Prague

---

*Paraphrased and reprinted from an interview for the programme of the Welsh National Opera.

†See also pp. 287–88.

within a few years. One was Gazzaniga's *Don Giovanni ossia il convitato di pietra*, to a text by Giovanni Bertati, which Da Ponte used as a model for his version. The famous Catalogue Aria is strikingly similar to Gazzaniga's, both musically and textually. (Da Ponte admitted in his memoirs that he produced it as a rush job.) The tenor who created the title role in the première of Gazzaniga's opera in Venice went on to create the part of Mozart's Ottavio in Prague.

The opera itself, particularly the second act Finale, contains several topical references whose meanings are now obscured for us. Mozart actually composed this whole scene *after* he arrived in Prague for rehearsals. The orchestra at Giovanni's supper party played excerpts from three works that were then current in Prague. The extracts from Martin y Soler's *Una cosa rara* (which also used a text by Da Ponte), is followed by a snatch from *I due litiganti*, where Mozart corrects some of Sarti's harmonic mistakes; Sarti had written rather rudely about one of Mozart's string quartets. The final item is an arrangement (in another key) of 'Non più andrai' from his own *Figaro*. Then there are references, or potential references to actual people. Don Giovanni remarks on a particularly savoury dish, 'Ah che piatto saporito' and it has been suggested that this is a play on the name of the first Donna Anna, Teresa Saporiti. The reference to Don Giovanni's cook ('Si eccellente é il vostro/mio cuoco')* could well be a kind of 'in' joke about F. X. Kuchař (*cook* in Czech), who sat in the orchestra pit at that first performance playing one of the fortepianos. Kuchař edited the piano score of five of Mozart's operas. He also arranged music from *Don Giovanni* for string quartet, which is particularly useful for us today because he wrote in many embellishments and appoggiaturas for the violin. This arrangement by a musician who actually played in the première of *Don Giovanni* seems to me to be an indication of Mozart's own practices.

As we know, in the eighteenth century singers were expected (or did themselves expect) to vary the melodic line of an aria so that when it was repeated, whether in the old-fashioned Handelian *da capo* aria or just when the first theme returned (as most of Mozart's do), they improvised something new of their own. It is not easy for modern singers to improvise, both musical interpretation and staging are strictly laid down. Occasionally a great composer like Mozart or Bach found it necessary to be explicit about ornaments and, as explained elsewhere, there are a few examples extant of Mozart ornamenting his own work. Unfortunately, since it is not his best-known music it is

---

*The stroke between vostro and mio signifies that one singer sings 'vostro' and the other 'mio'.

difficult to compare the simple and the ornamented versions. In the eighteenth century, numerous books were written on singing. The most famous in English was by the Italian, Domenico Corri, who actually set out to write down music the way it was performed with appoggiaturas and suggested embellishments; how the voices should begin *after* the orchestra has finished in a recitative; and how the orchestra should come in *after* the singer has finished. I do not believe in completely changing the melodic line, although many singers then did (and Mozart in embellishing the music of others did), but I feel that the second time round the line should, to some extent, be decorated, particularly in the arias of Don Ottavio and Donna Anna.

Characterization also plays a part in some of the embellishments. As we know, Garcia, the famous Don Giovanni and Rossini's original Count Almaviva, was the father of Manuel Garcia, a distinguished teacher and writer on singing. In his book, the son gives an example of an aria from *The Barber of Seville* as sung and embellished by his father, and as it might be embellished by another singer. He says, 'One can see that the one as sung by my father represents a noble count in love, whereas the other is just a lot of *fioriture*.' So there can be characterization in embellishment, even if nowadays we find it difficult to distinguish the styles, since both are equally florid.

In preparing an edition of a Mozart opera I always try to characterize the simple embellishments I put into the work. The comic as well as the noble characters have their chance for cadenza. Thus Leporello takes different liberties from those of his aristocratic master. Just as Mozart differentiated between comic and noble characters, so did the performers. The singer for whom the role of Donna Elvira was written was chiefly known as a soubrette; it was only when the opera went to Vienna and the role was sung by Caterina Cavallieri (who created the role of Constanze in *Die Entführung*), that Mozart wrote the florid aria 'Mi tradì'. Consequently, in the original performance there would have been a great contrast between the three ladies, Teresa Saporiti (Donna Anna), was an heroic singer, Caterina Micelli, the soubrette was Donna Elvira and Caterina Bondini, the wife of the director of the theatre, who played Zerlina, was a mezzo-soprano or possibly just a middle-voice, nondescript soprano. The role is not actually defined. (The category of mezzo-soprano was not specified until the late Romantic age of Verdi and Wagner.) There are several roles in Mozart which were regarded quite differently in his day; for example, the same singer sang Despina (in *Così fan tutte*) and Cherubino (in *Figaro*) in the first performance, and she also sang Zerlina in *Don Giovanni* in the Vienna production.

I think such parts were characterized much more in those days. There have been several attempts by singers, Emma Kirkby, for example, to reproduce the presumed sound of the eighteenth-century voice. The most notable difference is in the lack of vibrato which is also used in string playing. It makes that indefinable difference of tone between singers and between violinists. In the eighteenth century vibrato was not normally used by either singers or players, except as a special effect of trembling or shaking. The shaking effect — *Bebung* in German — is used in the violin part of *Don Giovanni* when the Commendatore is taking the Don down to Hell and there is a shaking of the earth.

Mozart's treatment of 'Deh vieni alla finestra' is interesting. Don Giovanni is using the aristocratic form of serenade, but since he is addressing a chamber-maid he sings it in a jaunty, earthy way, like a peasant dance. This serenade is often sung slowly and sincerely because singers find it not only beautiful, but *aristocratic* as well. Mozart caught exactly the right feeling of peasant jauntiness. Giovanni cannot completely disguise himself; he can be vulgar and raunchy, but never common. In its line, the melody could only come from an aristocrat. In Mozart's time singers played the instruments themselves. Luigi Bassi is shown in an old print playing his own mandoline, and the first Tamino played his own flute, but if the singer now is not actually playing the instrument himself I feel it is rather silly for him to pretend.

Bassi wrote his memoirs in which he claims that he saw a performance of *Don Giovanni* in Dresden and thought it was all far too po-faced. He said that when Mozart performed it they never kept to the beat, they made jokes all the time, they kept time with the orchestra but otherwise everything was done *parlando* and more or less improvised. This may not be quite true — all singers' memoirs must be taken with a pinch of salt — but it should be remembered that performances were a good deal more informal at that time. They were formal in the sense that actors had to go out of character to bow if the Emperor walked into the theatre, but informal in the sense that no one worried about the odd missed entry or note out of tune. Performers took operatic conventions at their face value. In fact, despite the aristocratic trimmings, the attitude of eighteenth-century performers seems to have been analogous to popular theatre today.

The libretto was always distributed first and people bought the text-book. Theatres were not darkened, they were lit by candles throughout the performance, consequently the only effects obtainable were with candles lit or candles out, or by covering up the floats —

lighted candles floating in candle-wax all along the stage, in glass. That is why there were so many fires in theatres. Also, the old type of keyboard-playing conductor could be *seen* easily by the artists with candlelight, whereas modern performances with darkened auditoria really need a baton-waving director if ensemble is not to suffer.

The conditions of performance in the eighteenth century cannot be imagined today. No modern composer with a reputation would allow the overture to the première of his opera to be performed without rehearsal as it was with *Don Giovanni*. Mozart said afterwards that a few notes fell under the stands but that in general it went very well.

In the eighteenth century, performances were often postponed if singers were ill, because they could not be replaced. There were no real repertory companies except perhaps in Vienna. In a city like Prague they would not have run opera in repertory. In one way the performance would have been immensely professional with highly accomplished singers and artists. On the other hand it was probably what we regard as rather amateurish in that performers talked to people in the audience and the singers would bow to the Emperor if he applauded. It was an attitude to performance completely unlike our own.

Tomaschek, who saw *Don Giovanni* within a year of the first performance, by the same Italian company, in the same theatre, later complained constantly that in all other performances and revivals the tempi were wholly wrong, mostly too slow. We know that this also happened in the nineteenth century to works of the previous period, like *Messiah* which was performed almost twice as slowly as Handel would have heard it. Tomaschek gave metronome readings for the tempi of *Don Giovanni* as he remembered them in his youth.

The most interesting feature of the tempi are the movements marked Andante (*alla breve*), meaning that the music was to be felt in two beats in a bar rather than in four. Time-beating conductors did not exist in Mozart's day and the leading violinist in the orchestra shared the responsibility with the musical director at the keyboard (see page 323). Mozart would have indicated the tempo by nodding his head as he played. The Andante *alla breve* sections in *Don Giovanni* are the Statue music, the sextet in the second act with Donna Elvira, also Don Ottavio's aria 'Il mio tesoro' and Donna Anna's aria 'Or sai chi l'onore'. I conduct all these quite a bit faster than 'normal' because, like Tomaschek, I believe that when Mozart writes the *alla breve* sign he means it to be played with two beats in the bar rather than four. If the Statue music is played at that speed the heavy tread of the Commendatore really does sound like the tread of a statue, and the melody of the Commendatore begins to sound like a line, not a series of long notes. The rushing scales of semiquavers do sound like leaping flames of Hell, and Leporello is able to sing his patter at a proper speed. (A particular singer in Prague was very adept at singing at a tremendous speed, like Gilbert and Sullivan patter songs.)

Since the overture was not rehearsed before the first performance, such details as whether a note was a crotchet or a minim were not considered important. Today we look at every little squiggle in a work by Mozart because he is among the greatest of all composers; but he wrote in a great hurry and might be rather surprised to know that people now discuss his markings in such detail. In the Statue music Mozart did in fact write a minim in the bass and a crotchet in the treble, but when he made his catalogue in the last years of his life, he wrote it as a crotchet (see examples of Mozart autograph, 27 and 28). I believe that this means that the tempo was so fast that it made no difference whether the note was written long or short. Music was not written down quite as accurately in the eighteenth century as it is now. The instruments have also changed. The practice of holding the note in the bass, which is done in almost all performances and recordings, is historically quite wrong; although people read all kinds of romantic ideas into it — the Statue's heavy tread etc., it could not have been performed like that in Mozart's time, and the fact that he wrote it in one instance as a minim and in another as a crotchet shows that he did not really care either way. I think it is far more impressive to play it as a loud terrifying chord and then stop all together.

In recent years there have been many experiments in the performance of eighteenth-century music, not only with authentic tempi and other features of the period, but with authentic instruments.

One does not have to use period instruments to obtain the springy rhythms and light sonorities of eighteenth-century music. Bowing according to the principles of Mozart's father, Leopold, plus the use of gut strings can make a huge difference to the sound of the violin section, while calf-skin timpani played with wooden sticks, and a fortepiano continuo, can bring the orchestral sound still nearer to that which Mozart would have known.

The tempi of operas have been measured metronomically by early nineteenth-century musicians like Tomaschek, but in fact others such as Czerny and Hummel list what they consider the right tempi for Mozart and Haydn's late symphonies and chamber music. Most of these are a good deal faster than has been customary in the twentieth century, especially the minuets, which are listed as being in *one-in-a-bar*, often as fast as a metronome setting of 72 or even 88 to the dotted

Ex. 27

(From the first page of Mozart's own manuscript of the overture, supposedly written during the night before the first performance.)

Ex. 28

(From Mozart's own catalogue of his works, showing the first bars of the overture.)

minim. In my recent recordings of the Mozart symphonies with the Prague Chamber Orchestra (June 1986), I adopted fast, scherzo-like tempi for the minuets and find them completely natural. So did the members of the orchestra, once they had got over the initial shock of unconventionality.

APPENDIX III

Handel

BY CHANCE, MY career has coincided more or less with the growth of interest in authentic performance of music of the past. There are now so many old music groups, each claiming their own brand of 'authenticity' that it is difficult for the present-day devotees of baroque music to realize how recent the whole concept really is.

It has already been mentioned that when I was growing up in Australia Handel's famous works were always played in some kind of re-arrangement with large forces: *Messiah* in Mozart's or even Prout's version, *The Water Music* in Hamilton Harty's orchestration and so on. This puzzled me, even as a boy, for though I found Handel's music just as great as Bach's, Bach was not subjected to quite the same treatment.* When, in my teens, I bought an early Boosey & Hawkes miniature score of *The Water Music* in the original orchestration I wondered why Sir Hamilton Harty had thought it necessary to arrange it for full orchestra and when, in 1946, I first saw the actual autograph of *Messiah*, in facsimile (see page 54), and noticed the huge difference between the way it was orchestrated by Handel and the way it was always played I began to realize that though interpreters of nineteenth-century works kept as closely as possible to the composers' intentions, the same could not be said of eighteenth-century music, particularly of the earlier part of the century, and that performances were very far from what the composers themselves would have wished.

Comparing the original *Messiah* with the Ebenezer Prout's re-orchestration I discovered that where Handel wrote his 'Sinfony' as dotted crotchet and quaver Prout transcribed it as a *double-dotted* crotchet and semiquaver. This, and certain choruses, such as

---

*It is true that even 'original' Bach, at that time, took on a rather romantic hue, as clarinets replaced oboes d'amore, the continuo, in the absence of a harpsichord, was played on the piano and the chorales in the *Matthew Passion* were sung very slowly and softly, unaccompanied . . . all very beautiful but with the cloying beauty of Delius rather than Bach.

'Behold the Lamb of God', were usually played double-dotted in my youth, but I had always attributed this to carelessness or even slovenliness, having been brought up in the orchestral school whereby every tiny mark was followed *exactly*. I was thus surprised that such an eminent Victorian pedagogue as Prout should actually *write in* the double dots which he claimed were traditional practice for a century and a half.*

I began to study Bach and Handel closely, as well as various commentators such as Terry, Schweitzer and very importantly Dolmetsch, so that on arrival in England after the war I was ready for the revaluation in baroque music that was being born. A great interest was developing in research and the correct performance practice of eighteenth-century music, especially the early eighteenth-century or baroque style.

Thurston Dart was one of the leaders in this movement. Sir Adrian Boult, conservative as he was, was the first person to record *Messiah* using the original orchestration and Joan Sutherland introduced some ornamentation into this recording. John Tobin, who had gone back to early versions of *Messiah*, added crisper rhythms and cadenzas to his performances. Anthony Lewis, a great scholar, introduced us to many unknown Handel works, particularly the operas, some of which he performed for the first time since Handel's day. He cast dramatic singers like Janet Baker in the castrato roles at a time when the Germans were still using baritones and basses, an unauthentic practice that has still not quite been stamped out.

By the time I was starting to make my career as a conductor in London, there was a wonderful new spirit. We were learning to see Handel as a much more virtuosic and dramatic composer. We dismissed the whole era of the Beechams and Sargents as unauthentic and therefore *wrong*, however much spirit and atmosphere their performances had created. The question of authenticity was becoming very, very important to us. The word 'authentic' was bandied about a great deal, although probably much of what we thought authentic was not. We were fired with enthusiasm, and read every contemporary pedagogical treatise we could. We learned much from theorists such as Quantz, C. P. E. Bach, Leopold Mozart.

We found that the orchestras of Bach's and Handel's day were very small by comparison with modern symphony orchestras; that the proportion of wind and strings was different, with strings only slightly

---

*In Mozart's version, on the other hand, it is virtually impossible to reconcile the long trombone and horn notes with double-dotting, leading one to the conclusion that, whatever the English tradition of Handelian performance, double-dotting was not normally practised in Vienna.

more numerous than oboes and bassoons; that rhythms, especially dotted rhythms, should frequently *not* be played as they were written — rests were substituted for dots and even notes were sometimes played as though dotted. Some baroque composers encouraged performers to embellish their melodies, add grace notes and generally show off their virtuosity. Others, like J. S. Bach, less flamboyant, wrote out all the ornaments and expected their tunes to be performed exactly as written. We learnt that eighteenth-century instruments (and voices) had less dynamic range than their modern counterparts, and that the massive effect of a huge modern chorus singing a work like *Messiah* or the *St Matthew Passion* was quite unlike the sounds Handel or Bach would have heard. In the same way large dynamic contrasts would have been beyond their experience. The mechanics of the harpsichord and organ of that period, the style of bowing of string instruments made short clipped phrases more practical than long drawn-out ones. The continuous broad style appropriate to a Brahms symphony or *The Mastersingers* would have been impossible in a long baroque melody such as the Air from Bach's D Major Suite or Handel's 'Largo', the opening aria in *Xerxes*.

I was anxious to put some of these exciting and fresh ideas into practice. The big chance to do something really original and spectacular came in the 1950's when I suggested to Ivor Walsworth, then Director of the BBC Transcription Service, whom I had met at Aldeburgh, that we should record the original orchestration of the *Royal Fireworks Music*. In order to have enough oboes and bassoons this was done late on a Sunday night. Handel had specified the exact number of instruments involved and Boosey & Hawkes had published the original orchestration, which I edited with double dots and various embellishments. This BBC recording was played on the Third Programme as well as the World Service and became quite famous. It was then recorded in St Gabriel's, Cricklewood, for Pye Records (see pp. 114–15) in 1965, the 200th anniversary of Handel's death. The *Concerto a due cori*, which I had also edited, was on the other side. It consists of choruses from the oratorios, including *Messiah*, beautifully arranged by Handel for two wind bands and strings, an ideal coupling. I often perform my version of both these pieces at concerts, as I have had no reason to change my editorial features of all those years ago.

Through Basil Lam, then in charge of early music for the BBC, I began working in oratorio. Lam was an academic as well as a harpsichordist, and I was a theatrical musician, so we complemented each other well. We worked together on many oratorios and cantatas, as well as on some Rameau (a special interest of his) for the BBC, always trying to achieve authenticity as we understood it. Lam would read the instructions about the various ornaments and describe them, but it was I who actually wrote out the music and explained to the singers exactly how it was to be sung. Because of Lam I was able to practise different baroque styles and also, to some extent, instruct the Goldsbrough Orchestra (later English Chamber Orchestra), in these styles. Arnold Goldsbrough, after whom the orchestra was named, was a distinguished pioneer in reviving baroque practices, but somehow lacked the professionalism to impart them to the enthusiastic, very professional young orchestra.

When we felt confident enough we decided to tackle *Messiah*, giving it a really new look with plenty of ornamentation. Basil, influenced by a keyboard reduction of Part I by the librettist Charles Jennens, extracted from it a number of types of ornamentation and put them into the orchestral accompaniment. This was a feature of my recording which was widely criticized by other Handel experts. However, most of the critics with a general as opposed to a specialized musical education, seemed inclined to sympathize with our aims, and I persuaded Peter Andry of EMI to take the plunge and record our version. Unfortunately for us, another recording with similar aims was released *ahead* of ours, conducted by Colin Davis and edited by Christopher Hogwood, who was just starting his career in the baroque field. The Davis recording was immensely fast, particularly in the choruses. Though we had both used fast tempi, his were extreme. It is hard to see how the choirs could have sung at that speed in the eighteenth century, but the choruses had a very beautiful lightness and buoyancy.

My recording was somewhat more 'meaty', especially in the choruses but in the solo parts I encouraged plenty of ornamentation from the singers, particularly in 'The trumpet shall sound' sung by Raimund Herincx, and in the two alto arias sung most beautifully by Janet Baker, 'Oh Thou that tellest good tidings to Zion' and 'He was despised'. This brought very heavy criticism from those who felt themselves expert in the baroque field. Handelian experts such as Stanley Sadie and Anthony Hicks claimed there was no evidence that the amount of ornamentation I included, particularly in the orchestra, was ever used in Handel's day. At that time I believed passionately that my method of interpretation was authentic, that it was what Handel himself would have expected, and further that it was necessary to *write out* the ornamentation rather than let the performers actually improvise, for fear that they might accidentally adopt an un-Handelian style.

Correspondence in various musical journals ensued in which I defended my use of ornamentation by referring to eighteenth-century embellished copies of *Messiah* (most of which appear in Watkins Shaw's marvellous edition), with copious quotes from eighteenth-century authors like Dr Burney: 'An Adagio . . . is generally little more than an outline left to the performer's ability to colour.' The only area in which I have revised my views since then is the *extent* of ornamentation practised by Handel. Every few years there are new perceptions of authenticity, as the *Zeitgeist* and the taste of the decade seem to merge dangerously with the 'Flavour of the Month'. It is finally a matter of taste, and Marpurg's dictum is as true today as it was in 1765:

Regarding the smaller ornaments, they are so essential at most places that without their strict observance no composition can please the more refined ears. But where does one learn what notes are given ornaments or at which point of the melody this or that ornament ought to be introduced? One should hear persons who are reputed to play elegantly, and one should hear them in pieces one already knows. In this way one may form one's own taste, and do likewise. For it is impossible to devise rules to meet all possible cases, and one man differs from the next in his appreciation. One should try to give a piece of music in which ornaments have not yet been marked to ten different people, each playing in the good style of the day, and ask them for their ornament. In certain cases, perhaps, many will agree; in the rest, they will all be different. (Donington: *The Interpretation of Early Music*)

Apart from questions like ornamentation, there are many other things we still do not know about Handel's oratorio performances. If, as we are told, he played an organ concerto throughout the intervals, when did he have a break, since he was also conducting the performance? When did the musicians take a break? We do not know whether the soloists in oratorio sang in the chorus or walked in and out between each solo. In old pictures that show how choirs were disposed it often seems that the voices were mixed, individual sopranos standing next to tenors etc., not arranged in groups. Although in Handel festivals at Westminster Abbey we may see the sopranos, altos etc. in proper ranks, in other performances string players seem to be sitting all over the place, particularly the bass. It was an important rule of the eighteenth century that the bass should always be very spread out so that if one set of continuo instruments could not be heard, at least there was another in a different position.

We may think we have answered many questions but I am not sure that we have. We know that the composers did not write accurately because they were themselves in charge of the performance and could always say what they wanted, but deciding *what* should be played, and *how*, poses even more insoluble problems. I feel in an odd way that these matters were possibly not considered very important by the composers: that Handel might have been rather puzzled by our great preoccupation with small details — as would Mozart; that like Janáček (who said 'I don't know whether it's forte or piano, make it sound like the wind whistling'), Handel might have said, 'I don't know why you're making such a fuss. Just *sing* it.'

Although I had conducted a great deal of Handel's music I came to his operas rather late, through his oratorios and instrumental works. It took me a little time to realize that Handelian *opera seria* was feasible as dramatic entertainment and not only as music. It is true, of course, that many of the operas are somewhat naive; the good characters are so unbelievably good and the bad so incredibly bad, but because Handel was the greatest composer of his time he could, through his music, give more depth to his characters than the librettist had allowed them — as Mozart was to do a couple of generations later.

In any case the exaggerated good or evil of the characters and their behaviour is really no harder for modern audiences to accept than many of the heroes and villains of Verdi or Donizetti. Success depends on how the work is presented — if there are genuine theatrical artists in the roles they will create a dramatic entity; if these are mere puppets singing the notes, making no attempt at acting, the audience will reject the performance as drama. On the other hand, producers do no service to Handel by staging the operas with tongue in cheek, or as a play within a play, with Handel's carefully planned sequences played out of order, or by changing the dramatic meaning, or by overloading the words with incomprehensible symbols. They should be played and sung with the immediacy, the panache and virtuosity which audiences must have felt when a Senesino held the stage, and Handel himself presided in the pit at the harpsichord.

Until the end of the 1970's all my performances of Handelian opera had been confronting the *musical* issues of these works long before I became involved with the much greater problems of *staging* them.

One of my first new productions as Musical Director of Sadler's Wells Opera at the Coliseum was not an opera but a secular oratorio, *Semele*. Anthony Lewis and I prepared an edition together which was published by Oxford University Press and the production was a relative success (see page 169). This gave me valuable experience in dealing with various problems of Handel's performance on the stage. There was quite a gap before I conducted *Semele* again, this time at Covent Garden. It was the first performance there since the première two and a half centuries before, and in the meantime there had been many changes in musical presentation. In Handel's 'real' operas the choruses are simple, almost primitive, hard to reconcile with the composer's mighty fugal structures of *Messiah* and other oratorios. In his operas the choruses were sung by any of the soloists who happened to be unoccupied at the time or by supernumeraries who could never have learned, let alone memorized, the complications of the choral writing in *Semele*. Handel's original performances at Covent Garden were in oratorio form and the chorus would have read from the music.

There are at present many singers, especially English and American, who take easily to the Handelian style and the 'aria' opera; they have a definite talent for delivering the arias which are extremely taxing, whether or not ornamentation is added. In the eighteenth century some singers improvised their cadenzas and 'graces', others had them written out and inserted them into arias as the fancy took them; today we need singers who are adept at ornamentation and able to make it sound as though improvised, even when it is not. In the eighteenth century performances were far less formal than they are now. There was more personal contact between singers and audience, less characterization and less 'production'. Improvisation was part of this general informality. The 'aria' opera is difficult today because modern producers expect singers to repeat exactly the same actions in each performance and conductors like to stipulate exactly the ornaments to be sung every time, what appoggiaturas on which note, always in the same way. I understand why some singers prefer to have their ornamentation written out; they say they have far more freedom to devote to their roles once they have thoroughly learnt them. However, it is all quite unlike the practice of the eighteenth-century theatre.

My first 'real' staged Handel Italian opera was *Julius Caesar* in 1979 at the English National Opera (see pp. 200–01). It posed many problems in its execution. Janet Baker, ideal from every point of view as Caesar himself, and around whose participation the whole production was geared, found that her voice was going up and that the original contralto *tessitura* of the role was much too low for her. Not only did we have to transpose almost every aria upwards but, to achieve the necessary brilliance, I had the impossible task of uniting a certain stylistic authenticity with very high lying embellishments. This applied to a lesser extent also to the other singers in the cast, who were among the ENO's best, Valerie Masterson, Della Jones, Sarah Walker and John Tomlinson.

A further problem was the actual length of the work. Uncut, it has Wagnerian proportions. When I once saw a complete performance even the experts were squirming in their seats. It is just too long. Among the revisions and cuts that Handel made in his own works there are only a handful of cases in which he shortened an aria by omitting the *da capo* section, so I decided it was better to cut complete arias altogether than to spoil his three-part aria scheme. In selecting the arias to be cut our objectives were to maintain dramatic continuity, to make the opera live again, to make it approachable and interesting to a modern audience, yet not overload the production with gimmicks or claptrap about social relevance. We also trimmed the sub-plots which left us with about three hours of music. Neither the producer/stage director, John Copley nor I claimed to be recreating the circumstances of the première of *Giulio Cesare in Egitto* at the Haymarket Theatre in London in 1724. As in all other aspects of my work with Handel, I felt that it was more important to capture his style and spirit than to be rigidly authentic. Too much rigidity leads to museum art.

The history of opera is full of composers whose works were too long and Dr Burney tells us that it was quite common for plenty of cuts to be made. Many of Handel's long operas need pruning. For festival performances they could be given complete but not for a season in a repertory house. I doubt if he would object: he was an extremely practical man, always prepared to cut his coat according to his cloth. The various versions of some of his operas, such as *Rinaldo*, show that he sometimes used the same famous arias but changed the action in order to accommodate the singers. He might have a soprano in a certain role one season and a mezzo in it the next. At that time the attitude to opera was quite unlike ours; the music was arranged round a particular artist, as it is now in West End or Broadway musicals. Handel, Mozart, Verdi, great musicians that they were, wrote their music with individual singers in mind. Their attitude was 'You are the singer — if what I write does not suit you I will write something else', whereas people like Wagner said 'Sing what I write and if you can't I will get another singer'.

I believe that anyone planning a baroque work these days should also adapt and adjust the roles according to the vocal gifts and limitations of his performers, as I did in *Julius Caesar* and have always done in every Handel opera.

A major problem in creating an historically accurate performance of a baroque opera is casting castrato roles. I solve it by trying to match the brilliance and timbre of the castrati as closely as possible. I believe it is quite wrong for their parts to be sung by a baritone or bass voice; it gives completely the wrong colour, even with a baritone who can sing with the requisite bravura. The real bass roles in Handel have a completely different and distinct kind of composition with the bass part of the harmony taking on the leading melodic line.

My principle in casting is to give the main castrato role to a strong woman. Even the most marvellous counter-tenor seems to lack the dash and vocal power required, so I reserve the counter-tenor for the second part, though it often means reversing Handel's original conception. For instance, when I conducted *Orlando* several times in different centres with Marilyn Horne in the title role, I gave the second part, Medoro, to Jeffrey Gall, though Medoro, a male role, was originally sung by a woman. I did the same with Arsamenes in *Xerxes*. This is done to achieve maximum dramatic power and vocal contrast.

There is no lack of precedent for the casting of female singers in male roles in eighteenth-century opera. In *Julius Caesar* the role of Sextus was originally sung by a soprano and his namesake in Mozart's *La clemenza di Tito* was sung by a mezzo-soprano.* The idea of travesty roles goes back such a long way that we are completely used to it. In the nineteenth century the title role in Rossini's *Otello* was sung by Malibran and Schröder-Devrient, among others! But it is essential to find the right type of woman, one who can be convincing as Caesar or Xerxes or some of the other legendary heroes and tyrants. The right *type* is more important than the ideal voice. This is particularly so in our large modern theatres.

At the Coliseum we were working in a theatre far larger than Handel had written for. Our orchestral forces were not really much greater than the original, and though Dame Janet's voice would have been larger than Senesino's we still had to alter the part so that her voice was 'singing high'. I was not attempting a notional reconstruction of what Senesino sang, who anyhow sang his roles in the small King's Theatre, Haymarket. La Fenice in Venice, where I did *Orlando* with Marilyn Horne in 1985, is approximately the same size and was ideal. The London Coliseum and the huge American theatres are all far too big, unless one has the right kind of singer.

*All my research has failed to elicit whether Caroline Perini sang Sesto or Annio.

Tatiana Troyanos, a singer with tremendous strength of personality and a large brilliant voice, was able to project the role of Caesar when she sang it at the San Francisco opera, though she also had to sing the high versions of Caesar's arias which I had arranged for Dame Janet.

When the role of Julius Caesar was taken over by Christopher Robson, one of our finest young counter-tenors, I not only put all Caesar's arias back into their lower original keys, but I rearranged and curtailed the ornamentation to suit the counter-tenor voice, lower than the big mezzos who had previously sung it, but still not quite as low as would have been Senesino's deep contralto. Robson was adept at improvising cadenzas which, in the aria 'Se in fiorito ameno prato', were echoed differently each time by the obbligato violin. Though there was almost no ornamentation and he rarely exceeded Senesino's range the 'fundamentalists' complained that there was too much ornamentation, apparently not noticing that it had been entirely re-cast to suit the different type of singer and voice.

There are, at the moment, very few female contralto singers who thrive on singing a very low *tessitura*. The genuine contraltos of today tend to be at home in slow-moving cantabile music. An exception to this is Marilyn Horne, but I have found that even she prefers to make a 'splash' with high notes and big leaps rather than low ones.

In the eighteenth century, singers always used the light head voice for their higher notes, the strong chest voice for the lower. Consequently, it created a bigger climax to end an aria on a low note rather than a high one. This rule applied throughout the eighteenth century and much of the nineteenth.

Not only do I try to adapt a role to suit a singer's capabilities, I try to make the embellishments of each character as individual as the characters themselves. However, when I am working with a singer whose voice and capabilities resemble those of Handel's original soloist in a role, I do encourage them to sing in the style of that soloist. Valerie Masterson, in *Semele*, had similar capabilities to the virtuosa '*La Francesina*' (Elisabeth Duparc, the celebrated French singer of Italian opera) for whom the role was written, so I encouraged her to take every opportunity to ornament her arias. Robert Tear as Jupiter was encouraged to sing simpler 'divisions' more appropriate to the oratorio style with which John Beard (an eighteenth-century English oratorio singer) would have been familiar. In short, I try to achieve a style as representative of Handel's own, and the spirit of the baroque, as is possible for performers so far removed from his time.

Handel composed at a tremendous speed (usually to a deadline), so it is no wonder that his calligraphy often shows haste, even carelessness with such details as length of notes, rhythms etc. These inconsistencies present difficulties for the modern performer. Are they no more than the result of haste, or are the differences intentional? Sometimes Handel uses a kind of shorthand, but there are also places where a desire for consistency can easily damage the great diversity of Handel's imagination. When I first realized that baroque rhythms were not always accurately notated, I used to change *everything* to make a melody agree with its first appearance, e.g. the trills in 'He was despised', the dots in 'I know that my Redeemer' and in 'The trumpet shall sound' in *Messiah*, or the short up-beats in Cleopatra's 'V'adoro pupille', from *Julius Caesar*. Experience has taught me to be more careful about this and to think very hard about every inconsistency. Several versions by Handel of a single piece of music (such as the *Fireworks*) have the same 'inconsistencies' in every version. Surely this must make one hesitate before changing his dotted rhythms, even though we know that such rhythmic alteration was very typical of baroque performing practice.

The problem of Handel's dotted notes and slurs has always puzzled scholars, and it is salutary to think that these questions, so vital to us today, probably weren't at all important to him! Even the famous double-dotting in the French style of all Handel's overtures occasionally results in un-Handelian consecutive fifths or sloppy rhythms (see bar 22 in *Belshazzar* for the former and bar 11 of *Messiah* for the latter). It also must be said that the tantalizingly few contemporary barrel organs that play Handel overtures *do not* perform the dotted rhythms as double dots. So the mass of contradiction proliferates, leading the performers to question almost every precept of the musicologist and the eighteenth-century pedagogue.

There is also the question of the *notes inégales* i.e. a row of notes written as apparently to be played evenly but in fact played *un*evenly, almost as though dotted. This is a particularly acute problem in Handel, who makes some notes dotted and leaves others undotted, apparently haphazardly. It is the same with slurs, which both Bach and Handel sprawled over three or more notes, with no precise indication as to how many notes should be played legato and how many staccato. This may be because they merely wanted to indicate that a particular passage be played smoothly. When it *really* mattered which notes should be smooth, they took good care to make it very clear.

The problem of interpretation of small grace notes (appoggiaturas) which is such a nightmare in composers as diverse as J. S. Bach, Gluck and Rameau, hardly exists with Handel, as he writes them only rarely.

Far more difficult is the decision as to where to insert them when he did not write them himself. Then there is also the problem of where to add trills. I think that probably the musicians used to put in the odd trill unconsciously, but we do not know how *much*, or whether there was a difference between the professional and the amateur, if the leader could add trills, but not the rank and file players; even how much was supervised by the composer/director. Both Quantz and J. A. Scheibe mention this in their writings.

There is the question of the bass line and its varying roles in arias and choruses. We believe (there are plenty of pictures to show us) that a double bass or *violone* played the bass line an octave lower than the basso continuo, but we do not know exactly when the bass played and when it was silent because very often in a chorus Handel does not bother to indicate in the *basso continuo* part that the bass singers in the choir have stopped and therefore the double bass and/or *violone* should stop playing.

Scores and parts of the period also give conflicting evidence on when the bassoon played alone with the general bass and when only with the other woodwind. The problem is even more puzzling in arias, where it is unclear if the bassoons played all the time or how often the *violone* played. Arias for continuo alone sometimes specify 'Violoncelli soli' or 'con Contrabassi' (usually the plural form e.g. in Orlando's first aria 'Stimolato dalla gloria'), but what are we to assume when nothing is written? When Handel writes a special part for bassoons, as in the introduction to the aria 'Se pietà' in *Julius Caesar*, he then writes 'col basso', to suggest that the bassoons, having played their tenorish cry of anguish, should continue to chug away unsuitably with the cellos for the rest of the aria. At the end of an aria there is usually an Adagio for voice and continuo alone, presumably to let the voice have complete freedom to improvise cadenzas with the minimum of accompaniment. Did the 'tutti' instruments then automatically stop, or was there only one instrument playing all along? One imagines that when rarely the orchestra continues to play the Adagio it is a sign that no cadenza be sung (see 'Aure' in *Julius Caesar*). Did a bassoon ever play in recitatives? Did the *violone* play? And if so, did they play long notes, as indicated in the score or did they play short notes to mirror the expressions of the words? (Bach, in the *St Matthew Passion*, wrote *long* notes in the *score*, but *short crotchets* in the continuo *part*. This creates problems when there are changing chords over the same bass note.)

One imagines that the recitatives were *spoken* a great deal more than is the custom today, and were probably done at great speed, in fact, at the tempo of speech and the declamation of spoken drama of the eighteenth century. Recitative endings are a great source of argument: whether the cadence should be played together with the voice or after it has finished, and at what stage sung appoggiaturas became the norm in recitatives. Various composers used different methods of writing things down, and it is difficult to know whether these are individual expressions of the same thing or whether they really intend a difference. (Bach, for instance, in his recits always writes that the chord comes after the voice has finished.) Handel *almost* always writes as though the voice should still be singing when the two cadential chords are played, yet tonic harmony simultaneously with a dominant chord does not sound very pleasant. Some writers of the period became so used to this idea that they say it is what one must do even though it is harmonically wrong, specifically that one must break a rule of harmony in order to avoid holding up the action.

I have often wondered about the chronology of the development of the recitative style. The 'secco' recitative hardly changed its form or style for more than a century which must be a phenomenon unique in musical history. The styles of Handel, Mozart and Rossini are poles apart, but their recitatives, particularly in their Italian works, are so similar as to be almost indistinguishable. The recitative style developed out of the narrative style of the Venetian type opera-ballets, and was used instead of speech to drive the action forward. It was accompanied by continuo instrument alone, lute, harpsichord or cello, which could follow the free declamation without difficulty. The practice of ending recitative periods with conventional cadences such as:

Ex. 29

developed gradually. We see examples of it in Handel's youthful works and we can trace how this style continues right up to the end of the nineteenth century. These recitative endings were accompanied by a full cadence V – I (see Ex. 29). As singers started to put ornaments into recitatives as well as airs, so they began to use the appoggiatura more and more on two-syllable words until it became established practice to employ the appoggiatura on *all* two syllable words. This meant often that the instrumental cadence at the end of phrases (such as in the example) became discordant with the 'appoggiaturized' melody, and so continuo players 'straightened it out' by playing a suspension 4 – 3

Ex. 30

4-3

thus making the harmony fit the melody. Later still, players took to playing the two chords *after* the voice had finished the phrase, particularly in the church and in oratorios where the recitatives were more sung than spoken, and consequently went slower. In the theatre, the recitatives were hardly *sung* at all, and I believe were spoken whether in comedy or tragedy, popular or heroic, and taken so fast that the ear would barely perceive that forbidden fifths and sevenths resulted in the two chords being struck *together* with the appoggiaturas.

The continuo playing of recitatives seems to have undergone great changes in style. In the seventeenth century the chords were played long, with slowish arpeggios suitable to the technique of the lute and theorbo. Later, during Handel's and Bach's time, even religious recitatives were accompanied by short chords. Still later, the serious recitatives of composers like Haydn and Beethoven seem to require *long* notes in the accompaniment, and the treatises on singing and accompaniment of the time seem to confirm this. It seems therefore that with Handel, who normally, though not always, indicated the cadences in recitatives to be played together, each case should be treated on its merits and dramatic context. It is just as wrong to play *all* cadences *with* the voice, as it was in the nineteenth century to play all of them *after*! A further point of doubt about recitatives in Handel and Bach (and even sometimes in Mozart) is how freely *accompanied* recitatives should be sung. Handel's setting of the text in all languages is somewhat idiosyncratic and I often wonder if the rather strange stops and starts that result from a recitative like 'Thy rebuke hath broken his heart' in *Messiah* being sung 'a tempo' can really be what Handel wanted. I feel that they should be sung freely, hardly noticing the difference between note values, though directors currently specializing in authenticity give their singers almost no freedom to express the words naturally and hardly an appoggiatura in sight. Similarly if the noble recitatives in the operas of Handel and Gluck are sung in a slow measured *bel canto* style reminiscent of Bellini or Donizetti, the difference between recitative and aria is lost.

My ideas on the tempi of baroque music in general changed considerably when I realized that our concept of tempo had been dictated by Romantic traditions. In Handel's day there were not such extremes of fast and slow. Tempo markings are more the feeling of expression, what the Germans called '*Affekt*' of the music. Contrasts of brilliance and expressiveness can be marked if the actual range of tempi is narrower, provided articulation and rhythm are carefully adjusted. For instance, overtures in the French style are now played at a relatively fast tempo even though sometimes the music is marked 'Grave'. I find it works very well if one regards the opening as being in four instead of in eight, making it less solemn and more sharp in rhythm, giving a rhythmic piquancy. Likewise in an Allegro, it is not simply the speed which gives it its spirit, but the kind of articulation, the buoyancy of expression with which it is played.

So far we have been concerned with general performing style. There are many questions regarding instrumental style which affect our understanding of baroque music. Twenty-four oboes playing in *The Fireworks Music* must have been rather out of tune and had a more 'quacky' sound than today's oboes. Modern players of the baroque oboe, playing the Hornpipe or the Bourrée in *The Water Music*, produce that sort of sound. When they play cantabile, as in the beautiful tenor aria in the *St Matthew Passion*, the sound has a 'straight' quality which, in modern players, is only approximated by the Viennese. It has no vibrato, and the expression comes out of the rise and fall of the pitch, the outline of the melody itself. It is the same on the harpsichord: there is little difference if you bang it harder. Early musicians had very little dynamic range to play with on their instruments, so expression was achieved by very subtle timing and an innate ability to follow the contours of the music.

Writers on baroque violin playing say that in order to bring greater expression to a note, one makes a crescendo and diminuendo rather as the singers did in the so-called *messa di voce*. The players of authentic instruments make such a feature out of this that it almost becomes a nervous tic. Yet, reading the same sources as they have, I note that Geminiani and Leopold Mozart said that one may *occasionally* do this in order to heighten the expression of one particular phrase, or even just one note. To me this does not mean that one *must* do it all the time. Again, those who use this effect continuously say that it was the method of playing expressively *before* vibrato was invented. They may be right. I can only say that to us today it does not have the same beauty as it must have had in the eighteenth century. Matters like these make one wonder how desirable it really is to be so preoccupied with authenticity.

Since the conductor as we know him did not exist in the eighteenth century, it might be asked why we need one now when Handel's music is played. For one thing, there could have been occasions when a conductor was needed, as with Handel's *Royal Fireworks Music* which was written for a huge band and performed in the open air. There must have been someone actually conducting to keep it all together. In performances today of large-scale baroque works, there must be a conductor to suggest the particular style in which it is to be performed. We have already remarked on how many different styles of playing baroque music now exist. There are such wide divergencies of opinion among the experts, that a conductor is required to tell the performers what type of interpretation is being adopted, so that everyone plays with one mind, one accord. In fact, two authentic-instrument orchestras have recently asked me to work with them, though we all know that the baton-waving conductor is an anachronism in such a context.

Arm-waving conductors were only used for the largest kind of oratorio. There is one picture in which Handel appears to be conducting, rather like a modern conductor, but normally he is seen playing the organ or harpsichord. The mammoth performance of *Messiah* in Westminster Abbey in 1784, in which there were about five hundred people, appears to have been conducted by the organist Joah Bates, who sat in the middle, apparently just keeping time with his head.

Although we should try to learn as much as possible about how eighteenth-century musicians performed, and try to imagine how the music sounded, we should not claim to be performing exactly as Handel and his singers would have done. We should not turn our knowledge into an inflexible dogma, but use it to vitalize our modern performances. Without reproducing exactly the performing conditions, acoustics, atmosphere and techniques of the eighteenth century, as some have attempted to do, we all, if we look at ourselves honestly, fall down in some respect of authenticity.

How often have we seen basic principles of authenticity thrown over for the whim of a modish stage producer, even admitting baritones and basses for castrato roles, or *da capo* arias reduced to their 'A' sections, thus neatly avoiding the problem of how much ornamentation would be appropriate to the *da capo*. Yet directors of 'authentic' ensembles constantly do all these things and finally succumb to the lure of the anachronistic baton, so much more glamorous than strumming on a harpsichord as Handel and Mozart did!*

I have come to the conclusion that as authenticity is a subjective not an objective concept, it is better to use the vast reservoir of knowledge that has been gained about the eighteenth century and its musicians, but express the music of the past in our own twentieth-century way.

I believe that my editions and performances are true to the spirit of the music and the eighteenth century, regardless of the necessary practical tailoring some of them have undergone to suit the instrumental and vocal resources I have had at my disposal. I have always tried to bring out the brilliant, the dramatic, the pathetic in Handel; above all, the *theatrical* side of his nature. Strangely enough, although critics of my generation seem to appreciate this in my performances (whether or not they like my embellishments), the younger generation of critics, who have grown up with quite different standards and values in these matters, have recently referred to my performances of *Julius Caesar* and *Solomon* as 'lacking in drama, bland, softened down, smoothed out' etc., by comparison with performances on authentic instruments. I find that all these criticisms describe precisely the faults of the 'authentic' performances themselves. The generation gap is never so evident in the musical profession as when young critics write about older performers.

New analyses of the minds of the great composers, new perceptions of what is authentic, new principles of interpretation appear every few years. Despite all our knowledge, what we can not recreate is the immensely theatrical and virtuosic feeling that the singers themselves engendered in the audience.

The singers with whom Handel worked were the greatest virtuosos of their day. Artists like Farinelli and Mrs Billington sang with a panache and commitment, a virtuosity and enthusiasm that made them

---

*Some modern conductors of baroque music have tried directing Handel operas from the harpsichord as the composer would have done. Since it means that the keyboard director is invisible to the singers on the stage, unless the eighteenth-century practice is revived of keeping the auditorium candles alight throughout the performance, authenticity usually gives way to practicality in the form of the baton.

the toast of Europe. They also had a quite tangible rapport with their audiences. Their singing was very far removed from the bland 'pure' expression of the modern baroque singers who discard all theatricality; yet it is this very quality that makes Handel's music so ageless and so alive. This is why I always try to bring it out as well as the brilliant, the tragic, the reflective and dramatic sides of his nature.

In the course of my career I have followed the bland white voice without ornamentation, once *de rigueur* for oratorio, through the operatic virtuoso style (which I still prefer), back to the 'pure' unornamented cathedral style of the 1940's. Isobel Baillie, the typical soprano of the Sargent era, is now replaced by the strikingly similar sound of Emma Kirkby. Once again, performers play baroque music almost exactly as written, with few trills and few liberties, though on authentic instruments, with small forces and faster tempi. The more I study the music of Handel and of the baroque era in general the more ironic it seems that so much concentration on authenticity has brought us almost full circle, back to where we were forty years ago.

APPENDIX IV

Janáček

I AM OFTEN asked what it was that drew me to Janáček as a composer; if perhaps it was the challenge of deciphering and editing his operatic music before it can be successfully performed. It is true that he wrote in a terribly careless way: he continually changed his music, he wrote out of the range of the instruments, he often wrote things that seem unplayable. Today, when technique has to some extent improved, much that was considered impossible in his time can now be played but it is still not easy. In order to perform Janáček properly one has to do almost as much editing as for a work by Handel or any baroque composer.

What drew me to him is the wonderful, dramatic, earthy human, personal, passionate quality in his attitude, not only to his music but towards everything; his pantheistic feeling for nature, for life itself; the extraordinary subjects he chose for his operas, his unique way of setting words, his different interpretations of commonplace everyday speech; in fact, his tremendous creativity, his absolutely original mind.

It has already been told how I heard my first Janáček opera during my student days in Prague, and how I brought back the score of *Katya Kabanova* to London, leading to its first performance in England on 10 April 1951. Now that Janáček is a classic in the opera house, it is amusing to read the reviews of that far-off première at Sadler's Wells. Most of the old guard seemed bothered by his short-windedness and apparent lack of lyricism. This was typified by the remark of the great Ernest Newman that 'Janáček is rather a scrap-by-scrap composer, finding it difficult to think consecutively for more than two or three minutes at a time; but there are enough good musical moments in his *Katya Kabanova*, of which Sadler's Wells gave us the first English performance on Tuesday, to keep the audience interested to the end.'

This, of course, was similar to Janáček's experiences in his own country about 40 years earlier, when he was trying to get recognition for *Jenůfa*, his first performed full-length opera.

However, the then younger critics found inspiration in these short phrases and Desmond Shawe-Taylor wrote in the *New Statesman*: 'The amazingly pregnant melodic germs are frequently built into ample, flowing phrases, and some of the leading themes of the opera are instrumental in origin. As in all the best of his later work, Janáček displays his peculiar structural power of allowing these brief germs to grow and spread like a thought in the mind, with all sorts of new and expressive harmonic subtleties, but without contrapuntal elaboration

Ex. 31

(*A sample of Janáček's score: from* The Makropulos Case.)

or thickening of the texture. The result is a kind of intimate eloquence which is the opposite of rhetoric: Janáček is like those rare people whose unselfconscious honesty of mind makes us ashamed of exaggeration or pretence. The most striking thing about *Katya Kabanova* is not the unusual technique, but the undiluted strength and purity of its human feeling.'

Katya, produced by Dennis Arundell, was successful enough to warrant several revivals and in 1973 a new production was staged at the London Coliseum. Between those two *Katyas* (1951 and 1973), Sadler's Wells produced most of Janáček's other operas, while Covent Garden gave two different productions of *Jenůfa*. Janáček was the staple diet at the Edinburgh Festival during two visits from Czech companies and there was a production of *Katya*, in Czech, at the Wexford Festival. The operas have become equally successful in Germany, Austria, Scandinavia and the USA, and it is a measure of his popularity outside his own country that Decca decided to record *Katya*, in Czech, but with international singers and the incomparable Vienna Philharmonic Orchestra.

When I first came to conduct *Katya* I found that owing to Janáček's extremely impractical, untidy way of writing down music, the scores and parts were full of mistakes and ambiguities. I knew that certain conductors, including Talich, had actually 'smoothed out' some of the rougher patches, rather as Rimsky-Korsakov did with Mussorgsky, but I had not realized how hard it would be to establish what the composer's intentions actually were. For those early performances of *Katya* I just had to make the best of it, using my common sense and feeling for Janáček's style when faced with problems concerning the text. It was not till 1960, when I returned to Czechoslovakia for the first time since my student days, that I really started to come to grips with the difficulties of establishing a correct text for the operas, particularly *Katya*. When one looks at a Janáček manuscript it is easy to see why there is so much uncertainty about his intentions. Even his so-called 'fair copies' are more like sketches than finished work and it is often very hard to tell which pages are part of a whole score and which merely discarded sketches. It is not unusual for a crossed-out sketch to be on the other side of a 'good' page, so that more often than not a manuscript score of an opera consists of alternate pages of correct and discarded material. Apparently he worked at an idea for a while, altering and rubbing out, then suddenly became impatient with it, crossed it all out and jotted down a completely different idea, which would become the final version.

He always composed straight into full orchestral score, then gave it to the copyist, who wrote out the whole work neatly, mistakes and all. Frequently Janáček added or scratched out things in the copy, sometimes correcting the copyist's misreading of his illegible manuscript and sometimes not. It is no wonder that ever since the first performances, at which Janáček was present, conductors have had terrible trouble deciding what the great man really wanted. Sitting in the Janáček Museum in Brno and looking at all this confusion I decided that if performances of the operas were going to proliferate as fast as they were doing in the 1960's, new editions of *all* his works would have to be made. Rafael Kubelik had started by re-editing *The House of the Dead* and the publishers, Universal Edition of Vienna, had reprinted *Jenůfa* in a new critical edition of Kovařovic's version. They then asked me to edit *The Makropulos Case*, which I was currently performing in London, and later *Katya Kabanova*.

On that visit to Brno I had discovered, or rather re-discovered, two intermezzi which Janáček composed, to give more time for quick scene changes in a new 1928 production, and I was able to include these in the new edition and on the recording. The correction of the vast number of errors for the new edition took Karl-Heinz Füssl, of Universal Edition, and me nearly seven years to complete: but even after much painstaking research, comparison of sources, etc., a few mistakes escaped us. During the Decca recording we had photocopies of both the manuscript sources of *Katya* at every session. Even at the very last session, when we recorded the double love duet of Act II, Scene 2, we found a wrong note in the oboe part which had escaped the notice, not only of the composer, but of all conductors since 1916, including myself.

For the recording it was possible for me to do away with almost all adjustments to Janáček's orchestration because Decca's fine engineers were able to achieve a perfect balance of sound, even when the composer had made realization so difficult as to be almost impossible. There was one instrumental point of which we were especially proud: Janáček often prescribes a viola d'amore in his work, especially in *Katya*, presumably because the name of the instrument inspired him to use it for his love themes: but the sound of the viola d'amore is too weak to be heard against a large orchestra and was always replaced by an ordinary viola, even in Janáček's time. Modern recording technique, however, has made it possible to realize his intention to the letter, and the plaintive tone quality of the viola d'amore may be heard at many poignant moments, lending 'amore' not only in name but in sound to *Katya* and *The Makropulos Case*.

In the theatre the problem of balance is very different. Janáček's unique treatment of the orchestra very often drowns the voices, with violins screaming up at the top of their register and trombones growling away at the bottom of theirs, with nothing in between. He apparently did not bother about the fact that brass instruments are naturally louder than strings. In a theatre performance one is therefore forced to do something to help the balance. Often it is enough to make the orchestra play *piano* rather than *forte*, but occasionally some retouching is necessary. I do not mean wholesale re-orchestration, as Talich did with *Katya*, or Kovařovic with *Jenůfa* for his Prague performance in 1916; I refer merely to small changes of balance produced by doubling some instruments in order to make the main part more audible, and/or changing the dynamics of subsidiary parts.

Thanks to modern technology, in recording *From the House of the Dead* we were able to create marvellous sounds in the second act which would never be possible in the opera house. With digital recording the quality remains equally good when it is copied, which means that one may superimpose all sorts of sounds over an already recorded tape, and the sound quality will remain equally beautiful. This again is a question of balance.

At the opening of the second act (*From the House of the Dead*), which takes place in Siberia, the prisoners are out working and we hear a tree being sawn, cracking and falling down with the music. It is actually written in musical notation in the score. Later, the Easter holidays are announced; the prisoners have time off and we hear the bells ringing. These sound effects had to be done separately, at a different time from the recording of the music, because the bells used by the Vienna Philharmonic are so huge that to play them someone has to stand at the top of a ladder. It gave a marvellous bell effect, whereas the normal tubular bells used in theatres sound much too high because they are comparatively short. Incidentally, during the making of this record, and while two percussion players were sawing a large piece of wood, the caretaker of the Vienna Sofiensaal came in, much alarmed, wondering if the Philharmoniker had decided to break up the place!

Before recording *From the House of the Dead* I re-edited the work with the invaluable assistance of John Tyrrell, the musicologist and Janáček specialist. In this case the reading of the manuscript proved more problematic than in any of the other works. As Janáček grew older he became more eccentric in his way of writing things down. When it came to *The House of the Dead*, which was his final opera, he was so afraid of over-orchestrating, of being tempted to fill in those blank staves that he made his own manuscript paper, drawing only the number of staves he thought he would need. Both the lines and the notes are crooked and one often wonders whether a note is on a line or in a space. How the copyists of his day managed to decipher his manuscript I really don't know, but at least they had him there to refer to — continually shouting at the musicians about interpretation and things to remember and think about when playing his music. As already described, he would go through the neatly copied score, cross things out, insert new ideas and generally revise, frequently *not* noticing mistakes made by the copyist. The original autograph sometimes provides proof that it *was* the copyist who got it wrong.

In *The House of the Dead*, however, Janáček died when he was only half-way through revising the copy made from his frightful autograph; so the whole thing looks like a sketch. It was later revised by two of his pupils, the conductor Bakala and the composer Chlubna. They filled in the orchestration and made it sound less eccentric; they also changed the vocal parts considerably and even went so far as to substitute an alternative, more optimistic ending. Every Janáček specialist, since then, has rejected their additions and tried to work out the original. This leaves no less than four different versions: three made by Czech conductors — Kubelik, Gregor (from Prague) and Nosek (from Brno) and the fourth by myself with John Tyrrell.

It is surprising that the Czechs should have such different views about their greatest national composer of this century; but this, in a way, seems to be Janáček's fate. People have felt that his compositions, although highly original and full of marvellous ideas, showed that he simply did not know how to orchestrate. Even my teacher, Václav Talich, considered his orchestration primitive. To me, this is the very quality that makes him unique; his orchestration is as basic a part of his style as are his melodies and other inventive ideas.

In the National Theatre in Prague today they no longer perform the version of *Katya Kabanova* re-orchestrated by Talich; however, like almost every opera house in the world, they still use Kovařovic's re-arrangement of *Jenůfa*. He, as musical director of the National Theatre, finally agreed that the work could be sufficiently interesting to revive, after it had been rather a failure in Brno in 1904, but he insisted on re-orchestrating it and making a great many cuts. Janáček submitted to everything because there was no other way of getting the work performed; but the question remains how much he gave in because he was forced to, and how much he actually did agree. Certainly his position over the whole issue is rather ambivalent. On one occasion he wrote to Erich Kleiber saying that he could never have imagined his work could sound so wonderful! (that of course was in Kovařovic's version, *further* retouched by Kleiber); on the other hand he said that he didn't see why Kovařovic's widow should have any of the royalties from the re-orchestrated edition when he, Janáček, had not asked for the changes in the first place.

It is a fact that *Jenůfa* sounds different from all the other Janáček operas simply because the only known version was that of Kovařovic. Now I have recorded Janáček's own version, after stripping the score of all Kovařovic's alterations to the orchestration and his cuts. The original overture, previously known as an independent piece entitled *Jealousy*, and the Kostelnička's lengthy Act I narration, can now also be heard. There are some dramatic differences between the two versions at the beginning and the end of Act II, and at the end of the whole opera. As Janáček did in fact work with Kovařovic on the revised version of the ending, we recorded the final love duet in both versions, firstly Janáček's simple, indecisive finish and then Kovařovic's triumphant ending with the horns blaring out the theme in canon.

With *Mr Brouček's Excursions* and *The Cunning Little Vixen*, the orchestration, though typically Janáček, involves no difficulties in reading his manuscript. This may be because the original conductors of these works were quick at spotting the wrong notes from the start. If so, I am more than grateful to Otakar Ostrčil (Prague) and František Neumann (Brno) for saving me further deciphering work, after the endless hours I spent on *Katya*, *The Makropulos Case* and *From the House of the Dead*; also, of course, his *Sinfonietta*, which is full of copyist's mistakes which Janáček once again failed to notice. In fact he even sanctioned this error-ridden copy as the only authorized edition of the work; since when, every Janáček conductor has tried to correct the mistakes. But our corrections are not necessarily the same; each individual can interpret the composer's hieroglyphics differently.

In the case of the *Glagolitic Mass* Janáček drew his own staves, as he did for *The House of the Dead*. After a fair copy had been made he simplified many of the rhythms, possibly because he thought the chorus would not be able to cope with the complications. However, he seems to have taken particular trouble over the exact details when the work came to be published. Despite this I found several important divergencies between the original manuscript and the fair copy — yet another example of Janáček failing to notice certain errors of the copyist. (These small errors have been corrected in my Supraphon recording with the Czech Philharmonic Choir and orchestra.)

The Mass itself is not only the product of a completely original mind — the Benedictus (*Blagoslovlen*, in old Slavonic) is set in the most extraordinary way a Benedictus could be set — but a perfect expression of the composer's feeling towards all nature, all life. It is a great pantheistic hymn of praise.

Shortly* after he had completed *The Cunning Little Vixen* Janáček wrote to his translator, Max Brod: 'A beauty 300 years old, and eternally young, but with all feeling burnt out of her! Brr-r! Cold as ice! I'm going to write an opera about such a woman.'

Even before the first production of *The Vixen* he was hard at work on *The Makropulos Case*, which he finished in November 1925. In *The Vixen* and *Mr Brouček's Excursions* he had already shown a predilection for the fantastic in opera; he was always attracted to plays and poetry which brood over the shortness of life, the inevitability of death and the timelessness of Nature. Karel Čapek's play about the 300-year-old Elina Makropulos must have had a very special fascination for him.

At the time that Čapek was dwelling on the problem of the elixir of eternal life Bernard Shaw was writing *Back to Methuselah*, but whereas Shaw regards longevity as a blessing without which Man cannot fully inherit the riches of the earth, Čapek's heroine has become soured and hardened by three centuries of living. She is torn between her longing for death and her desire to find again the recipe which will give her a further lease of life. This is the *věc* or 'thing' of the title: a literal translation of the title is *The Makropulos Thing*, rather than 'affair' or 'case'. Čapek intended his treatment of the subject as an optimistic one; in fact, he expressly called his play a comedy. His message is that the length of life is less important than Man's fulfilment of it, and in depicting his 300-year-old beauty as cynical and hard he wanted to show the moral degradation and spiritual decay of a human being in such a situation, rather as Aldous Huxley did in *After Many a Summer*.

Čapek himself was apparently very preoccupied with death, and his play was the outcome of much philosophical deliberation. He venerated Janáček as a composer and at once agreed with his wish to turn the work into an opera, although with misgivings as to the suitability of the subject for operatic treatment. Like many authors, he also feared the composer would distort the meaning of the play.

In fact Janáček used the play almost word for word, except for a few minor cuts and the compression of the third act from two scenes to one. The one important difference between play and opera is that, unlike Čapek, Janáček makes the long-lived heroine die at the end and presents the character less harshly than Čapek. The music infuses poetry into the somewhat prosaic plot and raises the whole plane of the work from a basically cerebral philosphical drama to a great

*What follows is reprinted from an article by Charles Mackerras in *Opera*, February 1964, and reprinted by kind permission of the Editor.

human tragedy, which the audience can feel as universal and enter into with sympathy.

Čapek linked his play to Czech history by starting the story in sixteenth-century Prague, under Rudolph II. This Hapsburg emperor employed alchemists and astrologers from all over Europe to search for the Philosopher's Stone, to produce gold and the Elixir of Life. Čapek imagined an alchemist, Hieronymus Makropulos, who actually did find the Elixir of Life and was forced by the emperor to try it on his own sixteen-year-old daughter, Elina. She lives for 300 years, until the early twentieth century, the period in which the drama takes place. Janáček's music lends further colour to the otherwise matter-of-fact ambience of the play by the marvellous prelude to the opera, which, in the mad, quasi-archaic fanfares for brass and kettledrums behind the scenes, suggests the fantastic court of Rudolph, surrounded by his astrologers:

Ex. 32

This off-stage fanfare reappears in the third act, when the whole sad history is narrated, and it accompanies the heroine's death (or redemption), in the final moments of the opera. The crazy fanfares are contrasted with great lyrical outpourings in the orchestra which mirror the tragedy of the alchemist's unfortunate daughter and her series of passionate loves through the centuries.

In this kind of drama an abundance of vocal lyricism would obviously be out of place. Throughout his opera-composing career we find Janáček gradually entrusting his broad, lyrical motivities to the orchestra, while the voices 'speak' at natural speed. Thus, *Jenůfa* and *Katya Kabanova* still contain much of the old 'operatic' *cantilena*, while *The Makropulos Case* and *From the House of the Dead* have hardly any at all. Janáček saw melody in all human speech, also in animal and natural noises. In fact, his attempts to write down the speech of various acquaintances in terms of music form the basis of many of his interesting articles. He even copied down in musical notes some of his daughter Olga's last tragic dying utterances, as if to preserve their sound in his memory. He read people's characters from their speech and painted each of his operatic personages in differing kinds of speech-melody and speech-rhythm.

It is never the purely musical idea which dictates Janáček's vocal writing. For instance, we may feel Albert Gregor's youthful, virile ardour in Act I of *Makropulos* in the upward-surging, widely ranging phrases which twice take him up to top C; but by Act II his passion for Emilia has become maudlin and his utterance is debased into a cringing, whining method of expression, just as it would be in ordinary speech. As Jaroslav Vogel has pointed out, in his excellent book on the composer, this is an example of how Janáček, like Wagner and Richard Strauss, uses the high register of the male voice to suggest weakness of character. With Prus, the remarkably high *tessitura* helps to suggest a scheming, tight-lipped, nervous character. Only once does Prus speak quickly and in the low baritone register, in Act II, when he enthusiastically explains to Emilia Marty how he chanced upon the true identity of 'Elian MacGregor'. The lawyer Kolenatý is one of the cleverest examples of Janáček's character-drawing through speech-melody. We note his fussy repetition of conventional phrases, the monotonous sing-song as he undramatically, almost boringly, narrates extraordinary events, and his slow, heavy humour, always at someone else's expense!

Janáček's genius in vocal music lies in his feeling for the rhythms and inflections of the Czech language. Czech words are all accented on the first syllable and often much lengthened on the second, as in the name Janáček itself. (It is suggested that when he often does not allow for the lengthened second syllable it is because he himself spoke a dialect in which that syllable is much shorter than in standard Czech.) Small, unimportant conjunctions and prepositions receive extra-ordinarily strong accents in speech and all these features of the language help to create the absolutely unique contours, the rise and fall of a peculiarly personal style. That this style is bound up with Czech inflection is shown, not only by the immense difficulty of translating his operas into other languages without distorting his vocal line, but also when he himself uses foreign words. In *The Makropulos Case*, Kolenatý reads from German legal reports, a half-witted old gentle-man called Hauk talks in Spanish and Elina speaks Greek, but in each case Janáček's genius for natural accentuation seems suddenly to have left him and he accents all these languages as though they were Czech. The very name Makropulos (Greek accent on the second syllable), is set by the composer as *Mak*ropulos.

Characterization of a different kind goes on more or less continu-ously in the orchestra; but Janáček's motives, unlike the leading-motives familiar to us in most symphonic opera since Wagner, grow from one into the other, by subtle changes of rhythm and melody.

Although the intervals and basic notes of a motive remain constant, it can thus be presented in ever-changing aspects, like a musical kaleidoscope. Stravinsky has also used this method (e.g. the minor third and the common chord motive in *Oedipus Rex*), and the 12-note idea in embryo had similar features. Nowhere is this technique of Janáček's more appropriate than in *The Makropulos Case*, where the same intervals are employed in different shapes to express E.M.* in all her myriad guises and situations. It is fascinating to follow the basic E.M. motive of seconds, fourths and fifths through the opera and to observe the number of forms it takes (see examples on pages 320 and 321).

If Janáček's treatment of themes and vocal characterization is original, his use of the orchesta is unique. The period in which he was composing was the high-water mark in lavish and colourful orchestration, so to his contemporaries his use of the orchestra must have seemed incredibly sparse and thin, almost clumsy. Perhaps this is what inspired Václav Talich largely to re-orchestrate *The Cunning Little Vixen* and *Katya Kabanova* so that they sound lush and gorgeous. Janáček, however, although he did not object to the occasional 'filling-out' of some passages by conductors, definitely did not want his works 'varnished with instrumentation' as he put it. It was to avoid the temptation to 'varnish' that he ceased using music paper and drew the lines of the staves himself on ordinary paper, and that, as he grew older, the scores grew sparser. *The Makropulos Case* abounds in such sparse effects — for instance the already-mentioned screaming violins, sometimes with flutes, and the growling trombones, tuba and double-basses with a huge gap in between.

This kind of scoring requires very careful balancing of the orchestral forces if it is to sound good, although it has become more familiar to musicians lately through its frequent employment in 'pop' music. Despite the great difficulty and awkwardness of many of Janáček's instrumental passages (due to their basis in the whole-tone scale and their habit of coming just after the beat), he knew how to orchestrate 'normally' if he wanted to, as his early Dvořák-like Suite and *Lachian Dances* show, but the listener should not be surprised if the lyrical and romantic parts of Janáček's operas do not sound like Puccini or Strauss. They simply are not orchestrated that way.

Nevertheless, his use of the orchestra fits the subject of this opera like a glove, and in particular the character of E.M. as Janáček saw her. During composition he wrote several times to Kamila Stösslová, his

*Elina Makropulos . . . Elian Macgregor . . . Emilia Marty.

Ex. 33

The Makropulos Case
transformations of the heroine's motive

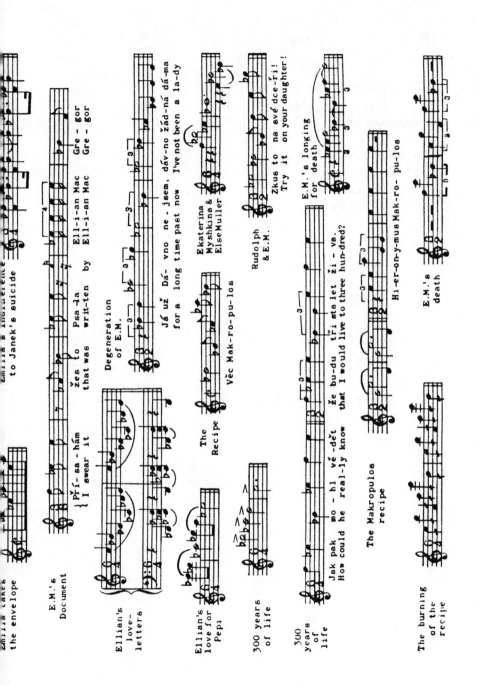

Immortal Beloved, so-to-say, and one of his images or models for Emilia Marty: 'I am already making Miss Brr-r. But I am making her warmer, so that people can have sympathy with her. I'll fall in love with her yet.' And again: 'But what about my 300-year-old! They all call her a liar, a fake, an hysterical woman — and in fact she's so unhappy! I wanted people to like her. With me it's no good without love . . . They call her dreadful names, they wanted to throttle her and what was her fault? That she had to live so long. I felt dreadfully sorry for her.'

The Makropulos Case is an extraordinary opera, but then everything about Janáček is different, new and original. He is difficult, but he is one of the greatest of composers and I am very glad he is becoming so popular with the public.

APPENDIX V

Aspects of Conducting

CONDUCTING, AS WE know it now, is the youngest of the musical performing arts, if we discount electronically-produced music. The modern conductor did not start to emerge as an important musical personality until about the middle of the nineteenth century, with Wagner and his associates. Before this, church choirs were frequently conducted by someone making arm movements, but the orchestra was led by the first violinist. Operatic and orchestral music was directed by the first violin, or *Konzertmeister*, and the *Kapellmeister* (often the composer) played the piano or harpsichord. When Haydn brought his symphonies to London he would have conducted from the keyboard (there is a famous painting which shows him at Esterhazy conducting opera in this way). The titles *Konzertmeister* and *Kapellmeister* are still used in Germany: in Hamburg, in the 1960's, I was called the '*Erster Kapellmeister*' and in American orchestras today the leader is referred to as *Concertmaster*.

The dual leadership of orchestras began to die out during the nineteenth century as the *Kapellmeister* at the piano took over more of the direction, but he was not yet responsible for interpretation in the manner of a modern conductor. At rehearsal he would say how he wanted the music played, but his job was mainly to keep things together, to see that everyone played in the same style, all had a *forte* at the same place and so on. The idea of interpretation, meaning different performers taking different views of how a work should be played, is relatively new, almost a twentieth-century concept.

In opera it became increasingly difficult to control the ensemble from the keyboard. The early baton-waving conductor stood in the centre of the pit, near the stage, which meant that while he conducted the singers on stage he had his back to the orchestra and when he turned to conduct the orchestra, his back was turned to the singers. The conductor's position near the prompter's box, with his back to the orchestra, lasted in some opera houses into the early years of the present century — for example, as shown on the two cover pictures of the Metropolitan New York in the recently issued Mapleson Cylinders recordings of Met singers from the turn of the century. As operas became more complicated, it became more difficult to keep singers and orchestra together. In the big Verdi operas the violin part of the leader contained every important melodic cue; every voice part was cued in, apart from passages in strict tempo, such as marches, so that the violin leader would know exactly where he was. If the conductor had to turn his back suddenly on the orchestra to help the singers the violinist could take over his old eighteenth-century job of actually keeping the orchestra together.

The change from the keyboard to the stick–waving conductor took place in the 1850's. For example, the programme for the Venetian première of Rossini's *Otello* in 1848 refers to a *Maestro al Cembalo*, whereas in 1851 for *Semiramide* he is called *Maestro Concertatore*, and presumably wielded a baton. In both performances there were still two violin-directors (one for the opera and one for the ballet), who helped to keep things together.

Modern orchestral musicians are so experienced in understanding baton technique that they can usually be relied upon to play together and in the same style, making opera performances possible without rehearsal. In German houses this has long been the norm and unrehearsed performances become second nature for any conductor who has worked in them. I often conducted *Fidelio* or *Aida*, say, in Berlin or Hamburg without rehearsal, twice in one week, each time with different personnel in the chorus and orchestra and possibly a different cast, yet would still give a good performance — provided productions were entirely 'traditional', i.e. without special aspects of style that demanded careful rehearsal. In opera it is accepted that players have the necessary confidence to perform together. In most cases there is a chorus–master conducting behind the stage to ensure that the chorus sings together. If soloists go wrong the prompter can usually put things right by gesticulating, shouting or even singing the solo parts to keep the performance going! A modern virtuoso conductor sees himself as an interpreter rather than a mere 'keeper-together'.

At the performance the orchestral musician's job is to play the notes in front of him as well as he can. The conductor's job is to mould those notes into a form so that the audience can grasp and understand the architecture of the music, whether it is a great symphonic movement or an act of an opera. He has to calculate the climaxes, the dramatic and emotional interpretation. Often it is not the obvious, brilliant moments that are the most difficult but the transitions between them, the subtle nuances of tempo.

As well as technique, experience, talent and personality a conductor needs the ability to persuade musicians to play the music as he imagines it should be played. This, in fact, is the whole art of conducting, welding a number of individuals with separate and different ideas and experience into one whole. It is largely the measure of a conductor's personality how successfully he can make the musicians submit to his will, voluntarily and with a good grace, for each one of them is an expert in his own field.

There have been great conductors like Walter, Beecham, Kleiber, who managed to give their players the illusion they were not being led at all but expressing themselves freely, so that naturally they all played their best. Others *drove* their orchestras. Shostakovich described conducting as 'the work of a born dictator'. Although this hardly applies now, it was certainly true at one time. In the years between the two world wars some conductors were absolute martinets. Toscanini, for instance, with his great tantrums, tearing up the score and breaking people's instruments over their heads, and the more Teutonic, psychological kind of dictator like Fritz Reiner and Georg Szell, though in fact these two great maestros were Hungarian, not German. They were terribly sarcastic and rude, even intentionally hurtful to players. In those days the conductor was boss and could hire and fire at a moment's notice. Objections were not tolerated, mutiny meant instant dismissal. Such tyrants were respected but feared, often resented, even hated. Some musicians actively hated Reiner and Szell, but their discipline was quite extraordinary and they really knew their music from A to Z. If all copies of the symphonic and opera repertoire had been destroyed they could have written them out again from memory with 100 per cent accuracy. The Cleveland Orchestra, which Szell conducted till his death only a few years ago, has never been the same since.

Now that life in general is more democratic, people are less likely to take orders without question. When I tried to impose my style of playing Mozart on the Paris Opera Orchestra, the leader said '*Nous n'aimons pas le style d'outre-Manche*'! This was such a monstrous insult to a British conductor that many of the orchestra members sniggered with embarrassment, waiting to see whether I would walk out in a huff or laugh it off. I decided to treat it as a joke and pretend I did not understand the insult. The dictator–conductor has been replaced perhaps, by the great charismatic type, such as Karajan. He moves very little; he conducts with eyes shut most of the time; he does not rehearse a great deal, yet he always produces *his* ideal performance and, because of his remarkable ability to communicate his own concept, he can produce a certain typical sound from any orchestra. It is this quality that makes the difference between one performance and another and between one conductor and another. The Germans call it *Ausstrahlung*, the Emanation of the Conductor. A vital part of conducting is projecting one's mind into that of the players. The more strongly a conductor can mentally transmit his interpretation into the minds of the musicians, the more successful he will be, whether or not they agree with his interpretation.

Emanation is a very mysterious process. In essence it is intense concentration or a combination of concentration and projection. Erich Kleiber (father of Carlos Kleiber, who has the same ability), had this inexplicable gift *par excellence* and there have been many with the same power. Furtwängler's performances of Beethoven symphonies and the big German works were mystical, utterly spontaneous, and with every performance quite unlike any other. When he conducted there was in the concert hall or opera house an extraordinary feeling that something immense was happening, something deeply mysterious going on on the stage. Both audience and performers felt it, yet there was nothing to be seen but a man gesticulating and that not even very clearly. Furtwängler believed that music was the revelation of the human soul. He saw in the form of classical music — from Haydn and Mozart to Brahms and Bruckner — with its conflict between the heroic and the lyrical, a profound statement of man's tragic predicament.

Bruno Walter was another poetic, philosopher-conductor, as in many ways was my old teacher, Václav Talich. Talich was very much one of those who regarded themselves as a channel or conduit, a translator of music from its bare notes to its spiritual content. Talich was a devout Catholic and Bruno Walter was Jewish but whether or not such men are religious in the orthodox sense they were certainly spiritual beings, like Mahler. Compare Mahler with Strauss: both were working, composing and conducting at exactly the same period but Mahler was a true mystic, a spiritual being, while Strauss was a clever professional. Strauss's attempts at spirituality and nobility, as with John the Baptist in *Salome*, have a touch of the commonplace, of *Hymns Ancient and Modern*; yet both composers were great in their own way. They expressed different attitudes and temperaments. There is room for both.

Most conductors have the ability to emanate to some degree; I have already mentioned unrehearsed performances in German opera houses and it is only through emanation that a conductor can hope to make each one of such performances different from every other.

Naturally he is more successful if his musicians are receptive; their responsiveness varies. Though it is possible to some extent to resist negative vibrations from an orchestra it can be psychologically very exhausting.

Sir Adrian Boult, who was very kind to me when I first arrived in London, invited me to attend his rehearsals with the BBC Symphony Orchestra and also went through certain scores with me. I was particularly interested in what he had to say about Elgar, who had been an idol of my youth. I asked him how the conductor can make it audible to the listener that the themes of the Scherzo and the Adagio of the First Symphony are made up of the same notes in a different rhythm. He said 'There is no way, except to *will* it, my boy. *Will* it enough and it will happen.' On one occasion, at the Coliseum, at the final dress rehearsal of *The Mastersingers* Edmund Tracey, one of my fellow directors, was concerned about certain aspects of my interpretation, although he was unable to be specific about what actually bothered him. On the first night the performance was quite different and very successful, although there had been no more rehearsal. Often, particularly in opera, at rehearsals, even up to the very last minute, the conductor must concentrate so completely on the work of others that he cannot think about himself, about measuring and pacing his own work. On the night, however, he must and does think of his own performance as well as that of the other artists. The pacing of an opera like *The Mastersingers*, which is so long, needs tremendous planning. If one section is taken the slightest bit slower, or the conductor gives way to a singer here and not there the architecture of the whole composition could be affected — and above all this, he must project to the singers and orchestra his own response to the music, how he wants the performance to be.

Many conductors have their own orchestral parts marked with dynamics, bowings and various other marks of interpretation. I have found that this saves an immense amount of rehearsal time. When I conducted frequently in East Berlin I amassed a large library of orchestral parts which I marked or had marked according to my interpretation. It includes about 50 famous symphonies, many other works which I often conduct (such as Janáček), as well as several operas, mainly by Mozart. I have also a large collection of various works by Handel which are marked so that non-specialist orchestras may quickly accustom themselves to baroque-style trills, overdotting, bowing and phrasing. This editing can save hours of explanation at rehearsals.

Frequently as conductors grow older their beat becomes slower.

This is sometimes taken as a sign of profundity. It is extraordinary how many audiences, orchestral musicians, and certainly critics, confuse slowness with depth. It applies to any musician, not only conductors: the slower he goes, the greater the meaning! For most of us, mind and body do slow down with age. This is particularly noticeable with conductors, and shows in the actual beat. In some cases, it may be through illness, as with Klemperer who was paralysed towards the end of his life. He still generated immense excitement, power and authority, but he had difficulty moving his hands, and his actual tempi became so slow as to be almost plodding. His earlier recordings reveal that he was not always like that. I have a tape of him conducting *Don Giovanni* in Budapest immediately after World War II, and he takes the opening, the Statue music, extremely fast by modern standards. I am sure he conducted it in two beats in a bar, as it should be; only later, when he was weak and ill did he conduct it in four.

This slowing down is quite marked with conductors in the great German Wagnerian tradition — Furtwängler, Klemperer, Hans Knappertsbusch. Though their minds were still alert, as they physically aged and weakened they became slower and slower; yet when one reads what Wagner himself said about conducting and tempo, one realizes that many famous Wagnerian conductors today would certainly not have met with his approval. Wagner said very definitely that, '*The whole duty of a conductor is comprised in his ability always to indicate the right tempo. His choice of tempi will show whether he understands the piece or not.*'[*] He mentions a performance of *The Rhinegold* which lasted exactly two and a half hours at rehearsals under a conductor he had personally instructed, while under the beat of the official *Kapellmeister* it lasted fully three hours. He also tells us that when he conducted the overture to *Tannhäuser* at Dresden it lasted twelve minutes, but 'now lasts twenty'. He adds tartly, 'No doubt I am here alluding to thoroughly incompetent persons who are particularly shy of *alla breve* time, and who stick to their correct and normal crotchet beats, four in a bar, merely to show that they are present and conscious of doing something.'

In the last article written by that famous musical commentator, Hans Keller, just before he died (in November 1985), he analysed what makes a really great performance — not only of conductors, but of all *performing musicians*. He speaks of the 'searching understanding' that is essential, the 'comprehension' of the way the composer wishes

*My italics — C.M.

his music to be 'read' which includes 'not only consistent phrasings, but also an ability to characterise logically — in other words to find the right tempo or perhaps we should say *a* right tempo, since there isn't a single piece of music in our Western tradition which requires a single right tempo.'

That of course is perfectly true — both Wagner in his day and Hans Keller, nearly 100 years later, realized that tempo is very flexible. Wagner constantly suggested modifications of tempo in the course of works which from the markings seem intended to be taken in strict time. He has given an exhaustive analysis of how to conduct the overture of *The Mastersingers* in which he tells us that certain phrases should become slightly slower, but he did not bother to mark them, assuming that any musical person would know what he meant.

Among 'authentic' performers of eighteenth-century music there is at present a reaction against slow tempi. Some groups even make a point of taking everything very fast, probably in an attempt to rid eighteenth-century masterpieces of the gravity and solemnity which have been grafted on to them in the two centuries since they were written. Although there is no doubt that tempi in the eighteenth and early nineteenth centuries were extremely fast by modern standards, the music taken at an authentic tempo runs the risk of becoming superficial. One has only to try taking Beethoven's symphonies at the tempi he prescribes by metronome marks to see how much taste in these matters has changed. The same can be said of the very fast metronome marks of Czerny and Hummel, in their arrangements of Mozart and Haydn symphonies.

Another factor which has significantly changed tempi in modern times is the marking of *alla breve* (₵), which means that the music should be felt in two beats in a bar rather than four. Mozart's music has often suffered from this misconception, but the outstanding example is the impressive opening of Schubert's Great C Major Symphony, of which no printed edition contains the correct *alla breve* markings of the autograph. Schubert never heard the work performed and it was not published until long after his death. It has been played at almost half the correct speed for a century and a half simply because publishers failed to notice that the opening time signature was ₵ and not C. Conductors have therefore had to make contortions of the transition between the Andante and the Allegro non troppo by doing a huge accelerando, instead of the basic pulse remaining the same throughout the two tempi.

Many twentieth-century conductors forget that much slow music is supposed to be conducted in two; because they see *andante* or *adagio* or *largo*, they tend to conduct it, mistakenly, in four.

I spent much of my childhood listening to old pre-electric recordings, including a good deal of Wagner, conducted by such people as Karl Muck and Siegfried Wagner. When I came to England in my early twenties I noticed that Wagner was being played far more slowly than I remembered. I assumed that I must have forgotten the tempi of those old recordings, yet when I heard them again I found it was not my memory at fault but that the conductors themselves had changed. If one listens to recordings of Furtwängler's great Covent Garden performances in the 1920's one finds they are really quite fast. It was only later that he slowed down, when he conducted his memorable broadcasts in Rome (which are all recorded), and later *The Valkyrie* with the Vienna Philharmonic and *Tristan and Isolde* with the Philharmonia. Marvellous as these performances are, they are far slower than they were in the 1920's when he was younger, yet even then he was a profoundly mystic conductor. No doubt he did gain in wisdom as he aged, but we should not necessarily think his later tempi are more correct, or chosen for some deep spiritual reason, just because they became slower.

It is said that the reason for the speed of the old pre-electric recordings which now seem so fast to us, was because they had to fit in so many minutes of music on one side of the record. I do not agree; I think our conception of time in music has slowed down very much, despite the fact that in many other ways life has speeded up. However, there have been conductors, Toscanini for instance, who did not grow slower with age, in fact he went to the other extreme and became faster. He had an absolute fetish about tempo, and he was always telling himself not to slow down. It was said that he was unyielding, did not give way to the singers and so on, but I believe he had the right view of the music. In *La Bohème* his tempi seem terribly fast compared to modern conductors, yet he conducted the original performance of *Bohème*. He also played the cello in the first performance of Verdi's *Otello*, so he must have known the right tempi.

It is an extraordinary fact that *all* composers of whom one has had personal experience, or knows their tempi through recordings, seem to favour faster tempi than conductors or soloists would find ideal. Of the former I would cite Britten, Shostakovich, Tippett and Henze; of the latter Strauss, Elgar, Bartók and especially Rachmaninov. The only famous exception to this seems to be Stravinsky, whose performances in his old age were always slower than his metronome marks.

The great composer-conductors like Strauss and Elgar were conducting their works at the right tempo at the end of their lives and both lived to a pretty good age! If one listens to Elgar conducting his

First Symphony and compares it with some of the later conductors one finds that they — including Sir John Barbirolli for instance, who was a great Elgar specialist — took Elgar's music much slower than the composer did himself.

Traditions and playing have also changed in other respects. Elgar's recordings of his own music are a good illustration. They are played with long swooping *portamenti*. I believe much of that swooping came from the way strings were played at that time. Players used an old-fashioned type of *portamento* which consists of sliding the finger *from* the note they were leaving whereas the modern string player slides *onto* the note he is approaching. The difference in sound is very great. In Elgar's recording of the *Enigma Variations*, which is one of the oldest, the Nimrod Variation sounds almost as though it is being played with one finger. Between every note in the tune there is a glissando.

There are great conductors who can still inspire orchestras to play wonderfully, even though the tempo may be too slow. A truly visionary mind can afford to go slower and still produce a superb performance. This is one of the ways in which young musicians can come to grief: trying to emulate the slowness of great conductors. A Furtwängler or a Klemperer starts life conducting at normal tempo, at the same time investing the music with a special dimension that only *he* possesses. As he ages and grows physically weaker he slows down; music he once conducted in a broad two-in-a-bar is taken in a fast four, then in a slower and slower four. Young aspiring conductors and musicians imitate him, thinking that slowness must be the key to understanding. The next generation hears them in their turn and decides that for profundity of interpretation they must take the music even slower, until eventually, after a couple of generations it is being played twice as slowly as the composer intended it. Meanwhile, the young conductor who has imitated the 'great old man', thinking he has found the answer, has not perhaps realized that the great old man also had something which the young one does not have.

I learned this lesson the hard way the first time I conducted *The Valkyrie*, taking over from Sir Reginald Goodall at the ENO. One of the Wagner recordings I grew up with was Bruno Walter's performance of this opera, with Lauritz Melchior and Lotte Lehmann. Walter took the opening (the storm where Siegmund is fleeing from his enemies), tremendously fast; there was a great sense of rushing, urgency, drama, excitement, but Goodall and Furtwängler whose recordings I had been studying, took it so slowly that, though it sounded spacious and grand, it did not in the least suggest a storm or someone fleeing from enemies. Because the ENO orchestra was accustomed to Goodall's slow tempo I tried to emulate him but I realized from the first performance that I was making a terrible mistake and I decided never to do it again. Thereafter at my Wagner performances for ENO I always took the more traditional, faster tempi.

A similar thing happened in Hamburg when I conducted a ballet choreographed to Furtwängler's famous recording of Schubert's *Unfinished Symphony*. The tempo of this recording was very slow, but, because Furtwängler was conducting, it sounded wonderful in its intense lyricism. The same tempo conducted by me sounded ludicrous. I realized that with my particular temperament I must move at what I considered a sensible tempo, even though the dancers cursed me!

I fell in love with opera when I was seven and it has really been my life. I find it very strange that some conductors regard it as a rather inferior branch of symphonic work and singers as just another orchestral instrument. Operatic conducting is an extremely difficult art, far more demanding than symphonic work, in fact it is so complex that I often wonder that it ever comes off. A good operatic conductor needs to have a certain kind of mind; one that allows him to develop an affinity with singers. He also has to realize *and not resent the fact* that, in effect, his job is to accompany them; certainly not to regard them as part of the orchestra. He has to know how to breathe with the singers; when to lead and when to follow them. Working with singers, whether soloists or in opera, demands tremendous give and take. The ideal I try for is to let the artists feel completely free when in fact they are being led. The conductor, and with him the orchestra, must be able to create a true rapport with the singers, one that, at its best, gives the feeling that singer and conductor are actually creating the music together. This is something intangible and unpredictable; it depends very much on the feeling of the moment, even with very great artists. One has to know and understand the singers' needs and problems during a performance. They are alone, exposed up there on the platform, far away from conductor and prompter. Anything can go wrong, even a voice can suddenly fail.

I had valuable training for operatic conducting during my days as an oboe player: I had to understand about breathing, about allowing time to phrase. Also, during my years as a repetiteur I had to learn all the parts of all the operas in the repertoire as well as off-stage noises and music; all the cues, so I could prompt if necessary, giving leads for singers to start or stop. If there is no prompter the conductor must give cues to the singers. They are singing from memory but they must be absolutely right; they must know *exactly* where to come in, whether a note is dotted or not, as well as act, often in positions from which they cannot see the conductor, who in any case is a long way away. It gives them a sense of security to know there is someone in charge who has the score in front of him which he knows inside out.

No matter how well I know an opera I always have the score with me. Apart from helping with cues and giving the singers confidence, too many things can go wrong. It is extremely confusing when one or more singers are a bar or two behind or in front, or if a musician who has not been to rehearsal is playing in two when the conductor is beating in four, or half a bar behind and the others half a bar ahead. It can really be very dangerous not to have the score. An eminent Italian conductor who never used the score of *Bohème* because he knew it perfectly, once had an unfortunate experience at the end of Act II: the off-stage fanfare of military fifes and bugles failed to sound. The young off-stage conductor did not bring it in, and because the maestro had no score in front of him he was completely lost and the performance had to stop. Exactly the same thing happened to me at the Coliseum during *Bohème*. The off-stage conductor missed bringing in the musicians for the fanfare (maybe they were in the canteen) but I was able to keep the performance together because I had the score and could see which bar I was conducting in. There was no fanfare, but orchestra and singers were able to go on and the fanfare did come in later.

It is extremely embarrassing when an important off-stage effect does not happen. Sometimes the mistake can be covered up, but at others there is nothing to be done. Probably no one would notice if the cannon in *Tosca* does not fire, the opera can go on, but if it is the cannon in Act II of *Butterfly*, which changes the whole direction of the plot—*At last! The Abraham Lincoln has returned!* — it is disastrous. I knew this to happen once. It is even worse if the trombones in *Don Giovanni* do not play in the Cemetery scene when the statue speaks, if there is dead silence or the statue has to sing alone. When I was conducting in Paris there were several occasions when the trombones did not turn up because they were in the bar. They just did not come in. They apologized afterwards, but the damage was done. The trouble is that they have such a long wait. Mozart only uses trombones at special moments, when he wants a solemn effect, and the Cemetery scene is the first time they play in the whole opera, after nearly three hours of music. The musicians come into the pit, play their phrases for the Statue scene with Don Giovanni and the Commendatore, then finish.

★

I have always enjoyed choral conducting, it appears to me a cross between the symphonic and operatic styles. During my career I have conducted nearly all the great choral works, most of them religious in character — since some of the greatest of all were written to be sung in church. Though I do not belong to any orthodox religion, no doubt my partly Catholic education influenced me to a certain extent where music is concerned. I am sometimes asked how one can conduct a religious work when one does not share the faith that inspired it. The answer could be that in trying to interpret a composer's work one has to get inside his mind and feelings as much as possible, identify with him and leave behind one's own personal views, including those on religion. The religious backgrounds of Haydn, Bach, Beethoven and Janáček were all quite different, yet their various responses to the words of the Mass are among the most sublime works of musical literature.

Associations

To me there is something particularly exciting about localities associated with music. I first came to appreciate this in Prague as a student when I heard Talich conducting Dvořák in the Rudolfinum (now House of Artists), where so many of the Master's works were first heard. In Prague, also, I remember my feelings on visiting the British Embassy where Mozart had played for the Thun family, and the Villa Bertramka where he composed the Overture to *Don Giovanni*; and in particular a performance of *Don Giovanni* (albeit a not very stylish one) in the very theatre where it first sounded in 1787. The Nostitz Theatre, now the Tyl Theatre, has since been seen all over the world in the horror film *Amadeus*, where the poor old theatre had to double as the Vienna Court Opera *and* as Schikaneder's Popular Theatre, all in the cause of Czechoslovakia's perennial need of foreign currency.

Associations are also very strong for any musician who performs Wagner's *Rhinegold* in Düsseldorf, as I did once. The barges floated by on the Rhine even as the first low E flat was heard, that primeval note 'that has been sounding for thousands of years, but is only just becoming audible'.

Another great river, the Volga, has the last word in *Katya Kabanova*. Once when I conducted the opera in Düsseldorf, imagine my horror when the chorus, in that final glorious Song of the Volga, failed to come in. I was told that the producer had cut it out, as being out of keeping with his 'concept' of the opera!

The Swiss lakes and mountains are very evocative in Delius's *Village Romeo and Juliet*, based on Switzerland's most famous novel. When I conducted the opera in Zürich I used to look out on to the lake and imagine Vreni and Sali drifting to their 'Love Death' (also in B major, like Wagner's) in a remote part of that same lake, with the cries of the bargees echoing around the mountains.

The thrill of the *Rosenkavalier Waltz* when it appears in all its glory at the end of Act II with the Vienna Philharmonic strings playing those lovely *glissandi*, is something I will never forget. To the Professors in the Vienna Phil, no doubt it was just another *Rosenkavalier*, but to me conducting it there was something very special.

These are a few of the myriads of associations which certain parts of Europe can lend to a musician, and which nothing in the New World can rival.

DISCOGRAPHY
& INDEX

DISCOGRAPHY
prepared by Malcolm Walker

Abbreviations & Symbols

ASV: Academy Sound and Vision
(bar): baritone
BE: recording/balance engineer
(c): contralto
CD: Compact Disc
CfP: Classics for Pleasure
CO: Chamber Orchestra
ECO: English Chamber Orchestra
LP: 33 1/3 rpm disc
LPO: London Philharmonic
    Orchestra
LSO: London Symphony Orchestra
(m): mono recording
P: recording producer/supervisor
PAO: Pro Arte Orchestra

PhO: Philharmonia Orchestra
PO: Philharmonic Orchestra
ROHO: Royal Opera House
    Orchestra, Covent Garden
RPO: Royal Philharmonic Orches-
    tra
RSO: Radio Symphony Orchestra
(s): soprano
(t): tenor
(T): pre-recorded reel-to-reel tape
VPO: Vienna Philharmonic Orches-
    tra
WRC: World Record Club
(4): pre-recorded cassette
45: 45 rpm disc
78: 78 rpm disc

alpha-numeric sequence/alpha-numeric sequence (e.g. XLP30022/
    SXLP30022) denotes mono and stereo catalogue numbers
    NB: all recordings are stereo unless otherwise stated

LAY-OUT
Recordings are listed by year, month and day(s) of recording; the recording
    studio or venue; participating artists including orchestra; recording
    company (and label).
An asterisk following a record number refers to the previously asterisked
    performer and/or work, and denotes appearance on this recording only.

Discography of Commercial Recordings made by Sir Charles Mackerras

1951 7-8 June. EMI Studio No. 1, Abbey Road, London NW8. Sadler's
Wells Orchestra. EMI/Columbia
SULLIVAN (arr. Mackerras): Pineapple Poll — Ballet (complete)
78: DX1765/70. LP: (m) 33SX1001
1955 4 May. EMI Studio No. 1. Peter Dawson (bass-bar); LSO. EMI/HMV
ARLEN: Clancy of the Overflow (a)
SPEAKS/HEDGECOCK/COBB/WILLEBY: Mandalay Scena (b)
45: (m) 7EG8157 (a, b).
LP: (m) SM411/414 (a). set PD1 (a, b).
1955 21, 22 and 30 June. EMI Studio No. 1. PhO. EMI/HMV
VERDI (arr. Mackerras): The Lady and the Fool — Ballet (complete)
LP: (m) CLP1059. (m) XLP30006. (T) HTC614
— excerpts — 45: (m) 7EP7081
1956 4 April. EMI Studio No. 1. LSO. EMI/HMV
HANDEL: Berenice — Overture (Minuet) (a)
HANDEL (arr. Harty): Water Music — Suite (b)
CLARKE: Trumpet Voluntary (Eskdale, trpt; Brass Ens) (c)
45: (m) 7EP7031 (a-c). (m) 7P269 (a, c)
1956 16 April. EMI Studio No. 1. ROHO. EMI/HMV
DELIBES: Lakmé — Ballet Music (Act 2)
VERDI: Otello — Ballet Music (Act 3)
45: (m) 7EP7069
1956 23 April. EMI Studio No. 1. ROHO. EMI/HMV
DELIBES: La Source — Ballet Music
LP: (m) CLP1195. (T) SCT1507. XLP30022/SXLP30022. CFP40298
1956 25 April. EMI Studio No. 1. PhO. EMI/HMV
COPLAND: Rodeo — Hoe Down (recording unpublished)
1956 25 and 28 April. EMI Studio No. 1. PhO. EMI/HMV
MESSAGER: Les deux pigeons — Ballet Music
LP: (m) CLP1195. (T) SCT1507. XLP30022/SXLP30022. CFP40298
— excerpts — LP: ESDW713 (4) TC-ESDW713
1956 30 April. EMI Studio No. 1. PhO. EMI/HMV
COPLAND: The Quiet City (recording unpublished)
1956 23-24 May. EMI Studio No. 1. LSO. EMI/Columbia
'Favourite Music of Eric Coates'
London Suite Again — Oxford Street: March (a); The Merrymakers
Overture (b); The Three Bears Fantasy (c); By the sleepy lagoon (d);

Summer Days Suite — At the Dance (e); The Three Elizabeths Suite —
Queen Elizabeth: March (f); Three Men — Suite: Man from the Sea (g)
45: (m) SED5539 (a, b, d, e); SCD2190 (a, d); DB8966 (d)
LP: (m) 33S1092. (T) BTD708. (m) XLP30071. CFP40279.
   CFPD414456–3 (b, c, d, e, g) (4) CFPD414456–5 (b, c, d, e, g)

1956 4 June. Kingsway Hall, London WC1. RPO. EMI/HMV
P. BURKHARD: Der Schuss von der Kanzel Overture
REZNIČEK: Donna Diana — Overture
45: (m) 7EP7037

1956 9 June. EMI Studio No. 1. PhO. EMI/HMV
'Gilbert and Sullivan Overtures'
Iolanthe (a); The Mikado (b); Ruddigore (c); The Yeomen of the Guard
(d) 45: 7EP7037/PES5254 (a, c). LP: (T) SCT1513 (a–d). CFP40279 (b, c)

1956 22 October. EMI Studio No. 1. PhO. EMI/HMV
GOUNOD: Faust — Ballet Music (Act 5)
LP: (m) DLP1177
WOLF-FERRARI: Il segreto di Susanna — Overture (a)
WOLF-FERRARI: I quattro rusteghi — Prelude (b)
WOLF-FERRARI: I quattro rusteghi — Intermezzo (Act 2) (c)
45: (m) 7EP7120 (a, c). LP: (m) DLP1193 (a–c)

1956 23–24 October.
COPLAND: El salón Mexico (recording unpublished)
WOLF-FERRARI: I gioielli della Madonna (Act 2) — Intermezzo (a); (Act 3)
— Intermezzo (b); Festa popolare (c); Danza napolitana (d)
45: (m) 7EP7120 (b, d) LP: (m) DLP1193 (a–d)
BERLIOZ: Les Troyens — Marche troyenne (Act 1) (a)
BERLIOZ: La Damnation de Faust, Op. 24 — Marche hongroise (b);
Menuet des follets (c); Ballet des sylphes (d)
45: 7EP7112/PES5269 (b–d)
LP: (m) DLP1168 (a–d). 35750/S-35750 (a–d)

1956 25 October.
MUSSORGSKY (orch. Lyadov): Sorochinski Fair — Gopak (a)
GLAZUNOV: Concert Waltz No. 1, Op. 47 (b)
GLIER': The Red Poppy — Ballet, Op. 70: Russian Sailors' Dance (c)
GLINKA: Ruslan and Ludmilla — Overture (d)
RIMSKY-KORSAKOV: Tsar Sultan — Flight of the Bumble Bee (e)
45: (m) 7EP7084 (a, d, e). LP: (m) DLP1170. (T) SCT 1524
WIREN: Serenade for Strings, Op. 11 — Scherzo; March

1956 26 October.
CHABRIER: Le Roi malgré lui — Fête polonaise
45: 7EP7109/PES5268. LP: (m) DLP1177. 35750/S-35750
IPPOLITOV-IVANOV: Caucasian Sketches, Op. 10 — No. 4, Procession of
the Sardar
RIMSKY-KORSAKOV: Snow Maiden — Dance of the Tumblers
45: (m) 7EP7084. LP: (m) DLP1170. (T) SCT1524. 35752/S-35752

1956 27 October.
BERLIOZ: Le Carnaval romain Overture, Op. 9 (a)
CHABRIER: España (b)

45: 7EP7109/PES5268 (b). LP: (m) DLP1177. 35750/S-35750

1956 2–3 November. Kingsway Hall. PhO. EMI/HMV
VERDI: Overtures — La forza del destino (a); Luisa Miller (b); Nabucco (c); Alzira (d)
45: 7EP7080 (b, d)
LP: (m) DLP1185. 35751/S-35751. XLP30019/SXLP30019. S-60354

1956 30 November. EMI Studio No. 1. PhO. EMI/HMV
WIREN: Serenade for Strings, Op. 11 — Scherzo; March

1957 25–26 May, 1 & 30 June and 1 July. EMI Studio No. 1.
Schwarzkopf (s); PhO & Chorus. EMI/Columbia
'The Elisabeth Schwarzkopf Christmas Album'
All items arr. Mackerras except Gruber
FRANCK: Panis angelicus. TRADITIONAL: O du fröhliche; Von Himmel hoch; In dulci jubilo; Easter Alleluia; Maria auf dem Berge; O come all ye faithful; The first nowell. HUMPERDINCK: Weihnachten. TRADI-TIONAL (arr. Brahms): Sandmännchen. F. GLUCK: In einem kühlen Grunde. GRUBER: Stille Nacht
LP: (m) 33CX1482. (m) 35530. S-36750. ASD3798 (4) TC-ASD3798. 100453–1 (4) 100453–4

1958 8 January. Kingsway Hall. PhO. EMI/Columbia
VERDI: I vespri siciliani — Ballet Music: The Four Seasons
LP: 35751/S-35751. XLP30019/SXLP30019. QIMX7021/SQMIX 7021. S-60354

1958 26, 27 and 30 May. Walthamstow Assembly Rooms. LSO. Decca
'Finlandia'
GRIEG: 2 Elegiac Melodies, Op. 34 (a); 2 Norwegian Melodies, Op. 63 — No. 2, Cowkeeper's Tune and Country Dance (b); Lyric Pieces, Op. 65 — No. 6, Wedding Day at Troldhaugen (orch. Huppertz) (c); SIBELIUS: Finlandia, Op. 26 (d); King Christian II, Op. 27 — No. 1, Elegie; No. 2, Musette (e); Kuolema, Op. 44 — Valse triste (f); Pelleas and Melisande, Op. 46 — No. 8, Entr'acte (g)
LP: LM2336/LSC2336 (a-g). RB16179/SB2069 (a-g). VIC1069/ VICS1069 (a-g). STS15159 (a-g). SPA91 (4) KCSP91 (8) ECSP91 (a-g). VIV44 (4) KVIC44 (a, f). SPA421 (4) KCSP421 (b). HBT1/1–2 (4) KHBC1/1–2 (d). DPA511/512 (4) KDPC511/512 (d)

1958 1 July. EMI Studio No. 1. PhO. EMI/Columbia
TCHAIKOVSKY: Symphony No. 5 in E minor, Op. 64 — (iii) Waltz (a); Eugene Onegin — Waltz (Act 2) (b); The Nutcracker — Suite, Op. 71a: Waltz of the Flowers (c); Swan Lake, Op. 20 — Waltz (Act 1) (d); The Sleeping Beauty, Op. 66 — Waltz
45: SED5564/ESD7252 (a, c). SED5566/ESD7258 (b, d)
LP: 35752/S-35752

1958 7 July. Kingsway Hall. PhO. EMI/Columbia
VERDI: Il trovatore — Ballet Music (Act 3)
LP: 35751/S-35751. XLP30019/SXLP30019. QIMX7021/SQMIX 7021. S-60354

1958 22–29 September. Herkulessaal, Munich. Streich (s); Bavarian RSO. Polydor International

'MOZART: Soprano Concert Arias'

Ah se in ciel, benigne stelle, K538; Mia speranza adorata!, K416; Nehmt meinen Dank, K383; No, no, che non sei capace, K419; Popolo di Tessaglia!, K316/K300b; Vado, ma dove? oh Dei, K582; Vorrei spiegarvi, oh Dio!, K418.

LP: LPEM19183/SLPEM138028. 2535 465 (4) 3335 465

1958 12 November. Kingsway Hall. PhO. EMI/Columbia

MEYERBEER (arr. Lambert): Les Patineurs — Nos. 1, 3, 5, 6 and 8

45: SED5563/ESD7254

PONCHIELLI: La Gioconda — Dance of the Hours

LP: 33SX1207/SCX3291. 35833/S-35833. MFP2085. ESD7115 (4) TC-ESD7115

1959 13, 14 April (23.00) — 15 (02.00). St Gabriel's Church, Cricklewood. Pro Arte Orchestra; *Wind Ensemble. Pye/PRT

HANDEL (ed. Mackerras): Concerto a due cori No. 2 in F

HANDEL (ed. Mackerras): Music for the Royal Fireworks*

LP: (m) CML33005. GGC4001/GSGC14001. GSGC2018 (4) ZCGC2018. SRV289-SD. Set MST27*

1959 16–17 April. EMI Studio No. 1. R. Lewis (t); (Masters) CO. EMI/ HMV

'Folksongs of the British Isles'

TRADITIONAL (arr. Dørumsgaard): Ar hyd y nos; Bingo; The Briery Bush; Buy Broom Buzzems; The Foggy, Foggy Dew; King Arthur's Servants; Leezie Lindsay; Mo nigheann, chruinn, donn; O Waly Waly; There's none to soothe; Dafydd y garreg wen; Fine flow'rs in the valley; Grad geal mo chridh; The Helston Furry Dance; I will give my love an apple; The Maypole Song; O love, it is a killing thing; She moved thro' the fair; The Stuttering lovers.

LP: (m) ALP1777

1959 25 May. Kingsway Hall. PhO. EMI/Columbia

CHOPIN (orch. Jacob): Les Sylphides — Ballet

45: SED5570/ESD7262. SED5571/ESD7263

LP: 33SX1207/SCX3291. (m) MFP2075. 35833/S-35833

1959 18–24 July. Walthamstow Assembly Rooms. PAO. Pye/PRT

DONIZETTI: La Fille du régiment — Overture (a)

DONIZETTI: Don Pasquale — Overture (b)

FALLA: El sombrero de tres picos — The Neighbour's Dance; The Miller's Dance; Final Dance (c)

SMETANA: The Bartered Bride — Overture (d)

45: CEM36016 (a, b). CSEM75007 (a). CEM36013 (c). CEM 36014/CSEM75007 (d)

LP: GGC4011/GSGC14011. SRV178/SRV178-SD

1959 18–24 July. Walthamstow Assembly Rooms. Cooper (piano); PAO. Pye/PRT

LITOLFF: Concerto symphonique No. 4 in D, Op. 102 — Scherzo (a)

SAINT-SAËNS: Wedding Cake — Caprice, Op. 76 (b)

TCHAIKOVSKY: Piano Concerto No. 3 in E flat, Op. 75 (c)

TURINA: Rapsodia sinfonica, Op. 76 (d)

WEBER: Konzertstück in F minor, Op. 79/J282 (e)
45: (m) CEM36015 (a, b). LP: (m) CML33006 (a, c-e)

1959 18 July. Walthamstow Assembly Rooms. PAO. Pye/PRT
MOZART: Divertimento in E flat, K113. Six German Dances, K 600.
March No. 1 in C, K408. March No. 2 in D, K408. Two Minuets,
K604. Les petits riens — Ballet, K299b
LP: GGC4033/GSGC14033. SRV186/SRV186-SD

1959 19–24 July.
JANÁČEK: Sinfonietta for Orchestra. Věc Makropulos — Prelude (Act
1). Katya Kabanova — Prelude. From The House of the Dead —
Prelude. Žárlivost — Prelude
LP: (m) CML33007. GGC4004/GSGC14004. GSGC15033. 71136.
GSGC2018 (4) ZCGC2018

1960 28 September. Kingsway Hall. PhO. EMI/Columbia
DVOŘÁK: Slavonic Dances — C minor, Op. 46 No. 1; A flat, Op. 46
No. 3; E minor, Op. 72 No. 2
LP: 33SX1389/SCX3427. SP8660. CFP40214

1960 3 and 5 October. EMI Studio No. 1. RPO. EMI/HMV
SULLIVAN (arr. Mackerras): Pineapple Poll — Ballet (complete)
LP: CLP1494/CSD1399. P8663/SP8663. ESD7028 (4) TC-ESD7028.
8016 (4) 9016. CD: (Arabesque) Z8016

1960 31 October. Kingsway Hall. PhO. EMI/Columbia
BARTÓK (orch. Szekely): Romanian Folk Dances (a)
BRAHMS (orch. Parlow): Hungarian Dances Nos. 5 and 6 (b)
DVOŘÁK: Slavonic Dance in E minor, Op. 46 No. 2 (c)
ENESCO: Romanian Rhapsody No. 1, Op. 11 (d)
SMETANA: The Bartered Bride — Polka (Act 1); Furiant (Act 3) (e)
45: SED5578/ESD7268 (b, e)
LP: 33SX1389/SCX3427 (a-e). SP8660 (a, c). SPB6061 (a). CFP 40214
(c, e)

1961 17–18 April and 9 May. EMI Studio No. 1. PhO. EMI/HMV
JOHANN STRAUSS II (arr. Dorati): Graduation Ball
LP: CLP1722/CSD1533. SXLP30011. CFP40268. P8654/SP8654.
8020

1961 8–9 May. EMI Studio No. 1. PhO. EMI/HMV
OFFENBACH (arr. Rosenthal): Gaîté parisienne — Ballet Suite
LP: CLP1722/CSD1533. SXLP30011. CFP40268. P8654/SP8654.
8020

1961 19–23 July. Walthamstow Assembly Hall. LSO. Philips.
'Kaleidoscope'
BRAHMS: Hungarian Dances No. 1 in G minor (a); No. 20 in E minor
(b); No. 21 in E (c). MEYERBEER: Le Prophète — Coronation March
(d). NICOLAI: Die Lustigen Weiber von Windsor — Overture (e).
OFFENBACH (arr. André): Orphée aux enfers — Overture (f). SMETANA:
The Bartered Bride — Dance of the Comedians (g). JOHANN STRAUSS I:
Radetzky March, Op. 228 (h). TCHAIKOVSKY: Mazeppa — Cossack
Dance (i). WEBER: Abu Hassan — Overture (j)
LP: (m) GL5698 (a-j). 6747 071 (a; h). 6747 204 (d).

DAL502/SDAL502 (e, f). 6747056 (i). 6747 327 (i). 6833 032 (i)
GLUCK: Orfeo ed Euridice — Ballet Music (k)
RAMEAU: Castor et Pollux — Ballet Suite (l)
LP: WS9002 (k, l)

1962 11–12 January. EMI Studio No. 1. Brannigan (bass); PAO. EMI/
      HMV
                          'A Little Nonsense'
      BINGE: The grand old Duke of York. The story of Cock Robin. HELY-
      HUTCHINSON: The owl and the pussycat. The table and the chair. LIZA
      LEHMANN (arr. Mackerras): Henry King. Matilda. TRADITIONAL: The
      duck and the kangaroo. TRADITIONAL (arr. Hely-Hutchinson): The
      jolly beggar. DIACK (arr. Mackerras): Jack and Jill. Little Jack Horner.
      DIACK (arr. Mackerras): Sing a Song of Sixpence. HELY-HUTCHINSON
      (re-arr. Mackerras): Old Mother Hubbard. TRADITIONAL (arr.
      Hughes): Doctor Foster
      LP: CLP1557/CSD1437

1963 14–23 August. St Vedast's Church, 4 Foster Lane, London, EC2.
      Germani (organ); PAO. EMI/HMV
      HANDEL: Organ Concertos (incomplete)

1964 26–27 April. EMI Studio No. 1. Harwood (s); Brannigan (bass);
      Hendon Grammar School Choir; PAO. EMI/HMV

                        'Sing the Songs of Britain'
      ARNE: Where the bee sucks. W. BOYCE (arr. Tomlinson): Hearts of
      Oak. DAVY (arr. Tomlinson): The bay of Biscay. HORN (arr. Macker-
      ras): Cherry Ripe. MORLEY (arr. Mackerras): It was a lover and his
      lass. TRADITIONAL (arr. Mackerras): The miller of Dee. The vicar of
      Bray. A-hunting we will go. The ash grove. TRADITIONAL (arr.
      Tomlinson): The oak and the ash. Ye banks and braes. Charlie is my
      darling. Early one morning. John Peel. The bailiff's daughter of
      Islington.
      LP: CLP1789/CSD1542. ESD7002 (4) TC-ESD7002. MFP1014 (4)
      TC-MFP1014

1965 1–2 November. Decca Studios, Broadhurst Gardens, London NW6.
      Cantelo (s); Brown (t); Tear (t); Partridge (t); Keyte (bass). St
      Anthony Singers; ECO. Decca/L'Oiseau-Lyre.
      PURCELL: The Indian Queen — Incidental Music
      LP: OL294/SOL294. 410 716–1DS

1966 19–22 June. Konzerthaus, Vienna. Forrester (Orfeo); Stich-Randall
      (Euridice); Steffek (Amor); Vienna Academy Choir; Vienna State
      Opera Orchestra. Vanguard
      GLUCK (ed. Mackerras): Orfeo ed Euridice
      LP: BGS70686/7. VSL11004/5. HM66/67

1966 29–30 June; 13, 15–16 July; 5–9 August. Kingsway Hall. Harwood (s);
      Baker (m-s); Esswood (alto); Tear (t); Herincx (bass-bar); Ambrosian
      Singers; ECO. EMI/HMV
      HANDEL (ed. Lam): Messiah
      LP: RLS693/SLS774. 0C 153 00635–7. (4) TC-SLS774. SCL3705.

Excerpts: YKM5007 (4) EXES5007. YKM1 (8) MCS11. (4) TC-EXE94. SEOM13. CFP40277. HQS1183 (4) TC-EXE24. S-36530. HQS1244. 1C 053 01881. SEOM17. 1C 047 28592. (4) TC-COS54258

1967 14–18 May. Hamburg PO. Checkmate (USA); Nonesuch★
BRAHMS: Symphony No. 1 in C minor, Op. 68
LP: 76001
TCHAIKOVSKY: Symphony No. 4 in F minor, Op. 36
LP: 76004
TCHAIKOVSKY: Symphony No. 6 in B minor, Op. 74 (Pathétique)
LP: 76009
DVOŘÁK: Symphony No. 8 in G, Op. 88★
LP: H71262 (4) ZCH71262

1967 30 September–4 October. Eberthalle, Harburg (Hamburg), West Germany, Troyanos (Dido); McDaniel (Aeneas); S. Armstrong (Belinda); Johnson (Sorceress); M. Baker (First Witch, Second woman); Lensky (Second Witch); Esswood (Spirit); Rogers (Sailor); Hamburg Monteverdi Choir; N. German Radio CO. Archiv Produktion
PURCELL: Dido and Aeneas
LP: SAPM198424. 2547 032 (4) 3347 032

1968 8–9 May. EMI Studio No. 1. New PhO. EMI
ROSSINI: Guillaume Tell — Ballet Music
DELIBES: Sylvia — Act 1: No. 3, Les Chasseresses; No. 4a, Intermezzo; No. 4b, Valse lente; Act 2: No. 16a, Pizzicati; No. 14b, Cortège de Bacchus
LP: TWO275. CFP40229. S-60284. No. 14b only: STW06

1968 9 May and 1–2 April 1969. EMI Studio No. 1. New PhO. EMI
GOUNOD: Faust — Ballet Music (Act 5)
LP: TWO275. CFP40229. S-60284

1969 9–11 January. Town Hall, Wembley (now Brent), Middlesex. Wolff (treb); Esswood, Tatnell (altos); Young (t); Shirley-Quirk (bar); Rippon (bass); Tiffin Choir; Ambrosian Singers; ECO. Archiv Produktion
PURCELL: Ode on St Cecilia's Day
LP: 2533 042

1969 30 January–1 February. EMI Studio No. 1. Lewenthal (piano); LSO. CBS
HENSELT: Piano Concerto in F minor, Op. 16
LISZT (arr. Lewenthal): Totentanz, S126
LP: 61115. Set MG-35183

1969 1 February. EMI Studio No. 1. LSO. CBS
HAYDN: Symphony No. 18
LP: 32 1603 42

1969 1–2 April. EMI Studio No. 1, New PhO. EMI
DELIBES: Coppélia: Act 1 — No. 1, Prelude & No. 3, Mazurka; Act 2 — Valse; No. 7, Czardas
LP: TWO275; CFP40229; S-60284

1969 27 April & 18 May. EMI Studio No. 1. Zukerman (violin); LSO. CBS
CHAUSSON: Poème, Op. 25 (a)
SAINT-SAËNS: Introduction and Rondo Capriccioso, Op. 28 (b)
VIEUXTEMPS: Violin Concerto No. 5 in A minor, Op. 37 (c)
WIENIAWSKI: Concert Polonaise, Op. 4 (d)
LP: 72828 (a-d). MS7422 (a-d). MP35125 (c)

1969 19–20 May. Town Hall, Wembley. ECO. Phonogram Inter-
national
VOŘÍŠEK: Symphony in D
LP: 6500 203. 6527 129 (4) 7311 129

1969 22–27 May. EMI Studio No. 1. Sills (s); RPO. ABC Records
CHARPENTIER: Louise — Act 3: Depuis le jour
MASSENET: Manon — Act 3: Voici les élégants (Chorus) . . . Suis-je
gentille ainsi (Air de Manon) . . . Je marche sur tous les chemins . . .
Oui, dans le bois (Fabliau) (with Fyson, bar; Ambrosian Opera
Chorus)
MEYERBEER: Les Huguenots — Act 2: O beau pays de la Touraine (with
Knibbs, Cable, Jennings (c))
THOMAS: Mignon — Act 4: Oui, pour ce soir je suis reine de fées . . . Je
suis Titania
MEYERBEER: Robert le Diable — Act 4: Robert, toi que j'aime (with Keith
Erwen, tenor)★
LP: ASD2513. 1E 063 90370. WST17163
CD: CDC7 47183-2★
THOMAS: Hamlet — Act 4: A vos jeux . . . Partagez-vous mes fleurs . . .
Pâle et blonde dort sous l'eau profonde
LP: ASD2513. 1E 063 90370. WST17163. ATS20019. AV34016 (4)
4XAV34016

1969 1 June. Town Hall, Wembley. ECO. Phonogram International
DVOŘÁK: Suite in D, Op. 39 (Czech)
LP: 6500 203. 6527 129 (4) 7311 129

1969 1–5 June. EMI Studio No. 1. Sills (Queen Elizabeth I); Glossop (Duke
of Nottingham); B. Wolff (Sarah, Duchess of Nottingham); Ilosfalvy
(Robert Devereux, Earl of Essex); K. MacDonald (Lord Cecil);
Garrard (Sir Walter Raleigh); Howell (Page); Van Allan (bass:
Cavalier); Ambrosian Opera Chorus RPO. ABC Records.
DONIZETTI: Roberto Devereux
LP: ASD2528/59 & ASDS2530 in set SLS787. ATS20003. WST323.
Excerpts: ATS20008 (4) ATS20020. AV34015 (4) 4XAV34015

1970 17–24 February. Kleiner Redoutensaal der Hofburg, Vienna. Troy-
anos (Anima); Prey (Corpo); Equiluz (Intelletto); Lackner (Consiglio);
T. Adam (Tempo); Esswood (Piacere); Resch (Compagne I); Spitzer
(Compagne II); Zylis-Gara (Angelo custode); Moser (Vita mondana);
Gutstein (Mondo; Anima dannata); Geszty (Anima beata); Auger
(Eco); Vienna Chamber Choir; Vienna Capella Academica. Archiv
Produktion
CAVALIERI: Rappresentazione di Anima e di Corpo
LP: 2708 016

1970 31 March–10 April. Kingsway Hall, London WC2. Caballé (s); ★Marti (t); LSO. EMI
'Caballé sings Puccini arias'
La Bohème — Act 3: Donde lieta uscì; Act 1: Sì, mi chiamano Mimì. Gianni Schicchi — O mio babbino caro. Madama Butterfly — Act 2: Un bel dì vedremo; Act 2: Tu, tu, piccolo iddio! Manon Lescaut — Act 2: In quelle trine morbide; Act 4: Sola, perduta, abbandonata. La Rondine — Act 1: Chi il bel sogno di Doretta. Tosca — Act 2: Vissi d'arte. Turandot — Act 1: Signore, ascolta; Act 3: Tu che di gel sei cinta. Le Villi — Act 1: Se come voi piccina
LP: ASD2632. S-36711. SXLP30562 (4) TC-SXLP30562. 0C 037 02099 (4) 0C 237 02099 CD: CDC7 47841
'Great Opera Duets'
DONIZETTI: Poliuto — Act: Ah! Fuggi da morte.★ GIORDANO: Andrea Chenier — Act 4: Vicino a te.★ PUCCINI: Manon Lescaut — Act 2: Tu, tu, amore.★ VERDI: Un ballo in maschera — Act 2: Teco io sto★
LP: ASD2723

1970 15–17 April. Town Hall, Leeds, Yorkshire. Harper (s); Clarke (s); Esswood (alto); Young (t); Rippon (bass), Keyte (bass); Leeds Festival Chorus, ECO. Archiv Produktion
HANDEL: Israel in Egypt
LP: 2708 020. 413 919–1GX2

1970 4 & 15 June. Barking Town Hall. LPO. EMI/CfP
GLINKA: Ruslan and Ludmilla — Overture
MUSSORGSKY (arr. Rimsky-Korsakov): A Night on the Bare Mountain
TCHAIKOVSKY: 1812 Overture (with the Band of the H.M. Welsh Guards and the guns of the Royal Horse Artillery)
WAGNER: Lohengrin — Prelude to Act 3★
LP: CFP101 (4) TC-CFP101. ★MFP 411036–3 (4) MFP411036–5

1970 28–29 December. Anvil Studios, Denham, Buckinghamshire. ECO. Archiv Produktion
M. HAYDN: Symphony in D minor, P27 (a)
M. HAYDN: Symphony in G, P16 with Mozart's Introduction, K444 (b)
M. HAYDN: Symphony in D — Turkish Suite for Voltaire's 'Zaire' (c)
LP: 2533 074 (4) 3310 101 (a–c)

1971 23 April. ABC Studios. Sydney, NSW, Australia. New Sydney Woodwind Quintet; Sydney SO. ABC/WRC (Australia)
SITSKY: Concerto for Woodwind Quintet and Orchestra
LP: R04694

1971 12–14 December. EMI Studio No. 1. Röhn (violin); ECO. Archiv Produktion
VIOTTI: Violin Concerto No. 16 in E minor, G85 (with Mozart's parts for trumpet and timpani, K470a)
VIOTTI: Violin Concerto No. 24 in B minor, G105★
LP: 2533 122

1972 Spring. Assembly Hall, Barking. Hunter (Brünnhilde); Remedios (Siegfried); LPO. EMI/CfP

WAGNER: Götterdämmerung — Act 1: Dawn; Zu neuen Thaten. Act 2: Siegfried's journey down the Rhine. Act 3: Siegfried's Funeral March; Starke Scheite schichtet mir dort
LP: CFP40008. CFP4403 (4) TC-CFP4403

1972 18–21 May. Town Hall, Leeds. McIntyre (Saul); Davies (Jonathan); Bowman (David); Winfield (Abner; Witch of Endor); M. Price (Merab); S. Armstrong (Michael); S. Dean (Doeg; Apparition of Samuel); G. English (An Amalekite; High Priest); Leeds Festival Chorus; ECO. Archiv Produktion
HANDEL: Saul
LP: 2722 008. 2710 014. 413 910–1GX3

1972 23 July. Town Hall, Watford. LSO. Vanguard
STRAVINSKY: Petrushka (1911 version)
LP: VSD71137 (4) ZCVSM71177 (4) CA-471177. VCS10113. VSQ30021 (T) VSS23

1973 15 January. Barking Town Hall. LPO. EMI/CfP
R. STRAUSS: Till Eulenspiegels lustige Streiche, Op. 26
R. STRAUSS: Don Juan, Op. 28
LP: CFP40042. CFP40307

1973 26 & 29 April. Barking Town Hall. LPO. EMI/CfP
MOZART: Symphony No. 36 in C, K425 (Linz)
MOZART: Symphony No. 38 in D, K504 (Prague)
LP: CFP40079. CFP40336 (4) TC–CFP40336

1974 31 January–4 February. Grosser Musikvereinsaal, Vienna. Mathis (s); Finnïla (c); Schreier (t); T. Adam (bass-bar); Austrian Radio Chorus & SO (Vienna); Archiv Produktion
HANDEL (orch. Mozart): Der Messias, K572
LP: 2710 016. 2723 019

1974 13 July. All Hallows Church, Gospel Oak, London. New PhO. Vanguard
MUSSORGSKY: Khovanshchina — Prelude (Dawn over the Moscow River) (a)
MUSSORGSKY (orch. Ravel): Pictures at an Exhibition (b)
LP: 71188(Q) (4) CA-471188. VCS10116. VSS24/25 (b)

1975 2 & 15 April. Barking Town Hall. LPO. EMI/CfP
MOZART. Symphony No. 40 in G minor, K550
MOZART: Symphony No. 41 in C, K551 (Jupiter)
LP: CFP40253 (4) TC-CFP40253

1975 16–17 April. Barking Town Hall. Schiller (pno); LPO. EMI/CfP
MOZART: Piano Concerto No. 23 in A, K488
MOZART: Piano Concerto No. 20 in D minor, K466
LP: CFP40249

1975 12–14 August. Henry Wood Hall, London SE1. LPO. Reader's Digest Association
'Orchestral Marches'
BAX. Coronation March (1953). BEETHOVEN: The Ruins of Athens, Op. 113 — Turkish March. BERLIOZ: La Damnation de Faust, Op. 21 — Hungarian March. CHABRIER: Marche joyeuse

ELGAR: Imperial March. GOUNOD: Faust — Soldiers' Chorus.
HALVORSEN: Entry of the Boyards. MEYERBEER: Le Prophète — Coronation March. RIMSKY-KORSAKOV: Le Coq d'or — March.
SIBELIUS: Karelia Suite, Op. 11 — Alla marcia. TCHAIKOVSKY: Marche slave.
LP: RDS8024

1975 1–7 October. L'Eglise Notre Dame de Liban, Paris. Freni (s); Berganza (m-s); Kuentz CO. Archiv Produktion
A. SCARLATTI: Stabat Mater
LP: 2533 324 (4) 3310 324

1976 4–12 April. Town Hall, Watford. Davies (Judas Maccabaeus); Palmer (Israelite Woman); Baker (Israelite Man); Shirley-Quirk (Simon); Keyte (Eupolemus); Esswood (Messenger); Wandsworth School Choir; ECO. Archiv Produktion
HANDEL: Judas Maccabaeus
LP: 2710 021. 413 909–1GX3

1976 22–23 May. Henry Wood Hall, London. André (trpt); ECO. Polydor International
STÖLZEL: Trumpet Concerto in D
TELEMANN: Concerto/Sonata in D*
TORELLI: Trumpet Concerto in D
VIVALDI: Double Trumpet Concerto in D, P75/RV537* (nb: both parts played by Maurice André)
LP: 2530 792 (4) 3300 792. 410 832–1GX (4) 410 832–4GX
CD: 415 980–2GH*

1976 May. Henry Wood Hall, London. Schiff (cello); New PhO. Polydor International
FAURÉ: Elégie in C minor, Op. 24
LALO: Cello Concerto in D minor
SAINT-SAËNS: Cello Concerto No. 1 in A minor, Op. 33
LP: 2530 793

1976 8 October & 19 December. EMI Studio No. 1. LSO (augmented). EMI
HANDEL (ed. Mackerras): Music for the Royal Fireworks
HANDEL (ed. Mackerras): Concerto a due cori No. 2 in F
HANDEL: Concerto No. 1 in F
HANDEL: Concerto No. 3 in D
LP: ASD3395 (4) TC-ASD3395. S37404 (Q) (4) 4XS-37404.
ED102894–1 (4) ED102894–4

1976 1–4, 6, 7, 13 & 14 December. Sofiensaal, Vienna. Jedlička (Dikoj); Dvorský (Boris Grigorjevič); Kniplová (Kabanicha); Krejčík (Tichon Ivanyč Kabanov); Söderström (Katěrina Kabanová); Švehla (Váňa Kudrjaš); Marová (Varvara); Souček (Kuligin); Pavlová (Glaša); Jahn (Fekluša); Vienna State Opera Chorus, VPO. Decca
JANÁČEK: Katya Kabanova
LP: D151D2 (4) K51K22. OSA12109 (4) OSA5–12109

1977 23–25 January. EMI Studio No. 1. André (trpt); ECO. EMI
HANDEL: Sonata for flute and harpsichord, Op. 1 No. 9 (reconstructed

as Trumpet Concerto in D minor by Jean Thilde)
ALBINONI: Oboe Concerto in B flat, Op. 7 No. 3
ALBINONI: Oboe Concerto in D, Op. 7 No. 6
TELEMANN (ed. Töttcher/Grebe): Trumpet Concerto in D
HERTEL: Trumpet Concerto in E flat
LP: ASD3394 (4) TC-ASD3394. EG290494-1 (4) EG290494-4

1977 26–27 March. Henry Wood Hall. LPO. EMI/CfP
VERDI: (arr. Mackerras): The Lady and the Fool (excs)
SULLIVAN (arr. Mackerras): Pineapple Poll (excs)
LP: CFP40293. CFP414490-1 (4) CFP414490-4

1978 1–4 February. D'ablice Studio, Prague. Prague CO. Supraphon/EMI
HANDEL: Water Music — Suites Nos. 1, 2 and 3
LP: ASD3597 (4) TC-ASD3597. S-37532 (4) 4XS-37532.
ED103271-1 (4) ED103271-4.
Excerpts: ESD143613-1 (4) TC-ESD143613-4

1978 18–19 February. D'ablice Studio
HANDEL: Concerti grossi, Op. 3
LP: ESD7089 (4) TC-ESD7089 EMX412086-1 (4) TC–EMX-
412086-4

1978 25–27 September and 2–4, 9–11 October. Vienna Film Studios.
Söderström (Emilia Marty); Dvorský (Albert Gregor); Krejčík
(Vítek); Czaková (Christian); Zítek (Baron Prus); Švehla (Janek);
Jedlička (Kolenatý); Joran (Strojník); Mixová (Polízečka); Blachut
(Hauk-Sendorf); Vítková (Komorna); Vienna State Opera Chorus;
VPO. Decca
JANÁČEK: Věc Makropulos
LP: D144D2 (4) K144K22. OSA12116 (4) OSA5-12116

1978 I. Dingfelder (fte); ECO. Enigma Classics/WEA/ASV
C. P. E. BACH: Concerto for Flute and Orchestra in D minor, Wq22
HOFFMEISTER: Concerto for Flute and Orchestra in D
LP: ACM2020 (4) ZCACM2020. H71388.

1979 24–25 November. Sofiensaal, Vienna. VPO. Decca
JANÁČEK: Taras Bulba
LP: SXDL7519 (4) KSXC7519. LDR71021.
CD: 410 138-2DH. 410 138-2LH

1979 26–27 November. Sofiensaal, Vienna. VPO. Decca
JANÁČEK: Sinfonietta
LP: SXDL7519 (4) KSXC7519. LDR71021.
CD: 410 138-2DH. 410 138-2LH

1979 27 November. Sofiensaal, Vienna. VPO. Decca
JANÁČEK (arr. Talich): Cunning Little Vixen — Suite
CD: 417 129-2DH2. 414 129-2LH2

1980 August. EMI Studio No. 1. LSO. Centaur
DEBUSSY: La Mer
RAVEL: Daphnis et Chloé — Suite No. 2
LP: CRC1007

1980 18, 21, 23, 24 August and 6, 21–23 September. EMI Studio No. 1.
Masterson (Violetta); Brecknock (Alfredo); Du Plessis (Germont);

D. Jones (Flora); Gibbs (Baron Douphol); Earle (Doctor); Dowling (Marquis); Pogson (Gaston); Squires (Annina); Byles (Joseph); ENO Chorus & Orchestra. EMI
VERDI: La traviata (in English)
LP: SLS5216 (4) TC-SLS5216
1981 25–28 February and 3–5 March. Sofiensaal, Vienna.
Zahradníček (Filka Morozov); Žídek (Skuratov); Zítek (Shishkov); Jedlička (Goryanchikov); Švorc (Commandant); Janská (Alyeya); Krejčík (Tall Prisoner); Novák (Short Prisoner); Blachut (Old Prisoner); Švehla (Voice; Cherevin); Zigmundová (Wench); Z. Soušek (Shapkin; Kedril); J. Šoušek (Chekunov; Don Juan); Vienna State Opera Chorus; VPO. Decca
JANÁČEK: Z mrtvého domu (From the House of the Dead)
LP: D224D2 (4) K224K22. LDR10036
1981 13, 14, 16–18 and 23–26 March. Sofiensaal, Vienna.
Jedlička (Gamekeeper); Popp (Vixen: Young Vixen); Randová (Fox); Marová (Dog); Zigmundová (Gamekeeper's Wife; Owl); Krejčík (Schoolmaster; Gnat); Novák (Priest; Badger); Zítek (Harašta); Blachut (Pašek); Mixová (Pašek's Wife; Woodpecker; Hen); Jahn (Cock; Jay); Šaray (Frog; Grasshopper); Ondraková (Cricket); Hřibková (Frantik); Hudecová (Pepik); Vienna State Opera Chorus; Bratislavá Children's Choir; VPO. Decca
JANÁČEK: Cunning Little Vixen
LP: D257D2 (4) K257K22. LDR72010 (4) OSA5–72010
CD: 417 129–2DH2 414 129–2LH2
1981 1–6 June. Stadion Hall, Brno, Czechoslovakia.
Mitchinson (Manolios); Field (Katerina); Tomlinson (Grigoris); Joll (Kostandis); Moses (Fotis); Davies (Yannakos); Cullis (Lenio); Savory (Nikolios; Old Woman); Lawton (Panais; Andonis); Harris (Michelis); Gwynne (Old Man; Patriarcheas); Jonášová (Despinio); Geliot (Ladas); Kuhn Children's Chorus; Czech Philharmonic Chorus; Brno State PO. Supraphon
MARTINŮ: The Greek Passion
LP: 1116 3611/2 (4) 3611/2
1982 15–16 February. Supraphon Studio, House of Artists, Prague. Prague Radio SO. Supraphon
MARTINŮ: Double Concerto for Two String Orchestras, Piano and Timpani
MARTINŮ: Les Fresques de Piero della Francesca
LP: 1110 3393 G. CO1056
1982 1, 10, 14 and 22 April. London Coliseum.
Baker (Mary Stuart); Plowright (Queen Elizabeth I); Rendall (Robert Dudley, Earl of Leicester); Opie (Sir William Cecil); Tomlinson (George Talbot, Earl of Shrewsbury); Bostock (Hannah Kennedy); ENO Chorus and Orchestra. EMI
DONIZETTI: Mary Stuart (in English)
LP: SLS5277 (4) TC-SLS5277. DSCX3927 (4) 4XSX-3927
1982 17, 19–21, 24, 24–29 April. Sofiensaal, Vienna.

Mrazová (Grandmother Buryjovka); Ochmann (Laca Klemeň); Dvorský (Steva Buryja); Randová (Kostelnička Buryjovka); Söderström (Jenůfa); Zítek (Mill Foreman); Jedlička (Mayor); Mixová (Mayor's Wife); Popp (Karolka); Soukupová (Old Woman); Pokorná (Barena); Jonášová (Jano); Vienna State Opera Chorus; VPO. Decca

JANÁČEK: Jenůfa
LP: D276D3 (4) K276K32. LDR73009 (4) OSA5–73009
CD: 414 483-2LH2
JANÁČEK: Žárlivost — Prelude
LP: D276D3 (4) K276K32. LDR73009 (4) OSA5–73009

1982 26–27 November. Kingsway Hall, London, PhO. Decca
SULLIVAN (arr. Mackerras): Pineapple Poll
SULLIVAN: Overture Di Ballo
LP: SXDL7619 (4) KSXDC7619. LDR71119 (4) OSA5-LDR71119

1983 13–14 February. St John's, Smith Square, London SW1. ECO. EMI/CfP
DVOŘÁK: Serenade for Strings in E, Op. 22
LP: EMX2013 (4) TC-EMX2013

1983 11, 12 & 15 August. Concert Hall, Opera House, Sydney, NSW, Australia. CBS Australia
HAYDN: Symphony No. 80 in D minor
HAYDN: Symphony No. 81 in G
LP: DBR005 (4) DBRC005

1984 20–21 January. House of Artists, Prague. Zítek (bar); Czech Philharmonic Chorus; Czech PO. Supraphon
MARTINŮ: Polní Mše (Field Mass)
LP: 1112 3576 ZA (4) 1922 3576
CD: C37 7735

1984 27–29 January. House of Artists, Prague.
Söderström (s); Drobková (c); Livora (t); Novák (bass) Hora (organ); Czech Philharmonic Chorus; Czech PO. Supraphon.
JANÁČEK: Mša Glagolskaja (Glagolitic Mass)
LP: 1112 3575 ZA (4) 1912 3575
CD: 33C37 7448

1984 30 January. House of Artists, Prague. Nemeckova (s); Vodička (t); Zítek (bar); Czech Philharmonic Choir; Czech PO. Supraphon
JANÁČEK: Amarus
LP: 1112 3576 ZA (4) 1922 3576
CD: C37 7735

1984 3–7 October. Hall of Artists, Prague. Prague CO. Telarc
MOZART: Serenade in G, K525 (Eine Kleine Nachtmusik)
MOZART: Serenade in D, K320 (Posthorn) (with Zdeněk Tyšlar, posthorn)
LP: DG10108. CD: CD80108

1985 26–27 January. St John's, Smith Square. ECO. ASV
MOZART: Symphony No. 32 in G, K318
MOZART: Symphony No. 35 in D, K385 (Haffner)

MOZART: Symphony No. 39 in E flat, K543
LP: DCA543 (4) ZCDCA543

1985 11–12 March. St Augustine's Church, Kilburn, NW8. LPO. EMI
ELGAR: Falstaff, Op. 68
LP: EL270374–1 (4) EL270374–4
CD: CDC7 47416–2

1985 13 March. EMI Studio No. 1. LPO. EMI
ELGAR: Enigma Variations, Op. 36
LP: EL270374–1 (4) EL270374–4
CD: CDC7 47416–2

1986 21–22 April. EMI Studio No. 1. Julian Lloyd Webber (cello); LSO. EMI
ELGAR: Romance for Cello and Orchestra, Op. 62
SULLIVAN: Cello Concerto
HERBERT: Cello Concerto No. 2, Op. 30
LP: EL270430–1 (4) EL270430–4
CD: CDC7 47622–2

1986 13, 14 & 16 May. Watford Town Hall. LSO. Telarc
TCHAIKOVSKY: The Nutcracker — Ballet, Op. 71
TCHAIKOVSKY: Pique Dame — Duet of Daphnis and Chloe
LP: DG10137
CD: CD80137

1986 11–16 June. Hall of Artists, Prague. Prague CO. Telarc
MOZART: Symphony No. 36 in C, K425 (Linz)
MOZART: Symphony No. 38 in D, K504 (Prague)
LP: DG10138
CD: CD80138
MOZART: Symphony No. 40 in G minor, K550
MOZART: Symphony No. 41 in C, K551 (Jupiter)
LP: DG10139
CD: CD80139

May 1987

INDEX